'This carefully co-ordinated t
history, religion, law and cul
Wales in 1920, and its iden
Wales, yet the underlying eng
relate has a universal relevance.

Robert Ombres OP, Blackfriars Hall,
University of Oxford

'The pre-eminent ecclesiastical jurist Norman Doe is uniquely placed to
confect this collection of essays to mark the centenary of a non-established
Anglican presence in Wales. Drawing on a rich array of scholars,
practitioners and clergy, the volume explores and celebrates the manner
in which the Church in Wales self-identifies as a national church, and inter-
relates with Welsh culture, society, politics, education and government. It is
required reading for historians, ecclesiologists and sociologists, both within
and beyond the Anglican Communion.'

Professor Mark Hill QC, Centre for Law and
Religion, Cardiff University

'In a series of sweeping studies over more than three decades, Norman
Doe has brought to brilliant light and life the extraordinary riches of law
and religion first in his native Wales, then in the United Kingdom, then in
all of Europe, and finally in all of global Christendom. In this learned but
accessible volume, Doe returns to his Welsh Anglican roots and leads a
score of distinguished scholars and churchmen in a close study of the
history, law, theology, liturgy, music, iconography, culture, education,
charity work and ecumenical efforts of the Church in Wales. This is not
a cheery tourist brochure, and some of the contributors pull no punches
when confronting some grimmer parts of this fascinating story. But
insider Welsh Anglicans and distant outsiders alike will find much to
savour, ponder and admire in these arresting pages.'

John Witte, Robert W. Woodruff Professor
of Law, Emory University

A NEW HISTORY OF THE CHURCH IN WALES

This book marks the centenary of the Church in Wales, following the disestablishment of the Church of England in Wales in 1920. Part I provides a historical overview: from the Age of the Saints to Victorian times; the disestablishment campaign; Christianity in Wales since 1920; and broad issues faced over the century. Part II explores the constitution, bishops and archbishops, clergy and laity. Part III examines doctrine, liturgy, rites of passage and relations with other faith communities. Part IV deals with the Church and culture, education, the Welsh language and social responsibility. Part V discusses the changing images of the Church and its future. Around themes of continuity and change, the book questions assumptions about the Church, including its distinctive theology and Welshness, ecumenical commitment, approach to innovation and response to challenges posed by the State and wider world in an increasingly pluralist and secularised Welsh society over the century.

NORMAN DOE is Professor at Cardiff University Law School. He studied at Cardiff University, the University of Cambridge and the University of Oxford, and is a barrister. His degrees include a PhD (Cambridge), DCL (Lambeth) and LLD (Cambridge). His books include *Fundamental Authority in Late Medieval English Law* (Cambridge, 1990), *Canon Law in the Anglican Communion* (1998), *Religion and Law in the United Kingdom* (with Mark Hill and Russell Sandberg, 2011), *Christian Law: Contemporary Principles* (Cambridge, 2013), *The Legal Architecture of English Cathedrals* (2017) and *Comparative Religious Law: Judaism, Christianity, Islam* (Cambridge, 2018). A visiting professor at Paris University since 1999, he was a visiting fellow at Trinity College, Oxford (2011), visiting scholar at Corpus Christi College, Oxford (2015), and visiting fellow at Jesus College, Oxford (2018), and acted as a consultant on canon law to the Anglican Communion, served on the Lambeth Commission (2003–4), and is Chancellor of the Diocese of Bangor. He directs the Cardiff LLM in canon law.

A NEW HISTORY OF THE CHURCH IN WALES

Governance and Ministry, Theology and Society

Edited by

NORMAN DOE

Cardiff University

CAMBRIDGE
UNIVERSITY PRESS

CAMBRIDGE
UNIVERSITY PRESS

University Printing House, Cambridge CB2 8BS, United Kingdom

One Liberty Plaza, 20th Floor, New York, NY 10006, USA

477 Williamstown Road, Port Melbourne, VIC 3207, Australia

314–321, 3rd Floor, Plot 3, Splendor Forum, Jasola District Centre, New Delhi – 110025, India

79 Anson Road, #06–04/06, Singapore 079906

Cambridge University Press is part of the University of Cambridge.

It furthers the University's mission by disseminating knowledge in the pursuit of education, learning, and research at the highest international levels of excellence.

www.cambridge.org
Information on this title: www.cambridge.org/9781108499576
DOI: 10.1017/9781108583930

© Cambridge University Press 2020

First published 2020

Printed in the United Kingdom by TJ International Ltd. Padstow Cornwall

A catalogue record for this publication is available from the British Library.

ISBN 978-1-108-49957-6 Hardback
ISBN 978-1-108-73087-7 Paperback

CONTENTS

vii

*The colour plate section can be found between pp. 202
and 203.*

PLATES

Chair of the Standing Committee of the Scottish Episcopal Church, with the
Archbishop of Wales, Barry Morgan.

16 June Osborne is consecrated as the 72nd Bishop of Llandaff, the first woman to hold
the office, at Brecon Cathedral, 15 July 2017, pictured with Joanna Penberthy, the
first woman to be consecrated as a bishop (St David's) in the Church in Wales,
amongst others.

The colour plate section can be found between pp. 202 and 203.

CONTRIBUTORS

ROGER LEE BROWN retired as vicar of Welshpool in 2007 and is well known as an authority on the ecclesiastical history of Wales, having written numerous books, monographs and articles on this subject. His books include *The Letters of Edward Copleston* (2003), *In Pursuit of a Welsh Episcopate* (2005) and *In Places Where They Sit: A Social History of the Church Pew in Wales* (2016). A fellow of the Society of Antiquaries, he holds the degree of Doctor of Letters from the University of Wales.

GREGORY KENNETH CAMERON has been Bishop of St Asaph in the Church in Wales since 2009. Ordained in the Church in Wales in 1983, Cameron has degrees in jurisprudence, theology and religious studies, and canon law, and has served in parish and educational ministries. He was Deputy Secretary General of the Anglican Communion between 2004 and 2009, during which time he guided the doctrinal and ecumenical work of the Communion. He was made a Doctor of Divinity (*honoris causa*) by the Episcopal Divinity School, Massachusetts, in 2007 for services to the Anglican Communion, and awarded the Cross of St Augustine by the Archbishop of Canterbury in 2009. In the Church in Wales he has held the educational portfolio, and now holds the Faith, Order and Unity portfolio, which includes Liturgy, on behalf of the Bench of Bishops. He is Co-Chair of the Anglican–Oriental Orthodox International Commission and dialogue, Chair of the Commission of the Covenanted Churches for Wales and a member of the Church in Wales Standing Liturgical Advisory Commission.

JOHN DAVIES is Bishop of Swansea and Brecon and also the 13th Archbishop of Wales. Born in Newport, he studied law at the University of Southampton prior to training for ordained ministry at St Michael's College, Llandaff, and worked, in private practice, as a solicitor specialising in criminal law. In 1995 he was admitted to the degree of

Master of Laws (LLM) in canon law. After serving in parishes in the Diocese of Monmouth, he moved to the Diocese of Swansea and Brecon where he served as Dean of Brecon Cathedral. He retains a personal interest in matters of social justice and the duty of the Church to speak out on such matters, where necessary demanding change. The rehabilitation of offenders and the treatment of prisoners are aspects of social justice about which he feels particularly strongly. The Church's duty to speak out must, he believes, be firmly grounded in the call of the prophets and in Christ's demand that all should have life, and have it in abundance.

NORMAN DOE, from the Rhondda, is Chancellor of Bangor Diocese and a Professor at Cardiff Law School where he set up the LLM in Canon Law (1991) and the Centre for Law and Religion (1998). A barrister, he studied at Cardiff, Cambridge and Oxford Universities. A visiting professor at Paris University since 1999 and founding member of the Colloquium of Anglican and Roman Catholic Canon Lawyers (1999) and of the Christian Law Panel (which works with the Faith and Order Commission of the World Council of Churches), he was President of the European Consortium for Church and State Research (2010). His books are mainly on law and religion. A consultant on canon law to the Anglican Primates, he served on the Lambeth Commission (2003–4) and has been a visiting fellow/scholar at Trinity (2011), Corpus Christi (2015) and Jesus (2018) Colleges, Oxford. His recent books include *Comparative Religious Law: Judaism, Christianity, Islam* (2018).

ARTHUR EDWARDS has been a priest in the Church in Wales for more than fifty years. He is an MPhil. London University, and Cardiff University awarded him a PhD in 2016. He trained for the ministry at St Michael's College, Llandaff, and was ordained in the Diocese of Monmouth in 1968, where he became a canon of the Cathedral in 1991. His publications include *Archbishop Green* (1986), *The Seven Bishops* (1996) and *Thomas Thomas of Pontypool: Radical Puritan* (2009).

JEFFREY GAINER is a native of Blaenllechau in the Rhondda. He was educated at Bablake School, Coventry, and Jesus College, Oxford, where he studied history before ordination training at Wycliffe Hall. After being made deacon in 1977, he served at Baglan and thereafter at Cwmbach and Tonyrefail in the Diocese of Llandaff. He taught New Testament Greek at St Michael's College, Llandaff, before becoming the incumbent of Meidrim and Merthyr in the Diocese of St David's in 1992. He became a cursal canon of St David's Cathedral in 2011. He has studied canon law at Cardiff University and Welsh at Aberystwyth University.

AINSLEY GRIFFITHS read mathematics and began his career as a mathematics teacher at a Roman Catholic sixth form college. Following discernment of his priestly vocation, he trained at Ripon College Cuddesdon, near Oxford. His entire ministry has been in the Church in Wales, serving as a cathedral minor canon, parish priest, university chaplain and Continuing Ministerial Development officer. Currently provincial Director of Faith, Order and Unity, he has day-to-day oversight of the Church in Wales' doctrine and its liturgy, as well as its commitments within the Anglican Communion and its relationships with other faith communities, Christian and non-Christian alike. His academic interests revolve around the themes of his doctoral research, namely theological perspectives on 'gift'.

RHIANNON JOHNSON grew up in Cardiff, studied at St Anne's College, Oxford, as an undergraduate, and holds the degree of Bachelor of Divinity and a doctorate from Cardiff University. Trained at St Michael's College, Llandaff, she was ordained deacon in 1997 and priest in 1998. After a curacy in the Diocese of Llandaff, she was chaplain at Trinity College, Carmarthen (1999–2000), in the Diocese of St David's, where she now serves in parochial ministry. She is also a canon of St David's Cathedral and the Diocesan Director of Ministry and Training.

BARRY MORGAN was brought up in the south Wales mining village of Gwaun-Cae-Gurwen, read history at University College London, theology at Selwyn College, Cambridge, and later studied for his doctorate at University College Bangor, where he was chaplain and lecturer in the Faculty of Theology for seven years, having previously been chaplain of St Michael's College, Llandaff, and lecturer in theology at University College Cardiff. He has spent his whole ministry in the Church in Wales, serving as incumbent and archdeacon and at one stage chairing its Doctrinal Commission. Elected bishop of Bangor in 1993, Llandaff in 1999 and Archbishop in 2003, he retired in 2017. He continues as Pro Chancellor of the University of Wales, is a fellow of several Welsh universities, and holds honorary doctorates in literature and divinity respectively from two of them.

D. DENSIL MORGAN is Emeritus Professor of Theology at the University of Wales, Trinity Saint David, at Lampeter. Previously he was Professor of Theology at Bangor University and Warden of Coleg

Gwyn, the North Wales Baptist College. An ordained Baptist minister, he has written extensively on Christianity in Wales, aspects of modern church history, and the theology of Karl Barth. Among his publications are *Theologia Cambrensis: A History of Protestant Religion and Theology, 1588–1760* (2018), *The Span of the Cross: Christian Religion and Society in Wales, 1914–2000*, 2nd ed. (2011), *Barth Reception in Britain* (2012) and *The SPCK Introduction to Karl Barth* (2010). He is a member of the Center of Theological Inquiry, Princeton, and a Fellow of the Learned Society of Wales.

ENID R. MORGAN, MA (Oxon), BD, MA (Wales), first lay woman editor of *Y Llan*, 1970–7, and the editor of interdenominational magazine *Cristion*, 1984–7. She was ordained deacon in 1984, priested in 1996, and became cleric in charge of Llanfihangel y Creuddyn, Llanafan, Gwnnws and Ysbyty Ystwyth (Diocese of St David's), 1987–93. She was the director of the provincial Board of Mission, 1993–2000, vicar of Llangynwyd with Maesteg (Diocese of Llandâf) 2000–5 and former chair of MAECymru, Chair of the Friends of the National Library of Wales, and Chair of Cristnogaeth21.

JOANNA PENBERTHY was elected on 2 November 2016 as the 129th successor of Saint David, being the first woman to be consecrated Bishop in Wales. Joanna read classics and modern history at Newnham College, Cambridge, and then trained for the ministry at St John's College, Nottingham, and at Cranmer Hall, Durham. Joanna was made deaconess in 1984 and deacon in 1988 and was ordained priest in January 1997 in the first ordinations of woman as priests in Wales. She has just completed a PhD in the theology of science at the University of Nottingham.

WILLIAM PRICE was an open scholar in history at Keble College, Oxford. He taught for twenty-seven years in St David's University College, Lampeter, and he was a residentiary canon of St David's Cathedral for eight years. He has published a two-volume history of St David's University College and has published widely on the history of the Church in Wales since 1920. He was formerly advisor on archives to the Church in Wales. In 2018 he was awarded an honorary doctorate in divinity by the University of Wales Trinity Saint David, Lampeter's successor institution. He is also an honorary canon of St Paul's Cathedral, St Helena, in the South Atlantic Ocean. He now lives in Shropshire and is Chairman of the Shropshire Historic Churches Trust.

PETER SEDGWICK studied history at Trinity Hall, Cambridge, followed by a year at Keble College, Oxford. He then returned to Cambridge where he took a second degree in theology while training for ordination. He has a PhD (Durham) in theology and moral philosophy. He lectured in modern theology and ethics at the University of Birmingham from 1979 to 1982, and was course director at the University of Hull for the MA in Theology and Society from 1988 to 1994. In 1994–5 he was vice principal of Westcott House, Cambridge, and was principal of St Michael's College, Llandaff, 2004–14. He was a member of the Doctrinal Commission of the Church in Wales from 2009, and chair from 2013 to 2016. He has been a member of the Anglican Roman Catholic International Commission since 2011. He is a provincial canon of the Church in Wales and has written widely on ethics and on Anglicanism.

MARY STALLARD, a priest who serves as the Archdeacon of Bangor, broadcasts, writes and presents a range of religious programmes for the BBC on Radio Cymru, Radio Wales and Radio 4. The daughter of a Church of England priest and a chemistry teacher, Stallard was born and educated in Birmingham. She studied theology at Selwyn College, Cambridge, and was a secondary school teacher before training for ordination. Stallard and her partner Revd Andrew Sully were the first ordained stipendiary clergy couple in the Church in Wales, and both are keen advocates of inclusion in the Church and in wider society.

ROSALIND WILLIAMS is the Director of Education and Lifelong Learning for the Diocese of St Asaph. She is a graduate of the University of Wales, has worked in a variety of roles in business, law and education, and is a member of the Ecclesiastical Law Society. She sits on the Welsh Government's 21st Century Schools Programme Board representing church schools and contributed to the development of the School Standards and Organisation (Wales) Act in 2013, working with the bill team to ensure that the rights and responsibilities of schools with a religious character were enhanced and preserved. Williams has worked with church schools since 2006 and is a passionate proponent of the role they play in the educational landscape of England and Wales. She has developed a comprehensive knowledge of the law and Christian distinctiveness of church schools and works to ensure their development and success. She is also a local councillor serving on St Asaph City Council.

ROWAN WILLIAMS grew up in Swansea and studied theology at Christ's College, Cambridge, before pursuing research in Russian religious thought at Christ Church and Wadham College, Oxford. He taught at the College of the Resurrection, Mirfield, then returned to Cambridge for nine years of academic and parochial work. In 1986, he became Lady Margaret Professor of Divinity at Oxford, and in 1992 moved back to Wales as Bishop of Monmouth. From 1999 to 2002, he was also Archbishop of Wales and, from 2002 to 2012, Archbishop of Canterbury. In 1990 he was elected as a Fellow of the British Academy, and as a Fellow of the Royal Society of Literature in 2003 and of the Learned Society of Wales in 2010. Since 2013, when he was made a life peer, becoming Lord Williams of Oystermouth, he has been Master of Magdalene College, Cambridge. His recent books include *Being Human* (2018) and *Christ the Heart of Creation* (2018).

CHARLOTTE WRIGHT grew up on a farm near Fishguard, in Pembrokeshire. She studied music at Magdalen College, Oxford, before completing her graduate diploma in law, and the Legal Practice Course at the College of Law in London. After a training contract with Barlow Lyde and Gilbert LLP in London, she qualified as a solicitor and worked in the firm's Professional Negligence and Financial Disputes department. Wright moved to Cardiff with her husband in 2015; having taking a year out after having their first child, Wright works as a solicitor specialising in professional negligence. She studied the LLM in canon law at Cardiff University, graduating in 2016, and has published an article on the English canon law relating to suicide victims in the *Ecclesiastical Law Journal*. Wright is currently working towards a doctorate at Cardiff University on the governance of music in Anglican churches, cathedrals and college chapels in England and Wales.

FOREWORD

THE RT REVD ANDREW JOHN, BISHOP OF BANGOR
THE RT REVD JUNE OSBORNE, BISHOP OF LLANDAFF

'The story of the Church in Wales might be seen as a story of battles won and wars lost.' So says Rowan Williams in this immensely readable and insightful book celebrating the centenary of the Church of which he first became archbishop. He is right that there have been dramas, triumphs and casualties. Tribute is paid to vivid leaders who have broken new ground and been 'Godsends' to this small but truly independent Anglican province. A remarkable fidelity in the worship, Christian ministry and outreach of parish churches has seen the Church in Wales become the largest Christian denomination in Wales with a joyful story to tell, taking us far beyond the contests which led to disestablishment in 1920.

Here it is acknowledged that Wales has been an intensely religious nation. For century after century, Christianity was the religion of the people, the majority of whom through a sense of obligation and duty would have attended worship at least once on a Sunday. Welsh Anglicanism was always an embedded part of that Christian identity – and the continuity of faith from the 'Age of the Saints' in the sixth century through to Diocesan Conferences and the Governing Body of the twenty-first century is told with clarity and affection.

There is also clear mapping of the social and ecclesial changes which have been shaping both that Christian identity and the diverse expressions of church life through the century we are celebrating. Wales is also the region in the British Isles where religion has declined the most. We are reminded that the Church which introduced a Constitution to order its life in 1920 in key ways does not resemble the Church in Wales we know today. The latter is more inclusive and compassionate and knows better its need to proclaim the Gospel afresh to each generation, in a way that future generations can access and to which they can authentically respond.

There are things to regret and lament – and the book is not shy in discussing these. Relationships with other communities of faith have often been marked by scepticism, even malign distrust and cynicism.

We have allowed the deeply bilingual nature of the Church in Wales to be misrepresented. Attitudes towards women and minority groups in society have not always matched up to the radical call for equality in the Gospel of Jesus Christ. A Church born from coercive origins needs to learn from the constant temptation to demonise or denigrate others and to strive to be a truly prophetic religion, healing a broken world.

Yet the pages of this book are also filled with heartening examples of things which make us proud and grateful to God for his mercy and grace poured out upon his people, the Body of Christ, within the Anglican tradition in Wales. For example, there are progressive rites of passage. With its new burial service came a more pastorally sympathetic approach to those who were unbaptised or had committed suicide, something the Church of England only introduced forty years later. Whilst other parts of the Anglican Communion continue to wrestle with the issues of same-sex relationships, some paralysed into an uncomfortable impasse, the Governing Body of the Church in Wales has concluded that it is pastorally unsustainable for the Church to make no formal provision for those in same-gender relationships. And which other Anglican province has women making up one-half of its Bench of Bishops?

Also, here you will find a good dose of realism about the challenges which lie ahead. Drawing plentifully on what has gone before, the future agenda is also seen in terms of both continuity and change. An appraisal of the Constitution to fulfil more effectively the mission and witness of the modern Church in Wales is overdue. Addressing with confidence the nature of Anglicanism will help us incorporate our disagreements into our life. We put evangelism at the heart of our ministry for the good of a society which is tempted to believe that faith is irrelevant or untrustworthy. As isolation and loneliness increase and mental anxiety, especially amongst the young, becomes a new epidemic, we will renew our commitment to the local church being in every way for the local community it serves. In the Rhondda Valleys, in Haverfordwest, in Wrexham, in the Llŷn Peninsula or in Builth Wells, the Church in Wales serves the people of Wales.

And so this volume stimulates us to ask ourselves: in celebrating the centenary of the modern Church in Wales, what will a properly catholic, reformed, mission-oriented, and thoroughly Welsh Christian community look like in its second century? It has been an exciting and joyful journey so far, and the best is yet to come.

EDITORIAL PREFACE

This book has been prompted by three factors. First, there is the opportunity to reimagine the lasting impact on Wales of the momentous events immediately leading up to the foundation of the Church in Wales in 1920. The enactment by Parliament of the Welsh Church Act 1914, which led to disestablishment of the Church of England in Wales in 1920, occurred in the most extraordinary and controversial political circumstances. Promoted by the Liberal government, and the subject of a protracted and publicly criticised royal commission, it was opposed by the establishment, including the House of Lords, which in 1909–10 also initially rejected David Lloyd George's 'people's budget', and was the first statute enacted under the Parliament Act 1911, itself of immense constitutional significance in enabling the House of Commons to present a bill for royal assent without the Lords' consent – and all this on the eve of the First World War. Intriguingly, the day of disestablishment was the same as that on which Owain Glyndŵr's 'Pennal Letter' to Charles V of France in 1406 proposed independence for the Welsh Church from Canterbury – the last day of March.

Secondly, there is the topicality today of the issues at the heart of the debate as it developed for fifty years prior to disestablishment, and in the persistence of similar issues since. It was the Welsh who agitated for disestablishment. Nonconformists represented the majority religion. They refused to pay tithes to the English Church. There was a belief that the minority and alien Church of England had an anglicising effect on Welsh life – on the heels of the 1847 report on education portraying the Welsh as backward, barbaric and bone idle. The Liberal Party supported the Nonconformists, inheriting from its Whig roots sympathy for their causes. It had a Nonconformist following and advocated religious freedom and equality, and separation of State and religion – and Gladstone's Liberal government had disestablished the Church of Ireland and dissolved its union with the English Church in 1869. In contrast, the 'throne and altar' Conservative Party defended establishment – and its unionism opposed Wales-only law on religion. As the nineteenth century closed, the English Church in Wales no longer had power to monopolise education, control university life or impose church rates on all resident in its parishes. Moreover, while the call of English Nonconformists to disestablish the Church in England waned there, it waxed in Wales, especially so after legislation about denominational education (1902–5) and the great Welsh Revival (1904–5) which increased dramatically numbers of Nonconformists in Wales. Similar issues persisted after 1920 and still persist today. As we shall see, the Church in Wales continued and continues to grapple with its role in the national life of Wales, its position *vis-à-vis* other faith communities, its institutional separation from the State, and its need to co-operate with the State over, for example, its secular equality legislation.

Thirdly, there is the appetite of the Church in Wales to reflect in scholarly and practical ways on its work and legacy over the past hundred years and look forward in light of this wisdom. One theme which emerges in this book is the slow numerical decline in the membership of the institutional Church in Wales, the pressures placed on it by its custodianship of much of the built heritage of Wales, its need to engage with the effects since 1998 of devolution, and the expanding jurisdiction of the National Assembly for Wales and of the Welsh government in areas such as the ecclesiastical exemption, church schools, the safeguarding of children and vulnerable adults, and equality and diversity in all areas of its life. The centenary, therefore, provides a good opportunity for the Church in Wales, as an institution and as a community of those faithful Christians who associate with it – together with its ecumenical partners and wider society – to evaluate its work and contribution to Welsh life as simply one religious organisation among many in a pluralistic Wales – that is to say, to reimagine itself as a church for the future.

I have enjoyed the support of a great many people in the process of editing this book. First, the contributors, each of whom took up the invitation to write without demur but with an enthusiasm and good will undaunted by the demanding *grille thématique* and the tight and relentless timescale. It was a great privilege and pleasure to work with such a distinguished, energetic and experienced team, and I thank each one of them for their industry, flexibility and patience in responding to queries, requests for further research, and suggestions for fine-tuning. Secondly, the staff at the provincial offices of the Church in Wales. Work on chapters required consultation of a host of primary and archival materials. The contributors and I are extremely grateful to John

Richfield, Lyn Chandler, Julian Luke and all their colleagues, and to William Price, for searching for, finding, and providing access to these materials. Thirdly, the Bench of Bishops, Representative Body and provincial secretary, Simon Lloyd, of the Church in Wales provided invaluable support and encouragement. Fourthly, at Cambridge University Press, I am especially grateful to Finola O'Sullivan, Editorial Director, Law, for her initial and positive response to the book proposal in the summer of 2018, for her continued faith in the project and for her support over recent months, as well as to her colleagues who have made production of the book such an enjoyable and expeditious experience. Finally, I thank for their constant support my long-suffering family – particularly my wife Heather who, as a doctor and legislator in the Church in Wales, provided much-appreciated insights into all the issues – as well as my own church community at St Edward's Church, Roath, in Cardiff, where I have had the very good fortune to serve as the organist for the past forty-three years. If the materials in this book have not been described accurately, explained adequately or assessed sensibly, I am solely responsible. Be that as it may, it is hoped this volume will be a lasting contribution to practical scholarship about the Church in Wales as it celebrates its foundation, fortunes and future.

~

Introduction

NORMAN DOE

This book marks the centenary of the foundation of the Church in Wales, *Yr Eglwys yng Nghymru*, as a separate province of the global Anglican Communion. It seeks to describe, explain and evaluate landmark developments in the life of the Church in Wales, following the disestablishment of the Church of England in Wales in 1920, as they have unfolded during the course of the century. The book focusses on key areas of activity of the Church over the years and the challenges and opportunities which these have involved as the Church has sought to carry out its mission and ministry in witness to the Christian faith and in service to the people of Wales. Each chapter seeks to explore the evolution of the mind and practice of the Church in each of these areas in terms of theology, law, policy, impact and experience.

The book is divided into five parts, each one dealing with a cluster of related topics. Part I provides a historical overview by way of general background. There are four chapters on: the church from the Age of the Saints to Victorian times; the campaign for disestablishment; the place of Christianity in Wales since 1920; and the broad issues faced by the Church in the course of the century. The four chapters of Part II explore matters of church governance and ministry, namely: the Constitution; bishops and archbishops; clergy (priests and deacons); and the laity and new patterns of ministry. Part III examines a further four areas: doctrine, liturgy, the rites of passage, and relations with other faith communities. Part IV – in its four chapters – deals with the Church and wider society: cultural debate; education; the Welsh language; and the Church's social responsibility work. The book ends with discussion, in the two short chapters of Part V, of the images of the Church as developed by it and by the media, how these have helped or hindered the Church in its mission, and with reflections by the archbishop of Wales on lessons learnt over the century, the Church today and its future.

In terms of method, while the first four chapters set the scene historically, the principal task of each subsequent specialist chapter is to identify

1

continuity and change within the particular field studied, in the form of landmark developments and issues. First, generally, the chapter sets out the position of the church on the topic at, and where appropriate immediately before, disestablishment, and then describes whether this position continued or changed over the century, until the present, indicating when change occurred. Chapters then either present developments in distinct periods or they do so thematically. Secondly, each chapter explains the continuity and/or change – typically, who drove it, the reasons and stimulus for it, the attendant debate, and justifications for and the extent of the continuity/change in theology, law and practice. Reasons more often than not include initiatives and pressures within the Church and its various constituencies, or responses to stimuli, including pressures, from outside the Church. Thirdly, each chapter evaluates the continuity and change in terms of the significance of the effects of these on the Church, its integrity, mission and place in society. This is the critical aspect of the studies – and various criteria are used to measure a position.

Within this methodological framework, therefore, the evaluative aspects of the studies often suggest (sometimes uncomfortable) conclusions about the national ministry of the Church, whether it has become more or less relevant to Welsh life, more or less liberal or tolerant, and more or less traditional. Some also express concerns about the extent to which the Church perpetuates elements of the former established position of the English Church in Wales (and how these have helped or hindered it in its mission across the decades), and the benefits and challenges of these for Anglicans (and other Christians) in Wales today and in the future. The book also questions various assumptions, in public debate and scholarship, about the Church in Wales. These include: the persistently articulated view that it is a disestablished church – it is not, but, rather, a new ecclesial institution – it was the English Church in Wales that was disestablished; the use of its freedom; its distinctive Welshness; its willingness to collaborate with other faith communities; its place in and contribution to global Anglicanism; its approach to innovation; and how it has faced challenges and opportunities posed by the State and wider world in the increasingly pluralist and secularised nature of Welsh society over the century. The book is, therefore, also designed to stimulate debate – some chapters propose changes. For example, there are explicit or implicit calls for the Church to deal with different visions within it of the nature of the church, for renewal of the Constitution (on the basis that it is better to have it and not need it than to need it and not have it), for the greater involvement of the laity in ministry, for more clarity on rights of admission to some rites of passage, for fuller engagement with other world religions represented in Welsh society, and for clearer appreciation of the impact of media portrayals of the Church on the effective discharge of its mission. In other words, whilst the book is designed to enhance our understanding of this institution of Welsh society, and at the same time to celebrate, it also seeks to generate thoughtful reflection on what has and has not worked across the century.

The contributors are all distinguished in various fields of expertise across a wide and diverse range of aspects of the Church's corporate public life – strategic and operational. An effort has been made to include contributors from as wide a spectrum as practicable. As a result, the contributors include: ordained people (archbishops, bishops, archdeacons and others); lay people and office-holders across the various levels of the Church (provincial, diocesan and parochial); educators, ministers, governors, theologians and historians; those still in active public ministry and those retired from it; and people from a range of theological positions and perspectives – traditional, liberal, catholic, evangelical and high and low church. One contributor is a distinguished historian from outside the Anglican tradition. What is also evident is the direct role played by many contributors in developments of more recent years affecting the Church – and, needless to say, their experiences add to the authenticity or richness of the book, subject to caveats about possible subjectivity. As will be seen, some chapters refer occasionally to the same historical events as treated in other chapters – it is hoped that such apparent repetition will be forgiven on the basis that all the topics treated are fundamentally interrelated and each event susceptible to new and different interpretations.

The book is ground-breaking as a centenary study and seeks to fill a gap in the academic literature. As the Bibliography shows, there is an abundant body of secondary literature on historical aspects of the life of the Church in Wales, both before and after disestablishment. However, there is little literature on the Church in Wales as it has developed in the past century in terms of the specialist areas covered in this volume.[1] Nevertheless, D. T. W. Price, *A History of the Church in Wales in the Twentieth Century*, is a notable exception and takes the story to 1990 in

---

[1] Of the eight excellent chapters in D. Walker, ed., *A History of the Church in Wales* (Penarth: Church in Wales Publications, 1976), only the final chapter deals with the twentieth century.

its masterly treatment of broad themes. This book studies a wider range of church activities and issues, and in greater depth, and to the present. There are also books on aspects of the life of the Church in Wales, from, for example, ecumenical, sociological and legal perspectives, such as G. Abraham-Williams, ed., *Towards Making an Ecumenical Bishop* (1997), or C. Harris and R. Startup, *The Church in Wales: The Sociology of a Traditional Institution* (1999), or Philip Jones, *The Governance of the Church in Wales* (2000). Our book draws on the learning of such scholars not only in re-examining topics such as these but also in continuing the story to the present. And it seeks to innovate in so far as studies in it are based on a very wide range of hitherto untapped primary sources, such as the minutes of provincial and diocesan bodies, including their commit-tees or commissions.

It is hoped that the book will appeal not only to those who wish to celebrate the centenary of the Church in Wales, but also to scholars and students of theology, ministry, church history, religious studies, Anglican studies, ecumenical studies, interreligious studies, the sociology of religion, and the study of religion and law. The book may also be relevant to those engaged in debate about the continued establishment of the Church of England, from which the four Welsh dioceses separated in 1920. Studies such as R. M. Morris, ed., *Church and State in 21st-Century Britain: The Future of Church Establishment* (London: Palgrave Macmillan, 2009), indicate vividly the topicality of the (dis)establishment issues in England today. As with the Church in Wales, the life of the Church of England too over the past hundred years has been characterised by continuity and change – of the latter, from the field of ecclesiastical law for instance, we might note: the setting up of the National Assembly of the Church of England under an Act of Parliament of 1919; the furore over the 1928 prayer book; the reconstitution of the Church Assembly as the General Synod in 1970 (under the Synodical Government Measure 1969); the passing of the Church of England (Worship and Doctrine) Measure 1974 (giving greater freedom to legislate by canon on doctrinal and liturgical matters); the rough parliamentary passage of the Churchwardens Measure 2001; and the requirement in relation to a host of areas of church life for the Church of England to obtain the consent of Parliament for the enact-ment of its legislation in the form of measures, and to obtain the consent of the Crown in the appointments of its bishops. For the Church in Wales (with the rare exceptions of such areas as marriage and burial law), the disestablishment of the Church of England in Wales and the separation of the Church in Wales from the State – both effected by the Welsh Church

Act 1914 – and the ecclesiastical separation of the four Welsh dioceses from the Province of Canterbury in 1920 provided the basic freedom which the Church in Wales still enjoys. And this book is about the use of that freedom over the course of one hundred years, a freedom to plan, articulate and live out its understanding of Christian faith.

The book is also designed to assist the bishops, clergy, officers and members of the Church in Wales, whether involved directly in its institutional administration and ministerial practice or as beneficiaries of its ministry, to learn about the church and to reflect on its legacy. It is hoped, therefore, that it will afford for policy-makers in the church an overview of the way in which the church has developed over one century of its activity, providing lessons to be learnt from the challenges it has faced, and elucidating the strategies it has evolved to deal with them, as well as evaluating the impact of these on the life of the church as it functions in wider society. Equally, it offers those engaged in training for ordained and other forms of church ministry – teachers and ordination candidates – essential reading to understand the historical development of the church since disestablishment. Finally, it is hoped that the book will provide for those beyond or in dialogue with the Church in Wales – ecumenical partners, interfaith interlocutors, and government officials – an opportunity better to understand the Church in Wales, its longstanding aspirations and its needs in a single accessible volume. This is so, not least, as to the opportunities and constraints which its own beliefs, practices, and rules place on the Church in Wales in developing relations with other churches, other faith groups, the government and society. Above all, however, the book is a lasting tribute to all those who have served and helped the Church in Wales as it embarks on its second century.

PART I

Historical Antecedents and Overview of the
Century

The Age of Saints to the Victorian Church

ROGER L. BROWN

This chapter presents an overview of the long history of the Church in Wales, from its earliest days to the mid-Victorian nineteenth century. Its concern is to identify those issues which became controversial during the time of the various campaigns which led up to disestablishment of the Church of England in Wales in 1920. Many of these issues had roots which lay in the past and, whilst they became significant during the disestablishment campaigns, many had proved contentious for earlier generations. We also need to note that there were considerable differences between the four Welsh dioceses, ranging from the poverty of St David's and Llandaff to the wealthier dioceses of Bangor and St Asaph.

The Early and Medieval Church in Wales

We know little of the history of the so-called Celtic Church or of its origins in Wales. However, we should remember that until the fourteenth century Wales was not a united nation in the modern sense of a single political unit. Rather, it comprised numerous lordships whose composition altered over the years. Much of the earlier history of the Welsh Church was bedevilled by Rhygyfarch (died 1099), a son of Bishop Sulien of St David's, and Giraldus Cambrensis (died 1223), both of whom endeavoured to promote St David as an archbishop of Wales, and so falsified the historical record, assuming that the early Welsh Church, particularly its religious communities, was akin to the Church of their own day.

It may be surmised that Roman soldiers and traders brought Christianity to Wales, and that missionaries arrived from the continent using the sea routes of their day. What evidence we possess of this period points to the existence of small Christian communities rather than an organised church. After the withdrawal of the Romans, Welsh Christianity embraced monasticism, which appears to have consisted of a tribal family under the leadership of an abbot, who may have been consecrated as a bishop. From these centres their members branched out, establishing places of worship and often naming them after the founder of their community. It was the 'Age of the Saints' of whom we may name Dyfrig, Illtyd, Cadog, Teilo, David, Deiniol and Beuno. They were more local than national figures, and the churches they served remained isolated from mainstream continental Christianity. At a later stage most of these monastic establishments had become *clasau* (singular, *clas*) or mother churches, with daughter churches linked to their community.

Even though these communities retained their independence, there are hints of a wider co-operation. Rhygyfarch records that 118 bishops attended the Synod of Brefi in west Wales, when Garmon (Germanus), Bishop of Auxerre, came to condemn the Pelagian heresy in either 429 or 447. A life of St David records two general synods in the sixth century, indicating some degree of co-operation between the various Welsh churches. There were also considerable links with the Breton Church.

When Augustine came from Rome to Kent in 597 to evangelise the English, he was unaware that in the west there already existed a strong Christian presence. When this became clear he desired to incorporate it into the mainstream Roman jurisdiction. Two meetings followed between Augustine and seven Welsh bishops in 601, but they rejected his demands to accept his authority and a concept of episcopacy foreign to them. Gradually the isolation was worn down. The Synod of Whitby of 664 accepted the Roman date of Easter, albeit in a Northumbria context, and in 768 Bishop Elbodugus of Bangor followed this example. By this time it appears that the Celtic Church in Wales had itself aligned to the liturgy and customs of the Western Church, but retained its own independent structures.

The Normans' conquest was gradual in Wales. They saw the Church as part of their secular arm, and managed in north Wales to end the ill-defined structures, not without opposition, to establish dioceses at Bangor and St Asaph. In south Wales, the diocesan structure was partly in place, and Bishop Herewald of Llandaff (1055–1107) introduced many of the continental developments. His successor Urban (1107–34), when consecrated with other English bishops by Anselm, Archbishop of Canterbury, made vows of obedience to him and thus became his suffragan. Urban's contemporary at St David's, Bernard (1115–48), followed suit, so ensuring that the Welsh Church was now part of the Province of Canterbury. Bernard, followed by Giraldus Cambrensis, unsuccessfully attempted to persuade the papacy that there should be a separate Welsh province with an archbishopric of St David's. Both Urban and Bernard found difficulties in defining their diocesan boundaries, but ensured that their diocesan structures were based on English models. The English Crown now determined the appointment of bishops in Wales and, while some were Welsh-speaking, others were English appointments, often rewarded because they were loyal officials of the Crown. By the fifteenth century, the papacy claimed the right of these appointments, with the result that few of these bishops were Welsh-speakers, and many were foreigners and absentees.

The *clas* churches did not survive. Many were taken over by Anglo-Norman lords and appropriated to monasteries in Normandy or to English monasteries such as Tewkesbury and Gloucester Abbeys, leaving a small income for the resident priests. The Benedictine order was supported by the Anglo-Normans and its houses were confined to urban areas, while the more austere Cistercian order, whose first Welsh foundation was at Tintern, was favoured by the Welsh princes and as a result became a champion of Welsh culture. Sadly, a decline set in, when these houses were given the advowsons of various churches, with rights of patronage, by the families who had founded them. These appropriations meant that the abbot became the titular rector of the parish – and the abbey took its main income and appointed a deputy or vicar to undertake its spiritual work, giving him a share of tithes, generally the most difficult to collect, or a small income. The origin of tithes is disputed, but it meant that a tenth of all agricultural produce was reserved for the parish priest. For example, Valle Crucis Abbey had appropriated the parishes of Wrexham, Ruabon, Llangollen and Chirk; and Margam Abbey gained the parishes of Llangynwyd, St Fagans and Afan. These appropriations continued after the Reformation and had a devastating effect on the Welsh Church.

Owain Glyndwr's unsuccessful campaign for independence and a parliament for Wales, which started in 1400 and was supported by Bishop Trevor of St Asaph, caused widespread devastation in Wales, not least to the Church. Had it succeeded, he and his advisors planned to establish the Welsh Church as an independent ecclesiastical province (but subject to Rome), restore the finances lost to the church, ensure that only Welsh-speakers were appointed to high office in the Church and establish two universities.

Though the monastic communities had declined by this time, popular devotion had not. Though the Mass was said in Latin, the local clergy were Welsh-speakers, and many must have encouraged their parishioners to establish shrines to various saints in their churches, often achieving a devotion far wider than their parish. Churches were rebuilt, and such places as St David's, Holywell, Penrhys, and Pennant Melangell became popular pilgrimage centres. The poetry of the period bears eloquent witness to these activities. If the administration of the Church in Wales was lacking in many respects, the parishes offered evidence of a rich spiritual life and fervour.

The Reformation in Wales

The Reformation commenced because of the dynastic concerns of Henry VIII, the second of the Welsh family of Tudor monarchs, and as such became a matter of royal policy and a legislative partnership with Parliament. The Act of Supremacy 1534 ended papal jurisdiction in England and Wales, and two years later the Act of Union formally united Wales with England. It is widely accepted that the Reformation had little impact in Wales. There is perhaps more evidence of bardic regret at the loss of pilgrimages and the outward aspects of medieval Catholicism than of popular support or enthusiasm for new doctrines and ecclesiastical order.

All the religious houses were suppressed by 1539. Their estates, including their impropriations, passed to the king, and were either sold to laymen or used to endow collegiate and ecclesiastical establishments. Men such as Rice Mansel or Edward Carne, who had leased these monastic estates previously, now bought them and thus became the lay rectors of Margam and Ewenni, while the earl of Worcester obtained the estates of Tintern Abbey. The parish of Llantrisant, with its outlying chapelries of Aberdare and Ystradyfodwg eventually passed to the new cathedral of Gloucester, and Christ Church, Oxford, obtained in due course the parishes of Meifod, Welshpool and Guilsfield. The Pickering family obtained the grant of the rectory of Wrexham, while over the course of many years the Chichester family of Devon acquired numerous parishes in Cardiganshire which were once in the possession of the abbey of Strata Florida. These new owners took their tithes and continued to pay the historic stipend to their curates. However, Henry VIII continued the liturgy, doctrine and practices of the Roman Church. Under his son, Edward VI, this policy was changed and a new order established.

There were many reasons why the Reformation was slow to make an impact in Wales. Three may be mentioned. The first was linguistic. The new order came in a foreign tongue for most of the inhabitants of Wales, and even the eventual publication of a Welsh translation of the New

Testament and Book of Common Prayer in 1567, and of the complete Bible in 1588, were permitted only because of a fear that otherwise Wales might remain an area owing allegiance to Rome rather than to Canterbury, as happened with Ireland. It was a political, not a linguistic concession.

Secondly, the native Welsh-speaking clergy were as scarce in learning as it appears in number, and caused anxiety even to their pre-Reformation bishops. Few of them were thought capable of preaching the new faith. Furthermore, the economic problems of the Church in Wales prevented an adequate maintenance for its clergy, 60 per cent of whom had less than £10 *per annum*. In turn, this poverty caused the university men, often the upholders and preachers of the new faith, to seek preferment outside their native land. Thus the men who could have introduced the new faith at ground level were either hostile, ignorant or absent.

Thirdly, there was a lack of clear episcopal leadership, at least in those vital early days. Anthony Kitchin of Llandaff was the only bishop who survived all the changes of the Reformation period. His enthusiasm for anything may be suspect while he allowed some of the episcopal estate to be forcibly alienated from the see by the machinations of the Matthew family.

Therefore, outwardly the familiar trappings of wall pictures, screens and vestments disappeared, images, chantries and shrines were destroyed, the doctrines of purgatory and the sacrifice of the mass were no longer officially taught, the altar was replaced by a communion table, and the Latin mass was displaced by an English observance at first (albeit with Welsh readings provided by William Salesbury). However, there was little or no understanding of Christianity as forming a personal religion. Habit replaced conviction. The pope may have been replaced by the king in Parliament, but the old order remained in the colour of the heart's associations and in the traditional cerebral imagery of the mind. The changes that had been made were *ffydd y saeson*, the faith of the English. It was as thin as their language, so they said.

Even with the translation and publication of the Welsh version of the Book of Common Prayer and Bible, the old and popular order remained. The new Elizabethan bishops found themselves unable to counteract the habits of popular religion, or to prevent their clergy from perpetuating in private what they were required to deny in public.[1] There were still

---

[1] G. Williams, *Wales and the Reformation* (Cardiff: University of Wales Press, 1997), 285.

isolated pockets of those who owed allegiance to Rome, especially in Monmouthshire, who were bitterly persecuted.

Matters were hardly better after another fifty years. Rhys Prichard, vicar of Llandovery (1602–44), in his popular *Canwyll y Cymry* ('The Welshman's Candle'), protested about prayers for the dead, belief in conjurors and the popular belief in purgatory. John Lewis, writing in 1646, referred to 'the swarm of blinde superstitious ceremonies that are among us, passing under the name of old harmless customs'. Vavasor Powell declared in the same year that not one in 500 families possessed a copy of the Bible. Preaching was almost non-existent.[2]

The late 1640s and 1650s saw the ascendency of the Puritan movement in Wales, following the execution of Charles I and the end of the civil war. The *gwerin*, who may not have minded the extinction of episcopacy, positively disliked the new usurpers – the sometimes jumped-up tradesmen (of some of whom even the later Puritans spoke with shame), who replaced the familiar good-humoured and complacent clergymen who used an ordered and well-known liturgy. More than 268 clergymen were ejected from their parishes.[3] Some were scholars. Many were not. Some were claimed to be drunkards and immoral, but many more were found to be unacceptable because of their churchmanship. Men such as these were replaced, but not always, by men who did as their consciences directed them, rather than that which was 'lawful and just'. A parish could find itself with a Baptist man who would allow only believer's baptism, or an Independent who allowed no outside interference, or a Presbyterian who took his orders from the local presbytery court. Some of these men were outstanding. One thinks of Philip Henry and Stephen Hughes. But time was not on their side. It was not possible to replace every ejected man. And so itinerants were appointed to preach here, there and everywhere. The good people of Guilsfield, Montgomeryshire, complained in 1652 that their church door was 'commonly shut on the Lord's day' and even on the previous Easter.[4] This was no isolated case. Where there might have been an ordered attempt to proclaim the Gospel, for such order was not lacking in the distribution of the Church's resources, instead, confusion reigned during the Commonwealth.

[2]   T. Richards, *The Puritan Movement in Wales* (London: National Eisteddfod Association, 1920), 9–12.

[3]   Ibid., 115–33.

[4]   D. R. Thomas, *A History of the Diocese of St Asaph* (Oswestry: Caxton Press, 1913), III, 145–6.

The Church and the Restoration of Monarchy

The churchmen returned after the restoration of King Charles II in 1660. The prayer book was revised, but spiritual fervour was controlled by the folk memories of the 'roundheads', the abolition of Christmas, and the oratorical powers of good, if sometimes misguided, men. Henceforth, the Puritan discipline would be associated with a denial of the good things of life, rather than with the enrichment of the whole of life in Christ. Alas, people had seen the outward veneer, not the inward conviction. A royalist Parliament determined on revenge. The Act of Uniformity 1662 required all clergymen to conform to the Book of Common Prayer (1662) and give consent to the Thirty-Nine Articles of Religion (1563). Those who declined to do so were ejected to the number of 118, though some had not been episcopally ordained.[5] Their number included such outstanding men as Philip Henry and Stephen Hughes. The so-called Clarendon Code forbade all non-Anglican meetings for worship and restricted the movements of ministers. At times there was persecution, especially of the Quakers who were a disruptive force throughout their early history. But the Toleration Act 1689 gave Dissenters freedom of worship though under carefully prescribed conditions. Roman Catholics were excluded. The established Church now had a rival if divided organisation, and this was to have major consequences in the years to come.

There were immense difficulties in the Dioceses of St David's and Llandaff, and although the other two dioceses were in a better condition they too continued to face similar issues. Those impropriators who had obtained the tithe income of the parishes continued to pay to the curates serving them the historic pre-Reformation stipend which was generally in the order of £10 or so *per annum*. In the county of Cardiganshire, in the Diocese of St David's, the Chichester family, already mentioned, possessed the tithe income of fifteen parishes, including the large and scattered parish of Llanbadarn Fawr. This tithe income amounted to £2,500 annually, but only a pittance of this was used for the historic stipends of the clergy who served these parishes. Bishop Nicholas Claggett remarked that this family had exhausted almost the entire revenue of the Church in those parts. The curate of Buttington, Montgomeryshire, received an annual income of £15 from the impropriators of his parish, Christ Church, Oxford, which received more than

---

[5] T. Richards, *Religious Developments in Wales (1654–1662)* (London: National Eisteddfod Association, 1923), 488, 495, 498.

£400 from its tithes.[6] Erasmus Saunders, in a book published in 1721, relating to the Diocese of St David's, noted the consequences of this state of affairs. The curates were forced to serve three or four churches for £10 or £12 a year, even though they were as many miles distant from each other. There was no time fixed for going to church, but the curate started as early as possible, hurried over as many prayers as might be accomplished in half an hour, and then returned to the road until he had finished his circuit. Saunders noted that it was unreasonable to expect these men to engage in a pastoral ministry, catechise, instruct or teach.[7] Consequently, there was much non-residence among the clergy – but this was mainly technical, for it has been possible to identify groups of parishes linked together where one cleric served as either incumbent of some and curate of others, and lived in a place from which he could serve this grouping.

The bishops were well aware of these problems, but could do little to alleviate them. However, some bishops were outstanding men, such as George Bull of St David's (1705–10), and William Beveridge (1704–8) and William Fleetwood (1708–15) of St Asaph. John Evans, Bishop of Bangor (1706–16), before his translation to Meath, was the last native Welsh-speaking bishop in Wales until 1870. As prime ministers effectively nominated bishops to the Crown, they began to choose those known to them and their partisans, and, with episcopal incomes varying greatly, those who remembered their 'makers' were translated to more lucrative sees. Between 1716 and 1800 Bangor had thirteen bishops, and St David's seventeen between 1710 and 1800. These were the Anglo-Welsh bishops – and although they have been given a bad press most were conscientious bishops according to the standards of their day, visiting their dioceses during the parliamentary recesses, and being young bishops were able to take initiatives to assist their dioceses. In the Diocese of St Asaph, for example, three of its bishops required their rural deans – an order which had survived in that diocese – to visit and report on each parish in their deanery, during 1729, 1749 and 1791. If these reports revealed dilapidated buildings and a lack of clergy houses, they also indicated, by and large, a conscientious clergy. However, these bishops were unsympathetic to the Welsh language and temperament, as illustrated by the presentation, by Bishop John Egerton of Bangor, of

---

[6] R. L. Brown, *A Social History of the Welsh Clergy* (Welshpool: privately published, 2017), Part 1, 200–4.

[7] E. Saunders, *A View of the State of Religion in the Diocese of St David's* (Cardiff: University of Wales Press, [reprint] 1949), 24–7.

Thomas Bowles to one of the most valuable livings in his diocese, to which Bowles was instituted in 1766. It was an almost monoglot Welsh parish and Bowles was an English-speaker. It became a *cause célèbre*.[8] Nevertheless, the bishops insisted that if Welsh services were required, then a Welsh-speaking curate had to be appointed to provide them.

Practical steps were required. Queen Anne's Bounty was made as a gift to the Church by the queen of that name in 1704. By it she returned the ecclesiastical taxes of first fruits and tenths to the Church which Henry VIII had secularised at the Reformation. These taxes, which continued to be based on the valuation of 1534, included a one-off payment on the induction to a benefice (originally of its first year's income) and an annual payment of a tenth of that income. Parishes founded since that date (1534), perpetual curacies and later those under a certain income were discharged from payment. These taxes were used to augment poor parishes, either by giving an equivalent grant to a benefaction, so doubling it, or distributed by lot amongst parishes under a certain income, at first under £10. Initially, this money had to be used in the purchase of land which would be rented out in order to add to the income of the benefice. Many parishes received numerous grants over the years, which slowly increased their income.

Further assistance came from the Society for Promoting Christian Knowledge (SPCK). Four of its five founders had links with Wales, some of whom were also founding members of the Society for the Propagation of the Gospel, a missionary society. Founded in 1698 and based in London, its aim was to provide charity schools and publish Bibles, prayer books and other spiritual works. Ninety-six schools were established in Wales, mainly in south-west Wales, but they taught in English, as did a previous charity supported by both churchmen and Nonconformists, the Welsh Trust of Thomas Gouge. Although the schools did not continue after 1727, its publication work continued, providing Welsh Bibles and prayer books for distribution at nominal cost (in 1752 it produced 30,000 copies of the Welsh Bible), and translations of English classics such as Nelson's *Festivals and Fasts* and Lewis Bayly's *Practice of Piety*. From the correspondence of the SPCK we also know it was supported by a substantial number of the Welsh clergy. Diocesan libraries too were supported by the society, enabling the clergy

[8] R. L. Brown, 'Pastoral Problems and Legal Solutions', in N. Doe, ed., *Essays in Canon Law: A Study of the Law of the Church in Wales* (Cardiff: University of Wales Press, 1992), 9–12.

to borrow theological books to supplement their education provided by the licensed grammar schools, such as at Carmarthen, Cowbridge and Ystrad Meurig. Few were able to afford a university education.

The demand for these Welsh Bibles and books was due to the circulating schools of Griffith Jones (born c. 1683), vicar of Llanddowror in Carmarthenshire. Deeply concerned at the spiritual ignorance of his parishioners he started a school at his church, and gradually this movement spread throughout Wales, although its main input was in the south. A schoolmaster, trained by Jones, at the invitation of the cleric, would set up a school in such places as a church, barn or farm kitchen, teaching the children by day and adults by night – to read the Bible, to take part in the liturgy of the church, to promote family and personal prayers, and to catechise the children each Sunday. From the late 1730s until Jones' death in 1761, when the schools were taken over by his associate Madam Bevan until her death in 1777, more than 6,465 schools had been held, some parishes holding numerous ones, and probably more than 200,000 people attended them. If this made Wales into a literate nation, Jones' real purpose was a spiritual one, to encourage people to seek Christ for their salvation and to grow in faith. Letters he published from clergy in his annual production, *Welch Piety*, indicated the encouragement the clergy felt through the work of these schools, with increased congregations and parishioners eager for a deeper spiritual ministry. None of the clergy could have been unaware of the spiritual nature of the schools, and it has been estimated that about 46 per cent of the working clergy in Wales supported these schools. Further support came from English benefactors who helped provide the finances required, as well as from the SPCK, but not so far as it is known from the Welsh bishops of the period.[9]

Although Jones played down the association of these schools with the Methodist Revival, there was a clear connection. Many of his schoolmasters were Methodist converts, and the spiritual fervour these schools imparted could not always be contained within the Anglican Church itself with its restricted liturgy and the difficulties of providing pastoral care.

The Age of Revival and Beyond

The Revival, part of a much wider movement through Great Britain, North America and parts of the continent, came to a Welsh Church that

---

[9] R. L. Brown, *Evangelicals in the Church in Wales* (Welshpool: Tair Eglwys Press, 2007), 33–44.

still held the loyalty of its people. Although some Nonconformists were affected by it, it was mainly an Anglican affair. In Wales it was linked with a Calvinistic theology associated with George Whitefield, who was frequently in touch with its Welsh leaders, unlike the Arminianism of the Wesley brothers, whose influence in Wales was limited. Its origin may be dated to 1735 when Howel Harris was converted, while Daniel Rowland, said to have been converted through a sermon of Griffith Jones, had walked to London the previous year in order to be ordained. They became the leaders of the Welsh Revival, which spread through preaching, the use of hymns, especially those of William Williams Pantycelyn, the *seiat* or experience meeting, and eventually the use of lay preachers termed 'exhorters'. Its adherents saw their societies as an extension of the Church's ministry and attended their parish churches Sunday by Sunday, as well as attending their own meetings. It is quite clear most of the clergy accepted this, for in their visitation returns, when asked about Nonconformity in their parishes, the majority ignored the often considerable Methodist presence in their midst.

The Anglo-Welsh bishops were not so accommodating. Failing to understand the Welsh temperament and being horrified by this enthusiasm and emotion, being Latitudinarians to the core, they acted accordingly. Howel Harris was refused ordination repeatedly, Daniel Rowland was ejected from his curacies for preaching in the open air, William Williams Pantycelyn and Thomas Charles, a later leader, were refused ordination as priests and remained permanent deacons, and pressure was put on others to conform, such as David Jones Llangan.

As a result, the Methodists built their own chapels, but initially arranged the times of their services so as not to conflict with those at the parish church. Later, concerned about the state of some of the clergy, and wishing to have ordained men celebrate Holy Communion for them, they became concerned at the scarcity of these men – and, finally, Thomas Jones, a Methodist exhorter, asked Thomas Charles which came first, the ministry of the Word or the celebration of the Lord's Supper, which derived from that Word. There was only one answer, and a reluctant Charles permitted the ordination of lay preachers in 1811, thus severing the final connection between Methodism and the Anglican Church. A number of Methodist clergy departed from the Church, while others remained within the fold, such as the influential David Griffiths of Nevern, Pembrokeshire. Two bishops, at least, took action to mitigate the loss. Bishop William Cleaver of St Asaph overturned his diocesan policy of admitting only university men to orders, and now ordained literate men from 'among the people', and, with Bishop Thomas Burgess of St David's, permitted many Methodist practices to continue within the Church, in the hope of retaining the allegiance of many lay people who might otherwise have gone over to the Methodists.[10] With the growth of the other Nonconformist bodies, the Church in the four Welsh dioceses was now a minority church, and its privileges began to be questioned.

The Church was seen as the moral guardian of the nation at a time when there was no standing army or effective policing. Its liturgy had the State prayers, the royal arms were a prominent feature of many church interiors, and the clergy were expected to preach morality and rebuke offenders. Nonconformity was suspect, however, of being seditious and there was a considerable if irrational fear that they might become akin to the roundheads of the civil war. High churchmen like Bishop Edward Copleston of Llandaff (1828–49) saw them as schismatics and as intruding upon the ministry of faithful clergymen. He could even describe Dissent as a 'sin'. His views were not uncommon and caused considerable resentment among Nonconformists.[11] Such views could not prevent the growth of Dissent. A Nonconformist body could establish a cause without difficulty, whereas to establish a new parish required vested interests to be respected, an Act of Parliament, a purpose-built church and an income for an incumbent. In many areas Nonconformity gained the field long before the Church was able to take action. Initiatives were needed and, while most of them were nationally based, others were more local.

One such initiative was taken by Bishop Burgess of St David's in the foundation of St David's College, Lampeter, which opened in 1827 to provide a theological training for the future clergy of his diocese. It replaced the traditional divinity classes attached to grammar schools but required a longer and more expensive training. However, the main initiative came from the government in the form of the Ecclesiastical Commission, established in 1835. Accepting that reform was required but that the Church had no central body able to take action, it took matters into its own hands, proceeding by Orders in Council. The commission took over the episcopal and capitular estates, giving the bishops and cathedral functionaries a stated stipend, and the surplus monies, as they became available (as existing interests and leases were respected), were used to assist the Church in populous and industrial

---

[10] Ibid., 94–95.
[11] R. L. Brown, ed., *The Letters of Edward Copleston* (Cardiff: South Wales Record Society, 2003), 29–31.

areas, and in parishes in which it held an interest, such as owning its tithes. This enabled new districts to be formed with an endowment for the minister, while the commissioners also offered grants to meet a benefaction of money, land or a tithe rent charge. They also assisted, in a similar way, the provision of grants for curates and for the building of churches, schools and parsonage houses. Without its assistance, the Church in the Diocese of Llandaff in particular would have faced an impossible task in catering for the increase in population which accompanied industrialisation. In Glamorgan alone the population increase was from 70,000 in 1801 to nearly 232,000 fifty years later. Much of this increase was in the large and scattered parishes of the upland, such as Ystradyfodwg, but it included such town as Merthyr Tydfil and Aberdare, where in the 1840s its one dilapidated church possessed 176 seats for a population of 13,000. The evangelical and London-based Church Pastoral-Aid Society also provided grants for curates, particularly in the industrial areas. The ministry of such men as David Howell at Cardiff and Wrexham, John Griffith at Aberdare and Merthyr, and Edward Squire at Swansea, which became 'church parishes' through their ministries, would have been impossible without the national resources of the commission, the Church Pastoral-Aid Society and the Church Building Society.

The government also tackled pluralism. The Pluralities Act 1838 limited the number of livings a man might possess to two, requiring him to reside in one of these parishes. Further legislation of 1850 reduced the distance from ten to three miles and one of the livings had to have an annual value of £100 or less. While this might have had caused much hardship to those in what were 'technical pluralities', new diocesan initiatives, as well as the work of Queen Anne's Bounty and the Ecclesiastical Commission, helped relieve the difficulties.

The Church was effectively comprised of individual legal corporations, such as parishes, cathedrals and bishops. Apart from the episcopal visitation of dioceses every third year, and an insubstantial diocesan administration, there was no sense of diocesan corporateness. This was changing by the 1840s and 1850s with the establishment of diocesan societies, such as the Bangor Church Building Society of 1838, and the later Llandaff Diocesan Church Extension Society which, supported mainly by the wealthy of the diocese, gave funds to establish new places of worship, augment the value of benefices, and provide curates in the populous areas. The lapsed archdeaconries were restored and others created, and rural deaneries and clerical chapters brought into being. The result was that a diocesan ethos was created – although Diocesan

Conferences appeared much later, the first, that of St Asaph, in 1879. The revival of the clerical Convocation of Canterbury in 1852 and the establishment of the national Church Congresses, held annually from 1861, enabled the four Welsh dioceses to be more involved within the framework of the national Church.

The Church had always seen itself as the rightful educator of the young, and the Dioceses of Llandaff and Bangor had established educational boards in 1839 and 1849 respectively. Assisted by government grants for schools, the church school became almost the handmaid of the Church. Most of the schools were affiliated to the National Society for the Promoting of the Poor in the Principles of the Established Church, founded in 1811 and immediately supported by the Welsh bishops. The society offered grants for these schools on condition their pupils were taught the church Catechism and attended the parish church on Sundays. One great advantage was that their buildings could be used for services on Sundays. By 1867 there were 808 National schools in Wales providing two-thirds of the elementary schools in the country.[12] As the government would only allow one grant-aided school in a locality, it was clear the Church had gained a monopoly in this field.

With a growing sense of nationalism within the country, the Church endeavoured to tackle the problems associated with non-Welsh-speakers being appointed to Welsh-speaking parishes. While bishops had insisted that Welsh-speaking curates be appointed, these men often felt themselves as the underdogs of the Church and deprived of its better livings. The Pluralities Act of 1838 endeavoured to prevent such appointments, but had its limitations.[13] At the same time, there was a growing pressure for the appointment of native Welsh-speaking bishops for the Welsh dioceses by the prime ministers of the day, who assumed that a man could learn Welsh in the same way as a classical language. Connop Thirlwall and Alfred Ollivant, who both learnt Welsh, could hardly be understood, and when William Gladstone eventually appointed Joshua Hughes to the Diocese of St Asaph in 1870 it was with the knowledge that he was deficient in some of the attributes required of a bishop.[14]

By the 1870s, the Church in the four Welsh dioceses was reviving and had done much to redress its previous plight. New parishes had been created, new churches built and others restored. Whereas in 1832 there

---

[12] J. Williams, *Digest of Welsh Historical Statistics* (Cardiff: Welsh Office, 1985), II, 201.
[13] Brown, 'Pastoral Problems', 13–24.
[14] R. L. Brown, *In Pursuit of a Welsh Episcopate* (Cardiff: University of Wales Press, 2005).

had been 450 resident incumbents, by 1879 the number had risen to 785 – a new army of assistant clergy had been employed, services had been revitalised, church schools established, mission churches built, stipends improved, and parsonage houses provided. Between 1840 and 1873, in the Diocese of Bangor, £160,000 had been spent on church building and restoration, and during the same period in St Asaph five new churches were built or restored on average each year.[15] Furthermore, the old pew system, which had deprived the poor of seats in their parish churches, was becoming a relic of the past. It was a massive achievement, but it was not enough.

The findings of the 1851 religious census organised by Horace Mann, a government official, came as a huge shock to the Church. Though its figures are disputed, it revealed that Wales was a nation of Nonconformists. The Church had 19.31 per cent of church attendances on the Sunday of the survey, outnumbered by both the Welsh Methodists and Independents, 29 per cent of places of worship and 31 per cent of sittings.[16] Nonconformists knew their strength, and their grievances were to be given an even greater prominence than before.

Each house owner or tenant was required to pay church rates, used to maintain the church building and provide the necessities of worship, though disputes arose about whether this included heating, lighting and the provision of music. Nonconformists opposed these rates, arguing that their purpose was to support a church they did not attend and that they had their own place of worship to support. It is not surprising that the Abergavenny Church Rate Abolition Association was formed in 1834. Nonconformists, attending the parish vestries, prevented church rates from being imposed in Swansea, Newport and Merthyr Tydfil in 1836, and this was followed in many other parishes. By 1864 half the parishes in Wales had ceased to demand church rates, and in 1868 an Act of Parliament abolished compulsory rates but permitted a voluntary rate. In most parishes it was replaced by a church offertory.[17]

Tithes, commuted to a money payment based on the value of corn in 1836, were another source of contention, though it was not until the agricultural depression of the 1880s that their existence became inflammatory, especially where a rebate was refused. Church laymen were often arbitrary in declining to allow sites for chapel buildings, and after the

[15] J. W. James, *A Church History of Wales* (Ilfracombe: Stockwell, 1945), 181–2.
[16] J. Williams, *Digest*, II, 352.
[17] Brown, *A Social History*, Part 2 (2018), 627–38.

1868 election, before the Ballot Act 1872 allowed a secret ballot, many who voted against their landlord's instructions were evicted from their tenancies. The landlords were Tories and churchmen, their evicted tenants Nonconformists and Liberals. The church schools, often the only school available to Nonconformist children, were regarded as proselytising agencies, while it was considered unfair that school buildings – often built with the aid of government grants – could be used for Anglican services and other activities.

The memory of the Anglo-Welsh bishops and clergy still resonated in Welsh circles, although the issues associated with them had been redressed already. The Church was regarded as an English institution, and the fact that, unlike Nonconformity, it was a bilingual church, at a time when English-speakers were migrating into Wales, was ignored. It was often impossible in multi-church parishes to hold a service in Welsh each week. Where separate services were held, their times were often inconvenient, and sometimes took place in schoolrooms, in mission rooms or in the ancient parish church. Too often the Welsh congregations felt they were given a second-class service. The truth was that the English congregations had the resources and the Welsh did not – and the understanding of many Welsh people was that English was the language of advancement and wealth. It is for this reason that church schools taught through the medium of English, which was a requirement for grant aid from the National Society, and later of the Board of Education. Nevertheless, however unfair, the Welsh Church was regarded as an Anglicising institution.

The Church's pronouncements about Nonconformity also aroused resentment. The famous Education Report of 1847 into Welsh education, though few disputed its findings about the poverty of its schools, was prepared by Anglican commissioners and revealed some hostility on their part to Nonconformity. It also attracted outright condemnation by several of the clergy whose opinions it quoted. But a few even linked the Welsh language and Nonconformity with backwardness and immorality. This 'Treachery of the Blue Books' was not to be forgotten even though churchmen attacked the findings of the report. The growth of Anglo-Catholicism, with its denunciations of Nonconformity as schismatic and its ministers as usurpers, became a focal point of concern, especially as the trustees of the Bute family (the industrialists) used their patronage to ensure that some of the leading parishes in the Diocese of Llandaff, such as Roath, Aberdare and St Mary's, Cardiff, were vested in the hands of Tractarian clergy. Nonconformists feared that these clergy were introducing the doctrines and ritual of the Roman Catholic Church, when that church, for many, was regarded as the anti-Christ. The inability of the bishops to control these practices only made the concern worse.

The Liberation Society, to liberate the Church of England from its state connection, became increasingly influential in Wales and, along with the Nonconformist press and the newly emerging newspapers, broadcast these anomalies and attacked the privileges of the Church. In 1862 the Nonconformists celebrated the great ejection of 1662 in a series of national and local meetings, during which the Church was vilified, while the Welsh Methodists cast in their lot with historic Nonconformity against the Church. Services, once held at different times from the church service, were now held at the same time, so that it was impossible to attend both Church and the chapel. Although the first bill for the disestablishment of the four Welsh dioceses was read in 1870, it was ineffectual, but the cause was not to be stopped. Yet, if there was bitterness, there also had to be some accommodation on the ground. Church and chapel united for meetings of the Bible Society and for temperance work. In marriage, the custom was for a wife to join the husband's denomination. And about one-quarter of the clergy ordained in the southern dioceses came from Methodist families, to the embarrassment and anger of the Methodists. The links were there, but the bitterness remained, and many churchmen felt that the reviving Church was challenging the Nonconformist position of Wales so that it was jealousy which was driving the campaign against it.

The myth that the Church in Wales was an alien institution was too sunk into the semi-conscious for it to be removed, although some had accepted a variation – namely, that the link with the Church of England had caused many of the problems faced by that Church. What was impossible to dispute was that the four dioceses collectively were in a minority compared to the overall strength of Nonconformity. The question then arose: was the Church in Wales justified in remaining an Established Church and in retaining its endowments for itself, when they were given, in times long past, for the work of religion itself?[18]

Conclusion

The Christian Church in Wales has an ancient history dating back to the Age of the Saints, pre-dating that of Canterbury. However, from the

---

[18] For the background to this period, see D. Walker, ed., *A History of the Church in Wales* (Penarth: Church in Wales Publications, 1976), and J. I. Morgans and P. C. Noble, *Our Holy Ground: The Welsh Christian Experience* (Talybont: Y Lolfa, 2016).

medieval period to the day of disestablishment, the four Welsh dioceses were part of the Province of Canterbury and thus a constituent part of the Church of England. The alienation of the historic endowments of many parishes, particularly the tithe income, to monastic bodies and, especially after the Reformation, to secular and English bodies, impoverished the Church in many parts of Wales and prevented it from offering an adequate pastoral ministry. While the wider Church endeavoured to counteract this, rather inadequately, and supported Griffith Jones' circulating schools, these schools helped promote the Methodist Revival. The bishops of the day, by misunderstanding and resisting this movement, caused the Methodists to enter the ranks of Nonconformity. Compared to Nonconformity, the Welsh Church was seen as a minority body, unable to compete with Nonconformity due to its position as an established church, whose privileges and income from the tithe were deeply resented by many. This conception was linked with the unfair assumption that the Church was an Anglicising body at a time when Welsh nationality was asserting itself. The mixture was explosive and led to the disestablishment campaigns.

2

The Road to Disestablishment

JEFFREY GAINER

The British State presents a curious combination of constitutional arrangements in respect of the Christian religion. In Scotland, Presbyterianism is the official religion, whereas in England Anglicanism is established. In Northern Ireland and Wales, there is no established church. This chapter considers how and why disestablishment and its concomitant disendowment took place in Wales – although only after a lengthy period of debate and division. In so doing, the chapter builds on the themes introduced towards the end of Chapter 1. Yet the story cannot be told unless we realise that Wales was then as now profoundly influenced by its neighbours within the British State with which it was historically and constitutionally closely connected. At the same time, the story bears witness to a continuing distinctiveness about the land of Wales and its people. This account begins in London with a pressing problem about Ireland and the leadership of a statesman whose home was in Wales.[1]

The Precedent of the Irish Church

In March 1869 William Ewart Gladstone argued in the House of Commons for 'the grave constitutional change' involved in disestablishing part of the United Church of England and Ireland. In his view, reached some years before, the establishment in Ireland could not continue with advantage to itself or without mischief to the country. Gladstone spent more than three hours expounding the principles and complexities of the legislation and showed a masterly grasp of detail.[2] He won the argument. He won the vote. He did so by emphasising the anomaly of continuing to endow that tenth of the Irish population who were episcopalian

---

[1] A useful and succinct account is found in K. O. Morgan, *Freedom or Sacrilege: A History of the Campaign for Welsh Disestablishment* (Penarth: Church in Wales Publications, 1966).

[2] *Hansard*, March 1869, vol. 19, cc. 412–70.

Protestants and who were wealthier than the Roman Catholics. There could be no dispute about the relative strength of the denominations – the 1861 census had demonstrated that the great majority of the Irish were loyal to Rome. Indeed, at no time since the Reformation had Anglicans formed a majority of the population. What Parliament had joined together it could also put asunder. So, on 1 January 1871, the union of the two churches was ended and the Irish Church was disestablished and disendowed. A matter which had been prominent in the election campaign of 1868 was thus implemented in a short period.

The advocates of this change had been helped by two factors: the attitude of the Roman Catholic bishops and the efforts of the Liberation Society. First, the Roman Catholic hierarchy in Ireland had come to the conclusion that their church should depend on the direct financial contributions of its adherents. The Roman Catholic bishops distrusted aid from a State which, as Benjamin Disraeli put it, had a Protestant Constitution. However, from 1856 the Irish hierarchy formed a curious alliance with the Society for the Liberation of Religion from State Patronage and Control. This organisation, commonly known as the Liberation Society, had succeeded an earlier one which sought to redress the grievances of Nonconformists. It had a clear ideological basis: the repudiation of the historic links between Church and State. Its guiding figure was Edward Miall (1809–81) who, as early as 1856, had tried in vain to persuade the House of Commons to consider the state of the Irish Church. He had considerably more success in organising the Liberation Society so as to choose suitable candidates at elections. His chance came with the increase of the electorate under the second Reform Act (1867). He was aided by another minister of religion and member of the Society, Henry Richard, elected to serve as the member of Parliament for Merthyr Tydfil in 1868. These men set out many of the arguments which were to be expounded at length over the decades until Welsh disestablishment came into effect after the First World War. So Miall had claimed in 1862 in his book *The Title Deeds of the Church of England to Her Parochial Endowments* that those endowments were in origin and nature public property that Parliament was entitled to dispose of as it saw fit.[3] Henry Richard too denounced the alien church which had been abandoned by the people. Both were encouraged by the successful campaign to disestablish the Irish Church.

---

[3] D. W. Bebbington, 'Edward Miall', *Oxford Dictionary of National Biography* (Oxford: Oxford University Press, 2004).

Yet, if Irish disestablishment was effected quickly, the same cannot be said about Wales where the move to follow the Irish example was protracted, bitter on occasions, and often marked by political as much as by religious factors. In 1862, the Liberation Society met in Swansea to commemorate the Act of Uniformity 1662. It agreed to promote a policy of breaking the link between the State and the Church in the Principality. However, it was not until 18 September 1914 that the Act to disestablish the Church of England in Wales received royal assent. Why did it take so long to bring about disestablishment in Wales, especially when there was precedent for such action in another part of the British State?

Part of the answer is that the Church of England in Wales from the time of Irish disestablishment was supported by the rest of the Church of England which saw an attack on the Welsh dioceses as an attack on itself. If Archibald Tait, Archbishop of Canterbury, had agreed to abstain in the vote on the Irish scheme, then his successors E. W. Benson and Randall Davidson did all they could to defend the establishment in Wales during their time at Canterbury. Thus, Benson spoke at a Church Congress in Rhyl in October 1891: 'I come from the steps of the chair of Augustine, your younger ally, to tell you that, by the benediction of God, we will not quietly see you disinherited.' The activities of the Church Defence League throughout England and Wales added force to his words, as did the stream of pamphlets arguing against disestablishment. At a large rally in the Albert Hall in 1912, we have notable expressions of the arguments used to defend the status quo. Sir Alfred Cripps MP argued that 'establishment is not to gain privilege for the Church; it is to procure Christianity for the nation'; and Lord Hugh Cecil stated that were the bill passed it would not be the Church that would lose and Nonconformity that would gain but that it would be 'the Christianity common to both that would be the true and real sufferer'.[4] This succour from the English side is hardly surprising inasmuch as the Welsh bishops had sworn allegiance to Canterbury from Norman times. The Irish dioceses, by contrast, had been united with the Church of England just some seventy years before disestablishment; these sees had their own provincial framework under the leadership of Armagh and Dublin; they even (in theory) had their own convocations. Above all,

---

[4] For Benson, see *The Times*, 7 October 1891; E. W. Benson, 'The Church in Wales: Shall We Forsake Her? A Speech to the Church Congress at Rhyl, Tuesday, 9 October 1891' (London: Church Defence Association, 1891); and Central Church Committee for Defence and Instruction, 'Mass Meeting of Churchmen in the Royal Albert Hall on February 20, 1912' (London: Central Church Committee for Defence and Instruction, 1912), 3–19.

as defenders of the Welsh Church often pointed out, the Irish example was no true precedent for Wales – and it was questionable whether disestablishment had helped Irish Anglicanism.

Gladstone too denied that the Irish precedent was appropriate for Wales when William Watkins proposed in the House of Commons in 1870 a motion to do for Wales what had recently been done for Ireland. Liberationists judged it ill timed. As a result of Watkins' poor tactics the motion was heavily defeated. It received but forty-five votes, seven of which were from Welsh members. Gladstone's influence was to be another factor in the slow progress of the disestablishment campaign. True, he was the leader of the Liberal Party with which Welsh Nonconformity was closely connected. But Gladstone was a keen churchman. He had other priorities which included settling the Irish Home Rule issue. In fact it was only towards the end of his political career that Gladstone unequivocally and publicly supported disestablishment of the English Church in Wales and it was only after his retirement in March 1894 that another disestablishment bill was introduced, although Gladstone had accepted the need for a prior measure, namely the Welsh Church Suspensory Bill 1893. In this respect Gladstone differed notably from the Liberal Unionist, Joseph Chamberlain, who in 1884 spoke in favour of 'disestablishment all round'. The following year, many Liberationists were returned to Parliament – 171 of them supported Chamberlain's policy. Of the thirty Liberals elected from Wales, twenty-nine were in favour of Welsh disestablishment. On 9 March 1886, Lewis Dillwyn (MP for Swansea) moved in the House of Commons yet another motion in favour of Welsh disestablishment. This time it was only narrowly lost – by 229 votes to 241. Pressure was increasing on Gladstone, and in October 1887 Welsh church disestablishment became official party policy.[5] Gladstone long equivocated on the matter but in the end his friend Stuart Rendel (Liberal MP for Montgomeryshire 1880–94) persuaded him to yield. Even so, Gladstone regarded the terms of disendowment presented by H. H. Asquith in 1894 as draconian, and when the Liberals lost power at the 1895 election any hopes of implementing disestablishment were dashed until the Liberal electoral triumph of 1906. Yet, as the electorate became more democratic, so it became more difficult to withstand the plea for disestablishment in the House of Commons. The House of Lords was a different matter and to the end

---

[5] K. O. Morgan, *Wales in British Politics, 1868–1922* (Cardiff: University of Wales Press, 1963), 80–1 and 90.

rejected disestablishment, attempted delaying measures and raised constitutional difficulties about Parliament unilaterally altering the composition of the Convocations of York and Canterbury.

The Influence of Dissent

To understand the continuing pressure for disestablishment over five decades it is important to realise the extent and reasons for the influence of Dissent in Wales. But who were the Nonconformists? They are sometimes described as consisting of old and new Dissent, the former congregationalist in their ecclesiology (Baptists and Independents) and the latter connexionalist (Methodists). The Calvinistic Methodists, who broke from the Anglican Church in 1811 by ordaining their own ministers, were aware that they had arisen as an energising movement to revive the state Church which they regarded as authentically Protestant in origin and ethos. Their leaders had agonised about the rightness of breaking away from the parent body. They believed that they were simply expounding the true evangelical Protestant meaning of the historic Anglican formularies (such as Article XVII of the Thirty-Nine Articles, 'Of predestination and election'). They were proud of being the only Nonconformist denomination to have started in Wales. The Calvinistic movement spread rapidly in north-west Wales under the direction of John Elias (1774–1841). In 1800 there were sixty-four Anglican churches in Caernarvonshire; in 1851 there were sixty-seven, an increase of 0.5 per cent. The corresponding figures for the Calvinistic Methodists were 30 and 221, an increase of more than 600 per cent. During the first half of the nineteenth century, a chapel was opened in Wales every eight days. Whereas the state Church struggled to adapt to the challenges of industrialisation and was hindered by the poverty and non-residence of its clergy and by a lack of lay involvement, the Nonconformists made great advances and used the press effectively. The rising generation was moulded by the Sunday School movement, so much so that Wales at this time has been described as a country centred on the Bible.[6]

As we saw in Chapter 1, the dominance of Welsh Nonconformity was confirmed by the voluntary religious census of 1851 which was organised by Horace Mann. It showed that about half the population of Wales was in a Christian place of worship on the census date, and chapel attenders

---

[6] K. D. M. Snell and P. S. Ell, *Rival Jerusalems: The Geography of Victorian Religion* (Cambridge: Cambridge University Press, 2000), 154–9, 205.

outnumbered Anglicans by four to one. This in itself was the basis for the agitation for disestablishment. How could it be right for such a minority church to be privileged by the State? Was not Wales a land of Nonconformists? What is also noteworthy about the census is the difference between England and Wales. True, there were regional variations within England; the Church of England was definitely stronger in the south; the areas with the highest Anglican attendances were those which voted for the Conservatives. Yet, despite its relative weakness in the north, the Church of England was easily the largest religious denomination in England. In Wales, however, the Church was weak everywhere – and Merthyr Tydfil had the lowest Anglican share of attendances at just over 6 per cent.[7] This difference in the patterns of religious observance between England and Wales meant that Nonconformists were able to argue that the Church of England in Wales was an alien institution, the Church of the anglicised and of the English settlers. Did not its very title say as much? At the beginning of his political career, David Lloyd George was able to appeal to this sentiment in Welsh-speaking Caernarvonshire. If in Ireland the patriots contended for Home Rule then, as the link between Welsh identity and Nonconformity strengthened, so did the push to disendow the minority church. In short, the disestablishment campaign served to focus and strengthen Welsh identity.

But there was also a theological rift concerning the proper relation between Church and State. In Ireland, the rift was in the context of the older division in Western Christianity between those who accepted the papal claims and those who rejected them. Matters were different in Wales, which was solidly Protestant. Here, the episcopalian Anglicans were confronted by fellow Protestants who had a markedly individualistic understanding of Christianity and who sincerely believed that their cause was righteous. This latter group argued that the State had no right to favour one particular form of Christianity. It should remain neutral. It should, however, ensure religious equality but in fact was failing to do so by maintaining a church establishment, something that was becoming ever more anomalous in a religiously diverse country. The days of the Anglican confessional state were numbered.[8] In addition, Nonconformists asserted the voluntary principle that churches should rely on the financial and moral support of their own members. These

---

[7] Ibid., 58.
[8] D. Caird, *Church and State in Wales: The Case for Disestablishment* (London: Liberation Society, 1912), Preface.

arguments were at variance with the assumption that Church and State were but different aspects of the same community, a belief articulated classically by Richard Hooker (1554–1600) and still influential in Anglican apologetics.[9] It is partly for this reason that, throughout the protracted controversy, the two matters of disestablishment and disendowment were always associated in people's minds and were embodied in the legislation. There was a precedent for distinguishing them – the Anglicans in North America had been disestablished but not disendowed – but it was the Irish precedent of combining the two that was followed. This not only added fierceness to the debate but also stiffened resistance on the part of the Church's defenders and made prompt resolution of the dispute more problematical. It is significant that a great deal of the heat in the period of 1909 to 1914 was fuelled by the terms of disendowment which were seen by John Owen and others as a secularisation of gifts made by individuals for Christian purposes and an assault on the right to hold property.[10]

There was a third factor which spurred on opposition to the status quo: the conviction that the Church of England, or at least much of it, was betraying its Protestant heritage by tolerating those attempting to catholicise it. Here again, deeply held religious beliefs and fears were active. And they led to a coalition of the Dissenters who, whatever their differences, were united by a resolve to safeguard Protestantism and the country against the Church of Rome. The emphasis of such Protestants was on the Word in Scripture and the words in the pulpit; the sacraments were occasional additions to their Sunday worship. The Mass was an abomination and the Roman Church the fount of idolatry and false teaching, and an authoritarian institution bent on suppressing the rights of the individual conscience.[11] In 1829, John Elias had censured some of his fellow Calvinistic Methodists in Jewin Street chapel, London, for favouring Catholic emancipation. Religious liberty had limits in the view of this leader. Elias himself was a natural conservative in politics. He abhorred the radical ideas which emanated from the French Revolution and professed loyalty to the Crown and constitution. In a session at Bala in June 1834, he supported a form of words which

---

[9] See N. Doe, 'Richard Hooker: Priest and Jurist', in M. Hill and R. H. Helmholz, eds., *Great Christian Jurists in English History* (Cambridge: Cambridge University Press, 2017), 115.

[10] John Owen, Bishop of St David's, and A. G. Edwards, Bishop of St Asaph, led the opposition to disestablishment; see e.g. J. Owen, *The Principles of the Welsh Disestablishment Bill* (Cardiff: Western Mail Ltd, 1909).

[11] D. Evans, *Cymru mewn perygl! Defodaeth yr un a Phabyddiaeth* (Dolgellau, 1869).

opposed disestablishment. The previous year he had written to the *Record*, an evangelical Anglican publication: 'we appreciate the liberty we enjoy to preach and to hear the Gospel . . . we believe that God did not ordain us to rule the nation, but to submit and to obey our King and rulers and we do not think it proper to dictate to our King and Senate'.[12] Yet within a decade the Calvinistic Methodists were turning towards those who argued vigorously for disestablishment and taking a more active role in politics. The change in attitude of the Calvinistic Methodists marks an important turning point on the road to disestablishment – but how did it happen and why?

The Oxford Movement and Its Effects

Much of the answer is to be found in the influence of the Oxford Movement in Wales. Ironically, this movement sought to emphasise the spiritual independence of the Church from the State. It was anti-Erastian and, in that respect, had some common ground with those Protestants who championed the spiritual independence of the congregation and the individual and protested against State control of the English Church. It was the government's action in uniting ten Irish dioceses in 1833 which had prompted John Keble's famous sermon on 'national apostasy'. However, the teachings of the *Tracts for the Times* were regarded by many within and without the established Church as contrary to the ideas and ideals of the Reformation. What may have appeared to be an academic exercise in Oxford soon enough touched the raw nerve of fear of Rome. As the *Tracts* appeared with their teaching about apostolic succession and the objective action of God through the sacraments, it became clear to many that they challenged the evangelical emphasis on the subjective element in religion. Pitted against the Tractarian teaching about baptismal regeneration, the apostolic succession of sacred ministers, and the real presence of Christ in the eucharistic species were the tenets of justification by faith alone and the centrality of preaching. Once again, deeply held convictions clashed. This may seem somewhat surprising as the movement was English in origin and academic in type. In fact, there was only one Welshman amongst the first Tractarians, Isaac Williams, who had known Keble from 1822 and who had links with north Cardiganshire.[13]

---

[12] R. Tudur Jones, 'The Origins of the Nonconformist Disestablishment Campaign 1830–1840', *Journal of the Historical Society of the Church in Wales*, 20 (1960), 39–76; quotation at 56.

[13] J. Boneham, 'Isaac Williams and the Welsh Tractarian Theology', in S. J. Brown and P. B. Nockles, eds., *The Oxford Movement: Europe and the Wider World 1830–1930* (Cambridge: Cambridge University Press, 2012), 37–65.

However, Williams himself was also markedly opposed to the papal system and his *Tract 80*, on reserve in communicating religious knowledge, was advertised along with the others as being directed against both Dissent and Rome. Nevertheless, the fear of Rome was a powerful religious and political factor in Victorian Britain. It served to mark British identity over against continental lands and the Irish, though in 1851 the Roman Catholics in Wales were but 3,000 in number. Nonetheless, the significant fact was that people thought that the Protestant constitution of the kingdom was under threat. Welsh Nonconformists were not alone in their alarm as the uproar at the time of the restoration of the Roman Catholic hierarchy in 1850 attests. The secession of prominent Tractarians such as John Henry Newman and Hurrell Froude alarmed good Protestants as did the conversion of Lord Feilding to Rome. The noble lord designated the church he was building in Tremeirchion as a place of worship for Roman Catholics. The Calvinistic Methodists reacted by sending a missionary there to counteract his influence.

The consequences were that the Calvinistic Methodists supported the criticism of the Church, published learned critiques of its theology in their quarterly *Y Traethodydd* and associated themselves with the protests to rectify Nonconformist grievances. These grievances included: the marriage law; the requirement to pay the church rate; the tithe system; the burial laws; and the establishment itself. Throughout the nineteenth century measures were taken to remove the causes of the ill feeling. In 1828 the Test and Corporation Acts were repealed. In 1837 civil registration of marriages was introduced. The Tithe Commutation Act was passed in 1836. In 1868 the Church Rates Abolition Act removed the obligation on Nonconformists to contribute to the maintenance of the parish church, a building which they might never or only rarely visit. In 1871 the Universities Tests Act allowed Dissenters to matriculate at Oxford, Cambridge and Durham and opened to them all degrees and offices save such as were tied to Holy Orders.[14] In 1880 George Osborne Morgan, a Liberal and the son of a vicar of Conway, succeeded in ensuring that chapel ministers would be permitted to officiate at the burial of Nonconformists in parochial churchyards.[15] It was a dispute about the implementation of this measure that allowed Lloyd George to make his name as a staunch defender of Nonconformist rights in the

---

[14] O. Chadwick, *The Victorian Church 1860–1901* (London: SCM Press, 1987), 443.
[15] M. Cragoe, 'George Osborne Morgan, Henry Richard and the Politics of Religion in Wales 1864–1874', *Parliamentary History*, 19 (2000), 118–30.

Llanfrothen burial ground court case.[16] A month after successfully challenging the rector and the Tory county court judge, Lloyd George was nominated as the Liberal candidate for Caernarvon boroughs. One by one, then, the causes of Nonconformist discontent were removed in the course of the nineteenth century as the structures of the Anglican confessional State were dismantled. There remained, however, the thorny matter of education.

If in the first half of the nineteenth century the Nonconformists were busy building chapels, then churchmen were busy founding schools where the church Catechism would be taught. A notable founder of National schools which existed to teach the children of the poor the principles of the Established Church was Dean James Cotton of Bangor. The result of such activity was that the church schools claimed the bulk of government grants and were often the only available school in rural areas. Some Nonconformists were content to send their children to such establishments – but not all. An early example of skirmishing was the controversy over Sir James Graham's Factory Bill of 1843 when chapel ministers organised petitions to Parliament against the clauses which would have favoured Anglican instruction in the workplace.[17] Such protests were successful. In the period after 1870 and William Forster's Education Act of that year, competition resulted between the National and the British or Board schools. In the latter the teaching was non-denominational. Nonconformists objected to public funds being used to teach the doctrines of any particular denomination. That, they argued, should be done by parents, by Sunday Schools and by the denominational authorities: it was not a concern of the State. Henry Richards was consistent in his adherence to this principle and argued on these lines, but in practice Welsh Nonconformists were content that the board school should teach about the existence of the Deity and ensure that children knew the Christian Scriptures. Just as they declined to use the catholic creeds in their worship, so Nonconformist ministers objected to church doctrine being taught in schools financed by the rates. Even more did they object to Roman Catholic schools being financed thus – there was to be no 'Rome on the rates!' All this came to a head in the fierce controversy that followed A. H. Balfour's Education Act of 1902, when the county councils in Wales adopted a policy of civil disobedience and refused to implement

[16] The matter is described in J. H. Edwards, *The Life of David Lloyd George* (London: Waverley Book Company, 1913), ch. VIII.

[17] P. Freeman, 'The Response of Welsh Nonconformity to the Oxford Movement', *Welsh Historical Review*, 20(3) (2001), 435–65.

its provisions. The Liberals were stirred into action. They had not won a majority of English constituencies since the 1880s but in 1906 they triumphed in what was called the Liberal landslide. No Conservative was returned for any Welsh constituency, and even though the electorate was only around 30 per cent of the adult population it was significant that more English Nonconformists were elected to Parliament in that year than at any time since the seventeenth-century Commonwealth.[18]

Not surprisingly, priority was given to changing the educational provisions made by the very unpopular government of A. H. Balfour. The effect of all this was to divert, for a time, the energies of the Welsh chapels into the education controversy and away from the disestablishment campaign. Likewise, Welsh Nonconformity had been gripped by the 1904 Revival which served to increase its adherents for a few years after a period of decline just before 1900. However, the new Liberal government, despite its huge majority, knew that it had other pressing measures to consider – Irish Home Rule, social and financial reform, and economic and naval rivalry with Germany amongst them – and accordingly was not eager to put disestablishment of the Welsh Church at the top of its agenda. There is once again an irony here in that one of the leading lights of the government was Lloyd George. A decade before, he had written to the elderly radical Thomas Gee on 9 October 1895: 'It is quite idle to expect Liberal legislation from the Imperial parliament – for Wales at any rate – as long as England dominates our law-making. Parliament has neither the time nor the inclination to attend to our wants … all our demands ought to be concentrated in the great agitation for National self-government.' By 1906, however, Lloyd George was preoccupied with issues affecting the whole of Britain rather than distinctively Welsh ones such as disestablishment. Instead, Sir Henry Campbell-Bannerman's government set up a royal commission to investigate the religious situation in Wales and thereby avoided the need for immediate action on disestablishment. Lloyd George knew that the powers of the House of Lords would have to be reduced first if his bold schemes were to succeed. Only then would the veto on Welsh disestablishment be removed. He was right.

Institutional Factors

But long before the final efforts of the Liberal government to settle the constitutional position of the Welsh Church, there had been other factors

---

[18] G. K. A. Bell, *Randall Davidson* (Oxford: Oxford University Press, 1952), 504.

which had hindered progress towards disestablishment. Some were related to structures and institutions – or rather the absence of them. Wales had very few of the institutional characteristics of a nation as compared, say, with Scotland. Everyone acknowledged that Scotland and Ireland were nations. Many, including Parliamentarians, doubted whether the same could or should be said about Wales. True, the bulk of the population still spoke Welsh to the curiosity, perplexity or indignation of their English neighbours. Yet in 1851 Wales had neither a capital city nor a separate legal system – unlike Scotland. It had no equivalent to the Scottish Kirk to articulate a distinct national identity. All it had were the four poorest dioceses of the Church of England which had in effect lost contact with most Welsh people, who had turned to Nonconformity instead. Yes, Wales had its own language and its provincial *eisteddfodau*; it also had learned societies founded in London for Welsh exiles. Nonetheless, the Acts of Union (1536 and 1543) and the general trend of policy had both treated Wales as a territory to be assimilated to England. It is no surprise, then, that as late as 1886 Basil Jones, Bishop of St David's, could say that Wales was a 'geographical expression'. In 1893 William Stubbs, the learned bishop of Oxford, in a speech to his Diocesan Conference described Wales as a 'district' albeit one where an ancient Celtic speech was still widely spoken – even though it had been described as a *natio particularis* at the Council of Constance 1417. One of those present on the same occasion, the notable theologian, R. C. Moberly, who was not antagonistic to disestablishment, also wondered whether there was sufficient reason to call Wales a distinct nation. Whatever the truth about that matter, it is evident throughout the years of controversy that both sides saw the future of Wales within the context of the British State and Empire. Here was another difference from Ireland, where the Fenians sought an independent republic and repudiated the authority of the British Crown. The consequence of this was that those advocating disestablishment had first to gain a fair representation in the British Parliament and then work towards acceptance of the principle of separate treatment for Wales.[19]

Another factor which enabled the Nonconformists to gain access to the corridors of power and thereby strengthen the disestablishment cause was the extension of male suffrage in various stages up to 1914. This was true to some extent in 1868 which marked a move away from the dominance of the landed gentry, invariably Anglican in sentiment, to the professional

[19]   P. O'Leary, 'Religion, Nationality and Politics: Disestablishment in Ireland and Wales', in J. R. Guy and G. Neely, eds., *Contrasts and Comparisons: Studies in Irish and Welsh Church History* (Llandysul: Gomer Press, 1999), 89–114.

classes, some of whom were Nonconformist. The politics of deference and of personal and family connection were being challenged. Chapel ministers in many areas were very active in Liberal politics and even allowed chapels to be used for political meetings. So in the Rhondda at one time the local Liberal association had 300 members of whom 29 were ministers of religion. Another significant political factor was the introduction of the secret ballot in 1872. This reform was the direct result of the revenge of the squires in rural Wales on those who had voted for Liberal candidates in 1868 and thereby defied what was called 'the screw' – the pressure on tenant farmers to side with the landed interest. In Cardiganshire and Carmarthenshire, there was clear evidence that some tenants had been turned out of their farms and this caused outrage on the part of the Liberal government. Even so, it took time for the electors to be assured of the effectiveness of the legislation, although with further extension of the suffrage with the third Reform Act (1884), the Liberals succeeded in dominating Welsh politics from the 1880s and were in government for almost a decade before 1915.

Unionists, however, were opposed to separate legislation for Wales – although at least one precedent existed: the ill-fated Act for the Propagation of the Gospel in Wales 1650. Advocates of Church Defence were not slow to point out that this was part of an earlier move to disestablish and disendow the Church and that it was a singularly unhappy precedent. Nevertheless, in 1881 the Sunday Closing (Wales) Act was passed, which met the wishes of the temperance movement in Welsh Dissent. Curiously enough, however, the Nonconformists of an earlier generation had been content to hold chapel meetings in public houses, and it had been the Anglicans who had been foremost in promoting legislation embodying Sabbatarianism in the 1830s. Likewise, the setting up of the University colleges and the calls for other national institutions such as a museum and a library all strengthened the case for separate treatment for Wales. The Welsh Intermediate Education Act 1889 was further recognition of Welsh needs and distinctiveness. It also honoured the principle advocated by the Aberdare Report of August 1881 which emphasised Wales' distinctive nationality and needs, and in effect repudiated the arguments of the earlier education commissioners of 1847. The cumulative effect of such moves was to establish the principle of separate treatment for Wales, something that undergirded the legislation that was passed eventually in 1914.[20]

---

[20] T. G. Watkin, *The Legal History of Wales* (Cardiff: University of Wales Press, 2007), 178–9.

Appeals to Identity, History and Numbers

Looking back after more than a century, we may see that there were three central arguments used by both sides: identity, history and numbers. All three are found together in the appeal of Henry Richard to the electors of Merthyr Tydfil in 1868: 'The people who speak this language [i.e. Welsh], who read this literature, who own this history, who inherit these traditions, who venerate these names, who created and sustain these marvellous religious organisations, the people forming three fourths of the people of Wales – have they not a right to say to this small propertied class . . . We are the Welsh people and not you? This country is ours and not yours and therefore we claim to have our principles and sentiments and feelings represented in the Commons' House of Parliament.'[21] This exclusive claim was challenged by defenders of the establishment and most notably by H. T. Edwards, vicar of Caernarvon and thereafter dean of Bangor, who in 1870 issued a public letter to Gladstone concerning the Welsh Church. His interpretation of the situation was very different: Wales had been an organic unity before the Methodist secession; the Church had expressed and reinforced that unity; Dissent was of but recent origin; and the Church was the oldest institution in Wales. What was needed was leadership that ministered to the needs of Wales and especially bishops who could speak the language of the people. The Commons had legislated to this effect in the 1830s in requiring that Welsh speakers should be appointed to Welsh-speaking parishes, although the Lords had subsequently weakened this provision. Gladstone, who had sympathy for the plight of small nations, appointed Joshua Hughes as the bishop of St Asaph, the first native Welsh-speaker to be appointed since the early eighteenth century.

Nonetheless, the claim that the Church was an alien body was used time and time again. Lloyd George was adept at using this argument, but he was by no means alone. Thomas Gee propounded the idea through his newspaper, *Baner ac Amserau Cymru*, which had a wide circulation in north Wales. In many ways this was unjust. The Tractarians, who were a powerful force in the Diocese of Bangor, taught through the medium of Welsh and produced a magazine in Welsh in the 1850s, called *Baner y Groes*, to spread their sacramental teaching.[22] But the advocates of disestablishment were astute. They pointed out too that none of the

---

[21] *Aberdare Times*, 14 November 1868.
[22] P. Freeman, '*Baner y Groes*, a Welsh-Language Tractarian Periodical of the 1850s', *Cylchgrawn Llyfrgell Genedlaethol Cymru*, 32 (2001–2), 305–316.

Welsh cathedrals held a parochial service in Welsh. However hard some might claim that the Church was sympathetic to Welsh culture – had it not given the Bible and Prayer Book in Welsh to the common people and so saved the language? – many claimed that the Church was a religious body for English settlers and the anglicised Welsh.

The appeal to history was also central. Amongst other things, it raised the issue of the continuity of the Church. Was the Church of England founded by the State in the sixteenth century or was it the continuation of the historic church of the Welsh people maintaining its unbroken line of bishops and its sacramental life from the earliest times? If the former, as some Nonconformists argued, then it had been endowed by the State and what the State had given it could take away. To strengthen the call for disendowment, some argued that the Church had failed in its use of its property and that it was right to confiscate its assets and turn them to humanitarian purposes such as founding schools and hospitals. Moreover, they argued: the Church's record after the Reformation was shameful; it had left the people in ignorance and superstition; evidence of clerical immorality was to be found in the bishops' visitation reports from the 1620s; the Church had persecuted those seeking to revive an experiential form of Christianity; it had lost the support of the people; an established church had to be the church of the majority, and the adherents of the Church in Wales were clearly a minority. Such polemic was noised abroad in the press and especially so during the anti-tithe agitation between 1886 and 1891. This interpretation of Wales' past had a powerful emotional appeal to those who opposed establishment. Their understanding of the very word was that it entailed privilege. In fact, the term arose in reference to maintaining liturgical uniformity in the Tudor period. Then it was used to translate Canon 3 of the 1603 Canons Ecclesiastical. The Latin was rendered as 'the Church of England by law established under the king's majesty'. That is, it spoke of providing legal security and not privilege. Each side used the past to justify its actions in the present. The controversy did stimulate learning in some respects – Charles Green, the vicar of Aberdare, delved deep into continental works of canon law and made an especial study of the origin and development of the tithe. He spoke on the subject at the Church Congress at Swansea in 1908 which had, not surprisingly, church endowments as its theme.[23]

---

[23] C. A. H. Green, *The Church's Title to Its Endowments* (London: Central Church Committee for Defence and Instruction, 1909).

In fact the appeal to history could not resolve a dispute about political action in the present. As so often happens, protagonists of a cause found what they wanted to see and ignored what they found inconvenient for their purposes. This also applied to the debate about numbers. The census of 1851 was important because it showed what observers had long noticed: Nonconformity was in the ascendant in Wales. Yet the Welsh bishops paid scant attention to the census findings or at least avoided mentioning them in their charges to clergy, even though Alfred Ollivant of Llandaff knew that his diocese had some parishes with the lowest Anglican attendance in the kingdom. The Church did, however, seek to respond better to a rapidly growing population in the industrial valleys and the cities. From the 1830s efforts had been made to reduce pluralism and absentee clergy. In the second half of the century strenuous efforts were made to subdivide large parishes in the mining areas, increase the number of resident clergy, and inaugurate the ministry of lay readers and deaconesses. There was much denominational rivalry at work here. By 1900, the Nonconformist denominations had saddled themselves with large debts and their ministers were inadequately paid. This did not inhibit their assemblies from pressing for disestablishment.

The whole controversy about numbers evoked an uncharitable spirit in many. Viator Cambrensis, writing in 1912, criticised his fellow Nonconformists for the asperity of their arguments whilst claiming that the Church Defenders had been more gracious.[24] In fact, some Church Defenders could be harsh – not least with their fellow churchmen who were prepared to accept that disestablishment might prove beneficial to the Church's mission and spiritual life. The lengthy controversy deepened divisions in Welsh society and strong emotions were aroused especially, but not only, at election time. The Nonconformist argument was simple enough. The church people were a minority and an established church made sense only if it was the church of the majority. To this was added another argument about numbers. Why should the Welsh people, who consistently returned decisive majorities of their elected representatives in favour of disestablishment, be expected to support financially a church which many of them saw as erroneous in doctrine and anglicising in effect?

Matters came to a head with the Liberal triumph at the election of 1906. The new government faced many problems – such as the education controversy and, as it turned out, the House of Lords. The government's

---

[24]   Viator Cambrensis [pseudonym], *The Rise and Decline of Welsh Nonconformity* (London: Sir Isaac Pitman and Sons Ltd, 1912).

legislative programme did not include a promise to implement Welsh disestablishment in the first session of Parliament. Asquith commended the bill in 1909. It was based on the 1895 proposals. Meanwhile, in 1906 the government had established a royal commission to enquire into the state of the Church and other religious bodies in Wales.[25] The commission's meetings reflected the divisions in wider society. One issue that had come up time and time again was the matter of holding a census of religious adherents. The Nonconformists opposed the idea. It was not the State's business to interfere. They suspected that a census would exaggerate Anglican numbers since nominal Christians would be more likely to describe themselves as 'Church of England'. The Nonconformists were not averse to collecting statistics of membership and published them in their annual handbooks. But their figures too came under suspicion. It was argued that they had been inflated by the influx of adherents during the 1904 Revival. The whole matter was complicated by different understandings of membership. When the commission's report was eventually published in 1910, it showed there were 549,123 Nonconformist communicants and 193,081 Anglican communicants. John Owen, Bishop of St David's, made three points in the Church's defence: the Church was 'far and away the strongest religious body in Wales'; church people in Wales outnumbered the two largest Nonconformist bodies put together; and the Nonconformists were less than half the population and the Church looked after the other half.[26]

The government, however, did not even wait for the report of its own commission to be published before bringing forward the disestablishment legislation. It wanted the matter settled. In fact, it had to settle the conflict with the House of Lords. Two general elections in 1910, and the passing of the Parliament Act 1911, resolved the issue and removed the Lords' veto on the disestablishment legislation reintroduced in 1912 and passed in 1914. Was it a triumph for Liberalism and for Nonconformity? In some ways we may see it rather as a step forward in the process of secularising Wales, a point that was noted at the time by some but obscured for others by the increase in Welsh Anglican strength from the 1870s onwards. We need to see what happened in Wales in a European and not just a British context. The French revolution had begun the process of breaking the traditional link between Church and State. Just a few years before the Welsh Church

---

[25] The Royal Commission on the Church of England and Other Religious Bodies in Wales and Monmouthshire: established on 21 June 1906, it reported 23 November 1910.

[26] J. Owen, *The Principles of the Welsh Disestablishment Bill.*

was disestablished, a government in Paris had terminated the concordat of 1801 between Church and State,[27] and the *laïcité* of the French State was summed up in its 1905 *Loi de la Séparation*.[28] As Timothy Ware wrote in 1963: 'The Christian Church in its early days was distinct from the State; and now in one country after another the traditional alliance between Church and State is coming to an end.'[29] The story of the half-century of disputes between Christians in Wales about the Church–State relationship is a sad one because what may well turn out to be of most significance in this particular protracted quarrel is that it is a small chapter in the story of the gradual de-Christianisation of Western Europe since the Enlightenment, a process which significantly means that all Christians now form a small minority existing in a predominantly non-Christian society.[30]

Conclusion

The history of the controversy over disestablishment also shows the persistence of arguments made at the beginning of the struggle. The plea for religious equality was confronted by the plea for a national recognition of religion, albeit of a particularly denominational type. Yet whilst many of the arguments changed little, the political tactics did vary. Thus, there was an increasing assertion of Welsh freedom of initiative, and the Liberation Society's influence on the disestablishment campaign diminished from the 1880s. More important still were the social changes within Wales in the course of the controversy: increased industrialisation, the great increase in population, the rise of Labour, the anglicisation of the industrialised areas, the alienation of the working classes from institutional religion, the last being nowhere near so marked a feature of Welsh life in 1851 as it had become by 1914. The controversy both expressed and deepened the divisions between Christians. It also diverted the attention of many, but not all, of them to the weakening of the hold of traditional belief on the mass of the people. Those who celebrated the enactment of the Welsh Church Act 1914 may have supposed that it marked the triumph of Liberalism and Welsh Nonconformity. Subsequent events may not have confirmed that judgment in the longer perspective of Christianity in Wales over the twentieth century.

---

[27] O. Chadwick, *A History of the Popes 1830–1914* (Oxford: Oxford University Press, 1998), 389–96.
[28] N. Doe, *Law and Religion in Europe* (Oxford: Oxford University Press, 2011), 34.
[29] T. Ware, *The Orthodox Church* (London: Penguin Books, 1997), 11.
[30] R. Tudur Jones, *Ffydd ac Argyfwng y Genedl* (Swansea: Ty John Penry, 1982), II, 234.

3

A Century of Christianity in Wales

D. DENSIL MORGAN

When the twentieth century began, Christianity was taken for granted as the religion of the people and an unassailable aspect of national life. It took the trauma of the First World War, the economic dislocation of the 1920s and 1930s, and ensuing social, political and cultural change to realise the rapidity of the secularisation process and its extent. This chapter describes the way in which the denominations, including the Church in Wales, responded to this challenge, and how the interpenetration between religion and society evolved. Ecumenism, evangelicalism and the development of a responsible social witness were among the pressing concerns of the second half of the century; thereafter one could add to the list the need to foster an effective witness in the context of a 'new' Wales, culturally diverse and religiously pluralistic.

Christian Religion 1900–1914

Wales, in 1900, was an intensely religious nation. That religion was Christianity, whether practised in a Nonconformist chapel or in a parish church, and few people questioned, much less challenged, the popular perception. Since the sixth-century Age of the Saints, throughout the Middle Ages, the Reformation and beyond, an unmistakably Christian consensus had prevailed. This had been intensified in the eighteenth century by the Evangelical Revival linked with the names of Howel Harris and Daniel Rowland, and by the creation less than a century later of a remarkable Nonconformist culture, the Revival having burst the bounds of the established Church and popularised a previously marginal Dissent. By the late nineteenth century, whether represented by the chapelgoers' 'nation of nonconformists' or by those whose Anglican commitment had never wavered, Christian faith and the characteristics of Welsh nationhood had virtually coalesced. Neither were there many obvious signs that this would change. According to one Baptist minister, writing in 1900:

There is good reason to believe that the sun will yet shine brighter on our land, and her religious life will show forth even more glory during the twentieth century than ever she did during the nineteenth. We can look forward with confidence to the even greater success of the Kingdom of God in the Wales of tomorrow.[1]

The 'four great nonconformist denominations' so described by the *Report of the Royal Commission on the Church of England and other Religious Bodies in Wales and Monmouthshire* (1910), namely the Calvinistic Methodists, the Congregationalists, the Baptists and the Wesleyans, had a shared communicant membership of some 535,000, to say nothing of the vast body of 'listeners' (*gwrandawyr*) or adherents, as many as 950,000, who though not baptised and confirmed members, were officially attached to the chapels and regularly attended services. Along with 500,000 children in Sunday Schools, Nonconformity commanded the loyalty of well over a million Welsh adults in a population of 2.5 million. Two out of every five Welsh people were Protestant Dissenters.

Anglicanism was also growing in confidence and numbers at the time. During 1914, 24,500 infants and adults were baptised in the four Welsh dioceses, 17,000 candidates were confirmed by their bishops, 155,500 worshippers attended Easter communion and 169,000 children were taught in the Church's Sunday Schools. In all, 13.78 per cent of the population belonged to the established Church. If this was less than the total number of Nonconformists, it represented considerably more than any other single denomination. Whatever separated the different religious traditions during these years, the presence and influence of mainstream Christianity, whether Dissenting or established,[2] were taken as fact. 'We think that from the evidence advanced before us', wrote the authors of the Royal Commission's *Report*, 'that the people of Wales show a marked tendency to avail themselves of the provision made by the churches of all denominations for their spiritual welfare.'[3] In surveying the key themes in the history of religion in Welsh society during the twentieth century, this is where we must begin.

---

[1] Quoted in D. D. Morgan, *Wales and the Word: Historical Perspectives on Welsh Identity and Religion* (Cardiff: University of Wales Press, 2008), 212.

[2] There were some 90,000 Welsh Roman Catholic communicants at the time while the smaller Protestant bodies together had a membership of some 20,000: D. D. Morgan, *The Span of the Cross: Christian Religion and Society in Wales, 1914–2000* (Cardiff: University of Wales Press, 2nd ed., 2011), 5–14.

[3] Royal Commission on the Church of England and Other Religious Bodies in Wales and Monmouthshire, *Report* (London: HMSO, 1910), I, 19.

The blithe confidence of the Baptist minister quoted above, soon to be boosted by the remarkable religious Revival of 1904–5,[4] and the undoubted strength of institutional religion as witnessed by the statistical evidence belied the fact that the consensus was even then being challenged. For the many who did avail themselves of the provision for worship afforded by the religious bodies, there remained scores of thousands who rarely, if ever, made their way into a chapel or church. Secularisation was growing apace. Industrialisation, which in its early nineteenth-century phase reinforced rather than undermined popular religiosity, was beginning to conform to the continental and English city-based pattern of weakening religious affiliation. Socialist and collectivist politics would quickly challenge *laissez-faire* Liberalism to say nothing of Tory paternalism, while politics itself was displacing spirituality as a basic concern of the people. Anglicisation was opening Wales up to new and formerly alien ideologies, while the theologians were having to fend off the challenge of Darwinism and other sceptical views. 'In the present condition of things in Wales', claimed Thomas Charles Edwards, first principal of the new University College in Aberystwyth and a highly perceptive religious leader,

> you have a people actually weary of contending systems, keenly alive at the same time to the fascination of new ideas, political and scientific, and, for this reason, in danger of drifting away from theological truth altogether. In our age agnosticism has come to the front as a conscious phase of the human intellect and teaches our young men not that this or that solution to the problem is fallacious but that the problem itself need not be solved either way.[5]

This claim was made as early as 1888. By 1914 the acids of modernity were dissolving the structures of Welsh religion in a most disconcerting way.

The First World War

The First World War broke upon the nation unexpectedly. If the Church of England (to which all pre-1920 Welsh Anglicans belonged), reflecting the

---

[4] Some 80,000 people sought baptism and church membership through the Revival; the best assessment remains that of R. Tudur Jones: *Faith and the Crisis of a Nation: Wales 1890–1914*, ed. R. Pope (Cardiff: University of Wales Press, 2004), 283–369.

[5] D. D. Williams, ed., *Thomas Charles Edwards* (Liverpool: National Eisteddfod Transactions, 1921), 110–11.

values of the establishment, threw itself into the war effort wholesale, a quasi-pacifist Nonconformity surprised itself by supporting the conflict so enthusiastically. Edwardian Wales partook of the imperialist spirit as much as any other part of the United Kingdom, while the presence of the Baptist David Lloyd George at the centre of government swayed the judgment of many. 'As the Lord liveth we had entered into no conspiracy against Germany', he assured a vast congregation at the City Temple, Westminster, in November 1914. 'We are in the war from motives of purest chivalry to defend the weak.' Belgium was, like Wales, a small nation, 'a poor little neighbour whose home was broken into by a hulking bully'. Were it not for the Christian resolve of her allies, she would surely perish. However regrettable, the war was just. 'We are all looking forward to the time when swords shall be beaten into ploughshares', but in the meantime there was no alternative but to fight.[6] Such rhetoric was replicated again and again, not only by those who sought to justify the war but also by others who would persuade young men to volunteer for military service. This was nowhere more so than in the Welsh-speaking heartlands of Caernarfonshire and Anglesey where Calvinistic Methodism's two most charismatic preachers, John Williams Brynsiencyn and Thomas Charles Williams, urged Christian youth to take up arms. Such uncritical zeal would prove their undoing. When the populace realised that the war would not be 'over by Christmas' and that the level of slaughter would be unprecedented, the reputation of such slick trumpeters of righteousness sank immeasurably.[7] So too did that of all who had tried to vindicate the war as a religious crusade. Whatever was true of Christianity more widely, the integrity of the Nonconformist cause would suffer considerably.

The counterpoint to the rhetoric of the jingoistic ministers and clergy was the stand taken by those who raised questions as to the unambiguous purity of the state's cause in waging total war. Thomas Rees, principal of the Congregational college at Bala-Bangor, and John Puleston Jones, a supremely gifted Calvinistic Methodist minister from Pwllheli,[8] suffered immense opprobrium for reminding the public of the moral ambiguities of war. 'I note that you have been expressing *Christian* views on this terrible European conflict', wrote one of Rees' correspondents in October 1914; and:

---

[6] Quoted in D. D. Morgan, *The Span of the Cross*, 2nd ed., 43.

[7] See H. Parri, *Gwn Glân a Beibl Budr: John Williams Brynsiencyn a'r Rhyfel Mawr* (Caernarfon: Gwasg y Bwthyn, 2014).

[8] H. Parri, *Cannwyll yn Olau: Stori John Puleston Jones* (Caernarfon: Gwasg y Bwthyn, 2018).

To find anyone with sufficient courage at the present time to stand boldly for such obsolete opinions is to me at any rate wholesome and invigorating. The 'neutrality of Belgium argument', as it has been presented on its altruistic side, is of course irresistible. At the same time, it takes a rather 'strong man' possessing any knowledge of the tortuous ways of diplomats, to believe that anything so disinterested is possible on the part of any European chancellery.[9]

Any blanket support for the government's cause belied the need for a measured view of national policy, the correspondent stated, while the present atmosphere of fevered patriotism made a mockery of the claim that the only absolutes within Christendom were Christ and the Kingdom of God.

Although not initially out-and-out pacifists, Rees and Puleston Jones became mainstays of the Fellowship of Reconciliation, the Christian (and overwhelmingly non-Anglican) society founded in 1914 to counter the claims of war. It received an undoubted boost in January 1916 with the government's decision to impose conscription, thus calling into question Nonconformity's core conviction concerning the rights of individual conscience. Those who refused to bear arms found themselves having to defend their stand before local tribunals and were often imprisoned. The one figure who came to personify pacifist absolutism was George M. Ll. Davies, the grandson of John Jones Tal-sarn, one of Calvinistic Methodism's mid-nineteenth-century prince preachers. Davies, whose Tolstoyesque conversion from bourgeois religiosity to a highly idealist (if dogma-free) form of Christianity inspired many,[10] while the pacifists' willingness to suffer for their convictions often elicited sympathy and respect even among those who remained unconvinced by their views. Although the pacificists were always a religious minority, their most substantial contribution was in helping create a post-war consensus, among Nonconformists at least, which put peace near the top of the political agenda. This fact was illustrated by George Davies' election, on a pacifist ticket, as MP for the University of Wales seat in 1923.

What, therefore, was the impact of the Great War on the future of Welsh Christianity? It is often said that the war destroyed people's faith in the reality of God and the goodness of humankind. Such an assessment is

[9] D. R. Daniel to Thomas Rees, 16 October 1914, Bala-Bangor MSS 65, Bangor University Archives.
[10] J. Llywelyn, *Pilgrim of Peace: A Life of George M. Ll. Davies, Pacifist, Conscientious Objector and Peace-Maker* (Talybont: Y Lolfa, 2016).

too stark and simplistic. Secularisation would have happened anyway. What the war provided was a convenient divide between a religious and a post-religious phase in modern Welsh history. There is no doubt that on returning from the front, disenchanted with the ideals with which they had grown up, many did abandon a belief in God, divine providence and the comforts of the Gospel. However, there were others – and the evidence points to the fact that they were many – who actually *found* their faith in the trenches. Whereas the question of how to justify God's existence in the face of human adversity has always been a conundrum, the biblical revelation contains unique resources to deal with (though never fully to understand) the fact of pain and suffering. This is especially true of a religion whose Saviour died on a cross. During the war the work of the military chaplains, both Anglican and Nonconformist, was mostly revered. The words 'This is my body broken for you' took on a new reality for many who partook of the Eucharist or Lord's Supper on the front line, having witnessed affliction, agony and extreme torment with their own eyes. One thoughtful Calvinistic Methodist ministerial student, soon to be killed, wrote to his college principal: 'The problems of war have always challenged faith, but a world organized for slaughter is something new.' Despite the horrors which the concept of total war had introduced, the religious questions being faced were more in scale than in kind: 'It would be truer as a general statement to say that the old difficulties have been intensified rather than new ones have arisen.'[11]

What was incontrovertible was that post-war Wales would be a different world and that the religious bodies would need to respond to its changes or face the consequences. 'The question that men will ask of the church when they return', wrote Alfred Jenkins, that same ministerial student, was:

> Are you prepared to lead in the social movement that has declared war on a system based on monopolism, which keeps the land locked up in the interests of a few and which condemns millions of our population to live in rack-rented, overcrowded dwellings? The church must not count on the devotion and loyalty that were merely a family tradition and heritage, for these have been shrivelled up in the experiences of war . . . [Moreover] if the basis of church membership will still invoke the pale ghosts of ancient creeds and musty dogmas rather than the challenge of the moral heroism of men, the church will not attract those who have learned to suffer and endure.[12]

[11] Alfred Jenkins to Owen Prys, sometime in 1917, Owen Prys Papers 22283, Calvinistic Methodist Archives, National Library of Wales, Aberystwyth.

[12] Owen Prys Papers 22283.

What was needed was a radical social message, genuine personal conviction and a realistic and pertinent theology. By 1920 there were many in the Welsh churches, both Anglican and Nonconformist, who agreed that this was the case.

The Post-War Challenge

On 1 April 1920 the newly disestablished and autonomous Welsh Anglican Church, soon to be called the Church in Wales, became a fact. The fractious disestablishment campaign had ended in 1914 but the creation of the new church had to be postponed until after the war. Having been cushioned from the worst effects of disendowment by the government's financial guarantee, Welsh Anglicans began to accustom themselves to their new status. Though disestablished, the new Church remained hierarchical in nature, in many places gentrified and very ambivalent about its status. In some quarters the old hostility towards the Welsh language persisted; many of its senior clergy and middle-class laity despised the vernacular as an uncouth throwback to the past, 'the last refuge of the uneducated', according to A. G. Edwards,[13] its first archbishop. Yet confidence was growing and churchmen began to appreciate, even to relish, their new-found independence.

If some of the senior clergy remained Anglophile and still establishment-minded high Tories, there were many among the parish ministers for whom a commitment to the Church was no bar to being wholly Welsh. Despite much social ambiguity, John Owen, Bishop of St David's and the most able of champions of Church Defence, was indisputably Welsh in language and culture,[14] as was Dr Maurice Jones, appointed in 1923 to a key position of influence, namely principal of St David's College, Lampeter.[15] Even more significant for the Church's profile was the unexpected election, in 1931, of Fr Timothy Rees, a monk of the Community of the Resurrection at Mirfield, Yorkshire, as bishop of Llandaff. As a Mirfield missionary based outside Wales since 1907, he had avoided the harsh polemics of the disestablishment campaign, while his social commitment, solidarity with the disadvantaged,

---

[13] Quoted in O. W. Jones, *Glyn Simon: His Life and Opinions* (Llandysul: Gomer Press, 1981), 55.

[14] See H. Williams, 'St David's and Disestablishment: Reassessing the Role of Bishop John Owen', in J. Morgan-Guy and W. Gibson, eds., *Religion and Society in the Diocese of St David's 1485–2011* (London: Ashgate, 2015), 179–202.

[15] D. T. W. Price, *A History of St David's University College, Lampeter* (Cardiff: University of Wales Press, 1990), vol. II *(1898–1971)*, 68–104.

and warm-hearted Welsh patriotism were felt to be something new. Less a prelate and autocrat than an evangelist and pastor, his Anglo-Catholic social radicalism blended perfectly with an evangelical piety to which Nonconformists warmed.[16] His death aged sixty-five in 1939 was a blow not only to the disestablished Church but also to the nation as a whole.

The context in which both the Church in Wales and the Nonconformist denominations would have to function, in the industrial south at least, was one of strife and depression, while in Wales generally a fundamental switch of allegiance occurred from the Liberal Party to Labour. By 1935 Labour controlled every single seat in the industrial south polling more than 45 per cent of the Welsh total. Since the first decade of the century, Christianity and the labour movement had striven to accommodate one another. Early socialists such as Keir Hardie, founder of the Independent Labour Party (ILP) and MP for Merthyr Tydfil, had used biblical language and a religiously inspired idealism in order to convince Welsh chapelgoers of socialism's compatibility with their faith. For Hardie, socialism was Christianity in action, the practical application of the Sermon on the Mount in order to usher in God's Kingdom on earth. It was above all a moral code rather than an economic dogma and was commended as such not least by T. E. Nicholas of Glais in the Swansea Valley, the ILP's most effective propagandist among the workers before the war. If Nicholas, a neo-Marxist poet-preacher in the romantic style, was a skilled populist,[17] there were other young Nonconformists such as the Baptist Herbert Morgan and the Methodist Robert Silyn Roberts whose *apologia* for the socialist creed was much more intellectually astute. James Griffiths, leader of the west Wales anthracite miners, later MP for Llanelli and a minister in successive Labour governments, recalled Silyn Roberts' immense influence on the youth of his generation:

> He preached God *and* evolution. He was a minister *and* a socialist . . . he became our inspirer and our justification. We could tell our parents, who feared this new gospel we talked of, 'but Silyn Roberts believes as we do'. How many devout but dubious fathers became reconciled to socialist sons by that assurance? He linked the South Wales of Evan Roberts to the South Wales of Keir Hardie.[18]

---

[16] J. Lambert Rees, *Timothy Rees of Mirfield and Llandaff: A Biography* (London and Oxford: Mowbray, 1945).

[17] Hefin Wyn, *Ar Drywydd Niclas y Glais: Comiwnydd Rhonc a Christion Gloyw* (Talybont: Y Lolfa, 2017).

[18] Quoted in D. Thomas, *Silyn (Cofiant Silyn Roberts)* (Liverpool: Gwasg y Brython, 1957), 77.

For these, there was no incompatibility between Labour and the chapels. 'There are thousands of Welshmen today', wrote one observer in 1923, 'who can find no inconsistency in singing *Diolch iddo* and *Ar ei ben bo'r goron,* with the Welsh *hwyl* at one meeting, and then proceeding to another meeting to sing *The Red Flag* with the same enthusiasm.'[19]

Theological Change

If some attempted to fuse socialism with chapel culture in order to retain the allegiance of the working class, there were others for whom a politicised faith was anathema and the social Gospel an abomination. The true Christian was called to withdraw from secular concerns in the interest of scriptural holiness. The intense spirituality of the 1904–5 Revival had, in some places, fuelled a separatist mentality which would transform itself into biblical fundamentalism. Originating in the United States, the series of booklets *The Fundamentals* (1910–15) had served to rally conservative-minded Protestants who believed that liberal theology was threatening the vitality of the cause. The movement soon became equated with a belligerent attitude to all aspects of secular culture, and by the early 1920s its militant temper and polemical defence of biblical inerrancy was being replicated in Wales. Its main exemplar was R. B. Jones, Baptist minister at the Tabernacle church, Porth, in the Rhondda, whose reputation as a stern prophet of the divine wrath had been consolidated during the Revival.[20] By the inter-war period, the mores of fundamentalism – a literalist biblical hermeneutic (a six-day creation, Adam and Eve and the serpent, the historicity of the Book of Jonah), post-millennialist eschatology, and the call to separate from the world and a worldly church – had become deeply entrenched among a section of Welsh Evangelicals. Its principles were upheld through such institutions as the annual Llandrindod Wells convention, 'the Keswick of Wales', which espoused a 'second blessing' holiness doctrine,[21] the Bible College of Wales at Derwen Fawr, Swansea, founded in 1924 by Rees Howells, another highly idiosyncratic Welsh Evangelical,[22] Jones' own

---

[19] Cited in R. Pope, *Building Jerusalem: Nonconformity, Labour and the Social Question in Wales, 1906–1939* (Cardiff: University of Wales Press, 2nd ed., 2014), 104.

[20] N. Gibbard, *R. B. Jones: Gospel Ministry in Turbulent Times* (Bridgend: Bryntirion Press, 2009).

[21] B. Pierce Jones, *The Spiritual History of Keswick in Wales, 1903–1983* (Cwmbran: Christian Literature Press, 1989).

[22] N. Grubb, *Rees Howells: Intercessor* (Cambridge: Lutterworth Press, 2013).

South Wales Bible Training Institute at Porth, and the bi-monthly periodical *Yr Efengylydd* ('The Evangelist'). The pugnacious nature of the fundamentalists' witness often made withdrawal inevitable, either from their parent denominations or from what they believed were 'worldly' local churches, and by the 1930s a plethora of independent 'mission halls' had sprung up throughout the south Wales valleys, though not further afield.[23] Due to its reactionary temper, its intellectual obscurantism and serious lack of balance, fundamentalism was never an adequate expression of evangelical religion, and outside a narrow circle it never became influential. With the death of R. B. Jones in 1933 it went into decline, though it too had its part to play in the development of religion in twentieth-century Wales.[24]

Despite the hardship of economic dislocation and the political upheavals of the period, there was much intellectual and cultural energy in inter-war Wales. An emerging 'Anglo Welsh' literature, spearheaded by novelists such as Rhys Davies, editors such as Keidrych Rhys, and a young Dylan Thomas among the poets, was moulding a new Anglophone identity: secular and industrialised but indisputably Welsh, while 'high' Welsh-language culture was enjoying a renaissance. These were the golden years of glittering icons such as W. J. Gruffydd, Saunders Lewis and their fellow litterateurs: R. T. Jenkins, Kate Roberts and the poets Gwenallt and R. Williams Parry.[25] A parallel strand of intellectual vitality was prevalent in the churches. The dominant theology within Nonconformity had been Protestant liberalism, and in some cases, among the Congregationalists especially, advanced Modernism. If the fundamentalists espoused a wooden biblical literalism, the liberal theologians thought that the only way to respond to the challenge of modernity was to reframe Christianity according to the norms of philosophical Idealism. Liberal theology with its optimistic world-view, its downplaying of human sinfulness and its non-miraculous bent, had become popular with a highly gifted generation of church leaders and by the 1920s had come to represent (for some) a new orthodoxy. It was being espoused in the seminaries, its principal scholarly manifestation was the *Geiriadur Beiblaidd* ('Biblical Dictionary') published

[23] B. Pierce Jones, *How Lovely Are Thy Dwellings* (Newport: Wellspring Publications, 1999).

[24] For the parallel development of another form of proletarian, pietistic religion during these years, see D. C. Jones, 'Pentecostalism', in R. C. Allen, D. C. Jones and T. O. Hughes, eds., *The Religious History of Wales: Religious Life and Practice from the Seventeenth Century to the Present Day* (Cardiff: Welsh Academic Press, 2014), 131–46.

[25] G. Jones, *The Dragon Has Two Tongues*, ed. T. Brown (Cardiff: University of Wales Press, revised ed., 2001).

in 1926 under the auspices of the University of Wales' Guild of Graduates, and its most winsome presentation was to be found in *Bannau'r Ffydd* ('Pinnacles of the Faith') (1928), an accomplished doctrinal treatise written by D. Miall Edwards, professor of theology at the Congregationalists' Memorial College in Brecon.

Yet soon this was all to change. Just as on the continent the Swiss Karl Barth was contesting the axioms of Protestant liberalism with his electrifying doctrine of 'the Word of God', one of Barth's earliest disciples, the 28-year-old J. E. Daniel, professor of theology at the Bala-Bangor college, was undermining all the maxims of Nonconformist liberalism with an exceptionally spirited critique of Edwards' work. Liberalism, he claimed, with its humanised God, its non-miraculous Saviour and its truncated concept of salvation, was a travesty of the true faith and as such had 'led to the theological and spiritual bankruptcy of Protestantism'.[26] What was needed was a fresh vision of God's transcendence, a full-blooded transformative Gospel and a restatement of classic orthodoxy according to a rejuvenated theology of the Word of God. There was nothing obscurantist about this response. Daniel, the most talented theologian of the upcoming generation, was an exceptionally powerful thinker who would combine extensive patristic learning with a unique commitment to the thought of the Welsh Protestant past.[27] By the late 1930s, younger ministers in each of the denominations would coalesce around this rejuvenated 'theology of the Word of God'.

By then and into the war years, 1939–45, and beyond, there occurred a partial return to a more balanced, biblical and orthodox faith by the Nonconformist pulpit, while an older conservative evangelicalism was revitalised, not least through the remarkable ministry of Martyn Lloyd-Jones, a London-Welsh physician who had relinquished his Harley Street practice in 1927 for the life of a lowly pastor-evangelist at Bethlehem Forward Movement Hall in Sandfields, Port Talbot. Even after returning to London as minister of Westminster Chapel in 1939, Lloyd-Jones would become a hugely revered figure in evangelical Nonconformity and wield enormous influence during the post-war years.[28] Among the congregations, the faithful

---

[26] J. E. Daniel, 'Diwinyddiaeth Cymru', *Yr Efrydydd*, 5 (1929), 174.

[27] For Daniel's contribution and the new doctrinal consensus, see D. D. Morgan, *The Span of the Cross*, 2nd ed., 230–47, and *Barth Reception in Britain* (London: T. & T. Clark, 2010), 48–62, 194–200.

[28] D. C. Jones, 'Lloyd-Jones and Wales', in A. Atherstone and D. C. Jones, eds., *Engaging with Martyn Lloyd-Jones: The Life and Legacy of 'the Doctor'* (Nottingham: Apollos, 2011), 59–90.

responded to the approaching war with quiet fortitude. The biblical categories of sin, redemption and the divine transcendence were seen to be infinitely more effective in interpreting the present crisis that those of a discredited liberalism. The striking difference between the quiet confidence of the mid-1940s and the facile optimism which had greeted the previous conflict was its note of realism. Optimism may have vanished, but there was little despair. Although Nazism was perceived to be an unmitigated evil, neither hatred nor jingoism marred the national response. The unspeakable horrors of Belsen and Buchenwald revealed the depths of human depravity which no ready-made theology could comprehend; nevertheless the proven realities of biblical faith did serve to offer consolation and a chastened hope.

The Period 1945–1979

Despite a measure of doctrinal retrieval among the Nonconformists, the one religious body that emerged from the war with most confidence was the Church in Wales. By now quietly assured of its identity, it was becoming ever more popular with worshippers and was attracting a highly talented generation of new leaders to the ranks of its clergy.[29] This contrasted with Nonconformity which, by the 1950s, was showing serious signs of internal decay. In a perceptive if gloomy analysis published in 1962, the tercentenary of the birth of modern Dissent, R. Ifor Parry, a senior Congregational minister, showed how Nonconformity was suffering due to its cultural captivity to 'the Welsh way of life' which was currently in decline; that it was wedded to 'the Nonconformist Conscience', the puritanism of which was everywhere regarded as being antiquated and hypocritical; that the plainness of its worship had bred a negativity towards beauty and the senses which contemporary Welsh Anglicanism was exploiting to the full; and that growing economic affluence was dissolving the moral seriousness on which Dissenting conviction had always been built: 'This is the atmosphere in which nonconformity is having to exist, and today it is fighting for its very life.'[30]

There were, nonetheless, attempts to stem the decline. The Evangelical Movement of Wales, established in 1949 following a spiritual awakening among university students at Bangor, had become the focus of considerable religious verve. Through its magazines, Y Cylchgrawn Efengylaidd

---

[29] D. T. W. Price, A History of the Church in Wales in the Twentieth Century (Penarth: Church in Wales Publications, 1990), 25–34; D. D. Morgan, The Span of the Cross, 2nd ed., 181–7.

[30] R. Ifor Parry, Ymneilltuaeth (Llandysul: Gomer Press, 1962), 175.

and the *Evangelical Magazine of Wales*, its annual conferences, well-attended preaching meetings and local evangelistic campaigns, the movement provided a network through which evangelical believers could share fellowship and nurture a vision for the nation's Christian renewal. Its tendency from the beginning, however, was to mark itself off from those who did not fully endorse its aims, and it seriously curtailed its own effectiveness as a means of cross-denominational renewal by espousing a restrictive concept of biblical infallibility and increasingly a separatist ecclesiology.[31] This was especially true after 1966–7 and the secession of some of its affiliated churches from their parent denominations following Martyn Lloyd-Jones' call for evangelical believers to secede from what he had come to believe were apostate religious bodies.[32] Thereafter evangelical witness within the denominations tended to occur outside the ambit of the Evangelical Movement of Wales, not least within the Evangelical Fellowship in the Church in Wales.[33]

A second focus for renewal was ecumenism. Ever since the great Edinburgh Missionary Conference of 1910, the conviction had increased that for mission and evangelism to be effective, they must stem from a single and united Christian church. The British Council of Churches had been established in 1942 and the World Council of Churches had been inaugurated in 1948, while the Council of Churches for Wales was formed in 1956. Just as the evangelical awakening among the Bangor students had led to the birth of the Evangelical Movement of Wales, lively evangelistic activity of a less restrictive kind had been happening there under the auspices of the Student Christian Movement (SCM), its focus being *Yr Ymgyrch Newydd yng Nghymru* ('The New Campaign in Wales').[34] As well as emphasising the necessity for personal commitment, it was socially involved and held to the ecumenical vision of fashioning a single and unified Welsh church. The path to create such a body was tortuous and complex, and though it led, by 1975, to the ratification of a covenant for union between the Methodists, the United Reformed Church, the Presbyterian Church in Wales, the Congregationalists and the Church in

---

[31] See D. C. Jones, 'Evangelicalism and Fundamentalism in Post-War Wales, 1947–1981', in D. Bebbington and D. C. Jones, eds., *Fundamentalism and Evangelicalism in the United Kingdom during the Twentieth Century* (Oxford: Oxford University Press, 2013), 289–308.

[32] D. C. Jones, 'Lloyd-Jones and Wales', 81–5.

[33] R. L. Brown, *Evangelicals in the Church in Wales* (Welshpool: Tair Eglwys Press, 2007), 271–91.

[34] E. Jones, *Croesi Ffiniau: Gyda'r Eglwys yn y Byd* (Swansea: Gwasg John Penri, 2000), 63–88.

Wales, in the end it amounted to little.[35] Organic union, or the abolition of denominational Christianity in favour of a single ecclesiastical body, would never happen, while the main contribution of the Ecumenical Movement would be to foster mutual respect among Welsh Christians whatever their church background, and to share a knowledge of the riches of the various traditions.[36]

The theological tumult which affected Western Christianity generally during the 1960s did not bypass the Welsh churches. The Second Vatican Council, Bishop John Robinson's radical and unexpectedly popular paperback *Honest to God* (1963), the 'Death of God' movement and various secular theologies had their devotees within the land. A particularly vigorous theological discussion took place in the Welsh-language monthly *Barn* in 1963–4 between J. R. Jones, a Calvinistic Methodist layman and professor of philosophy at the University of Wales, Swansea, and H. D. Lewis, also a Calvinistic Methodist and professor of the philosophy of religion at King's College, London. Heavily influenced by the radical theologian Paul Tillich's 'Protestant Principle' and some of the most enigmatic sections of Dietrich Bonhoeffer's *Letters and Papers from Prison,* Jones championed a highly idiosyncratic existential humanism which was openly antagonistic to Christian orthodoxy.[37] As well as reflecting faithfully each of the religious predilections of the 'secular Sixties', this altercation was intensified by being linked to the concurrent crisis of nationhood and that within Welsh Dissent. Within the Church in Wales, Glyn Simon, Bishop of Llandaff and soon to become Archbishop, lamented 'the theological ferment of our days' and its destabilising effect on ordinary worshippers: 'Men' he stated, in 1966, 'have been made to feel unsure of the Scriptures, the Creeds, the Church, the Ministry, even Christianity itself ... Many writers have used misleading and sometimes wild phrases such as "the Death of God", "the Abolition of Religion", and "our image of God must go" and so forth, which have caused great confusion.'[38] Although this ferment did not affect the immediate witness of most church people or chapelgoers, it contributed towards the increasing feeling of unease with

---

[35] D. D. Morgan, *The Span of the Cross,* 2nd ed., 243–7.

[36] N. A. Davies, *A History of Ecumenism in Wales, 1956–1990* (Cardiff: University of Wales Press, 2008).

[37] See R. Pope, 'Dolur Dwfn Diffyg Ystyr: J. R. Jones a Chrefydd', in E. Gwynn Matthews, ed., *Argyfwng Hunaniaeth a Chred: Ysgrifau ar Athroniaeth J. R. Jones,* vol. 6 in the series Astudiaethau Athronyddol (Talybont: Y Lolfa, 2017), 31–59.

[38] G. Simon, *A Time of Change: The Second Visitation Charge of the Bishop of Llandaff* (Penarth: Church in Wales Publications, 1966), 42.

traditional expressions of religious faith which would endure into the 1970s.

By then industrial Wales was being progressively more secularised and church attendance was plummeting, while rural Wales was suffering depopulation and economic decline. Those who cherished the Welsh language had become seriously anxious about its survival, and many were reminded of the nation's defencelessness when Liverpool Corporation was given permission, in the teeth of wholesale opposition, to expel the inhabitants of the Tryweryn Valley in Merionethshire and drown the valley itself in order to provide water for its citizens. Saunders Lewis' radio appeal of 1 March 1962, 'The Fate of the Language', sounded the alarm and Gwynfor Evans' election in 1966 as Plaid Cymru's first MP signalled the stirrings of a nationalist awakening. This was not welcomed everywhere, not least among Labour's centralisers and Tory unionists, though the report of the Kilbrandon Commission on the United Kingdom's constitution, in 1973, recommended the setting up of Welsh and Scottish Assemblies. The failure of the first devolution referendum of 1 March 1979 to secure a majority was a huge blow to those who were committed to home rule. What with significant immigration from England into the rural heartlands and the ambivalence of those who lived in the industrial and urban centres concerning a specifically Welsh future, it seemed that Wales as a separate national entity was courting oblivion. Their despair was voiced vividly in the historian Gwyn A. Williams' description of 'that people, which are my people and no mean people, who have for a millennium and a half lived in [those two western peninsulas of Britain] as a Welsh people, are now nothing but a naked people under an acid rain'.[39] This too was to have repercussions for the churches.

Towards the Millennium

By the 1980s one of the two strongest pillars of the Welsh economy for over a century, namely, steel and tinplate making (along with slate-quarrying in the north) was contracting, while an even greater social and psychological threat had to do with the future of coal. The monetary policies of Margaret Thatcher's government (which came to power in May 1979) demanded sweeping changes in the coal industry, represented by coalfields and their communities in both south and north-east Wales. Emboldened by her election victory in 1983 following the Falklands War,

---

[39] G. A. Williams, *When Was Wales?* (London: Penguin Books, 1985), 305.

Thatcher implemented the closure of innumerable pits, an action which was to cause catastrophic unemployment. The policy of gradual, consensual and negotiated change led by local leaders of both the National Coal Board and the National Union of Miners was now superseded by the twin intransigencies of Thatcher on the one hand and the extreme left-wing leader of the miners, Arthur Scargill, on the other. The coal strike of 1984, which in south Wales lasted into 1985, was disastrous. Thatcher had her way, the miners were forced to yield and the mainstay of Welsh communitarian life since the nineteenth century came to an end. Yet – ironically – it was not to be the end. By the late 1980s newer, technology-based industries, were being established, the Welsh Office (paradoxically) was being afforded more powers, and Cardiff, since 1982 the home of S4C, the Welsh fourth channel, and latterly a flourishing media industry, was gaining ever more confidence as a metropolitan centre. By the time of Thatcherism's expiration in the early 1990s, Labour's centralisers were in a minority, an appetite for devolution was abroad, and the referendum of 1997 laid the basis for a Welsh Assembly and parliament, its inaugural elections being held in 1999. In short, a national future had been secured.

Decline among the mainline churches, however, continued apace. Between 1980 and 1995 the Church in Wales shrank in membership from 131,600 to 96,000, the Roman Catholic Church from 57,000 to 47,000, and the older Nonconformist denominations – Presbyterians, Congregationalists, Baptists and Methodists including by now the United Reformed Church, established through a merger between English-speaking Presbyterians and Congregationalists in 1972 – from some 250,000 to around 170,000. Observers were hardly impressed: 'As the diminishing Christian community staggered into the twenty-first century, mainline churches continued a decline which had begun at the beginning of the twentieth century . . . While the churches debated details of belief, church discipline and ministry, the world journeyed rapidly towards secularism.'[40] Although newer bodies, mainly Pentecostalist, charismatic and evangelical, made sometimes impressive gains during these decades, it was nowhere near enough to offset the overall loss in church membership.

By the 1990s, the ecclesiastical landscape had changed. The 'new evangelicalism', socially engaged, more inclusivist and less doctrinally rigid than formerly, found an institutional manifestation in the

---

[40] J. I. Morgans and P. C. Noble, *Our Holy Ground: The Welsh Christian Experience* (Talybont: Y Lolfa, 2016), 176.

Evangelical Alliance Wales, established in 1986 as an umbrella organisation attracting support not only from congregations of the older denominations (including the Church in Wales) but also from classic Pentecostal
bodies such as the Assemblies of God, the Elim Church and the newer
charismatic networks as well. Ecumenical realignment occurred in 1990
with the formation of Cytûn: Churches Together in Wales, taking the
place of the old Council of Churches for Wales. It emerged from the 'Not
Strangers but Pilgrims' initiative of 1986 when an unexpectedly large
number of Christians from across the denominational spectrum came
together during Lent for prayer, Bible study and mutual enrichment,
culminating in the 20,000-strong 'Teulu Duw' festival in Llanelwedd in
which Archbishop Desmond Tutu thanked the Welsh people for their
support for the anti-apartheid movement in South Africa. The Roman
Catholic Church, engaged since the Second Vatican Council of 1962–5 in
ecumenical co-operation, had been fully involved in 'Not Strangers but
Pilgrims' and, following the nationwide consultation at Bangor in 1987
and the corresponding English event at Swanwick, committed itself to
full membership of the incipient body. The same would be true for
Catholic membership of Churches Together in England. For ecumenical
enthusiasts this was a huge breakthrough: 'The creation of Cytûn was
nothing short of miraculous.'[41] Miracle or not, widespread Christian
renewal did not ensue.

As the millennium dawned, the basic shape of Christian presence in
Wales was now manifest. It would be smaller and more variegated than it
once was, more a diverse mosaic of different denominations, sects and
ecclesial traditions than the stark twin slabs of Chapel and Church (with
a substantial Roman Catholic bloc, though very much to the side).[42] It
would be more self-effacing than previously, unassuming in the face of
religious pluralism and a sometimes strident secular consensus, though
still faithful (at best) to the Christian verities of the past.[43]

Conclusion

Throughout the twentieth century, the Church in Wales functioned side
by side with other Christian denominations in the service of the people of

[41] Ibid., 189.
[42] The authoritative study is T. O. Hughes, *Winds of Change: The Roman Catholic Church and Society in Wales, 1916–1962* (Cardiff: University of Wales Press, 2nd ed., 2017).
[43] See D. D. Morgan, *The Span of the Cross*, 2nd ed., xi–xviii; Morgans and Noble, *Our Holy Ground*, 194–201.

Wales. Sometimes there was contention, as during the disestablishment campaign when two different visions of the relation between Church and State vied with one another for ascendancy. Often this bred acrimony, especially when linked with the financial considerations of disendowment, and resentment when mixed with matters of status and class. At other times the Church and Nonconformity seemed oblivious to one another, content to witness to their own constituencies and according to their own religious and liturgical norms. Happily, there has more often (and more recently) been co-operation and partnership based on a common Christian commitment and a shared sense of mission to an ever-evolving Wales. In celebrating the centenary of the modern Church in Wales, all will join together endeavouring to keep the unity of the Spirit in the bond of peace.

4

The Church in Wales across the Century

WILLIAM PRICE

This chapter provides an outline account of developments in the Church in Wales since 1920, to assist readers to place the more specialised chapters which follow in their broader ecclesial context. As with Chapter 3 of this book, on Christianity in Wales over the century, this study too uses the tried-and-tested technique of periodisation as a convenient way of approaching the subjects treated. The landmark developments in the first period (1920–45) involve creating the administration of the Church, forming two new dioceses and establishing a sound financial basis for the Church. In the second period (1946–70), we see more self-confidence in the Church, some liturgical developments and the beginning of ecumenical co-operation. The third period (1971–95) is characterised by further liturgical and ecumenical progress, the ordination of female deacons and an increasing reduction in clergy numbers. The final period (1996–2020) deals with the ordination of female priests and bishops, a reorganisation of parochial structures and a severe decline in church membership.

The Early Years: Proceeding with Caution 1920–1945

On 31 March 1920, the Wednesday in Holy Week, four dioceses – Bangor, Llandaff, St Asaph, and St David's, in the Province of Canterbury in the Church of England – became, for the overwhelming part unwillingly, an autonomous province in the Anglican Communion.[1] The early years of the

---

[1] For fuller accounts, see D. Walker, ed., *A History of the Church in Wales* (Penarth: Church in Wales Publications, 1976); D. T. W. Price, *A History of the Church in Wales in the Twentieth Century* (Penarth: Church in Wales Publications, 1990); D. D. Morgan, *The Span of the Cross: Christian Religion and Society in Wales, 1914–2000* (Cardiff: University of Wales Press, 1999; 2nd ed., 2011); D. P. Davies, 'Welsh Anglicanism: A Renewed Church for a Reviving Nation', in N. Yates, ed., *Anglicanism: Essays in History, Belief and Practice* (Lampeter: Trivium Publications, 2008), 105–123. The province is not quite coterminous with Wales, since some border parishes with churches geographically in Wales chose to remain in, or join, the Church of England.

newly disestablished Church were marked by caution. Its leaders, clerical and lay, were elderly, and they had been opposed to disestablishment, but it was necessary to provide what were no more than four separate dioceses with mechanisms for their governance as a new province. In October 1917 a Convention had approved the establishment of a Governing Body to be the legislative authority of the new Church and also a Representative Body to hold in trust the property of the Church. Both bodies had first met in January 1918, when the Governing Body passed the following resolution: 'The Governing Body does hereby accept the Articles, Doctrinal Statements, Rites, and Ceremonies, and save in so far as they may be necessarily varied by the Welsh Church Act, 1914, the formularies of the Church of England.'[2] The new office of archbishop of Wales was not tied to one particular diocese, and on 7 April 1920 the four bishops elected Alfred George Edwards, Bishop of St Asaph, to the position. He remained archbishop and bishop of St Asaph until his retirement in 1934.

The name of the Church was finally established in 1921 as the Church *in* Wales. The Constitution, largely the work of the future Lord Sankey, accorded great power to the bishops, especially in the exercise of patronage and in the right to veto resolutions of the Governing Body. During its first seven years the Governing Body dealt with many issues – the creation of two new dioceses, and chapters in the Constitution on vestries, Parochial Church Councils, Ruridecanal and Diocesan Conferences, the Electoral College for choosing the archbishop and bishops, a scheme for training ordinands, schemes for administering the cathedrals, a dilapidations scheme, a patronage system, a series of courts, and a clergy pensions scheme for incumbents and curates. There was, however, almost no consideration of liturgical, ecumenical or social issues, although in 1928 the members of the Governing Body did give £500 to the National Fund for the Relief of Distress in the Coalfields.[3] The Book of Common Prayer 1662 of the Church of England, in English and Welsh, remained the legal prayer book of the Church in Wales until the 1980s, although some services were revised, for experimental use, from the 1950s.

Perhaps the major achievement of the new Governing Body and Representative Body was the creation of two new dioceses – Monmouth, out of Llandaff, in 1921 and Swansea and Brecon, out of St David's, in 1923. No new dioceses have been created since, although the

---

[2] Constitution of the Church in Wales (hereafter Constitution), Prefatory Note.
[3] Church in Wales, *The Welsh Church Year Book, 1929* (Cardiff: Representative Body of the Church in Wales, 1929), 82.

matter was considered by the Governing Body in 1980. Raising clergy stipends was seen as more important than creating new dioceses. It had been decided in 1917 that each diocese should have equal representation in the Governing and Representative Bodies, so that the less populated northern dioceses would not feel that they might be outvoted by the southern dioceses, but the creation of two additional dioceses in the south did give south Wales twice as many delegates as north Wales. Once the two new dioceses had been established, there were 502 members of the Governing Body, with 25 clergy and 50 laity from each of the 6 dioceses, together with *ex officio* and co-opted members. Since the 1920s the dioceses of the Church in Wales have often been seen as six kingdoms, each jealous of its autonomy. Indeed, as one commentator has written: 'One feature of the Church in Wales is that individual dioceses have a greater cohesion and individual character than the Province as a whole.'[4]

Disestablishment had been accompanied by disendowment. By an amending Act of 1919, passed by a House of Commons with a Conservative majority, some endowments were preserved, and the Church was awarded a grant of £1 million by the Treasury to enable it to survive financially.[5] Eventually more than £4 million was transferred to the Welsh counties and county boroughs and to the University of Wales. At disestablishment an appeal was launched to raise £1 million, to provide an income of about £48,000 a year to make up for the financial loss at disestablishment. By 1923 £661,730 had been subscribed, an impressive sum in the dire economic climate then prevailing in Wales. The appeal was closed in 1935, when £722,552 had been raised. In the words of one distinguished historian: 'By the late 1930s it had become apparent that the Church, though far from being opulent, was on as sound an economic footing as it had been prior to 1914.'[6]

Most of the income of the Church went to pay clerical stipends, now on a standard scale, except for those clergy who had been in post in 1914. By 1929 the average annual stipend of an incumbent was £335 and of an assistant curate £200. Until the Second World War there was no shortage of clergy, with about 1,000 incumbents and almost 500 assistant curates. Most of the clergy had studied in St David's College, Lampeter. In 1927 it was calculated that 66 per cent of Welsh clergy

---

4 D. P. Davies, 'Welsh Anglicanism', 107.
5 For the best account of the financial complexities of the Act, see P. M. H. Bell, *Disestablishment in Ireland and Wales* (London: SPCK, 1969), 308–18.
6 D. D. Morgan, *The Span of the Cross*, 2nd ed., 81.

had trained, in whole or in part, at Lampeter.[7] Others graduated in the University of Wales, and some in Oxford and Cambridge. Many had completed their training in St Michael's College, Llandaff. During this period, the worship in most churches was of a 'low-church to central prayer book' nature, reflecting the tradition of Lampeter, with Morning and Evening Prayer as the usual Sunday services. Holy Communion as a main Sunday service was usually monthly. In some parishes, especially in south-east Wales, the tradition was of a more eucharistic nature. Evangelical Anglicans were few.

In 1926 there were 22,427 baptisms, 14,931 confirmations and 184,568 Easter communicants. The total population of Wales in 1921 had been 2,648,356. Other statistics showed a vibrant Church, with 1,775 church buildings, 135,432 children in Sunday Schools and 41,486 people attending Bible classes.[8]

The Welsh language was not often heard in the higher echelons of the Church in Wales. A considerable number of influential lay members of the Governing Body in the 1930s were of the aristocratic, gentry and military classes, most of whom did not speak Welsh. In the parishes, however, the Welsh language was widely heard in much of Wales. In 1930 only eight churches in the Diocese of Bangor had no Welsh services. In the neighbouring Diocese of St Asaph, 125 churches had Welsh services and 69 did not. In the Diocese of St David's, 308 churches had Welsh services (37 being monoglot Welsh) and 106 did not.[9]

In 1929 a Joint Committee for the Promotion of Mutual Understanding and Co-operation between the Christian Communities in Wales was founded, with the aim of ensuring denominational co-operation in social, moral and spiritual matters, of encouraging interdenominational study circles, prayer and social service, and of deepening spiritual life throughout Wales. The committee was made up of representatives of Anglicans, Baptists, Congregationalists, Methodists and Presbyterians, but the wounds of the long disestablishment conflict made it difficult for the Church in Wales and the free churches to work together. The Church in Wales claimed

---

[7] D. T. W. Price, 'The Contribution of St David's College, Lampeter, to the Church in Wales, 1920–1971', *Journal of Welsh Ecclesiastical History*, 1 (1984), 63–83, and *A History of St David's University College, Lampeter* (Cardiff: University of Wales Press, 1990), vol. II, *(1898–1971)*.

[8] Church in Wales, *The Welsh Church Year Book, 1929*, 349.

[9] Church in Wales, *The Official Handbook of the Church in Wales* (Cardiff, 1930), 194–243, and D. T. W. Price, 'The Modern Diocese of St Davids', in W. Gibson and J. Morgan-Guy, eds., *Religion and Society in the Diocese of St Davids 1485–2011* (Farnham: Ashgate, 2015), 207.

to be the Ancient Catholic Church in Wales. An incumbent was charged at his institution to minister to all residents in a parish, whatever their religious affiliations. The Church in Wales was not a sect. Disestablishment did not destroy the parish system in the Church's mind, and the Church retained a favoured position with regard to marriage law. These matters and, for example, the use of cathedrals for civic occasions gave the Church in Wales what has been termed a 'post-established' character,[10] although only communicants aged eighteen years and older were able to vote for parochial, diocesan and provincial representatives.

Archbishop Edwards eventually retired in 1934, and was succeeded by Charles Alfred Howell Green, Bishop of Bangor. Undoubtedly the finest bishop during these years was Timothy Rees, elected to the Diocese of Llandaff in 1931. Rees had been a member of the Community of the Resurrection at Mirfield in Yorkshire. He sought to bring relief to those in his diocese who were suffering from the economic depression and to provide support for clergy ministering in deprived areas.[11]

By the end of the second decade of the Church's independence, Wales was beginning to experience increasing secularisation, particularly affecting Protestant Nonconformity, where the loss in membership was hastened by the serious decline in the number of Welsh-speakers. In terms of Anglican baptisms, numbers showed a decline, from 25,454 in 1920 to 17,917 in 1939. It is striking that the number of Easter communicants rose from 159,957 in 1920 to 193,668 in 1939, but this reflects the replacement of Morning Prayer by Holy Communion in many churches on Easter Day.[12]

The Governing Body met on 27 September 1939, but thereafter, because of the onset of the Second World War, its routine work was delegated to a War Committee, which met on eight occasions before Archbishop Green summoned a special meeting of the Governing Body in Cardiff on 2 October 1942. The Representative Body and each Diocesan Conference also set up war committees. The archbishop died on 7 May 1944. His high view of episcopacy was perpetuated until at least the 1980s by several archbishops and bishops. His successor, David Lewis Prosser, Bishop of St David's, was elected in September 1944. The Church suffered in the war, with much devastation in Cardiff and Swansea,

---

[10] C. Harris and R. Startup, *The Church in Wales: The Sociology of a Traditional Institution* (Cardiff: University of Wales Press, 1999), 7.

[11] J. Lambert Rees, *Timothy Rees of Mirfield and Llandaff: A Biography* (London and Oxford: Mowbray, 1945), and D. D. Morgan, *The Span of the Cross*, 2nd ed., 88–91.

[12] D. D. Morgan, *The Span of the Cross*, 2nd ed., 93.

including the bombing of Llandaff Cathedral and St Mary's Church, Swansea.

The Years of Optimism 1946–1970

The Church in Wales emerged from the Second World War with a new sense of looking forward, rather than back to the golden age of establishment, with younger leaders, and a rash of new committees and commissions. The financial state of the Church in Wales was, however, less healthy than many thought, and in 1945 a new Reconstruction Committee was established to investigate how clerical stipends might be increased. This had to be through the reduction in the number of benefices by grouping. Other commissions were set up. That on Religious Education in Wales led to the creation of a provincial Council for Education to watch over all aspects of education in Wales from primary schools to universities. In 1947 the Commission on the Nation and Prayer Book was formed, and in 1948 a Commission on Cathedrals followed. By 1949 the new archbishop, John Morgan, Bishop of Llandaff, was pleading, without success, for a respite in the number of new committees and commissions.

The report of the Commission on the Nation and Prayer Book was received by the Governing Body in September 1949. The Church, it stated, faced many challenges. The Church in Wales had not been in the forefront of theological thinking in Wales for more than a century, and preaching in the Church was not effective in contemporary Wales. Perhaps more fundamentally, the Church in Wales was felt to be isolated from the 'Welsh way of life' in Welsh-speaking areas, and it made very little contribution to Welsh academic and intellectual life.

Another concern considered in the report was liturgy. Almost thirty years after disestablishment, the Church in Wales was still using the Book of Common Prayer of the Church of England. The report's authors were sure that the Church had 'reached a position in which practical and pastoral needs require both the amendment and enrichment of our present Prayer Book in certain directions'. Liturgical revision should begin with changes urgently needed in the prayer book to reflect current 'pastoral and practical' conditions. However, there ought not to be any 'large-scale revision' at one time, but rather liturgical reform should be carried out by stages. This proposal was accepted, and it would take the Church in Wales many years to replace the entire Book of Common Prayer.

The report requested the archbishop to set up what became known as the Standing Liturgical Advisory Commission to advise the Bench of Bishops on possible revisions of liturgy. It was established in January 1951 and sent its recommendations to the bishops. If they approved, the proposals were to be debated by the Governing Body. If the Governing Body approved the proposed revised services, each bishop had the authority to permit their use in his diocese. The whole process was very slow, but gradually the liturgical texts of the Church in Wales were introduced into the parishes, in each case for an experimental period. The first revised services were those for infant and adult baptism and for confirmation, introduced from 1 January 1958 for use for ten years. By 1965 revised marriage, churching and burial services had been published.

After the Second World War a major problem for the Church was the low level of clergy stipends. They had scarcely been raised since 1939, and an increasing number of clergy moved to the Church of England, where stipends were considerably higher and where free housing was provided for assistant curates. Between 1947 and 1954, 276 priests left Wales for England, and in 1962 700 priests ordained in Wales were serving in England, but only 10 priests ordained in England were serving in Wales. In 1954 the editor of *Crockford's Clerical Directory* made the observation that 'not a few parsons seem to prefer the shackles of an Established Church to the "freedom" which some within it seem to desire'.[13] Other clergy in the Church in Wales left parochial ministry, usually for teaching posts. The number of ordinands also fell sharply. To maintain clerical numbers after the Second World War, the Church in Wales needed to ordain 70 deacons a year, but only 163 were ordained between 1947 and 1952, an average of about 27 each year.[14]

Most of the income of the Church from endowments, investments and the Provincial Levy, or Quota (payable through the dioceses), went on clergy stipends, but it was not easy to raise stipends to pre-war levels. At the meeting of the Governing Body in September 1949, for the first time the lay members met without the clerical members, and in 1952 they launched the Laymen's Appeal, to raise £500,000 for the express purpose of increasing clergy stipends, and as an addition to the Quota. By the summer of 1953 the target had been exceeded. The Quota was a relatively heavy demand on the parishes. In 1954, for example, the total Quota levy was £145,000 a year, which was only £51,000 less than the equivalent in

[13] *Crockford's Clerical Directory* (London: Oxford University Press, 1953–4), xx.
[14] Price, *History of the Church in Wales in the Twentieth Century*, 30.

the Church of England, a Church with fourteen times as many parishes as its Welsh sister.

Archbishop John Morgan died in 1957, and the election of his successor aroused some strong feelings. The new archbishop was Alfred Edwin Morris, an Englishman, born in Worcestershire, a professor at Lampeter since 1924, and elected bishop of Monmouth in 1945. He did not speak Welsh. Shortly afterwards Archdeacon Jack Thomas was elected bishop of Swansea and Brecon. He did not speak Welsh either. Bishop Glyn Simon of Llandaff, whose own command of Welsh was limited, wrote in his 'Diocesan Leaflet' that the elections of two bishops who could not speak Welsh came 'as a severe blow to the confidence of many Welsh-speaking Church folk'. He saw the elections as revealing 'an anti-Welsh and pro-English trend' in the Church in Wales. The new bishop of Bangor, G. O. Williams, wrote of 'the ambiguous attitude of our Church to the Welsh language'. Of course about 80 per cent of the people of Wales did not speak Welsh, and to have restricted the post of archbishop to a bilingual bishop would have made the great majority of clergy in Wales ineligible for the role.[15]

In 1966 the Governing Body approved an experimental form of the Holy Eucharist, first used at a meeting of the Governing Body on 5 April 1967. It won praise from liturgists throughout the worldwide Anglican Communion and beyond. The Book of Common Prayer 1662 of the Church of England remained an authorised rite in the Church in Wales, although the new experimental rite quickly became the usual service in most churches. At last the Church in Wales had a eucharistic rite published which was not 'According to the Use of the Church of England'. Some pastoral reorganisation also began during Edwin Morris' tenure of the primacy, especially the creation of Rectorial Benefices, mainly in urban areas, where a rector, assisted by vicars and curates, served several parishes. It was also at this time that stipendiary clergy were required to retire at the age of seventy years, reducing still further the number of serving clergy. Edwin Morris retired in 1968, and for the first time the senior bishop, David Bartlett of St Asaph, was not elected archbishop. At the age of sixty-eight he would have had to retire in just two years' time. The new archbishop was Glyn Simon, Bishop of Llandaff. He was certainly the first archbishop of Wales to be regarded as the leader of most Christians in Wales, Welsh-speaking and English-speaking. In September 1968 he addressed the Governing Body on Wales

---

[15]   For fuller accounts, see J. S. Peart-Binns, *Edwin Morris, Archbishop of Wales* (Llandysul: Gomer Press, 1990), 106–37, and D. D. Morgan, *The Span of the Cross*, 2nd ed., 190–4.

and the Welsh language. He made it clear that he wished the Church to become truly bilingual. He spoke out on the social and economic issues of the day, and he was deeply moved by the tragedy of Aberfan in 1966 when a coal tip collapsed, killing 116 children at school and 28 adults.

Having participated in 1956 in the formation of the Council of Churches for Wales, a successor to the Committee for Mutual Co-operation and Understanding, in 1966 the Church in Wales established a provincial Council for Mission and Unity, although without much enthusiasm on the part of the Bench of Bishops, most of whom still saw the Church in Wales as the 'Ancient Catholic Church of this land'. To them Christian unity meant the return of 'Nonconformists', whose numbers were continuing to decline, to the bosom of Mother Church. Archbishop Morris had said in his first visitation charge, in 1946, that 'Roman clergy and Nonconformist ministers [are], strictly speaking, intruders' in Wales. It is clear, however, that Glyn Simon was beginning to adopt a more liberal attitude towards the end of his archiepiscopate. At the end of the 1960s the possibility of Anglican–Methodist reunion became a live issue, at first in England and then in Wales, where there was considerable support for it among lay people and some clergy – but when it came to nothing in England it fell also in Wales. Nonetheless, steps were taken at this time to frame regulations whereby Nonconformists were permitted to receive Holy Communion in Anglican churches in Wales.[16]

The Winds of Change 1971–1995

Glyn Simon was diagnosed with Parkinson's disease in 1971, and he was obliged to resign after a mere three years as archbishop. By the time of his resignation, much of the optimism of the Church in Wales in the 1950s, when the future archbishop, G. O. Williams, had been moved to declare that the future belonged to the Church in Wales, had gone. Glyn Simon's final address to the Governing Body acknowledged the diminishing influence of all denominations in an ever more secular Wales.[17]

Glyn Simon's successor as archbishop was Gwilym Owen Williams, Bishop of Bangor, a convert from the Presbyterian Church of Wales and thoroughly bilingual.[18] His crusade was to see greater visible unity among

[16] Church in Wales: Governing Body, *Highlights* (Penarth: Church in Wales Publications), April 1967, October 1969 and May 1970.
[17] O. W. Jones, *Glyn Simon: His Life and Opinions* (Llandysul: Gomer Press, 1981), 122–5.
[18] D. T. W. Price, *Archbishop Gwilym Owen Williams, 'G.O.': His Life and Opinions* (Cardiff: Church in Wales Publications, 2017).

the denominations in Wales. A Joint Committee to consider Covenanting for Union was established in Wales, and in 1974 the Governing Body approved joining in a Covenant with the Presbyterians, the Methodists and the new United Reformed Church. On 18 January 1975 the Covenant was signed by the participating denominations. This was not an agreement to become one united institutional church, but a declaration to work and pray that the churches might become one visible church 'to serve together in mission to the glory of God the Father'. In 1977 some English-speaking Baptist congregations in south-east Wales also signed the Covenant. The years since have seen virtually no further steps towards visible unity. However, in most places there has been much more evident good will and co-operation between denominations, including those which did not enter into the Covenant, among them the Roman Catholic Church, especially after the visit of Pope John Paul II to Wales in 1982. In 1990 the Roman Catholic Church in Wales became a founding member of Cytûn: Churches Together in Wales, successor to the Council of Churches for Wales.

The Governing Body resolved, in April 1975, that there was no fundamental theological objection to the ordination of women to the priesthood, but a motion was passed 'that it would be inexpedient for the Church in Wales to take unilateral action in this matter at the present time'. Five years later, however, the Governing Body approved the ordination of women as deacons, before any other Anglican province in the British Isles took this step. The first women deacons were ordained in Wales in 1980.

There were also liturgical developments in G. O. Williams' time. In 1971 the revised services of baptism and confirmation were made compulsory after thirteen years of experimental use, and in the same year there appeared a volume of services for Candlemas, Ash Wednesday and Holy Week. By 1975 new services of matrimony and burial had been published, and these were not to be alternatives to rites in the Book of Common Prayer, but obligatory services. Experimental ordination services appeared in 1977. The gradual publication of so many services led to a desire for a new Book of Common Prayer for the Church in Wales. The production of such a volume was delayed, however, by the failure of a revised form of the Eucharist to gain the necessary two-thirds majority in the Governing Body in September 1979. The 1966 version had been widely praised throughout the Anglican Communion, as we have seen, but the 1979 version was clearly regarded by some in Governing Body as too radical an adaptation of 1966 and by others as too conservative a revision. A very conservative revision of the 1966 version was finally approved by the Governing Body in September 1981.

One matter which increasingly concerned G. O. Williams was the location of the archiepiscopal see. The framers of the Constitution had opted not to create a permanent see for the archbishop. G. O. Williams was the first archbishop based in north Wales since 1944, and he found it increasingly challenging to attempt to combine care of the Diocese of Bangor with his archiepiscopal responsibilities, which involved working with the staff in the Church in Wales' headquarters in Cardiff, and also his commitments as a primate in the Anglican Communion. One possible solution was to divide the Diocese of Swansea and Brecon into two, with a seventh diocesan bishop and a cathedral in Swansea. The archdeaconry of Brecon would become a separate diocese, permanently attached to the archbishopric. It was proposed that the Diocese of Llandaff and the Diocese of Swansea and Brecon would become 'collegial dioceses'. This made members of the Governing Body even more cautious than usual, and the proposal was defeated.[19] The matter of establishing a permanent archiepiscopal see has been actively considered ever since, with no resolution.

The 1970s saw a crisis in the Church's financial position, during a time of rapid inflation. In 1975 a Committee on Inflation was established, and in 1976 the annual diocesan Quota assessment on the parishes was doubled, from £258,000 to £516,000. The parishes met the challenge, and between 1979 and 1984 clerical stipends were also doubled, a target achieved in part because of a decline in the number of stipendiary clergy.

Archbishop G. O. Williams retired in 1982 and was succeeded by Bishop Derrick Childs of Monmouth. During his tenure, at last, more than sixty years after disestablishment, the Church in Wales had its own complete prayer book. *The Book of Common Prayer for Use in the Church in Wales* was published in two volumes in 1984. The first contained the Eucharist and Morning and Evening Prayer. The second contained Baptism, the Catechism, Confirmation, Ordination, Marriage, the Ministry of Healing, and Burial. These two volumes replaced the Book of Common Prayer 1662 of the Church of England, although the services of Holy Communion and Holy Matrimony in that book could still be used in Wales. All the newly published English services of the Church in Wales, except that for marriage, addressed God as 'Thou', when all other

---

[19] Church in Wales: Governing Body, *Highlights* (Penarth: Church in Wales Publications), August 1980.

Anglican provinces had moved to using 'You'. The archbishop strongly defended the traditional form, but in 1984 a version of the Eucharist in modern Welsh and English was made available for experimental use.

A reshaping of the management of the Church began in 1984 with the creation of the Board of Mission, and in the following year a lay provincial secretary-general took office. The Board of Mission was headed by a full-time director, and it was divided into six divisions – Communications, Ecumenism and World Mission, Education, Evangelism and Adult Education, Social Responsibility, and Stewardship. As the number of officers in the Board of Mission increased, the number of parish clergy decreased rapidly. In 1930 there were 969 incumbents and 376 assistant curates in the Church in Wales. In 1969 there were 748 incumbents and 182 curates. In 1989 numbers had fallen to about 526 incumbents and 116 curates. These figures reflected a serious decline in the number of those training for ordination. In 1961 there were about 135 in training, not all of whom completed the course and were ordained. In 1974 there were 101 in training, in 1989 only 50. The decline was most marked in the number of ordinands who were fluent in Welsh. Of the fifty in training in 1989 only five were fluent in Welsh. Between 1976, when Bishop Burgess Hall in Lampeter closed,[20] and 2016, the only theological college in Wales was St Michael's in Llandaff, although some ordinands trained in England. The parochial system survived only through the grouping of parishes and also from the late 1960s by the ordination of non-stipendiary clergy, at first in the Diocese of Bangor.

Archbishop Childs retired in 1986. His successor was George Noakes, Bishop of St David's. George Noakes was the first archbishop to come from an evangelical background, albeit he was a 'gentle Evangelical'. A prayerful man of deep personal spirituality and a stimulating preacher in both languages, he never entirely lost the persona of a parish priest. Sir William Gladstone, Chairman of the Representative Body, considered, in 1999, that George Noakes offered the Church in Wales 'quite exceptional leadership of a quality which was not seen before and has not been seen since'.[21] Alwyn Rice Jones, Bishop of St Asaph, succeeded Noakes as archbishop in 1991. During his leadership, perhaps the most notable development was the ordination of women to the priesthood, which the archbishop strongly supported, as did the bishop of Monmouth, Rowan Williams. Following a long debate in the Governing Body in April 1994,

[20] D. D. Morgan, *The Span of the Cross*, 2nd ed., 254.
[21] J. S. Peart-Binns, *Gravitas with a Light Touch* (Durham: Memoir Club, 2009), 238.

however, the bill to enable women to be ordained as priests was defeated – because the clerical vote narrowly missed the required two-thirds majority.

The Need to Change 1996–2020

The issue of the ordination of women to the priesthood returned to the Governing Body in September 1996. The bill needed a two-thirds majority in each order, and it reached this by one vote among the clergy. While the Church in Wales had led the way in the British Isles in ordaining women deacons, it was the last Church to ordain women priests. Before the vote was taken in September 1996, a document containing guidelines for the spiritual care of those unable in conscience to accept the ministry of female priests was distributed to all Governing Body members. This stressed that there would be a continuing place in the Church in Wales for those who could not accept the sacramental ministry of women priests, and the bishops undertook to appoint an assistant bishop in Wales to take pastoral oversight of the minority. Canon David Thomas was consecrated as such in December 1996.

Archbishop Rice Jones, whose final years in office were clouded by ill health, retired in 1999, and in December of that year the bishop of Monmouth, Rowan Williams, began what was to be a fairly short tenure of the archiepiscopate, during which a radical proposal to create an ecumenical bishop in east Cardiff was defeated in the Governing Body.[22] In 2003 Rowan Williams became archbishop of Canterbury, and Barry Cennydd Morgan was elected archbishop, having been bishop of Bangor between 1992 and 1999 and then bishop of Llandaff. The number of serving clergy, of ordinands and of active lay members of the Church, especially young active members, all continued to fall in the new century, and in September 2010 the Governing Body, by then much reduced in the number of its members, 143, called for changes.

As a result an external review was appointed which opened with a statement by Archbishop Barry Morgan and Philip Price QC, Chairman of the Standing Committee of Governing Body, that 'The Church in Wales cannot go on doing the same things in the same way; some things need to change and we are open to – and indeed

---

[22] Church in Wales: Governing Body, *Highlights* (Cardiff: Church in Wales Publications), September 2002; R. Shortt, *Rowan's Rule: The Biography of the Archbishop* (London: Hodder and Stoughton, 2008), 202–3.

encourage – that possibility.' The task of the review was to make recommendations, 'with particular reference to its structures and use of resources, to increase the effectiveness of the Church's ministry and witness'. The reviewers were Lord Harries of Pentregarth, former bishop of Oxford, Professor Charles Handy, and Professor Patricia Peattie. Their lengthy report was published in July 2012. The reviewers had no doubt that there was a great desire for change in the Church, but there were, of course, many different and sometimes conflicting ideas about what changes were desirable and how they should be made. There was also a general feeling that the organisation and structure of the Church were hampering reform: 'One overwhelming impression we have received is that the Church in Wales continues to have the structure and organisation appropriate to an established church 100 years or so ago, but which is now stretched beyond what it can or should properly bear now.' Furthermore the culture of the Church in Wales was, in the opinion of the reviewers, too deferential towards the bishops in their dioceses and towards the clergy in their parishes. This was not a novel observation. The need was clear: 'What is needed is a new, more collaborative, style of leadership, modelled by the Bishops and reflected at parish level.' There was real leadership in the Church, but the gifts of lay members were not fully used. The reviewers felt certain that the Church could 'only continue into the future' if it took advantage of the 'human resource' available in lay people.

The report looked at many aspects of the Church's life, but the most fundamental recommendation dealt with the creation of Ministry Areas: 'The parish system, as originally set up, with a single priest serving a small community is no longer sustainable.' A radical change was needed. The parish had to be replaced by a larger unit, and the single priest had to be replaced by a team of clergy and lay people. A Ministry Area ought to be large, something like the catchment area of a secondary school, with about twenty-five congregations or churches. Each Ministry Area would be made up of perhaps three stipendiary priests, working with non-stipendiary priests and lay ministers, and the Ministry Area should pay for its own leadership team if possible. Full-time Ministry Area workers should be appointed to reach out to the unchurched, especially young people. Moreover, each individual congregation or church would have a leader, who would usually be not an ordained but a lay person.[23]

---

[23]   Church in Wales, *Review* (July 2012), www.churchinwales.org.uk/review/, Preface and 3, 4 and 6.

Among the many other matters considered by the review were cathedrals, training for leadership and ministry (clerical and lay), clergy appraisal, worship (and each Ministry Area should hold at least one non-traditional service each week, not necessarily on Sunday), the number of dioceses (not to be changed for 'at least the next four years'), the archiepiscopal see (which should be fixed at Llandaff), closing church buildings, and permitting clergy to buy their own homes. They also recommended establishing a separate pensions fund, abolishing fees as additional income for clergy (later debated by Governing Body and defeated), assisting ordinands to learn Welsh, establishing a Board of Mission and Ministry, developing ecumenical partnerships, changing the method of electing bishops and the archbishop, simplifying the Constitution, and strengthening the role of Governing Body's Standing Committee.

The reviewers stressed that the major changes proposed by them needed to be implemented with urgency. For the regular churchgoer, the most important change was the replacement of the parish by the Ministry Area. Each diocese worked at a different speed in introducing Ministry Areas, Bangor being the first to complete the process throughout its territory. True to the tradition of diocesan autonomy, the Diocese of St Asaph used the term Mission Areas to denote the new system. Some Ministry/Mission Areas were made up of about the twenty-five congregations or churches proposed by the report, but most were smaller. Some had two or three stipendiary clergy, but some, especially in the Diocese of Bangor, had only one. Whether the abandonment of the centuries-old parish system and the creation of the much larger areas of ministry will be to the benefit of the Church remains to be seen. With a serious decline in the number of stipendiary clergy, however, it is difficult to see how the traditional parish system, with ever larger groups of parishes, and possibly many vacant benefices, could have survived. The day must surely come when many churches will have to be closed.

Barry Morgan had long been a very vocal proponent of women's ordination, including to the episcopate. In 2008 the Governing Body debated the matter, but it failed to secure a two-thirds majority in the Order of Clergy. The issue was debated again on 12 September 2013, when it was passed. To care for those clergy and laity who could not accept female bishops, a Code of Practice was produced by the Bench of Bishops, although no successor had been appointed to Bishop David Thomas after his retirement in 2008. The Church was committed to ensuring that those members who could not accept the sacramental ministry of women as bishops and priests could remain and flourish within the Church, and appropriate provision would be made for them. All members had to recognise 'unreservedly and without qualification' the jurisdiction of a woman bishop, to whom was due 'respect and canonical obedience' by all members. The Code of Practice was not enshrined as a canon, and the bishops reserved the right to amend its provisions if that were necessary in the future. Joanna Penberthy was elected bishop of St David's in 2016 and, following a meeting of the Electoral College which failed to elect to Llandaff in 2017, the Bench of Bishops appointed June Osborne to that see. In 2019 Cherry Vann was elected as bishop of Monmouth. The Church in Wales now has the highest proportion of female bishops in the Anglican Communion.

St Michael's College in Llandaff closed in 2016, and training for clerical and lay ministry was entrusted to St Padarn's Institute, with courses and tutors throughout Wales, but with the buildings in Llandaff. An increasing number of clergy and ordinands were Evangelicals, a development which had begun in the 1970s.

Archbishop Barry Morgan retired in January 2017, and his successor was Bishop John Davies of Swansea and Brecon. As the Church approaches the centenary of disestablishment under his leadership, the statistics do not look favourable. The number of Easter communicants fell from 85,304 in 1999 to 48,540 in 2017. In 1927 there were 187,178 Easter communicants in the Church in Wales, with 47,007 in the Diocese of Llandaff alone. Between 1927 and 2017 annual baptisms fell from 20,804 to 5,487, and annual confirmations from 13,261 to 559, doubtless in part reflecting new social mores. On 31 December 2017 there were 423 stipendiary clergy and 149 non-stipendiary clergy in Wales, 154 under fifty years of age and 418 over fifty, and on the same date there were 25 candidates in training for stipendiary ministry and 38 for non-stipendiary ministry. Twenty-five deacons were ordained in 2017. There are certainly differences of opinion among church members on issues of human sexuality, especially in relation to same-sex relationships, with a Bench of Bishops following clearly a 'liberal' agenda in what had been in the past at least a conservative Church.

Conclusion

Regardless of all these developments since 1920, the Church in Wales is today the largest Christian denomination in Wales with an average

Sunday attendance of 33,265 in 2017 – the Roman Catholic Church in Wales had a Mass attendance of 25,107 in 2017. The Church in Wales still covers the whole country, with much enthusiasm in the leaders, clerical and lay, of its new Ministry/Mission Areas. It is not a 'gathered church', but it seeks to serve people of any faith or denomination or none, in both languages, and it ministers in hospitals, universities and prisons. During the century, however, there has been 'a shift from a culture of obligation or duty to a culture of consumption or choice',[24] and the Church has to share the good news of the Gospel in a totally new social context. The Church in Wales faces a far more fundamental challenge to its very existence in 2020 than it did in 1920.

---

[24] G. Davie, 'Establishment', in M. D. Chapman, S. Clarke and M. Percy, eds., *The Oxford Handbook of Anglican Studies* (Oxford: Oxford University Press, 2016), 292.

PART II

Governance and Ministry

5

The Constitution of the Church

NORMAN DOE

The Constitution is the legal instrument made by the Church in Wales to facilitate and order its public life. When first drafted, on the eve of disestablishment, it was intended to provide the essentials for institutional stability, to enable the Church to carry out its mission. However, the Constitution was never intended to be a static instrument of church governance. At the outset, provision was made for the Constitution to be revised as the years unfolded, in order to adapt to whatever changes and chances were to face the Church. As such, whilst today its fundamentals remain much the same as they did at disestablishment, there have been numerous landmark changes which indicate well how the Constitution is a living document. This chapter describes, explains and evaluates the century-long evolution of the Constitution, from the perspective of the role of key figures in its development, in relation to five themes, namely: (1) the sources and foundations of the Constitution in civil law; (2) the formation and drafting of the Constitution; (3) the structure, systematisation and revision of the Constitution; (4) the purposes and enforceable nature of the Constitution; and (5) the institutional organisation of the Church in Wales. These are explored, where appropriate, in the context of principles of canon law common to the churches of the Anglican Communion.[1]

The Civil Law Foundations of the Constitution

From the twelfth century the four Welsh dioceses of Bangor, Llandaff, St David's and St Asaph came under the jurisdictional control of Canterbury and Rome. Alongside local law, the church was subject to papal law until the Reformation. The Henrician legislation of the 1530s ended papal

[1] I am grateful to the Principal and Fellows of Jesus College, Oxford, for a short-term Visiting Fellowship in 2018 which enabled me to prepare for key aspects of this study, and to Robin Darwall-Smith, the College Archivist.

authority and prepared the way to establish the Church of England under the royal supremacy (consolidated and developed under Elizabeth I). But by statute Roman canon law continued to apply to the church unless contrary to the law of the realm. The Canons Ecclesiastical 1603 were passed by the Convocation of Canterbury, of which Welsh bishops and clergy were part. These canons, with any papal law surviving the Reformation, decisions of church (and state) courts and, particularly in the nineteenth century, a host of Acts of Parliament, together formed the ecclesiastical law regulating the Church of England in Wales and, within the framework of the common law, defined the terms of ecclesiastical freedom. These were the legal sources applicable to the English Church in Wales until 1920.[2]

The legislative battle to disestablish was long and hard – it took half a century from the first bill to disestablishment day. Two Welsh barristers and Liberal MPs were at the forefront: in 1870 George Osborne Morgan sought reform of burial law, and Watkin Williams proposed the first (failed) disestablishment bill. Disestablishment became official Liberal Party policy in 1887. However, after its election success in 1892, the Liberal government was reluctant to proceed; as a result, four Welsh MPs (including David Lloyd George) refused the party whip. In turn, disestablishment bills were introduced in 1894 (and Lloyd George was largely responsible for it) and 1895 – both failed: the House of Lords opposed them and the Liberals lost the 1895 election. But a landslide Liberal election victory in 1906 led to the appointment of a royal commission reporting in 1910, itself a delaying tactic – the commission was heavily criticised, and its proposals were not unanimous. A disestablishment bill was introduced by H. H. Asquith in 1909 but, along with Lloyd George's budget, it was rejected by the Lords. The Parliament Act 1911 was passed, therefore, enabling the Commons to present a bill for royal assent without the Lords' consent – itself a radical constitutional change. Another Welsh church bill was introduced in the Commons in 1912 – it was rejected twice by the Lords. The Commons then invoked the Parliament Act, the first time to do so, and the Welsh Church Act 1914 was enacted.[3] Its implementation was delayed until after the Great War, and so the Church of England in Wales (and Monmouthshire) was disestablished on 31 March 1920.

---

[2] See e.g. R. Phillimore, *Ecclesiastical Law* (London: Sweet & Maxwell, 2nd ed., 1895).

[3] Welshman Ellis Jones Griffith, KC and Liberal MP, steered the bill in the Commons and chaired the Executive Committee of the Central Campaign Committee for Disestablishment of the Church of England in Wales.

The Welsh Church Act 1914 provided that the Church of England in Wales and Monmouthshire ceased to be 'established by law'. No person was to be appointed by the monarch to any ecclesiastical office in the Church in Wales. Every ecclesiastical corporation was dissolved. Its bishops ceased to sit in the House of Lords. Bishops and clergy could be elected to the House of Commons, and they ceased to be members of or represented in the Convocation of the Province of Canterbury. The Act also disendowed: English church property was transferred to Welsh church commissioners to redistribute – church buildings and parsonages were vested in the Church's Representative Body; churchyards were transferred to local authorities (but this changed in 1945); other property passed to county councils, the university and bodies such as the National Library of Wales.[4] Importantly, though, 'vestiges of establishment' remained for the Welsh Church: the duty of clergy to solemnise marriages of parishioners; the right of parishioners to burial in the churchyard; and the duty to provide prison chaplains. Further Acts of Parliament followed during the century.[5] Following devolution, legislation of the National Assembly for Wales and of the Welsh government also touches the Church either directly or indirectly.[6] Indeed, in 2013 an Assembly committee proposed exploring how the constitutional convention that Parliament will not legislate for the Church of England without its consent might be developed to apply to the Welsh Church.[7]

Importantly, the Welsh Church Act 1914 provides that, from the date of disestablishment, 'the ecclesiastical law of the Church in Wales shall cease to exist as law' for the Welsh Church (section 3(1)). Before 1920, English ecclesiastical law, applicable to the established Church of England in Wales, formed one part of the law of the land: 'the ecclesiastical law of England . . . is part of the general law of England – of the common law – in that wider sense which embraces all the ancient and approved customs of England which form law'.[8] However, this ecclesiastical law (found in both

---

[4] See N. Doe, *The Law of the Church in Wales* (Cardiff: University of Wales Press, 2002), ch. 1.

[5] See Chapter 11.

[6] E.g. Ecclesiastical Exemption (Listed Buildings and Conservation Areas) (Wales) Order 2018.

[7] National Assembly for Wales: Constitutional and Legislative Affairs Committee, *Report on the Inquiry into Law-Making and the Church in Wales* (June 2013), par. 77: 'We note the constitutional convention referred to by Professor Doe in his evidence and consider that there would be merit in exploring a similar solution for the Church in Wales while vestiges of establishment relating to marriage remain.'

[8] *Mackonochie v Lord Penzance* (1881) 6 App Cas 424 at 446.

state-made and church-made law) did not lose all its authority for the Welsh Church. The statute provides that pre-1920 ecclesiastical law continues to apply to the Church in Wales as if its members had assented to it (section 3(2)); this was to continue unless and until altered by the Church in Wales. This was to fill the juridical vacuum to be left by disestablishment and to ensure a degree of continuity.

Nevertheless, the 1914 Act also provides for the Church to regulate itself by its own legal system. Nothing in any Act of Parliament, law or custom is to prevent its bishops, clergy and laity from holding synods or electing representatives to them, nor from framing 'constitutions and regulations' for its management, government, property and affairs (section 13(1)). The power to alter ecclesiastical law includes power to alter such law as is contained in any Act of Parliament forming part of pre-1920 ecclesiastical law (section 3(4)). The Constitution still lists pre-1920 Acts of Parliament which the church has dis-applied since 1920, and it classifies the pre-1920 terms of its statutory contract as the 'received ecclesiastical law', and those made by the Church since disestablishment (post-1920 instruments) as 'enacted ecclesiastical law'.[9] Early editions of the Constitution used to carry a Note reciting verbatim the terms of sections 3(2) and 13(1) of the 1914 Act (as does its Prefatory Note today: see below). The 1914 Act was modelled largely on the Irish Church Act 1869 which dissolved the constitutional union between the Church of Ireland and the established Church of England.

The Formation and Drafting of the Constitution

The postponement of bringing into force the Welsh Church Act 1914 enabled Anglicans to prepare for disestablishment. A convention of about 400 delegates met at the City Hall in Cardiff in 1917 to discuss a new constitutional order for the Church. Moreover, whilst it was Parliament in the Welsh Church Act 1914 which separated the Church from the State, it was by an ecclesial act on 10 February 1920 that the archbishop of Canterbury declared the Welsh dioceses to be 'separate from the Province of Canterbury and (they so desiring it) a distinct ecclesiastical Province' of the Anglican Communion.[10] And so, by 31 March 1920 the Welsh dioceses had a Constitution, a Governing

---

[9] See e.g. Scheme for the Cathedral Church of St Davids, II.1.

[10] The archbishop had earlier released the Welsh bishops from obedience to the See of Canterbury: M. Lane, 'The Legal Extent of the Disestablishment of the Church in Wales' (LLM Dissertation, Cardiff University, 2018).

Body (legislature), Representative Body (provincial trustees) and courts (ordered hierarchically), then elected an archbishop.

Three Welsh judges were active in drafting the Constitution. James Richard Atkin (1867–1944), later Law Lord (Baron Atkin of Aberdovey), discussed drafts, was an original member of the Governing Body and Representative Body, and judge of the Provincial Court (1922–38); in 1937 he secured statutory relief for clergy who refused to solemnise the marriages of divorced persons, and opposed the Welsh bishops' blanket ban on clergy to do so on the basis of this statutory right as a matter of individual conscience.[11] The second was John Eldon Bankes (1854–1946), of Flintshire, a Court of Appeal judge, diocesan chancellor of St Asaph (1908–10), active at the 1917 convention, and chair of the Representative Body (1928–43).

The most prominent, however, was John Sankey (1866–1948) of Roath in Cardiff. Diocesan chancellor of Llandaff (1909–14), he spoke against disestablishment – and called disendowment 'morally wrong'. Appointed as High Court judge (1914) and knighted, he chaired the Enemy Aliens Advisory Committee (1915) and a coal industry commission (1919) proposing its nationalisation, and later served as Lord Chancellor (1928–35). Sankey worked unsparingly on the Constitution, and at the 1917 convention spoke positively of 'the privilege ... seldom given to a generation [of] shaping the course of the Church, it may be, for centuries'. But he warned of 'chaos' if it had not framed its constitution. His team 'consulted every constitution of every disestablished Church'. His drafts included only the 'absolutely essential', with 'no originality' and 'not running after any new thing' – 'with a few exceptions every paragraph is taken from some [existing] constitution which has been tried in the balance and found not to be wanting'. The drafts of the constitution were 'based on the assumption that the Church in Wales is part of and will remain a member of the Catholic and Apostolic Church', he said.[12]

Sankey's diaries attest to the intensity of his work on the Constitution. For example, on 1 October 1917: 'At Cardiff for Welsh Church Convention'; on 2 October: 'I proposed chief resolution. Spoke for 70 minutes. Bankes CJ seconded'; on 5 October: 'A unanimous vote of thanks was given to me'; and on 18 October he was at the Welsh Church Drafting Committee in London. In January 1918 he attended the first meeting of Governing Body, at

---

[11] Matrimonial Causes Act 1937, s. 12, for 'the relief of conscience among the clergy': see Chapter 11.

[12] *Official Report of the Proceedings of the Convention of the Church in Wales Held at Cardiff* (Cardiff, 1917), 11, 13, 17, 18, 25. See also J. Gainer, 'John Sankey and the Constitution of the Church in Wales' (LLM Dissertation, University of Wales Cardiff, 1994).

Westminster, and on the second day 'spoke about 2 hours in the morning, explaining a chapter of the constitution'. The next day was the first meeting of the Representative Body: 'I had to speak often.' Later that month he dined with Atkin and Bankes, and 'determined not to work so much at Welsh Church affairs'. In September he attended the first meeting in Wales of the Governing Body, at Cardiff: 'I made many speeches in introducing the various clauses of the further chapters of the constitution. Greatly helped by Bankes.' In 1920, he continued to consult John Bankes and Frank Morgan on a temporary scheme for Welsh church tribunals, chaired the Legal Committee of the Representative Body, presided at the Welsh Church Legal Committee, and spoke on new chapters of the Constitution at the Governing Body.[13]

His contribution in drafting the Constitution is summed up by Bishop Lloyd Crossley (formerly of Auckland): 'He is not only a lawyer but behind the legal acumen shines the brilliancy of his loyal churchmanship and his profound and humble reverence for his God'; and from a woman in Llandovery: 'We in Wales owe you a great debt ... for your powerful aid and wise counsel during the crisis in the history of our beloved Church, and for your strong hand in drafting its new constitution and consolidating its present position.'[14] By 1936, in a letter about possible publication of his 'reminiscences', Sankey himself recognised that when he 'drew up the constitution of the Church in Wales', this was one of the top ten 'points' of his legal career.[15]

The Systematisation and Revision of the Constitution

The Constitution was originally and remains composed of 'chapters', 'canons of the Church in Wales', and 'rules and regulations made from time to time by or under the authority or with the consent of the Governing Body'. Governing Body was and is still empowered 'to add to, alter, amend, or abrogate any of the provisions of the Constitution'. Altering *chapters* in matters of faith, order and discipline is by making a *canon* under bill

---

[13] P. J. Bull, *Catalogue of the Papers of John Sankey (1866–1948)* (Oxford: Bodleian, 1973). For his *Diaries*, see Bodl. MS Eng. Hist. e. 271 (1917); e. 272 (1918); e. 273 (1919); e. 274 (1920); *Diary* 7 Oct. 1920: 'Made a long speech on churchwardens! The meetings have gone fairly well except for episcopal disputes and jealousies.'

[14] Crossley returned to minister near Cardiff due to ill health; the Llandovery letter is dated 9 June 1929.

[15] Bodl. MS Eng. Hist c. 515: fol. 36: 21 Sept. 1936: it appears at number 5 and 'took me about 5 years'.

procedure. Once promulgated by the archbishop as president of Governing Body, a canon becomes 'a law of the Church in Wales'.[16] The Constitution is published in two volumes: volume I with chapters and regulations; and volume II, canons, rules and regulations, and other instruments.[17] It was intended that it be published in both Welsh and English – but it was not until 1972 that the chapters were published in Welsh, and the canons, rules and regulations, not until 1980.[18]

The subject matter and ordering of the chapters changed little over the century. The original Constitution comprised chapters titled: General (I); Governing Body (II); Representative Body (III); Diocesan Conference (IV); Ruridecanal Conference (V); Vestry Meeting and Parochial Church Council (VI); Appointments and Patronage (VII); Election of Bishops (VIII) and Archbishop (IX); and Dilapidations (X).[19] However, in 2010, bill procedure was used to reorganise the chapters – fundamentals were retained in chapters, outdated materials omitted, and other materials transferred into regulations (both alterable by a motion of Governing Body, unless involving faith, order and discipline when bill procedure is used). As a result, today volume I contains: General (e.g. definitions) (I); Governing Body (II) and regulations on it; Representative Body (III), but there are no associated regulations; the Diocesan (IVA) and Deanery Conferences (IVB), Parochial Administration (IVC) – and there are associated regulations for each of these – and Territorial Arrangements (IVD), but there are no associated regulations. Next come: the Archbishop and Diocesan Bishops (V); Appointment and Nominations (VI) and associated regulations; Parsonages (VII) and related regulations; Retirement (VII) and the Tribunal and Courts (IX) – rules and regulations about the last two matters are found in volume II. There is also an index containing information on the derivations of the new chapters and destinations of old references in new chapters.[20] It is typical of Anglican churches to treat subjects of the kinds set out here in their constitutions.[21]

---

[16] Constitution I.I.1 and II.IV (Governing Body powers), V (Bill Procedure), VI (Motions), VII (Regulations).

[17] See www.churchinwales.org.uk/resources/constitution-handbooks/constitution-of-church-in-wales/.

[18] E. P. Roberts, 'The Welsh Church, Canon Law and the Welsh Language', in N. Doe, ed., *Essays in Canon Law: A Study of the Law of the Church in Wales* (Cardiff: University of Wales Press, 1992), 151–173.

[19] Constitution (dated, in handwriting, 21 August 1920). See below for chapter XI.

[20] Divided between Parts I and II. Volume I has an Index.

[21] See N. Doe, *Canon Law in the Anglican Communion* (Oxford: Clarendon Press, 1998), ch. 1.

While volume I of the Constitution does not specify the dates when chapters were revised,[22] volume II gives a legislative history of the canons, rules, regulations and other instruments. Forty-three canons were promulgated 1949–2016 to amend chapters of the Constitution or the Book of Common Prayer.[23] They indicate both the intensity and preoccupations of legislative activity. Sixteen canons amended chapters (1974 to 2017), namely: two on appointment and patronage (1980, 2001); two on bill procedure (1980, 1999); two on the election of the archbishop (1987, 2013); six on the courts, and, latterly, the tribunal (1980, 1987, 1996, 1997, 2000, 2006); two on retirement and pensions (1993, 2001); and two on miscellaneous matters (1974, 2009). Six dealt with clerical matters: one on the resignation of incumbents (1949) was followed by a fallow period until a canon on better distribution and use of clerical 'manpower' (1968); fourteen years of inactivity were followed by canons on the incapacity and absence of the archbishop (1982), incapacity of incumbents (1985), terms of service (2010) and women bishops (2013). As to revisions to the Book of Common Prayer 1662 and 1984, there were six canons in the 1970s, seven in the 1980s and none in the 1990s; there were also five on liturgical matters (2003–14), one on marriage (1987) and one on ecumenism (2016).[24]

In addition, thirty-three canons dealt with matters not involving changes to the chapters of the Constitution. Eighteen are on ecumenical relations (1937, 1966, 1973–7, 1985, 1991, 1995, 2000, 2005 and 2016). The other fifteen deal with: experimental use of proposed liturgical revisions (1955); removing doubt about irregularity of birth as impeding ordination (1961); use of versions of the Bible (1974); ordaining women deacons (1980); incapacitated incumbents and ordination days (1982); clerical disabilities, and age for ordination (both in 1990); ordaining women priests (1996); removing doubt on divorce as impeding ordination (1998); ecclesiastical offices (2010); the tribunal and courts (2010 and 2017); ordaining women bishops (2013); and the Book of Common Prayer (1984) as an alternative Ordinal (2014).[25]

---

[22] But the church website gives dates of recent revisions – e.g. Chapter II: Governing Body, Part 1:3 amended Dec. 2016, Sections 6(1) and 6(4) amended April 2015; Chapter II: Regulations on Governing Body, Section 22 amended April 2015. See www .churchinwales.org.uk/resources/constitution-handbooks/constitution-of-church-in-wales/volume-i-amendments/.

[23] These were not required by the Standing Committee of Governing Body to be printed in full.

[24] Constitution II.1.2: Canons (Part 2).

[25] Constitution II.1.1: Canons (Part 1).

Most of these canons have lengthy preambles and brief enacted norms. A few have detailed enacted norms or schedules. These arrangements do not represent a 'code of canons' typical of Anglican churches nor do they mirror methodically the principles of canon law common to churches of the Anglican Communion.[26] Indeed, on subjects commonly treated in Anglican codes of canons, the Welsh Church still has to resort to pre-1920 ecclesiastical law. The Constitution provides that the 'ecclesiastical law as existing in England', at 1920, 'shall be binding on the Members' and determine 'any question or dispute' between them, if it is not in conflict with the Constitution; but its church courts are 'not to be bound by any decision of the English Courts in relation to matters of faith, discipline or ceremonial'.[27] Consequently, pre-1920 sources which continue to bind the Church, unless in conflict with the Constitution, disapplied or abrogated since disestablishment, include: Acts of Parliament (e.g. Sacrament Act 1547); the Canons Ecclesiastical of 1603; and pre-Reformation Roman canon law, if it is both consistent with the laws of the realm and incorporated as custom into ecclesiastical law.[28] The Church in Wales has disapplied only twelve Acts of Parliament since 1920.[29]

Next, there are those further constitutional instruments for the whole province contained in volume II. Whilst there is a 'regulation' for lay persons to administer elements of the Holy Eucharist, most *rules* and *regulations* relate to property or finance, namely: rules made by the Representative Body under the Welsh Church (Burial Grounds) Act 1945; regulations on: churchyard administration; removal of monuments and gravestones; application of proceeds on the sale of churches, church sites and churchyards; chancel repair funds; accounting; church fabric; redundant churches; and resources to train for ordained ministry. They also include the *constitution* of Diocesan Churches and Pastoral Committees and the Cathedrals and Churches Commission *rules*. Then

---

[26] Anglican Communion Legal Advisers Network, *The Principles of Canon Law Common to the Churches of the Anglican Communion* (London: Anglican Communion Office, 2008): e.g. ministry (Part IV), doctrine/liturgy (V), rites (VI), ecumenism (VIII).

[27] Constitution I.I.5; nor 'any special contract as to glebe between the Representative Body and an Incumbent'.

[28] See G. K. Cameron, 'The Church in Wales, the Canons of 1604 and the Doctrine of Custom' (LLM Dissertation, University of Wales, Cardiff, 1997).

[29] In 1972, nine were listed. Today, Constitution I.I.5 lists: Clergy Ordination Act 1804; Church Discipline Act 1840; Ecclesiastical Commissioners Act 1840; Clerical Subscription Act 1865; Clerical Disabilities Act 1870; Colonial Clergy Act 1874; Public Worship Regulation Act 1874; Sales of Glebe Lands Act 1888; Clergy Discipline Act 1892; Benefices Act 1898; and the Pluralities Acts and Incumbents Resignation Acts.

come *schemes* for the support of ministry (2007), the maintenance of ministry (e.g. stipends, pensions) and the cathedrals (one scheme for each), followed by *rules* of the Tribunal and Courts (on composition, jurisdiction, and processes).[30]

As to liturgy, in the mid-1980s it was provided that: 'The law of worship of the Church in Wales is contained in the Book of Common Prayer' (1984); the *rules*, *rubrics* and *general directions* in the prayer book, itself authorised by the Governing Body by means of a canon, therefore, had constitutional authority. However, such entities as *notes* and *guidelines* (while normative in their language) found in the more recently authorised service books seem rather in the nature of soft law than constitutional norms.[31] Ecclesiastical *custom*, though a minor source of regulation, is also still recognised by the Constitution as having binding authority.[32]

The Constitution also empowers various church bodies to make regulatory instruments which do not apply throughout the province but represent what may be styled proper laws applicable to units within it in the form of delegated or secondary legislation. The Governing Body may make *Standing Orders* for its own procedures. A bishop with Diocesan Conference consent may make a *decree* on territorial arrangements, and the conference may make *rules* to effect resultant changes. A Deanery Conference or Parochial Church Council may make *rules* and *regulations* for its own procedures and committees – but these may be overridden by the Diocesan Conference.[33] Cathedral *constitutions*, *statutes*, *ordinances* and *customs* operate under *schemes* (one for each cathedral) which are part of the Constitution – and, the bishop may, with the consent of the cathedral chapter, abrogate, alter, enlarge, interpret and add to these, and abolish cathedral custom. These schemes also allow cathedrals to make *orders*, *regulations* and *bye-laws*, and to revise, annul or add to these. However, cathedral governance was the subject of a review in 2016; and as a result a canon was promulgated in September 2019 to take the cathedral schemes outside the Constitution and to replace them with a single canon on core matters: for example, the rights of the bishop in the

---

[30] Volume II, Section 2: Rules and Regulations, 1–12; Section 3: Schemes, 1–3; Section 4: Disciplinary Tribunal, Provincial Court, and Diocesan Courts.

[31] Church in Wales, *The Book of Common Prayer for Use in the Church in Wales* (Penarth: Church in Wales Publications, 1984) (hereafter BCP), v; see also e.g. Church in Wales, *An Order for the Holy Eucharist* (Norwich: Canterbury Press, 2004): 15 (Notes), 21 (Guidelines for the Eucharist with Children).

[32] See e.g. Constitution IV.C.IV.13(1): Churchwardens.

[33] Constitution II.IV.17: Standing Orders; IV.D.2, 4 and 5: Decrees and Rules; IV.A.IV.21(2): Deanery etc.

cathedral, and empowering the trustee body of each cathedral to make its own constitution and regulations.[34]

Any statement of the forms of regulation supplemental to the Constitution should also include soft law which is used as an informal means of rule-making in the Church. This includes codes of practice, guidelines and policy documents, presented as 'advice', what 'should' or 'should not' be done, 'recommendations', 'expectations' or what is 'good' or 'best practice'. There was a dramatic increase in its use in the 1990s. *The Cure of Souls* (1996), commended by the Bench of Bishops, was typical, a policy document providing for good clerical practice, with general statements and interpretations of both civil and church law; there were others on, for example, child protection, children and Holy Communion, clergy expenses, and the ministry of a provincial assistant bishop for those opposed to women priests.[35] The past twenty years have seen further proliferation of such documents, but it is often not easy to identify their provenance, date, author or which elements of them are declaratory of law. They deal with a host of matters. At provincial level, for instance, there is guidance on: Parochial Church Councils and policies to protect the environment; parochial expenses and fees; record-keeping; parsonage security; and safeguarding. The handbook for clergy (following a 2004 review) has particularly detailed provision with regard to: terms of service; procedures (e.g. grievance); the benefits of office; learning, development and ministerial review; welfare; and interregnum duties.[36] At diocesan level too soft law has increased.[37]

The Purposes and Enforceable Nature of the Constitution

In the decades before disestablishment, commentators on ecclesiastical law (with their focus on parliamentary statutes, common law and canon

---

[34] *The Cathedrals of the Church in Wales: Report of the Review Group* (June 2016); the Constitution of the Church in Wales (Cathedral Schemes Amendment) Canon 2019. For possible models for the new constitutions, see N. Doe, *The Legal Architecture of English Cathedrals* (London: Routledge, 2017).

[35] See Doe, *The Law of the Church in Wales*, 19–20.

[36] Parish Green Guide (undated): it is not 'prescriptive'; Care of Area Deanery and Parish Records (2013, updated 2017); Parochial Fees Guidance (2015); Parsonage Security (undated); Mediation Service (set up in 2014); and the Code of Practice on Episcopal Ministry (2014) on care for those opposed to women bishops.

[37] E.g. Diocese of Bangor, 'Guidelines for Governance in Ministry Areas' (2013): this is prescriptive and based on the model of the United Parish; Diocese of Llandaff: Ethical Investments Policy (undated).

law) approached the subject descriptively and largely uncritically; and its relationship with theology was usually unexplored. Typical was the refrain that a commentary was simply 'to enunciate rather than to criticise the law'; or to elucidate 'general principles'.[38] However, the principal Welsh exponent of canon law in the nineteenth century, Robert Owen (within the Oxford Movement) was more discursive and theological as he develops the idea that 'Canon Law . . . reveals the true nature of the cleavage in our continuity with the Catholic Church'; and he criticises books on ecclesiastical law as either 'ever in humble vassalage to the Statute Law' or else 'spoilt by homely vulgarity'.[39] The Welsh Church Act 1914 provided, in mechanical terms, for the church to legislate for its 'general management and good government' as well as for its property and affairs (section 13(1)). A more theological approach to the Welsh Church Constitution evolved after 1920, especially in the thought of three bishops – Charles Green, Roy Davies and Rowan Williams.

Charles Alfred Howell Green (1864–1944) was a scholar of canon law and consulted by those drawing up the Constitution. His book, *The Setting of the Constitution of the Church in Wales* (1937), written when he was archbishop of Wales, was the first comprehensive work on this subject.[40] Green explains that one purpose of his book is to enable 'our countrymen' to 'value the Constitution even more when they perceive how well it stands in its setting'.[41] Three themes express the nature and purposes of the Constitution as understood by Green. First: 'The Constitution . . . neither confers, nor is meant to confer, any authority or power upon the Bishops which did not already belong to them, by Divine Command'; since: 'The Church is a Theocracy, not a Democracy . . . The totality of Christian Ministry stands in the Bishop alone'; 'all ministrations, clerical or lay . . . derive their validity from the Bishop, in whom is vested the plenitude of Apostolic authority' – but 'in the exercise of his Ministry, the Bishop is regulated by the Ecclesiastical Law'. Secondly: 'Ecclesiastical Law is a System of Rules, for soul and body, which governs the relation of member to member, and of all the members

---

[38] H. W. Cripps, *A Practical Treatise on the Law relating to the Church and Clergy* (London: Sweet & Maxwell, 1849); and Phillimore, *Ecclesiastical Law*.

[39] N. Doe, 'Rediscovering Anglican Priest-Jurists I: Robert Owen', *Ecclesiastical Law Journal*, 21 (2018), 54–68.

[40] However, see Frank Morgan, Oxford don (1868–1935), *A Short Summary of the Constitution of the Church in Wales* (Cardiff: Western Mail Ltd, 1920); he helped draft the Constitution and was the Representative Body secretary.

[41] It was published in London by Sweet & Maxwell. A. J. Edwards, 'Building a Canon Law: The Contribution of Archbishop Green', in Doe, ed., *Essays in Canon Law*, 49–67.

to the entire Church'; it is 'necessary for the intellectual outfit of every member' and enables 'the conservation and development of that Common or Mutual Faith which animates the Body of Christ'; and: 'breaches of this Law are punishable, spiritually, by the dread of Divine Displeasure [and] temporally, by varying degrees of exclusion from [its] common life'. Thirdly: 'In the nineteenth century the Church of England found herself on the verge of Democephalism, so far had she departed from the Discipline of the Primitive Church.' While the ecclesiastical law the Welsh Church 'took over' in 1920 includes statutes, canon law and common law (in that order), the church 'is not irrevocably tied to' these – they 'can be revised, altered and enlarged'. He saw the Welsh Church Act 1914 as having 'secured the Spiritual liberty of the Church in Wales', albeit one limited in its exercise by catholic order.[42]

A second landmark in developing critical understandings of the nature and purposes of the Constitution occurred in the last decade of the twentieth century. This was stimulated partly by renewed academic interest in church law.[43] In 1992, for Thomas Glyn Watkin: 'Regrettably, it would be misleading to pretend that the Church [in Wales] perceives its Constitution as a theological document'; rather, it is seen as 'a necessary but unwelcome legal guest'. This reflects 'its genesis in an ecclesiastical law . . . not of the Church's own making', and 'the fact that the Constitution and canon law are not sufficiently studied, criticized and appreciated from a theological standpoint'. But, the Constitution 'has a theological as well as a legal integrity' as 'the law of the Church, made by the people of God for the people of God'. Anthony Lewis was also critical: the constitution is 'like a suit of clothes' but gives the impression of having been handed down from earlier generations and a 'more prosperous bygone age'; the Church 'moves awkwardly' in them and 'an entirely new suit' is needed. So: 'Constitutional renewal should be a priority if the Church . . . is to be ready for the challenges of the 21st century.' This led Roy Davies, Bishop of Llandaff, to write about the perception that 'the Constitution is a necessary evil', of reluctance to

---

[42] C. A. H. Green, *The Setting of the Constitution of the Church in Wales* (London: Sweet & Maxwell, 1937), 13, 14, 21, 22, 80, 82–93, 97–8, 279, 285, 297; he cites e.g. O. J. Reichel, *The Canon Law of Church Institutions* (London: SPCK, 1922); Z. B. Van Espen, *Jus Ecclesiasticum Universum*, 5 vols. (Louvain, 1753).

[43] E.g. the Master of Laws (LLM) in Canon Law at Cardiff Law School set up in 1991 and delivered at St Michael's College Llandaff under its warden, John Rowlands: F. Cranmer, M. Hill, C. Kenny and R. Sandberg, eds., *The Confluence of Law and Religion: Interdisciplinary Reflections on the Work of Norman Doe* (Cambridge: Cambridge University Press, 2016), 1–15.

tamper with it, and of 'Making things possible without resort . . . to the legislative grind'. He too anticipated the Church would develop a better understanding of the aims of its Constitution.[44] He was right.

The Constitution now has a Prefatory Note (as from 1998). It states the twin purposes of the Constitution: 'to serve the sacramental integrity and good order of the Church and to assist it in its mission and . . . witness to . . . Christ'. Its 'chief features' are 'synodical government, episcopal oversight, canonical ministry, the participation of the laity, and access to the ministrations of the Church'. It says these are 'shared' with all other Anglican churches, give 'an essential focus of unity' and are a 'product of the freedom given to the Church' by the 1914 Act. In 2002, Archbishop Rowan Williams captured the new outlook: 'Canon Law, in Wales or anywhere else, is for: the advancing of God's Kingdom and the holiness of God's people.'[45]

One effect of the civil law foundations of the Church in Wales is that – still the case today – its internal law (both pre- and post-1920) has the status of a contract: 'It is binding upon all members of the Church in Wales, both clerical and lay, but not upon the people of Wales generally, and, in common with the rules of other voluntary associations, it is enforceable in certain circumstances in the civil courts.' Moreover, the Church in Wales 'remains bound by the secular law . . . regarding such matters as the ownership and management of property, the solemnisation of marriage and rights of burial in its churchyards'.[46] However, the Human Rights Act 1998 means that, if a civil court entertains a challenge to the Constitution or decisions made under it, it must have particular regard to the importance of the right of freedom of religion and act compatibly with that right.[47] In terms of enforcement within the Church, alongside systems such as visitation, the Church in Wales may establish courts, but not with coercive jurisdiction – submission to them is voluntary and complying with their decisions is by way of declarations made by prescribed

---

[44] T. G. Watkin, 'Disestablishment, Self-Determination and the Constitutional Development of the Church in Wales', in Doe, ed., *Essays in Canon Law*, 46, 48; A. T. Lewis, 'The Case for Constitutional Renewal in the Church in Wales', ibid., 175–89; R. T. Davies, 'Some Reflections', ibid., 191–4.

[45] R. Williams, 'Foreword', in Doe, *The Law of the Church in Wales*, xiii.

[46] Constitution, Prefatory Note and I.I.2; Welsh Church Act 1914, s. 3(2); see also *Welsh Church Commissioners v Representative Body of the Church in Wales* [1940] 3 All ER 1 at 6: the 'quasi-contractual obligation'.

[47] Human Rights Act 1998, s. 13; European Convention on Human Rights, Article 9: religious freedom.

classes.[48] These church courts 'shall not be bound by any decision of the English Courts in matters of faith, discipline or ceremonial'.[49] A landmark civil judicial decision of 1998 held that in church disciplinary cases the High Court lacks jurisdiction over the consensual jurisdiction of the church courts.[50]

From the outset the Constitution provided a complex of church courts. The Archdeacon's Court handled disputes about parochial elections. The Diocesan Court exercised the faculty jurisdiction and limited discipline over some lay officers. The Provincial Court heard appeals from Diocesan Courts and disciplinary cases. The Special Provincial Court treated cases on episcopal discipline. The Supreme Court was the final appeal court. However, in 2000 the Disciplinary Tribunal was introduced for clergy (and initially lay) discipline with appeal to the Provincial Court; the Archdeacon's, Special Provincial, and Supreme Courts were later abolished.[51] Diocesan Courts' ancient faculty jurisdiction, over work to be carried out on consecrated and associated property such as church buildings and churchyards, was retained on disestablishment. That the Church had a developed faculty procedure led to ecclesiastical buildings being exempted from secular planning processes when they were introduced in civil law, including the ecclesiastical exemption from listed building controls and ancient monuments legislation. Despite disestablishment, the Welsh Church continues to enjoy the ecclesiastical exemption which is regulated today by the Welsh Assembly and Government.[52]

The Institutional Organisation of the Church

In 1920 the Church in Wales decided that then existing territorial arrangements of dioceses and parishes were to continue except as provided by the Constitution; this is still the rule.[53] The Governing Body, Representative

---

[48] Welsh Church Act 1914, s. 3(3). See e.g., for clergy, Constitution VI.III.10.

[49] Constitution I.5: no definition of 'the English Courts' is given.

[50] *R v Provincial Court of the Church in Wales, ex p Reverend Clifford Williams* (1998) CO/ 2880/98. See also *R v Dean and Chapter of St Paul's Cathedral and the Church in Wales, ex parte Williamson* (1998) *Ecclesiastical Law Journal*, 5 (1998) 129: a challenge, to the Church in Wales' decision to ordain women priests, was dismissed as vexatious litigation.

[51] They were abolished in 2010 following a report in 2008. For later changes, see e.g. Chapter IX: Tribunal and Courts, Part 3, Disciplinary Tribunal, Section 9 amended April 2017; the former Chapter XI became Chapter IX.

[52] See n. 6 for the ecclesiastical exemption. It is also regulated by the Constitution.

[53] Constitution IV.D.1.

Body and Bench of Bishops remain the chief bodies at provincial level. The Governing Body, with its three orders (Bishops, Clergy and Laity), may add to, amend or abrogate the Constitution. Its decisions on faith, order and discipline are made by bill procedure with three readings and a committee stage, before Governing Body holds a final vote in each of the three orders; a two-thirds majority is required for it to pass. An expedited process (introduced 1998) may be used if a bill is certified as non-controversial. Governing Body meets twice a year. Between meetings it is supported by a Standing Committee, and Business, Appointments and Drafting Sub-committees. After reviews in 2001 (rejected), 2003 and 2004, its membership was reduced in phases from 350 to 144 by 2008.[54]

The Representative Body continues to hold assets in trust on behalf of and for the benefit of the whole Church. A charity, it must observe civil law. Its investment income provides grants to support each diocese and to pay towards clergy pensions. It works with dioceses and parishes, such as in maintaining church buildings and churchyards (owned by the Representative Body and looked after by parishes) and in advising on compliance with civil law, e.g. disability and health and safety law. Its members include persons elected from each diocese. It meets thrice a year, and once with the Bench of Bishops and Diocesan Boards of Finance staff. A lot of its work is carried out by committees (e.g. investment, property, and human resources). It is accountable to and must comply with Governing Body directions. Various reviews this century have resulted in a reduction of its size from seventy-five to twenty-six members.[55]

As well as being chief pastors in their dioceses, diocesan bishops are members of Governing Body, and have a particular role as to matters of faith, mission and ministry when they meet together four–six times a year as the Bench of Bishops to consider such issues as: plans to use new forms of ministry; current ethical issues; ecumenical matters; the process of selection for ministry and the appointment of clergy; advising other bodies on issues impacting on church teaching, mission and ministry; and new liturgies. Since disestablishment, various structures have emerged to support the Bench, including the Bishops' Advisors (provincial or diocesan officers specialising in areas such as education, church and society, world

---

[54] Constitution II. See https://law.gov.wales/constitution-government/intro-to-constitution/ecclesiastical-church-in-wales/the-constitution-of-church-in-wales; Church in Wales, *Review* (July 2012), www.churchinwales.org.uk/review/, 39.

[55] Constitution III. See www.churchinwales.org.uk/structure/repbody; Church in Wales, *Review* (2012), 40.

mission, stewardship, and evangelism), the Standing Liturgical Advisory Commission, the Doctrinal Commission, and the Archbishop's Registry which holds records of for instance Tribunal and Provincial Court decisions and arranges for the Electoral College to elect diocesan bishops.[56]

At diocesan level, there are Diocesan Conferences, Deanery Conferences and, at the level of the parish, Parochial Church Councils, each institution with its own members and functions. The Diocesan Conference is involved in parochial reorganisation and elections to Governing Body. The Deanery Conference is by and large a deliberative not determinative institution. By way of contrast, a Parochial Church Council is responsible for governance of the parish.[57]

Although there had been earlier institution-specific reviews,[58] as seen elsewhere in this book, an 'external review' of 2012 criticised the Church in Wales as having 'the structure and organisation appropriate to an established church 100 years or so ago, but which is now stretched beyond what it can or should properly bear'. While the 'legacy of establishment has good features', such as a continuing ministry to the wider community, 'as a disestablished church, [it] has, and ought to claim, the freedom that comes from this in making necessary changes'. Present structures are 'hindering people from making visible the Word'. Crucially, the review recognised 'a feeling that the constitution is an unhelpful constraint on changes that might be necessary'.[59] It is 'large, complex and unwieldy', 'an inhibitor of necessary change', though two working parties since 1998 have sought to make it 'more manageable'; the second in more than 100 meetings 'succeeded in distinguishing regulations and core material'. The review, therefore, recommended: 'In due course a small working party should be framed to re-examine the Constitution' and 'seek to produce a document which is shorter and simpler, and . . . would build on the principles, already established, of distinguishing between Canons which could be changed only with difficulty and Regulations which could be changed by the Standing

---

[56] For the Electoral College, see Constitution V.

[57] Constitution IV; Deanery Conference was formerly Ruridecanal Conference; see also Church in Wales, *Review* (2012), 5: the Church should consider restyling the Diocesan Conference a Synod. For revisions to the Constitution, see e.g. Chapter IVA: Diocesan Conference, amended age of members from eighteen to sixteen, Jan. 2015.

[58] E.g. Archbishop's Commission on the Boundaries and Structures of the Church in Wales: Governing Body debated its report in 1980, rejecting most of its proposals; Working Group on the Future Role of the Archbishop (1992): making a permanent archiepiscopal see at Llandaff (with further reports 2007 and 2008): no change yet.

[59] Church in Wales, *Review* (2012), 1, 3, 4, 5.

Committee' of the Governing Body.[60] No such working party has been set up yet.

Conclusion

Over the past century, the dominant features of constitutional development in the Church in Wales have been stability, piecemeal amendment, and reaction to innovations in theology and wider society. The legislative and other norm-making processes and debates are themselves often the testing grounds of theological liberalism or conservatism, values and pragmatism. Five landmark developments may be highlighted. The Welsh Church Act 1914, separating the English Church from the State, is the civil law foundation of the Constitution of the Church in Wales. The liberating effect of the statute led to the release of the dioceses by the archbishop of Canterbury to form a separate Anglican province, and the formation of a Constitution drafted principally by John Sankey. Innovation was avoided, and continuity protected. Pre-1920 ecclesiastical law then and still continues to apply alongside the Constitution unless and until modified by it – but we await a modern statement of it. The original structure of the Constitution also continues to this day – a bewildering complex of chapters, rules, regulations and schemes dealing principally with government, ministry and property. The Constitution itself generates at least fifteen types of regulatory instrument. Over the years these have been the subject of piecemeal but not comprehensive and systemic reform – unlike most other Anglican churches, the Church in Wales still has no modern code of canons. The advent of soft law, to supplement the Constitution, has increased dramatically as a mode of regulation, driven not only by the demands of civil law but also to regulate matters (such as clerical ministry), usually treated in other Anglican churches in their code of canons. Understandings about the nature and purposes of the Constitution have changed radically: from seeing it as a largely functional instrument to a vehicle of applied theology. Moreover, the pace of constitutional change has quickened over the past three or so decades, particularly with regard to the institutional organisation of the church as to, for example, the size and bill procedure of Governing Body (but its original functions remain), extra-constitutional introduction of ministry areas around the classical

[60] Ibid., 33–4 (namely, Section 24 and Recommendation XLIX).

parish, and reshaping the court system. The review of the Church in Wales in 2012 recommended an appraisal of the Constitution, for the church to fulfil more effectively its mission and witness. Models for any such constitutional renewal are readily to hand in the principles of canon law common to the churches of the Anglican Communion and even, perhaps, in the principles of Christian law.[61]

---

[61] Ecumenical Panel, *A Statement of Principles of Christian Law* (Rome, 2016), is being fed into the work of the World Council of Churches Faith and Order Commission: M. Hill and N. Doe, 'Principles of Christian Law', *Ecclesiastical Law Journal*, 19 (2017), 138–53. Agreed by an Ecumenical Panel (meeting annually in Rome, 2013–16), it is based on N. Doe, *Christian Law: Contemporary Principles* (Cambridge: Cambridge University Press, 2013), Appendix.

6

The Bishops and Archbishops

ARTHUR EDWARDS

'The greatest problem the Church will have to face in the future, will be to find a Bishop.'[1] Those were the words of John Owen on the eve of disestablishment in 1919. Then aged sixty-five, he had been bishop of St David's since his appointment in 1897. Both John Owen and Alfred George Edwards, Bishop of St Asaph since 1889, had fought tirelessly against the disestablishment of the Church of England in Wales. That did not prevent them from bravely preparing for disestablishment during the Great War. What both bishops feared most was the separation of the four dioceses of Bangor, St Asaph, St David's and Llandaff from the Province of Canterbury. To Edwards what mattered most about disestablishment was that the 'Welsh bishops and clergy were no longer members of the Convocation of Canterbury.'[2]

In spite of Owen's doubts, no fewer than forty-seven bishops have been elected to the dioceses of the Church in Wales since 1920. Six were translated from another diocese in Wales. Twelve were elected archbishop of Wales while remaining bishops of their respective dioceses. The seniority of Edwards made his selection as archbishop obvious to his fellow bishops in 1920.

When he retired in 1934, Archbishop Edwards, in the forty-fifth year of his consecration, was the senior bishop in Wales and England. He knew everyone who mattered, especially David Lloyd George, who was a personal friend for forty years. It was through Lloyd George that Edwards married Winston Churchill to Clementine Hozier in St Margaret's Church, Westminster, in 1908, and Edwards encouraged Lloyd George with the spectacular investiture of the Prince of Wales at Caernarvon Castle in 1911 'to unite and inspire the Welsh nation'. John Owen and his episcopal colleagues had no hesitation in proclaiming Alfred George Edwards the first archbishop of Wales. Charles Green

---

[1] E. E. Owen, *The Later Life of Bishop Owen* (Llandysul: Gomer Press, 1961), 469.
[2] A. G. Edwards, *Memories* (London: John Murray, 1927), 328.

compiled the service for Edwards' enthronement and moved the official welcome to him as archbishop at the Governing Body meeting at Llandrindod Wells on 9 April 1920. Green, who succeeded Edwards as archbishop in 1934, praised him for his 'courage, foresight, tact and splendid leadership'.[3]

The enthronement of Edwards as archbishop, which he described as 'a national festival', took place on 1 June 1920. It marked the inauguration of an independent autonomous ecclesiastical province whose disestablished status placed it as an equal alongside all the other Christian denominations in Wales. Yet the establishment was out in force. Everybody was there including Prince Arthur, representing the king, the archbishops of Canterbury, York and Dublin, the bishop of London, and Lloyd George, the prime minister. The following Sunday in parish churches and cathedrals throughout Wales it was worship as usual according to the Book of Common Prayer 1662 and Hymns Ancient and Modern (unrevised). Archbishop Edwards had campaigned against disestablishment on the premise that the Anglican Church alone provided worship and pastoral care for every person in Wales through its parochial structure.

What follows deals with the bishops and archbishops within the framework of the thirteen archiepiscopates across the century. It seeks to blend biographical sketches with landmark developments in episcopal and archiepiscopal ministry.

The Archiepiscopates of Green, Prosser and Morgan

The three archbishops who succeeded Edwards were all present at his enthronement service. Charles Green, Archdeacon of Monmouth, had many gifts, not least in liturgy, canon law and ecclesiastical administration, which guaranteed his future. David Lewis Prosser, Archdeacon of St David's, succeeded John Owen as bishop in 1927 and Green as archbishop in 1944. John Morgan, vicar of Caernarvon, became bishop of Swansea and Brecon in 1934 and bishop of Llandaff in 1939. He succeeded Prosser as archbishop in 1949. Morgan was a disciple of Green.

The freedom which gave the new province the courage to set up two much-needed new dioceses, Monmouth in 1921 and Swansea and Brecon in 1923, was hindered by a shortage of money. The Diocese of Monmouth was created from the archdeaconry of Monmouth in the

---

[3] *Rhyl Journal,* 31 July 1937.

Diocese of Llandaff. Green became its first bishop. The Diocese of Swansea and Brecon was formed from the archdeaconry of Brecon and a new archdeaconry of Gower. Its first bishop was the former archdeacon of Brecon and suffragan bishop of Swansea, Edward Latham Bevan.

The Church in Wales also had the freedom to produce its own liturgy by bill procedure in the Governing Body, as Green observed. Green steadied many nerves over disestablishment, not least those of the bishops, who were assured of their greatly enhanced new status in the catholic Church in Wales. In his book *The Setting of the Constitution of the Church in Wales* in 1937, Green described the exclusion of the Welsh dioceses from the Convocation of Canterbury as 'a situation of extreme delicacy' because, he said, the State had done it without the consent of the Church, but the archbishop of Wales 'took over the Metropolitical Authority and all other ecclesiastical rights and privileges hitherto enjoyed in Wales by the Archbishop of Canterbury' sanctioned by the Constitution of the Church in Wales. The law of the land no longer applied, but canon law made up for its deficiencies.[4]

Green had style and scholarship. He earned the degree of Doctor of Divinity from Oxford while he was vicar and rural dean of Aberdare and was responsible for Church Defence in the deanery. Green brought his friend Gilbert Joyce to Aberdare as sub-warden of St Michael's College there. Joyce was later appointed as archdeacon of St David's and succeeded Green as bishop of Monmouth in 1928. Charles Green also supported and encouraged Timothy Rees, chaplain of St Michael's College. When Rees joined the Community of the Resurrection at Mirfield, Green invited him to be a missioner for his crusade to the Diocese of Monmouth in June 1928. It was to Father Timothy Rees of Mirfield that Green sent a recorded letter in January 1931 when he knew that the bishop of Llandaff would be retiring in February. The Electoral College promptly elected Timothy Rees as bishop of Llandaff in March. Rees was an outstanding bishop in the dark days of the 1930s, a Catholic Evangelical with a profound spirituality and love of God, clarity of vision and speech, a social conscience and a pastoral heart. Added to that was his bravery, which earned him the Military Cross as an army chaplain in the Great War. He wrote hymns presenting the theology of the suffering God to the troops at the front. Timothy Rees died at the relatively young age of

---

[4] C. A. H. Green, *The Setting of the Constitution of the Church in Wales* (London: Sweet & Maxwell, 1937), 210.

sixty-five in 1939.[5] The election of Rees is evidence of the Church in Wales broadening its sympathy and understanding of its mission as it overcame its isolation. It was Green who first expressed his confidence that the fears created by separation from the English Church had been overcome by 1935. It would take much longer for the Church in Wales to settle down to its new status after disestablishment.

Green's successor as archbishop, David Lewis Prosser, was the most senior bishop in Wales. Like his two predecessors as archbishop, Prosser had attended public school (Llandovery College) and Oxford (Keble College), and was past his seventieth birthday. His entire life, apart from his time at Keble College, had been spent in the Diocese of St David's. Prosser was praised by Derrick Childs, a future archbishop, for his unsurpassed example of 'unpretentious piety, deep humility and pastoral love'. Prosser was also a favourite with Eric Roberts, one of his successors at St David's. Yet, unlike Roberts, Prosser still wore gaiters, and he did not allow the clergy to grow beards or moustaches, or appear out of doors without hats. The diocesan representatives on provincial bodies were mostly peers, baronets, knights and senior army officers.[6]

Prosser's sermon at his enthronement as bishop had been in Welsh, on the subject of Christian unity. The sermon held out an olive branch after disestablishment, but it was too early for the denominations to respond. Prosser still stuck to his principles as an Anglo-Catholic churchman and he was suspicious of Evangelicals, but he gave his full support to John Charles Jones, a former Calvinistic Methodist, during his training at Wycliffe Hall, Oxford, and his time at Bishop Tucker Theological College, Uganda. Prosser made J. C. Jones vicar of Llanelli in 1945 and he was elected bishop of Bangor in 1948. Jones was a popular pastoral bishop who died at a young age in 1957.[7]

Another popular bishop who died relatively young was William Thomas Havard (1889–1956), Bishop of St Asaph and later of St David's. Like Jones, Havard was a fluent Welsh-speaker and the product of a Nonconformist home. He was confirmed before training at St

---

[5] A. J. Edwards, *Archbishop Green: His Life and Opinions* (Llandysul: Gomer Press, 1986), 77–8; D. D. Morgan, 'Lampeter, Mirfield and the World: The Life and Work of Bishop Timothy Rees (1874–1939)', *Welsh Journal of Religious History* (2013), 100–17.

[6] D. T. W. Price, 'The Modern Diocese of St Davids', in W. Gibson and J. Morgan-Guy, eds., *Religion and Society in the Diocese of St Davids 1485–2011* (Farnham: Ashgate, 2015), 204, 212–14, 220.

[7] E. Lewis, *John Bangor – The People's Bishop: The Life and Work of John Charles Jones, Bishop of Bangor 1949–1956* (London: SPCK, 1962), 26–7, 83, 141.

Michael's College, Llandaff, and ordained to a curacy in Llanelli before becoming a chaplain to the forces in 1915. Like Timothy Rees, he was awarded the Military Cross for bravery. After the war, Havard served as an incumbent in the Diocese of Southwark before returning to Wales as vicar of St Mary's, Swansea. In 1934 he was elected bishop of St Asaph. Havard had played rugby at university in Aberystwyth, and he was capped for Wales against New Zealand in 1919; he went on to play soccer for Swansea Town. Havard brought new energy and vitality to the Diocese of St Asaph after the long reign of Archbishop Edwards, and he did the same for the Diocese of St David's after Archbishop Prosser. The youth pilgrimage to St David's in August 1955 was greatly enjoyed by the young people of the province.

Charles Green's influence on the Church in Wales continued when John Morgan, Bishop of Llandaff, was elected to succeed Prosser as archbishop in 1949. Aged sixty-three, he was the youngest archbishop of Wales and the first archbishop to be trained for ministry at a theological college (Cuddesdon, Oxford), but his education was the traditional one of public school (Llandovery College) followed by Oxford (Hertford College). Like Edwards and Green, Morgan was the son of a clergyman. Like his predecessors at Swansea and Brecon, and at Llandaff, Morgan was a bachelor, but there the similarity ended. Unlike Edward Latham Bevan and Timothy Rees, Morgan had a gift for admin-istration and so much admired Green's system at Bangor that he adopted it. Questionnaires were addressed to clergy and new filing cabinets were filled with so much detail that he did not appear to need an archdeacon.

'Martinet and Shepherd', the title of an article written about John Morgan, is very apposite. Morgan instilled discipline, even fear, in his clergy. He told them what to wear, especially black wide-brimmed hats, but never sports jackets, and they should never smoke on the street. Attention to detail was essential: all services must be conducted with dignity, order and solemnity. He was quick-tempered with any clergy-man who did not obey his instructions. At the same time, he had great personal charm. He could be understanding, compassionate and thoughtful. When clergy needed a holiday, Morgan would take their services for them. He enjoyed music, and he could hold a large congrega-tion with his musical voice and preaching skills. Morgan died on 27 June 1957.[8]

---

[8] J. S. Peart-Binns, 'Martinet and Shepherd: John Morgan Archbishop of Wales', *Welsh Journal of Religious History*, n.s. 4 (2004), 41–64.

The Archiepiscopates of Morris, Simon and Williams

The Church in Wales had found its feet by 1957. The next three arch-bishops were all ordained after 1920. They all had first-class honours degrees in theology from Oxford. All three made a significant difference to the life of the Church in Wales. All three have biographers.[9] The fact that the backgrounds, personalities and outlooks of these successive archbishops were so different is evidence that there was no lack of variety in bishops appointed by an electoral college and no mediocrity either. Edwin Morris became bishop of Monmouth in 1945 at the beginning of a post-war rejuvenation in the Church in Wales. He put much personal effort into mission in the diocese in 1951, which was a great source of renewal. The Diocese of Monmouth reflected the range of activities throughout the province in the many organisations for all ages in the 1950s.[10]

In 1957 Edwin Morris inherited an efficiently organised province which regarded itself as little different from the Church of England, except that it was much poorer and increasingly short of clergy, partly because so many of them left Wales for England.[11] The Laymen's Appeal in 1952 for half a million pounds from the parishes, in addition to the Quota, to increase clergy stipends, had passed its target by the summer of 1953. By 1960 the number of communicants throughout the province was 182,864, compared with 155,911 in 1945.

As we see elsewhere in this book, this increased confidence, which Morris himself exuded, and the establishment structure, together with Green's high doctrine of episcopacy, made the Church in Wales' relationships with the other Christian denominations difficult. Morris taught that the 'Church in Wales is the Catholic Church in this land, and we cannot, without denying our very nature, yield one iota of this claim.' He caused great offence to both Roman Catholics and Nonconformists by calling them 'intruders' with no rights of spiritual jurisdiction in their own land.

---

[9] J. S. Peart-Binns, *Edwin Morris Archbishop of Wales* (Llandysul: Gomer Press, 1990); O. W. Jones, *Glyn Simon: His Life and Opinions* (Llandysul: Gomer Press, 1981); D. T. W. Price, *Archbishop Gwilym Williams 'G.O.': His Life and Opinions* (Cardiff: Church in Wales Publications, 2017).

[10] D. D. Morgan, *The Span of the Cross: Christian Religion and Society in Wales, 1914–2000* (Cardiff: University of Wales Press, 1999), 181–96.

[11] D. P. Davies, 'Welsh Anglicanism: A Renewed Church for a Reviving Nation', in N. Yates, ed., *Anglicanism: Essays in History, Belief and Practice* (Lampeter: Trivium Publications, 2008), 113.

Morris' long charges at his visitations were published as *The Church in Wales and Nonconformity* and *The Catholicity of the Book of Common Prayer*. Morris was not an Anglo-Catholic but a prayer book Catholic. His booklet, *The Christian Use of Alcoholic Beverages*, was widely read before the vote on Sunday opening in Wales in November 1961.[12] Morris was opposed to unilateral nuclear disarmament. He wrote many letters to newspapers and became well known as the leader of the Church in Wales, which he loved and where he spent his whole ministry, but he did not speak Welsh. As his biographer shows, his lack of empathy with Welsh culture affected his relationships as archbishop, particularly with Glyn Simon, Bishop of Llandaff.

The son of a Welsh clergyman, Glyn Simon was educated at Christ College, Brecon, and Oxford (Jesus College and St Stephen's House). After a curacy in Crewe, he became warden of the Church Hostel in Bangor in 1930 and an examining chaplain to Bishop Charles Green, whom he admired. Simon was then a celibate Anglo-Catholic with a high reputation as a teacher, preacher and confessor. At Bangor and St Michael's College, Llandaff, where Simon became warden in 1939, he enforced strict discipline in a semi-monastic atmosphere. He was softened and improved by his marriage in 1941 and his move to the deanery of Llandaff in 1948. With architect George Pace he planned the restoration of the cathedral after its wartime damage, and they collaborated to produce a church designed as a setting for liturgy. Simon became the first chairman of the provincial Standing Liturgical Advisory Commission.

As bishop of Llandaff, Glyn Simon made his greatest contribution to the Church in Wales between 1957 and 1967. He won high praise for his unprecedented engagement with the world of industry, as his biography reveals, and he appointed an Anglican industrial chaplain at Port Talbot steel works. In October 1966 his personal intervention in the Aberfan disaster, when he spoke on television, visited bereaved families and denounced the negligence of the National Coal Board, won him wide respect and admiration. Glyn was always popular with students, ordinands and younger clergy.

Glyn Simon was the first archbishop of Wales not to be the senior bishop at the time of his election. Bishop David Bartlett of St Asaph was already sixty-eight, and clergy retirement at seventy came in 1969. Simon's first presidential address to the Governing Body on 25 September 1968, 'Wales, the Welsh Language and the Church', was

---

[12] Risca: Starling Press, 1961.

published in Welsh and English. It was a timely appeal for 'a genuine bilingual policy in Wales with parity of esteem and usage for both languages at all levels'. Simon gave his support to the campaign for bilingual road signs in Wales. He was himself a determined Welsh-learner who later achieved proficiency. He had publicly expressed his concern that an archbishop of Wales (Edwin Morris) had been elected in 1957 without the ability to conduct a service in Welsh, words which divided the Bench of Bishops. Outside Wales, Simon was better-known than any archbishop since Edwards. He was opposed to nuclear weapons and to apartheid in South Africa and the proposed cricket tour there in 1970.

Archbishop Gwilym (G. O.) Williams came from a Welsh-speaking home although he was born in London. The family returned to north Wales, and Gwilym went from there to Jesus College, Oxford. He earned first-class honours degrees in English and theology and intended to become a minister of the Calvinistic Methodist (Welsh Presbyterian) Church. As a research student at St Deiniol's Library, Hawarden, he was conditionally baptised in Hawarden parish church and confirmed by Bishop Havard, who ordained him in 1937. Gwilym Williams lectured at St David's College, Lampeter, until 1945, when he returned to Bangor as warden of the Church Hostel and of ordinands. In 1948 Williams became warden of Llandovery College where he made Welsh compulsory in the first three years. At the Welsh Church congress in 1953 he urged 'a thorough-going bilingualism' to halt the decline in the Welsh language.

G. O. Williams was elected bishop of Bangor in 1957, perhaps as a counterbalance to Edwin Morris, the new archbishop, about whose appointment he was more cautious than Glyn Simon. Another bishop who remained loyal both to the Welsh language and to Morris was John Richards Richards of St David's. Yet on a divided Bench it was Simon with whom Williams was friendly. He disagreed with Morris over nuclear weapons, Sunday opening and ecumenism. Williams was the first arch-bishop to take ecumenism seriously and to work for a full reunion of the Christian churches in Wales without asking the free churches to capitu-late and come home to 'the old mother'. When he became archbishop in November 1971, he was already vice president of the British Council of Churches and chairman of the joint committee on covenanting. The importance of covenanting was urged in his presidential addresses to the Governing Body in 1972, and in April 1973. He was accepted as the leader of Welsh Christians in a way no previous archbishop had been.

Gwilym Williams' understanding of the importance of the language in the culture of Wales led him to express his concern at the Governing Body in September 1980 that the government had not apparently honoured its manifesto commitment to provide programmes in Welsh as the fourth TV channel in Wales. Soon after his address he received a telephone call to tell him of the government's decision to allow the birth of S4C. His intervention had done much to bring about the decision. His concern for the Welsh language brought him much hard work as chairman of the joint committee for the new translation of the Bible into Welsh from 1961 until its publication in 1988.

G. O. Williams was not the only bishop of Bangor to realise that he lived five hours away from the offices of the Church in Wales in Cardiff, and the demands of his diocese did not allow him to stay long in his flat there. He had the help of Bishop Benjamin (Binny) Vaughan who came from Belize to Bangor as assistant bishop in 1971 until Vaughan became bishop of Swansea and Brecon in 1976. Archbishop Gwilym[13] suggested the appointment of John Poole-Hughes as assistant bishop of Llandaff on his return from the Diocese of South-West Tanganyika. Poole-Hughes became bishop of Llandaff in 1975. Williams then urged Poole-Hughes to find an assistant bishop, and Bishop David Reece was consecrated at Bangor in 1977.

Gwilym Williams enjoyed the fellowship of the Bench of Bishops which changed little during his twelve years as archbishop. He was distressed by the resignation of the bishop of Llandaff, Eryl Stephen Thomas, in 1975 after he was found guilty of an 'act of gross indecency'. Archbishop Gwilym showed his leadership by commending the work of 'Bishop Stephen Thomas' in the *Welsh Churchman* of February 1976, saying that 'nothing could wipe out the worth of his outstanding work for the Church' in the parishes he served, as warden of St Michael's College, Llandaff, as dean of Llandaff and as a diocesan bishop. Archbishop Gwilym, while condemning the offence, also mentioned the 'very heavy workload that bishops find themselves carrying'. He then praised Thomas' contribution to the province as chairman of the liturgical commission and in matters of Christian social responsibility. In the end, Eryl Thomas returned to public ministry as an assistant bishop in Swansea and Brecon Diocese in 1988.

---

[13] From the time of Archbishop Alwyn, most people have referred to the archbishop by his Christian name rather than his surname. As such, in this and occasionally other chapters in this book, the Christian name is used.

The Archiepiscopates of Childs, Noakes and Rice Jones

G. O. Williams had been Wales' youngest archbishop at the age of fifty-eight. His successor Derrick Childs started at sixty-five. Childs was alert to the need to group parishes where teams of clergy could work together, and leadership and service would be shared with lay people. Compulsory retirement after 1969 had already deprived the province of more clergy than were being ordained to fill the vacancies. As we see in Chapter 7, the Church in Wales had no objection to the ordination of women to the priesthood in April 1975, but decided that it was inexpedient to do anything about it at that time.

Derrick Childs was a native of the Diocese of St David's, where he was ordained in 1941 after achieving a first-class honours degree in history from Cardiff and training at Salisbury. He broke Oxford's monopoly on the archbishops. He worked on publications and education and was principal of Trinity College, Carmarthen, when he became bishop of Monmouth in 1972. As archbishop, Childs presided over the publication of volumes I and II of the *Book of Common Prayer for Use in the Church in Wales* in 1984. He urged the acceptance of the new prayer book by all the clergy of the Church in Wales. In his presidential address to the Governing Body in April 1985, Archbishop Derrick contrasted the Church in Wales under its first archbishop with its current 'awareness of its identity within the worldwide Anglican Communion'. He referred also to the challenges that the Church faced in a society where the Christian message and the duty to apply that message were questioned. This had been obvious in the aftermath to the miners' strike of 1984 where the attempted reconciliation and the 'small efforts of the Church in Wales to help families in the coal-strike still had some of the papers screaming'.[14]

Childs was archbishop for only three years and was tragically killed in a car accident soon after his retirement. As archbishop, he shared the frustration of his predecessor over the failure of the ecumenical Covenant for Unity to make much difference in the parishes, but he did not have the latter's frustration of living so far from 39 Cathedral Road, Cardiff, where the provincial offices of the Church in Wales were located (until 2018).

That frustration was shared by Childs' successor, George Noakes, Bishop of St David's from 1981 until his election as archbishop in 1987.

---

[14] A. J. Edwards, *The Seven Bishops* (Newport: Diocese of Monmouth, 1996), 61.

After university in Aberystwyth, George trained at Wycliffe Hall, Oxford. He was vicar of Dewi Sant, the Welsh-language church in Cardiff, before becoming archdeacon of Cardigan until his election as bishop. The 1980s were characterised by the appointment of faithful pastoral bishops, including Cledan Mears, Bishop of Bangor, Roy Davies, Bishop of Llandaff, Clifford Wright, Bishop of Monmouth, and Dewi Bridges, Bishop of Swansea and Brecon, all of whom served as bishops with George Noakes, himself loved and respected as a humble and faithful pastor. His time as archbishop lasted only four years and was dogged by ill health, although he returned to work after suffering a heart attack.

As archbishop, Noakes reminded the Governing Body of the urgent need for evangelism. He said that 'the present state of our country is the measure of the Church's opportunity'.[15] He stressed the importance of preaching and said that the churches which were growing were those in which preaching and teaching were taken seriously. The new Board of Mission was important, and he welcomed the new director of mission, Revd David Jones. In 1988, Noakes commissioned Professor Chris Harris of Swansea to conduct a study of the 'State of the Church' in preparation for the 'Decade of Evangelism'. He also asked the dioceses and parishes to prepare for this and in 1990 invited them to discuss the issues involved in the ordination of women to the priesthood, and to submit their reasoned responses by March 1991.

The ordination of women to the priesthood was resolved under Noakes' successor, Alwyn Rice Jones, Bishop of St Asaph since 1982. He was the senior bishop but the youngest on the Bench, aged fifty-seven when elected as archbishop in 1991. A native of Caernarvonshire, Rice Jones read Welsh at Lampeter and theology at Cambridge (Fitzwilliam College). He trained for the ministry at St Michael's, Llandaff, before his ordination at Bangor by the new bishop, Gwilym Williams, with whom he shared his love of Welsh culture, education and ecumenism. Rice Jones' vision of the Church went beyond bilingualism to what, in his presidential address in September 1993, he called 'equilingualism'.

Archbishop Alwyn was a warm, approachable, open and engaging personality with bushy eyebrows and a good sense of humour. He did not stand on his dignity, but he reminded the Governing Body in April 1995, when the first bill to ordain women to the priesthood had

---

[15] Presidential Address, April 1987, in *Highlights* (Cardiff: Church in Wales Publications), May 1987. Presidential addresses quoted in this chapter were all published in the editions of *Highlights* for the respective Governing Body.

just failed, that synodical government may have replaced the former autocratic manner in which the bishops exercised authority, but in questions of doctrine, faith and order the episcopate still had particular authority. That applied to the two bills before them: to allow the ordination of women to the priesthood and the remarriage of divorced persons in church under certain circumstances. He emphasised that he and his fellow bishops were unanimously in favour of both bills, which were passed successfully. In 1996 David Thomas was consecrated as provincial assistant bishop for those who could not accept the ordination of women priests. Archbishop Alwyn ordained his first women priests in 1997 and celebrated with them in St Asaph Cathedral on the tenth anniversaries of their ordination. As a member of the Gorsedd of Bards, he regularly attended the National Eisteddfod and was a strong supporter of devolution in Wales.[16]

The Archiepiscopates of Williams, Morgan and Davies

Overtures were made to secure the election of Rowan Williams, Lady Margaret Professor of Divinity at Oxford, to a Welsh diocese while George Noakes was archbishop, but it was Alwyn Rice Jones who consecrated Williams at St Asaph on 1 May 1992 after the latter's election as bishop of Monmouth. A native of Swansea, Williams was already a distinguished theologian, a doctor of divinity of Oxford University and a fellow of the British Academy. Aged forty-one, he was the youngest bishop elected in Wales.

In his biography, *Rowan's Rule* by Rupert Shortt, one chapter is titled 'The Newport Years', when Rowan Williams and his family lived in Bishopstow while he was bishop of Monmouth and archbishop of Wales. In a chapter of forty-six pages, only the first eighteen really say anything about Rowan Williams in diocese and province. The rest is concerned with his role at the Lambeth Conference in 1998, his tribulations over issues of human sexuality, his direct involvement in the events around 9/11 in New York, his prolific publications during his Newport years, his poetry and his visit to Uganda with four others from the Diocese of Monmouth in September 2001. The chapter does contain descriptions of his character, with observations about his work as a bishop in a small diocese where easy access to the bishop was a mixed blessing. Rowan Williams soon knew everyone and showed pastoral

---

[16] *The Independent,* Obituaries, 16 August 2007.

concern for them. He had an excellent memory for faces and names. He was kind and generous and helped many lame dogs over stiles. In a diocese with limited resources, he attended more meetings than many other bishops; he was an excellent chairman and much of his management was performed by his words, not least in telling his hearers to listen to one another.[17]

Rowan Williams made an important contribution to the work of the Governing Body. Like Glyn Simon, whom he admired, that contribution was made mostly while he was a bishop because, like Simon, his time as archbishop was short. At his second Governing Body meeting in April 1993, he seconded the motion in favour of women priests, spoke convincingly, stating that nothing could be gained by further delay, and discounting the objections from 'male headship' in the New Testament. Whilst describing Glyn Simon as 'arguably the greatest ornament of the Welsh bench since disestablishment',[18] Williams himself was a great bonus. He was welcomed to his first Governing Body as archbishop in 1999 by Barry Morgan, as 'a scholar of international standing ... well known and respected throughout the whole Anglican communion already ... not least because of his own spirituality and holiness'. Morgan wrote similar words in his foreword to Williams' *Addresses and Sermons* delivered while he was archbishop and published by the Church in Wales in 2003.[19]

Archbishop Rowan's first presidential address to the Governing Body warned that: 'the Church has been trapped into sharing the sex-obsession of the age ... so that all that most people ever know about the Church is the attitudes of some Christians to some kinds of sexual behaviour'. Those words haunted the Church for decades and there are still unresolved issues. When Barry Morgan of Llandaff succeeded Rowan Williams as archbishop in April 2003, he inherited these issues and others, including the continuing decline in membership in the Church in Wales.

Archbishop Barry did not shirk the task. He was intellectually able and well qualified as a graduate of London and Cambridge Universities; he trained for the ministry at Westcott House. After ordination in Llandaff,

[17] R. Shortt, *Rowan's Rule: The Biography of the Archbishop* (London: Hodder and Stoughton, 2008).

[18] R. Williams, 'Simon, (William) Glyn Hughes', *Oxford Dictionary of National Biography* (Oxford: Oxford University Press, 2004).

[19] R. Williams, *Addresses and Sermons delivered by The Most Revd and Rt Hon. Dr Rowan Williams while Archbishop of Wales* (Cardiff: Church in Wales, 2003), 3–4.

he served as a university and theological college lecturer and university chaplain, as rector of Wrexham and archdeacon of Meirionnydd before his election as bishop of Bangor in 1993 and bishop of Llandaff in 1999. He also served on the central committee of the World Council of Churches and on the primates' standing committee of the Anglican Communion. Barry Morgan brought to his role as archbishop in 2003 wide experience of the Welsh Church and personal gifts of pastoral care, social concern and courageous leadership to make the changes that were necessary.

In his first presidential address to the Governing Body in September 2003, Archbishop Morgan said that the resolution against homosexual practice passed at the Lambeth Conference of 1998 had become the 'defining resolution', as if the conference had 'discussed nothing else'. In the absence of a centralised system of government in Anglicanism, the most constructive way forward would be through conversations on the subject. He was eager to listen to the Governing Body and stressed that 'the witness of the Gospel and of Jesus is to an inclusive community'. At the Lambeth Conference, the Anglican bishops committed themselves 'to listen to the experience of homosexual persons' because 'all baptised faithful persons, regardless of sexual orientation, are full members of the body of Christ'.

The Governing Body, much reduced in size after 2004, was often divided into groups to discuss together such issues as same-sex partnerships, the review of the Church in Wales, or the ordination of women as bishops. In 2010, after his presidential address, the Governing Body divided into three groups to discuss: what they thought was potentially the Church's greatest gift to the nation in the next ten years; what they wanted the essential evidence of Anglican Christianity to be in 2020; and what each member could do to help the Christian presence in Wales. Seven groups also discussed the role of the bishops and archbishop. Group discussions had been used at the Lambeth Conference in 2008.

As a result of these discussions, and the decline in membership and finances, the archbishop's presidential address in April 2011 flagged up the review of the Church in Wales to be undertaken by Lord Harries of Pentregarth, a former bishop of Oxford, and Professors Charles Handy and Patricia Peattie. They were to provide external, independent advice about how the Church might reshape itself to be more effective. As we see elsewhere in this book, their report in 2012 made many recommendations, including the development of ministry areas where teams of clergy and lay people from groups of parishes would work collaboratively with a leader. This would change the traditional parish structure of the Church in Wales and provide a programme of '2020 Vision' throughout Wales.

Archbishop Barry Morgan had anticipated the need for change long before 2012. By 2007, he was also aware that a decision would have to be made about the ordination of women bishops. In his presidential address to Governing Body he said he did not 'personally see how having agreed to ordaining women to both the diaconate and priesthood the church can logically exclude women from the episcopate'. That Governing Body requested a review of the representation of women in the Church's structures, and the archbishop noted the low percentage of women on the Church's decision-making bodies. The bill to enable women to be ordained as bishops failed in 2008, but it passed in September 2013, and a code of practice was provided by the bishops in 2014. Before Archbishop Morgan's retirement in January 2017, the first female bishop in the Church in Wales, Canon Joanna Penberthy, was elected as the bishop of St David's in November 2016 and consecrated in January 2017.

As a result of devolution in Wales, Archbishop Morgan reported in his presidential address in 2008 that 'the Church in Wales, through the Bishops, had produced a response' to the 'ONE WALES' document, the legislative agenda of the third-term Welsh Assembly Government. He also said that he and his fellow bishops were 'talking to cabinet ministers about a whole range of issues to do with the life of Wales' such as health, housing, poverty and education. His services were also used extensively in the Anglican Communion. He was the longest-serving archbishop in the Communion at the time of his retirement.

Archbishop Barry bravely spoke out about many moral and social issues. He personally condemned the government's renewal of the Trident nuclear weapons programme, and the Governing Body supported his views. His support for the government in Wales did not extend to its policy of 'presumed consent' for organ donation at the time of death. He said that climate change was the most important issue facing our world and, in 2009, spoke strongly about children growing up in relative poverty in Wales. Morgan also chaired a commission on housing for Shelter Cymru. His proposal that the archiepiscopal see should be permanently located in the Diocese of Llandaff was not accepted. Llandaff is the most populous diocese. As archbishop, Glyn Simon had an assistant bishop, T. M. Hughes, and Barry Morgan had David Yeoman (2004) and David Wilbourne (2009) as assistants.

Barry Morgan retired at seventy in January 2017, a year after his wife Hilary had died. His presidential address to the Governing Body in April 2016 contained a deep personal reflection on facing grief and death. He had been archbishop for nearly fourteen years, a record equalled only by the first archbishop, Alfred George Edwards. Bishop Dominic Walker, who served on the Bench with Morgan for ten years (from 2003), described him as a very strong leader who knew everyone and was a very good pastor to the bishops. Morgan had obtained a doctorate from the University of Wales in 1986. When he retired he was pro-chancellor and a fellow of University of Wales Institute in Cardiff. Morgan's 'engagement in the public life of Wales' has been praised by his successor, Archbishop John Davies.[20]

John Davies was acting archbishop after Morgan retired until elected archbishop on 6 September 2017 when the vacant Diocese of Llandaff had been filled by the consecration of June Osborne, former dean of Salisbury, in July. The enthronement of the archbishop took place in Brecon Cathedral on 2 December when the archiepiscopal throne came to Brecon for the first time. John Davies had been in Brecon for seventeen years, as dean from 2000 and as bishop since 2008. A cradle Anglican, he grew up in the Diocese of Monmouth's parishes of Risca (where he was confirmed by Archbishop Morris) and Bassaleg, and, as a layman, he came to serve in a variety of capacities at parish, diocesan and provincial levels. In his early years he acquired and has never lost a keen interest in the musical inheritance of the Anglican Church. One of his regrets is the decline, in so many places, of church music, a rich source in years past of vocations to the ordained ministry, his own included. He was ordained in the Diocese of Monmouth in 1984 and had served in four parishes there. After graduating in law from Southampton University he practised as a solicitor, specialising in criminal law, before training for ministry at St Michael's College, Llandaff. John Davies obtained a Master of Laws degree in canon law at Cardiff University in 1995, like Gregory Cameron, later bishop of St Asaph (in 1997) and Dominic Walker, Bishop of Monmouth (in 2004); Bishop Andy John of Bangor is also a graduate of Cardiff Law School.

John Davies challenged the Governing Body, in his address as senior bishop in April 2017, to 'Put evangelism at the heart of your ministry.' And so Governing Body affirmed the central place of evangelism in church life. His first presidential address in September that year continued the same theme. 'Inclusivity' was stressed as the mission objective so that there would be concrete things to celebrate during the Church's centenary in 2020. Despite the challenges, he emphasised that the Church had the finances and human resources in its local communities to support new ministries and to achieve its 2020 Vision strategy.

---

[20] See www.churchinwales.org.uk/news/2017/01/archbishop-of-wales-retires/.

As bishop of Swansea and Brecon, John had been the 'lead bishop' for church and society issues. He chaired the Ethical Investment Group and the Wales National Committee of Christian Aid, of which he was a national trustee, and he also chairs the steering group of Housing Justice Cymru. His background in criminal law leads him to hold strong opinions about the administration of justice and, in particular, the rehabilitation of offenders.

Conclusion

There is no real conclusion to this chapter because the Church goes on. John Davies is the thirteenth archbishop. Andy John, Bishop of Bangor, leads on mission and evangelism, highlighted as the chief priorities in a post-Christian society. Bishop Gregory Cameron of St Asaph looks after liturgy, about which he writes in this book. The Bench is now balanced by three female bishops with their own provincial responsibilities, Bishops Joanna Pemberthy of St David's, June Osborne of Llandaff and Cherry Vann of Monmouth. The bishops meet together, formally as a Bench, over two or three days, four times a year. In former times they met together less often and often less harmoniously. After 1920, the bishops ceased to be appointed by the Crown, and all lay patronage ended in the Church in Wales. That gave the bishops much greater power. Directly or indirectly, they are involved in every appointment from assistant curate to assistant bishop. Their word is treated as law in their dioceses.

The Electoral College has remained essentially unchanged since 1920. An age limit of seventy was imposed on members in 1996. College meetings are private and discussions are confidential, but frequent breaches of confidentiality have been revealed, not least in the biographies of archbishops quoted in this chapter. In recent years some effort has been made to insist on electors observing their oaths of secrecy. Until 1996, if the College failed to elect a bishop or archbishop, the right to appoint passed to the archbishop of Canterbury. No such failure ever occurred. In 1996 that right of appointment passed from the archbishop of Canterbury to the Bench of Bishops in Wales. Since 1996 there have been two elections when the Bench had to appoint, to Bangor in 2004 and to Llandaff in 2017.

The archbishop, elected from the six bishops, is *primus inter pares*, with authority but no power outside his or her own diocese except when another diocese is vacant. The Church in Wales has been fortunate in its bishops. For the most part they have rejected prelacy and been people with pastoral hearts and a love for Christ and his Church. They have usually been well in advance of their dioceses in leading a reluctant flock to pastures new. That has been particularly true in ecumenism, and attempts to develop an ecumenical bishop, collegial bishops or an archiepiscopal see. Archbishops Alwyn Rice Jones and Barry Morgan both commissioned studies into the role of the archbishop. Among the many recommendations of the Harries Report in 2012 is that of collaborative, collegial bishops. Harries revisited the issue raised in the Partners in Mission Consultation in 1978, of undue deference to bishops in the Church in Wales. Society today is much more informal and less respectful than it was forty years ago. Bishops, like their clergy, have had to become more collaborative in a less deferential age. For the most part, the bishops have adjusted appropriately as conditions have changed.

APPENDIX

Archbishops and Diocesan Bishops of the Church in Wales, 1920–2020

Archbishops of Wales

1920	Alfred George Edwards (St Asaph)
1934	Charles Alfred Howell Green (Bangor)
1944	David Lewis Prosser (St David's)
1949	John Morgan (Llandaff)
1957	Alfred Edwin Morris (Monmouth)
1968	William Glyn Hughes Simon (Llandaff)
1971	Gwilym Owen Williams (Bangor)
1983	Derrick Greenslade Childs (Monmouth)
1987	George Noakes (St David's)
1991	Alwyn Rice Jones (St Asaph)
1999	Rowan Douglas Williams (Monmouth)
2003	Barry Cennydd Morgan (Llandaff)
2017	John David Edward Davies (Swansea and Brecon)

Bishops of Bangor

1899	Watkin Herbert Williams
1925	Daniel Davies
1928	Charles Alfred Howell Green

1944   David Edwardes Davies
1949   John Charles Jones
1957   Gwilym Owen Williams
1982   John Cledan Mears
1993   Barry Cennydd Morgan
1999   Francis James Saunders Davies
2004   Phillip Anthony Crockett
2008   Andrew Thomas Griffith John

Bishops of Llandaff

1905   Joshua Pritchard Hughes
1931   Timothy Rees
1939   John Morgan
1957   William Glyn Hughes Simon
1971   Eryl Stephen Thomas
1975   John Richard Worthington Poole-Hughes
1985   Roy Thomas Davies
1999   Barry Cennydd Morgan
2017   June Osborne

Bishops of Monmouth

1921   Charles Alfred Howell Green
1928   Gilbert Cunningham Joyce
1940   Alfred Edwin Monahan
1945   Alfred Edwin Morris
1968   Eryl Stephen Thomas
1972   Derrick Greenslade Childs
1986   Royston Clifford Wright
1992   Rowan Douglas Williams
2003   Edward William Murray (Dominic) Walker
2013   Richard Edward Pain
2019   Cherry Elizabeth Vann

Bishops of St Asaph

1889   Alfred George Edwards
1934   William Thomas Havard

1950   David Daniel Bartlett
1971   Harold John Charles
1982   Alwyn Rice Jones
1999   John Stewart Davies
2009   Gregory Kenneth Cameron

Bishops of St David's

1897   John Owen
1927   David Lewis Prosser
1950   William Thomas Havard
1956   John Richards Richards
1971   Eric Matthias Roberts
1982   George Noakes
1991   John Ivor Rees
1996   David Huw Jones
2002   Carl Norman Cooper
2008   John Wyn Evans
2016   Joanna Susan Penberthy

Bishops of Swansea and Brecon

1923   Edward Latham Bevan
1934   John Morgan
1939   Edward William Williamson
1954   William Glyn Hughes Simon
1958   John James Absalom Thomas
1976   Benjamin Noel Young Vaughan
1988   Dewi Morris Bridges
1999   Anthony Edward Pierce
2008   John David Edward Davies

7

The Clergy: Priests and Deacons

BARRY MORGAN

Two things immediately stand out when writing about priests and deacons from the time of disestablishment of the Church of England in Wales to the present day. The first is the huge reduction in their number. In 1924 there were 1,416 stipendiary clergy. At the end of 2017 there were 320 stipendiary and 140 non-stipendiary clerics – the latter category was unknown in 1924. Admittedly there was a corresponding decline in church membership, from 196,389 Easter communicants in 1938 to 48,986 in 2017 – but that is still a huge drop in clergy numbers. The second point is that it was four dioceses which were disestablished, not a province, for there was no Welsh province at that time and, therefore, no Welsh provincial structure. The newly formed Church in Wales had to set up its own structures so as to ensure the wellbeing and care of its clergy, cut off as it was from the Church of England and its organisation and protection. Although the Welsh Church Act 1914 provided that the then existing ecclesiastical law of the Church of England should be binding on members of the Church in Wales, as if they had agreed to be so bound, and that it was free to alter that law through whatever procedures it adopted, the first task was to find ways of doing so. Essentially, the Church set up two main bodies: the Governing Body, which dealt with the policies, Constitution and governance of the Church; and the Representative Body, in which was vested all the property of the Church and which was tasked with paying clergy stipends and pensions now that it was no longer part of the English Church. One side effect of disestablishment was to remove the legal disability hitherto preventing clergy from election to the House of Commons. They did, however, retain their previous status of being registrars for marriages and could, as before, conduct marriages after banns, by common licence or by special licence from the archbishop of Canterbury. This chapter examines those landmark changes that have occurred as to the deployment, pay and conditions of service of clergy.[1]

Clergy Appointments and Stipends

Although the parish system was retained in 1920, patronage by the Crown and all other private patronage to any ecclesiastical office was abolished (except for newly created or newly endowed parishes where the person endowing it was allowed to nominate). Each diocese set up a Board of Patronage (of Nomination from 2002) and a Provincial Board of Patronage was set up in 1927, to encourage the movement of clergy around Wales. The right to appoint was vested with the bishop once in four vacancies, the Diocesan Board twice and the Provincial Board once. The bishop of each diocese, however, appointed the dean, the archdeacons and cathedral canons. Since the Church had been disendowed as well as disestablished, an appeal raising £722,252 was launched in the 1920s and a further appeal in the 1950s raised £600,000. Nevertheless, it was still necessary for parishes to be amalgamated to pay the clergy. All incumbents in post on the date the Welsh Church Act received royal assent (18 September 1914) retained the old endowed stipend of their parishes until they retired, died or moved to another benefice. All appointments after that day received the same stipend until 1920 when they received the standard stipend, with no option, set up that year. In 1930 there were still 1,345 clerics – by 1969 only 930, and 642 in 1989. In addition to provincial money, dioceses contributed a little to the stipends through a Provincial Levy or Quota. This was £45,000 a year from 1922 to 1943; £130,000 from 1954 to 1959; but £258,000 by 1970. This still only amounted to around 20 per cent of the total cost of clergy, whereas today dioceses contribute more than 70 per cent to this through the parish share.

In spite of that, no other province in the worldwide Anglican Communion still subsidises the costs of its clergy as greatly as the Church in Wales. In this province, all clergy are paid centrally, and different formulas have been used at different times for diocesan contributions. At one stage, the province paid for various kinds of expenditure in the dioceses,

---

[1] For the purposes of this chapter, I have consulted a wide range of primary sources held by the Church in Wales, including: Bench of Bishops and Bishop of Llandaff papers concerning the ordination of women; Doctrinal Commission and Governing Body papers on marriage and divorce; Representative Body and Bench of Bishops papers as to Terms of Service and clergy numbers; minutes of Standing Committee of Governing Body; and *Highlights* (published after each meeting of Governing Body with details on the issues and decisions made).

money that could only be spent in that way. Today it is a more flexible
system in which each diocese is given an equal sum for general expenditure
amounting to a quarter of what the province sets aside as a block grant; each
diocese is then allocated money based on its clerics, the number of whom
has been negotiated and agreed by the bishops for each diocese.

In 1920 the standard stipend of an incumbent was £282, which rose to £345
by 1938 with the minimum in 1945 set at £300 and the maximum at £600
a year since dioceses and parishes could augment them. From 1938 to 1952
the stipend hardly increased – a mere £75 in fourteen years and in real terms
worth less than half of what it had been before the Second World War. In
1961, it was still only £600. The result was that many clergy left for the Church
of England or to teach. By 1962, there were 700 Welsh priests serving in the
Church of England, whereas only 10 priests ordained in that Church were
serving in Wales. Over the years there has been a determined attempt to
ensure stipends have kept pace with inflation. This was originally made
possible through the sale of prime London property in 1972, but thereafter
through shrewd and careful investments managed by the Representative
Body. In 2019 the standard stipend of an incumbent is £24,259 and an
assistant curate £20,620. It is now adjusted annually in line with the consumer
prices index. Archdeacons and deans are paid roughly one and a half times
the stipend but, unlike other clergy, receive no fee income.

Although this is modest in comparison with many other professions, it
compares favourably with stipends in the Church of England. Clergy are also
given houses in which to live and do not have to pay either for their external
maintenance or council tax and water rates. Up to 1980, curates were paid by
parishes, although grants were given to dioceses and parishes by the province
to help pay for them.[2] Clergy in the Church in Wales, unlike in the Church of
England, also receive fees for occasional offices – but an attempt to pool these
and give each incumbent an additional non-pensionable allowance of the
same amount failed in 2015. This was attempted, not for the first time, to
abolish the huge differential in fee income of rural and urban clergy. By 1939,
clergy were assured of a non-contributory pension, and grants were available
for their widows. A non-contributory pension is today paid both to a cleric
and his or her spouse based on the highest pensionable office held in the five
years preceding retirement with a lump sum payment equivalent to one and
a half times the stipend for forty years' service. For pensionable service for

---

[2] Curates were paid centrally (i.e. from the Provincial Office) from October 1980. The
Constitution was updated to reflect this change only in 1991, which is the first reference
to curates in the list of minimum stipends in the Maintenance of Ministry Scheme.

those ordained before January 2006, it is 60 per cent of the final stipend; after that date it is 50 per cent. Pensionable service before January 2006 is increased by the same percentage as an incumbent's stipend; and after that date by the same percentage as the increase in the retail price index over the previous year up to a maximum of 5 per cent.

Death-in-service benefits were also introduced by 1978, paying the equivalent of three times the annual stipend. Spouses and civil partners receive 60 per cent of the pension of the deceased cleric. In 1968, retirement became compulsory at the age of seventy. These provisions would, of course, have been impossible had the Church in Wales not reduced the number of stipendiary clergy. Various housing retirement schemes were made for clergy at different times by both the dioceses and the province. At present, provincially, anyone over the age of fifty on 31 December 2010, having completed ten years' service at retirement, is eligible for an equity loan up to one and a half times the nationwide Welsh average house price index with interest repaid at half the Bank of England's base rate.

In 1982, amended in 1985, 1996 and 2006, a Disabilities Canon was passed by Governing Body making provision for incapacitated clerics. The full stipend is given for the first twenty-six weeks and a half stipend for the next twenty-six weeks of illness. Provision was also made for appearance before a medical board, should the diocesan bishop require it after an absence of more than four weeks. Parochial ministry was the only kind of ministry envisaged until the 1960s. There were no specialist posts of chaplains serving in schools, universities or hospitals and, indeed, the Governing Body in the 1960s voiced its opposition to such ministries. The only specialist post was that of warden of the Church Hostel in Bangor who also had responsibility for ordinands in the two northern dioceses at that time. In the 1960s a bold initiative was taken in the Diocese of Llandaff in appointing an industrial chaplain to Port Talbot steelworks. Since that time, dioceses have appointed chaplains to various institutions such as universities and hospitals, funding the former but the latter being paid by the State.

Yet the story of the fall in the number of clergy is more complicated than it seems. As before 1920, until the late 1980s clergy continued to be appointed to parishes with populations of fewer than 500 parishioners. In the long term, this was not a financially sustainable policy and there was no real concept in the Church in Wales that the task of ministry belonged to every member of it by virtue of baptism. Ministry was seen as the sole prerogative of the ordained. Archbishop C. A. H. Green (1934–44), in his book on the Constitution, took the view that the work of mission and pastoral care belonged solely to the clergy who offered ministry to the laity who, in turn, simply received it. In fact, so entrenched was this concept of ministry that the revision of the eucharistic liturgy in 1960 was opposed by some clergy on the grounds that it undermined the ministry of the ordained. Letters in the 1960s in *Y Llan*, the Welsh language paper of the Church in Wales, claimed clergy were demoralised because the new service, involving lay people as it did, diminished the sacerdotal power of the priesthood and reduced their authority to satisfy the spiritual needs of parishioners – on the basis that it encouraged the congregation to participate in the liturgy on much the same level as the priest.

Over the years the Church in Wales, whilst holding a high view of ordination, has come to stress the importance of the ministry of all the baptised. But a Partners in Mission Consultation in 1978 concluded that the Church was over-clericalised. Yet, the Ordinal of 1984 emphasised that all baptised persons were called to make Jesus Christ known as Saviour and Lord. The Catechism too teaches that the Church carries out its mission through the ministry of all its members. A Governing Body motion of 2006 encouraged the development of partnerships in ministry between clergy and laity. However, the Harries Review of 2012 found that there was still a culture of deference to clergy. As a result, Governing Body in 2013 welcomed the recommendation to establish Ministry Areas served by teams of clergy and laity, and that concept has been embraced by every diocese. The Bench of Bishops produced a paper on ministry the same year emphasising the call of every member to discipleship and seeing the role of the ordained as enabling and equipping lay members for ministry. The aim was not just that clergy should work collaboratively with teams of fellow clergy, as had happened with rectorial benefices created in 1968, but that clergy and laity together should form teams in areas larger than conventional parishes to minister to their communities. The cynical have interpreted this as a reaction to fewer clerics, but it is a return to a New Testament concept of every member ministry.

Training for Ministry

It was only after the First World War that formal theological training, generally within a theological college, became obligatory and then only for one year. St David's College, Lampeter, founded by Bishop Thomas Burgess in 1822, was a university college – but to all intents and purposes it was a seminary for the Church in Wales. During its first fifty years, the college produced over half of the Church's clergy. In 1914, it had 150 students preparing for ordination, and, since the college was affiliated to

Oxford and Cambridge, some went on from an arts degree at Lampeter to read theology at Oxford or Cambridge.

In 1892 St Michael's was founded as a Tractarian Theological College in Aberdare to provide devotional training for graduate ordinands. In 1907 it moved to Llandaff. Lampeter and St Michael's trained most people for ministry in Wales – although until 2011 people could also train at English theological colleges. That is now a rare exception. All of the ordinands of the Diocese of Llandaff in 1999, for example, were at St Stephen's House, Oxford. In the 1970s some, especially those being prepared for non-stipendiary ministry (NSM), a ministry that came to the fore in Wales during that decade, were trained at St Deiniol's, Hawarden, essentially a library but with a cleric as warden. Some NSM students were trained on diocesan courses set up especially for them. The advent of NSM ministry meant ways had to be found of training people locally since they continued in their employment.

The Diocese of Monmouth in the 1990s, followed by some other dioceses, ordained non-stipendiary local ministers to serve in parishes where they lived as opposed to the usual practice of having them serve elsewhere in the diocese. The aim was that NSMs should help in parishes but also offer ministry in their places of work. Lectures were organised during evenings and weekends, and a residential component was built in to enable fellowship and corporate prayer. The courses varied in quality, and some of the southern dioceses used the facilities and staff of St Michael's for teaching. When St Michael's became part of the University of Wales' Faculty of Theology in 1958, many ordinands combined academic and vocational training there. In 1976, Bishop Burgess Theological Hall, at St David's University College, Lampeter, closed, the latter having become a constituent college of the University of Wales in 1971. The Dioceses of St Asaph and Bangor had courses for stipendiary and non-stipendiary ministry linked to Glyndŵr University, Wrexham, and its predecessor the North East Wales Institute of Higher Education, from 2005.

Eventually, St Padarn's Institute was set up in 2016 to oversee every kind of ministry in the Church in Wales, with a small residential community based at St Michael's (now called the St Michael's Centre). Although all ministry training is now overseen and organised by the institute from that centre, it is delivered in various places and in different ways throughout the province and its degrees are validated by the University of Wales Trinity Saint David and its staff appointed in cooperation with the dioceses. The name change to St Padarn's was deliberate in order to indicate a different way of providing ministry for the whole of the Church in Wales and to mark a departure from the conventional way of training. A great deal of this takes place in parishes, so that people combine practical work and theological reflection. For years the provincial church had provided subsidies of various kinds to St Michael's. With a small coterie of students, however, it found it difficult to be financially viable, especially during the years when Welsh students trained outside the province. Eventually, in 2011 the Representative Body invested heavily in refurbishing St Michael's in return for an equity stake and now owns all of it, because it paid off its yearly deficits.

Before a person is accepted for training, each diocese has its own selection process and people also have to attend a residential provincial panel, first set up in 1974, which makes recommendations to each bishop about a person's potential for training, defined in terms of vocation, faith, devotional life, personality, leadership skills, quality of mind, relationships, and pastoral and communication abilities. Normally, one has to be twenty-four years of age to be ordained as a priest, but in 1990 a canon was passed allowing the archbishop to permit those aged over twenty-three to be priested. The costs of training are borne by province and diocese. The formula has also changed over the years but the province bears the greater part of the costs. The Church in Wales was prevented by canons, which it had in common with the Church of England, from ordaining some classes of people until it changed them by introducing canons of its own by bill procedure at the Governing Body. This it proceeded to do at various times. In 1961 a canon for the removal of doubt concerning irregularity of birth as an impediment to admission to Holy Orders was promulgated. Previously, the ordination of those born out of wedlock was not permitted. The new canon removed this prohibition.

Women and Ordained Ministry

Legislation had to be framed to allow women to become deacons in 1980, priests in 1996 and bishops in 2013, since women were barred by canon law from admission to Holy Orders. The proposed legislation did not have an easy passage in the Governing Body. In the latter half of the nineteenth century, because of industrialisation and population growth, Dr Richard Lewis, Bishop of Llandaff, had seen the need for a ministry to women by women and revived the order of deaconesses. It was regarded as the restoration of an order begun in New Testament times but which had lapsed by the twelfth century. The *Official Handbook* of the Church in Wales in 1933 stated they were ordained, and a small community of deaconesses ran a House of Mercy and Retreat in Penarth from the 1890s to 1939. Deaconesses needed both theological and spiritual training, but also had to have a professional qualification in teaching or social work, to be twenty-five years of age and to undergo selection. They were to assist pastorally in parishes, prepare people for baptism and confirmation, preach, administer the chalice and give communion to the sick. Some organised diocesan Sunday School work. In exactly the same way as male deacons, they were ordained by prayer and the laying-on of hands, given letters of orders and a licence, and asked the same questions at the examination at the same service. The Doctrinal Commission on Women and Ministry in 1972 recommended that, since that was the case, they should be recognised as belonging to the order of deacons and referred to as such. The commission also advocated the opening up of all three orders to both genders. The lawyers, however, held a different view.

The 1980 bill to enable woman to be ordained deacons stated that canon law had hitherto prohibited women from being admitted to Holy Orders and that that impediment was now to be removed. Until 1970, no pension had been paid to deaconesses, they had to retire at sixty, and they were not *ex officio* members of their Parochial Church Councils or Rural Deanery Conferences, nor were they allowed to baptise. The Constitution was amended in 1974, allowing assistant curates and deaconesses the same rights. By 1978, deacons and thus deaconesses could be members of the Representative Body, Governing Body and Electoral College, rural deans, canons and archdeacons. Although Wales was the first province in the United Kingdom to ordain women as deacons, there was still no question of ordaining them as priests. Effectively they were permanent deacons without the Church even having discussed the desirability of creating such a permanent order. Male deacons, though, were automatically priested after their diaconal year. This was in spite of the fact that the 1972 Ordinal referred to the order of deacons as an inferior order and as a step towards the higher ministries of the Church. This too in spite of the fact that in 1975 the Governing Body had passed a motion by a large majority that there were no fundamental objections to the ordination of women to the priest-hood, but that it would be inexpedient for the Church in Wales to act unilaterally. This was slightly disingenuous since the Anglican Church in Hong Kong had already done so, soon to be followed by other provinces of the Anglican Communion, whose deliberations must have been known.

However, even after the bill was promulgated as a canon, the ordination of a woman as deacon caused a huge furore in the Diocese of Llandaff but in no other diocese. A number of senior Anglo-Catholic clergy threatened resignation if the bishop went ahead with it. They regarded the canon to ordain women as deacons as 'heretical', and although they conceded it had become canonically possible for a woman to be ordained as deacon, the bishop was not compelled to ordain: the bill merely provided that he could, not that he must. Under pressure, the bishop of Llandaff decided not to proceed initially, but then in 1980 ordained the woman deacon concerned, persuaded by those who took a contrary view. It was an unedifying episode in the history of the diocese since there was only one woman deacon, and it was therefore difficult for the matter not to become personalised, especially since some senior clergy attended the ordination with the deliberate aim of walking out, which they did. Although the bishop reminded some of the latter that they had declared to observe the Constitution and that the time for protest was during the passage of the bill, he did not ordain any other woman for fear of defections to Rome. Two priests did indeed leave for Rome, but one returned soon afterwards. From this point, the Constitution styled clergy 'clerics'. In this context, it is worth remembering that the Lambeth Conference had approved the ordination of women to the diaconate in 1968 and that the Anglican Consultative Council had in 1976 recommended that provinces make provision for this.

The Church in Wales had to wait a further sixteen years before women could be priested. A bill was introduced in 1994 – but at its report and vote stage it failed to obtain a two-thirds majority in the House of Clergy, in spite of hardship provisions being made for those, who in conscience could not accept such a move if it succeeded, as well as making provision for those who might want to leave in the event of the bill failing. The present bishop of St David's, Joanna Penberthy, informed the then archbishop of the intention to set up a movement for the ordination of women to the presbyterate. The bill was reintroduced in 1995. The bill contained the same hardship provisions as had appeared in the 1994 bill, and no bishop was to be obliged to bring proceedings against clerics who dissented in conscience from it. The Bench of Bishops also promised to appoint a bishop who would care pastorally for parishes and clerics unable to accept women priests in order to assure them of a continuing place within the Church in Wales. The bishops issued a protocol as to how the pastoral ministry of an assistant provincial bishop should operate. The bill was passed in September 1996, and the first women were ordained priests in all six cathedrals in January 1997.

Women as Bishops

In 2006, the Bench of Bishops signalled its intention to introduce a bill to Governing Body enabling women to be ordained to the episcopate. It commissioned a special edition of *Theology Wales* looking at the arguments for and against. The report and vote came in April 2008. Recognising that there were different views on the matter, the bishops issued a statement setting out some pastoral principles in the event of the bill being passed. In it they made clear that a woman bishop had the same jurisdiction and authority within her diocese as her male counterparts. The latter would also make themselves available to her should she ask for episcopal sacramental help in her diocese. Those against the bill proposed an amendment to set up a parallel alternative episcopate. Whilst the Select Committee rejected this, it proposed an amendment of its own, that the Bench provide pastoral care and support for those who in conscience could not accept the ordination of women by providing an assistant bishop, as had been provided before, when women were ordained to the priesthood. The Governing Body rejected this amendment but at the report and vote stage the bill was defeated in the Order of Clergy, having passed the necessary two-thirds majority in the other two orders.

The bishops did not bring back another such proposal until 2012. They proposed two bills. The first would allow women to be ordained as bishops but this would only come into effect on the same date as a second bill addressing the question of the consciences of those who could not accept it. The first bill required the bishops to set up a working party to make provisions to be incorporated into this second bill addressing such concerns. The third reading took place at Governing Body in September 2013. However, an amendment was moved, so that instead of having a second bill the bishops were entrusted with drafting a code of practice within a year of promulgation of the relevant canon making such provision. The amendment was carried as was the bill itself. Consultations were held in the dioceses and Governing Body itself about such a code, and this was issued by the bishops in September 2014 very much along the lines of what had been proposed in 2007. Provision was made for individuals, not parishes, to ask for the sacramental, as opposed to the jurisdictional, ministry of a male bishop for confirmations and ordinations. This needed a letter of support from the parish priest, and the bishops agreed to cover for one another – male bishops would make themselves available to a woman bishop but if individuals asked for confirmation or ordination by a woman bishop her male colleagues would allow it.

The first two vacancies on the Bench after passing the canon in 2013 were in 2016 and 2017: 2016 saw first the election of a woman bishop to the Diocese of St David's and then the appointment of a woman bishop to Llandaff by the Bench in 2017 after the Electoral College failed to reach a two-thirds majority for any candidate. No one expected this a mere three years after passing the legislation since it had taken far longer in Ireland and Scotland. In September 2019 a woman was elected as bishop of Monmouth. Half the Bench now consists of women.

Clergy, Divorce and Civil Partnerships

Marriage after divorce was regarded as an impediment for admission to Holy Orders, and a bill to remove it was introduced in Governing Body in 1995. It was withdrawn by the bishops immediately after a preceding bill allowing the marriage of divorced people in church during the lifetime of a former spouse was lost in the Order of Clergy by two votes. The bishops believed it would also be lost if it were not withdrawn. The issues were complicated and had to do with civil law duties of the clergy to solemnise the marriages of parishioners, acting also on behalf of the State as registrars. In 1938 the Bench of Bishops had instructed the clergy effectively to excommunicate any church member remarrying during the lifetime of their former partner, and forbade clergy from remarrying divorced people in church or allowing their churches' use for such marriages. A Bench letter in 1951, revised in 1966, modified this stance, by counselling and advising clergy not to solemnise such marriages and advising parishioners in those situations not to receive Holy Communion during the lifetime of a former spouse. The clergy obeyed their bishops whose directions they took as instruction rather than advice, without realising their civil legal right to ignore it if they wished. At the same time, any divorced cleric who wanted to remarry during the lifetime of their former spouse had to leave the ministry of the Church in Wales. A Governing Body motion in 1978 allowing the remarriage of divorced people in church had been lost, but in 1979 the Governing Body asked the bishops to provide a service of blessing in church after the civil marriage of a divorced person. This was provided in 1980 and called as such by the then archbishop in a letter to his clergy in the Diocese of Bangor. In 1985, however, a memorandum from the Bench called it a service of prayers and stated that marriages after divorce should not be blessed, although that is what Governing Body had asked for. Indeed, the service provided by the Bench, as the Doctrinal Commission in 1994 pointed out, contained more than one blessing. Clerics had to ask permission of their bishops to use it – copies of it were not distributed but kept in bishops' offices, to be requested and returned – and the instruction was that only close relatives and friends were to attend the service.

Although the 1994 Doctrinal Commission unanimously recommended that divorced people be remarried in church, a Governing Body bill of 1995 making that possible was lost, as has been stated. After taking legal advice, the Bench issued a statement that the law of the land permitted clergy to solemnise the marriages of divorced couples and that since this was a civil statutory discretion, the bishops did not wish to prohibit clergy from exercising it. They realised that they had no power to stop clergy using the rights given to them by the State, and so they withdrew their previous advice. Clerics could, as they had always been able to, had they but realised it, remarry divorced people during the lifetime of a former spouse whatever the views of the bishops or the Governing Body. A Governing Body bill allowing the remarriage of divorced people in church was therefore unnecessary because clerics had the right to do so if they wished. The Bench statement merely declared the statutory rights of clergy.

However, there was genuine legal doubt as to whether marriage following a divorce during the lifetime of a former spouse, or marriage to a divorced person during the lifetime of their former spouse, was an impediment to Holy Orders. The bishops produced a bill in 1998 removing such canonical impediments. It was amended by the Governing Body to declare both of the above as impediments but gave the bishops power to grant dispensations in individual cases, following consultation and consideration by a provincial panel of advisors. At the same time, although no dispensation was necessary for serving clergy wanting to remarry after divorce, requests to do so came to the Bench as a whole to ensure uniformity of practice and to avoid the possibility of scandal. In 2004 the bishops appointed a divorced and remarried person to the see of Bangor after the Electoral College had failed to elect.

When the Civil Partnership Act 2004 came into force in December 2005, allowing people of the same sex to be so registered, the bishops stated that they could not and would not want to prevent what the civil law allowed to clerics of the Church in Wales. Clergy could enter civil partnerships since the statute left open the nature of the commitment couples chose to make to one another in such partnerships. Those who entered civil partnerships in 2005 had a legal claim to some of their partner's pension in the event of death. In 2011, the Governing Body agreed to extend that right to the period before 2005 even though it was not legally obliged to do so. So, civil partners could have the same pension benefits as clerics' widows. In 2011, too, the government made provision for civil partnerships to be registered in religious premises if the denomination concerned desired it. The only body allowed to give permission for churches of the Church in Wales to be so used was Governing Body, and it has not done so. This was consistent with the policy of not registering civil marriages on church premises.

In 2014, the State gave by statute the right to marry to same-sex couples. After lobbying by the Church in Wales, the government agreed in its primary legislation that should the Church in Wales want to allow same-sex marriages in its churches in the future, the Lord Chancellor would be obliged to bring secondary legislation before Parliament, in the form of an Order, to enable this. The original draft primary legislation had proscribed both the Church in Wales and the Church of England from doing so. The Church of England, being established, could place a measure before Parliament enabling that. The Church in Wales could only do so by private Act of Parliament – a long, costly process even if the government allowed time for it. By getting the bill changed, the Lord Chancellor is now required to frame an Order allowing the Church in Wales to marry same-sex couples should it decide to do so.[3]

In 2015 the bishops authorised prayers for same-sex couples for public use in churches, making no distinction between clerics and laity. In September 2018, in a secret ballot, Governing Body approved a statement that 'it was pastorally unsustainable for the church to make no formal provision for those in same-sex relationships'. This contrasts sharply with the 1988 statement of the Bench on homosexuality that: 'basing its teaching on scripture, Christian tradition and the example of Jesus, the Church identified as sinful, promiscuity, fornication, adultery and homosexual acts'. The Bench did distinguish the latter and homosexual orientation, which it did not deem sinful. Candidates were not to be accepted for ordination if a serious moral charge of any of the aforementioned was substantiated against them, and serving clerics would not be allowed to remain in office for the same reasons.

Terms of Service for Clergy and Clerical Discipline

In civil law, clerics do not generally have the status of employees, but are deemed to be office-holders, and their life and work are governed by the

---

[3] See also Chapter 11.

law of the Church. They therefore do not benefit from the protections and rights provided by civil law to employees and have no automatic recourse to the State's employment tribunals. Under pressure to respect civil employment rights, and to protect the clergy in a similar way, a Terms of Service Canon was passed in 2010 governing the terms and conditions of all clerical appointments.[4] It outlined their terms and conditions of service such as stipend, accommodation, sickness, pension, holidays, sabbatical, training, retreats and expenses, as well as a grievance and disciplinary policy. It also outlined maternal, paternal, adoption, compassionate and emergency leave as well as a ministerial development review. For the first time as well, a generic job description was provided for incumbents, area deans, archdeacons and bishops. The aim was to ensure that clerics had no less a standard of rights and protection than those provided under civil law for employees. This canon came to the Governing Body only after wide consultation with clerics over many years. Clerics in post had the choice of opting either in or out of Common Tenure, as it was called, except that everyone appointed to any post after 2011 had to opt in.

This canon had been preceded in 1996 by a policy statement issued by the bishops: *The Cure of Souls*, on the calling, life and work of the clergy. It was meant as authoritative advice and guidance on what might be expected of ordained people, consistent with their vocation, outlining a theology of what it meant to be a minister of the Gospel. The aim was to protect those with whom the clergy worked as well as the clergy themselves and their families, and to encourage personal, professional and ministerial development. It was both theological and practical – and it included, for example, advice on how to observe appropriate boundaries in pastoral relationships and a statement of the need for safeguarding training. The latter became mandatory for all serving clerics and retired clergy wishing to receive permission to officiate in later years; all clerical files in dioceses were reviewed by someone seconded from the secular

---

[4] The Clergy Terms of Service and Reform of the Courts Bills, circulated to the Governing Body in January 2010, refer to a document, 'Draft Statement of Clergy Terms of Service'. Subsequently, the paper circulated to the Governing Body for its April 2011 meeting states that Governing Body passed the Clergy Terms of Service Canon at its last meeting. It has two purposes: to identify the ecclesiastical offices to which the new terms of service apply and make arrangements for bringing Common Tenure (the new Terms of Service) into effect; and it provided that 'the Representative Body shall prepare and publish a statement of Terms of Service for Common Tenure' which was laid before Governing Body and approved by it in a motion in April 2011.

Childrens' Commissioner's office and action taken in individual cases. The Church later appointed its own safeguarding team.

The Ordinal gave liturgical expression, theologically and practically, to what was expected of clerics. The Welsh Church Ordinal 1984, like the Book of Common Prayer 1662, declared the Church in Wales' intention of maintaining the three orders of bishops, priests and deacons. Before ordination, or indeed appointment to any ecclesiastical office, a declaration of canonical obedience to the bishop is required and a promise to uphold the Constitution of the Church in Wales. All clerics declare that they will use only those services prescribed by the Church in Wales. A more modern Ordinal was produced in 2004 for experimental use, and for ten years; it became definitive in 2014. This expressed more clearly than previous Ordinals the responsibility of clerics to be involved in mission and in pastoral work.

The Cure of Souls had recommended 'a more effective way of enforcing professional standards of conduct' among the clergy since the vehicle for doing so, namely the Provincial Court, had fallen into disuse by 1996. Ironically it had to be used in 1998, as the only vehicle the Church had of disciplining a cleric for behaviour causing scandal and offence. It proved to be long-drawn-out, expensive and a very public affair. What was proposed instead was a tribunal to which all complaints against clerics could be referred. This was set up in 2000. However, a new Disciplinary Canon was passed in 2010. This was to deal with issues causing scandal and offence, whilst neglect of duty or incompetence was handled by the relevant bishop with an appeal to the Appeal Panel of the Disciplinary Tribunal. The tribunal consists of elected lay and clerical members from every diocese, as well as appointed members (who must be lawyers or doctors) and a legally qualified president. The tribunal investigates complaints and then decides if there is a case to answer. It has the power to discharge, rebuke, suspend, depose and expel persons from the exercise of Holy Orders.

There have also been developments with regard to ministerial review. Individual bishops had held reviews with their clergy from the mid-1990s, sometimes combining them with parochial reviews. The introduction of Common Tenure led to three-year ministerial reviews throughout the province in 2012 to help clergy to see where they needed support and further training with trained reviewers. Retired clerics who were still resident in their dioceses had been allowed to be members of Diocesan Conferences and so had a vote in electing clerics to the Governing Body, Electoral College and diocesan committees – even though they themselves could not be so elected. This was ended in 2000 in most dioceses.

Finally, in 1974 the Church in Wales entered into a Covenant for Union with the Methodist, Presbyterian and United Reformed Churches and with certain Baptist churches in 1977. By 1985, clerics of the Church in Wales could officiate at marriage services in places of religious worship registered for marriage (i.e. chapels) with episcopal consent, provided the service was not according to the rite of the Church in Wales. In 1991 with the passing of a canon setting up ecumenical projects, clerics of the Church in Wales and accredited ministers of other churches could take services in one another's churches, provided the rite for Holy Communion was that of the covenanting churches. In 2005, under the Local Ecumenical Partnership Canon, the eucharistic rite of any participating church was allowed to be used by both its own clerics and accredited ministers of other churches. This was a far cry from the 1960s, when one bishop had forbidden his clergy from allowing Nonconformist ministers to take part even in church funerals, and when in the 1950s Archbishop Edwin Morris had urged all Protestant denominations to return to the one true church – the Church in Wales.

Conclusion

It is not easy to assess how the clergy responded to the vast changes in both Church and society during this period. As S. H. Jones and L. J. Francis point out, the clergy of the Church in Wales entirely escaped empirical research until the 1990s.[5] The 2011 census revealed Britain to be a secular and post-Christian society, with Wales as the region where religious belief had declined the most. In the same study, Jones and Francis showed that between 1971 and 1992 a quarter of those ordained in Wales were either serving in another part of the Anglican Communion or had taken up secular employment – with 15 per cent having left during the first four years of ministry. Fifty-six per cent of male clerics active in full-time stipendiary ministry felt the Church in Wales to be too con-servative, whilst 22 per cent and 12 per cent felt they had been ill prepared for ministry in the valleys on the one hand and for rural parishes on the other. In another study, 25 per cent of clergy admitted suffering from depression, and 43 per cent to overwork at some point. Yet the same study showed that 95 per cent of them enjoyed their pastoral work.[6] The

---

[5] S. H. Jones and L. J. Francis, 'The Fate of the Welsh Clergy: An Attitude Survey among Male Clerics in the Church in Wales', *Contemporary Wales*, 10 (1997), 182–99.

[6] D. W. Turton, *Clergy Burnout and Emotional Exhaustion: A Socio-psychological Study of Job Stress and Job Satisfaction* (Lampeter: Edwin Mellen Press, 2010).

Church responded by trying to provide courses for the personal and professional development of clerics as well as appointing, provincially and in dioceses, specialists to advise on various aspects of ministry such as youth, school and adult education, stewardship, mission, evangelism and social responsibility. It provided training courses for important transitional periods, such as first incumbency, mid-ministry and retirement, as well as for curates. A provincial officer was appointed to oversee all this work. It part-funded an independent counselling service for many years and sought to train ordinands to better equip them for future ministry. All in all, the Church in Wales, in its structures, discipline and organisation, is a totally different church from that of 1920. It is, one hopes, more compassionate in its attitudes towards its clerics (and laity). It is certainly a more inclusive church and more willing to experiment. It realises – unlike the Church of 1920 – that its continuation as an institution depends on its ability to commend the Gospel in ways that resonate with a society vastly different from that of the previous millennium.

8

The Laity and Patterns of Ministry

RHIANNON JOHNSON

It is said that a Roman Catholic cardinal once told the lay faithful that it was their duty simply to 'pray, pay and obey'. It is not that lay people in general reject these obligations, but there is a feeling that this language inadequately captures and belittles how lay people live out their faith. This chapter will use the headings of praying, paying, obeying and more to look at continuity and change within the role of the laity of the Church in Wales since 1920. It will then go on to consider patterns of ministry, particularly as they are developing in Ministry or Mission Areas following recommendations of the Harries Report of 2012. First, though, some definitions and some trends that impact on all these matters will be discussed.

Definitions and Trends

It is simultaneously both easy and difficult to define who the laity are. The laity are the People of God. We become part of the People of God through baptism. Therefore, it is reasonable to define the laity of any church as those baptised within it (although baptism confers membership of the universal church rather than any particular denomination). However, as Archbishop C. A. H. Green notes in his commentary on the Constitution, even in the Old Testament the people are contrasted with the priests and the rulers.[1] So, although by the dignity of their baptism clerics are part of the laity, the term 'laity' usually applies only to those who are not ordained to the order of bishop, priest or deacon. This is reflected in the Constitution of the Church in Wales which uses the category of 'lay person' and provides that a 'cleric' means 'a clerk in Holy Orders'.[2] This 'usual definition' is the one that this chapter will explore.

---

[1] C. A. H. Green, *The Setting of the Constitution of the Church in Wales* (London: Sweet & Maxwell, 1937), 61.
[2] Constitution I.I.7.

Even then, however, the Church in Wales, in common with many other denominations, baptises more people than become active members. So many lay members, as defined by baptism, take little further part in church life. This is not a new problem. Bishop Glyn Simon noticed that if he took the number of baptisms in the Diocese of Llandaff and the number of live births in 1938, it appeared that half the population in the diocese were being made members of the laity – although he did this with the caveat that the figure for baptism also included adults. Just over half the number of those baptised were subsequently confirmed by the bishop in the laying-on of hands, but only 5.5 per cent of the total population of the diocese received Holy Communion at Easter. In 1959, by comparison, he calculated that 42 per cent of live births were brought to baptism in the diocese, a larger proportion were confirmed than in 1938, but the proportion of the population making their Easter Communion was only 4.66 per cent.[3]

This means that, in practice, many denominations have to make a further distinction between those who act on their baptism and those who do not, and tend to think of these active members as the laity. For the purposes of the Constitution, a member of the Church in Wales is defined by implication as a person on whom 'the Constitution shall be binding' which would include lay office-holders and those whose names are entered on the electoral roll of a parish. But church law also recognises other classes – 'parishioners, residents in a parish, habitual worshippers, communicants, qualified electors and persons holding office in the church who are not members of religious bodies not in full communion with the Church in Wales'.[4]

All this makes counting the laity of the Church in Wales, or indeed characterising them, a problematic business. Should it be on grounds of attendance at worship, baptism numbers, Easter communicants, membership of the electoral roll? Different figures have been captured at different periods of the Church in Wales' life, which makes comparisons difficult. Furthermore, there are factors which might skew any figures returned. Many coastal parishes, for example, experience an influx of visitors at Easter which make the Easter communicant figure unrepresentative of the normal life of the church. Where figures are used to calculate how much a church pays towards the central costs of the Church, the ministry share, there is an undeniable temptation to underreport attendance.

[3] G. Simon, *Then and Now* (Penarth: Church in Wales Publications, 1961), 28–9.
[4] N. Doe, *The Law of the Church in Wales* (Cardiff: University of Wales Press, 2002), 179–80.

Nevertheless, some broad trends can be observed. The Church in Wales had experienced considerable growth, measured in terms of Easter communicants, in the years before disestablishment. In the Diocese of St Asaph, there had been 14,214 Easter communicants in 1890. In 1912, there were 312,669. In the Diocese of St David's in 1912, Easter communicants were 8.68 per cent of the population. This was the largest proportion anywhere in England and Wales, where the average for both was 6.28 per cent of the population. An analysis of data provided by the Representative Body of the Church in Wales compared against population data in the nearest census year suggests that by the late 1920s around 1 in 14 of the population of Wales made their Easter Communion. There were around 1,500 people per each church building and 1,950 people in the population as a whole to each stipendiary priest.

However, by the early 1960s, the figures for Easter communicants were 1 in 15, the population per church building had dropped slightly to 1,480 but per stipendiary priest had risen to 2,432. The overall population had dropped slightly, and the number of church buildings had increased but both the number of clergy and Easter communicants had declined. By 1990, the population had increased considerably but the numbers of clergy, Easter communicants and church buildings had declined. The proportions were now around 1 in 26 of the population making Easter Communion, 1 church building to 1,806 people. By this stage non-stipendiary ministry had become a settled aspect of the life of the Church in Wales – so the figures are 1 stipend per 4,040 people or 1 cleric per 3,680. A similar trend can be seen in the 2002 figures: Easter communicants were 1 in 39, 1,980 people per church building, 4,512 per stipend, and 3,919 per cleric. Again, comparing the 2017 church figures against the 2011 census returns for the population of Wales, gives a figure of 1 in 63 for Easter communicants, 2,377 per church building, 7,364 per stipend and 5,510 per cleric.

In 1927, there were 1,775 church buildings in Wales served by 1,367 stipendiary clergy, and the Easter communicant figures were 187,178. This meant that the laity could expect to worship at Easter in congregations with an average size of 105, served by a cleric who divided attention between 1.3 church buildings. By 1958, 1,785 church buildings housed Easter communicants totalling 170,695 and there were 1,087 stipendiary clergy. The size of congregations based on the Easter figure was 96 and the cleric now served in 1.6 buildings. By 1990, there had been a considerable change. While the general population had grown hugely, church congregations continued to dwindle. Easter communicants were

108,174 and there were 696 stipendiary clerics and 68 non-stipendiary. The number of church buildings had also dropped, but not at the same rate, to 1,557. So the average size of an Easter congregation had dropped to 69 and there was one stipend to 2.24 buildings, one cleric to 2.04 buildings. This trend galloped on in the 2002 figures, with 51 Easter communicants per building, 2.28 church buildings per stipend and 1.98 per cleric, the raw figures being 74,894 Easter communicants, 1,470 buildings, 645 stipendiary clerics and 98 non-stipendiary. By 2017, the figures stood at 48,986 Easter communicants accommodated in 1,289 church buildings served by 416 stipendiary and 140 non-stipendiary clerics. This equates to 38 Easter communicants per building served by a stipendiary cleric with an average responsibility for 3.01 church buildings or 2.32 buildings per cleric. While, rightly, a great deal of attention has been paid to the decline in clergy numbers, it is the decline in faithful laity that shows the most severe drop. The Easter communicants in 2017 were 26 per cent of those in 1927. The clergy were 41 per cent of the 1927 figure – and 30 per cent if only stipendiary clerics are considered. At the same time, moreover, the general population of Wales has risen by 15 per cent.

The Church in Wales is not unique in this. Peter Brierley shows that, overall, membership of churches in Britain is declining and ageing.[5] Indeed, there has been a decline in almost all forms of voluntary association, and churches have shared in this. Grace Davie's influential book on religion in Britain since 1945 characterises this as an attitude of 'believing without belonging'. In churches, Davie notes, this can cause deep structural problems. Those who 'belong' turn up regularly, get involved and can be consulted, but do not necessarily represent those who do have an affiliation but do not attend regularly. Davie believes they will have different priorities than the attenders concerning – 'to give but a few examples – liturgy, the occasional offices, parochial structures and, most of all, regarding buildings'.[6]

The truth of this is often witnessed at the closure of a church building. For example, when All Saints' Church, Maerdy (in the Rhondda), faced a bill of £400,000 in 2011 to repair the building, the Parochial Church Council voted to close it, sadly but unanimously. The backlash made national news with a sit-in and claims that other options had not fully

---

[5] P. Brierley, *Major UK Religious Trends 2010 to 2020* (Tonbridge: Brierley Consulting, 2010).

[6] G. Davie, *Religion in Britain since 1945: Believing without Belonging* (Oxford: Blackwell, 1994).

been explored by the parish and the diocese. The incident left a legacy of bad feeling.[7] This is a pattern often repeated elsewhere.

In the 2011 census, 58 per cent still described themselves as Christian, but the proportion of those self-identifying as having no religion had grown significantly – in 2001, it was 15 per cent (around 7.7 million), and in 2011, it was 32 per cent (around 14.1 million). Furthermore, in Blaenau Gwent, in the south-east Wales valleys, for instance, the proportion of non-religious was 41.1 per cent but in Flintshire, in the north-east, it was 25.4 per cent.

In the disestablishment debate, the Church of England in Wales was often characterised, unfairly, as a church of the few and the rich. Glyn Simon claimed that the Church in Wales – in contrast to what he saw as the puritanism of Nonconformity – was 'the church of the poor and feckless, so seldom at home with puritans'.[8] The Church in Wales' laity have also been characterised as conservative both in theology and in practice, often more conservative than the clergy who serve them; as Simon wrote: 'no one would call the clergy revolutionary, but compared with the laity they are far out on the left, recklessly progressive'. He also remarked that 'there is no part of Christendom more clericalised, more priest-ridden than we are',[9] an opinion echoed fifty years later in the Harries Report's finding of a 'culture of deference' to the clergy.[10] What follows questions how fair or unfair such characterisations have been.

More than Praying, Paying and Obeying

Throughout the whole Church in Wales, it is the lay people at the local level who keep things running. Parochial Church Council members, treasurers, secretaries and church wardens are those who ensure that the church building and churchyard are maintained and cared for, and that bills are paid. Then there are those who play music and sing, offer hospitality and see that newcomers are welcomed. These things are so commonplace that they almost go without saying. In the rural parishes I have served, it is often church events, ostensibly fundraisers, which help give the wider community its sense of focus and identity. Often individual lay members of the

---

[7] See www.bbc.co.uk/news/uk-wales-14001902.

[8] Quoted in D. T. W. Price, *A History of the Church in Wales in the Twentieth Century* (Penarth: Church in Wales Publications, 1990), 35.

[9] Simon, *Then and Now*, 37 and 39.

[10] See https://cinw.s3.amazonaws.com/wp-content/uploads/2013/03/Church-in-Wales-review-English.pdf.

church are heavily involved in running many other community events and groups. Such matters will rarely fill the pages of a history, and, indeed, the Church still operates a restrictive approach to recognition of the work of the laity in the form of installing memorial tablets in church buildings.[11] But that does not mean they are unimportant or unappreciated.

In his 1961 visitation address in the Diocese of Llandaff, Bishop Glyn Simon set out his own expectations of churchwardens, and ended by paying tribute to them, saying that they should be 'faithful and regular in attendance at Divine Service, men or women of high character, well respected in the parish for their life and conduct, and morally above reproach'. Also: 'They must also be men of courage and conviction, loyal to their clergy, but loyal above all to the church they serve, always ready to put the wellbeing of the church above their loyalty to or affection for any single individual and ready, too, in the parish to give a lead to the parishioners generally in any way that will be for the good of church and people. We may indeed thank God that in so many of our church-wardens these qualities are plain to see.'[12]

This praise goes well beyond what the Constitution of the Church in Wales expects. The qualities it requires of churchwardens are, simply, to be over eighteen years old and qualified electors of the parish.[13] Once in post it envisages the churchwardens' role as being 'foremost in represent-ing the laity and in consulting and co-operating with the Incumbent', using 'their best endeavours to promote peace and unity amongst the parishioners, and by example and precept to encourage the parishioners in the practice of true religion', maintaining 'order and decency in the church and churchyard, especially during the time of public worship', as well as discharging 'the duties placed upon them by the Church Fabric Regulations'.[14]

On a larger scale, beyond the parish, much of the mission of the Church has been carried out through groups that, while having some clerical members or chaplains, are essentially lay in character. Five such groups are discussed here. First, the Mothers' Union which, founded in 1876, came to Wales before disestablishment. Its objectives have been rephrased and have grown over its history but reflect Christian concern for marriage

---

[11] See e.g. the ten criteria set out in the faculty case of *Re St Gwenfaen, Rhoscolyn* (2014), Bangor Diocesan Court, Doe Ch., reported in *Ecclesiastical Law Journal*, 17(1) (2015), 124–6.

[12] Simon, *Then and Now*, 7.

[13] Constitution IV.C.IV.13.1.

[14] Constitution IV.C.IV.13.4.

and family life, maintaining a worldwide fellowship of Christians united in prayer and service, and promoting conditions in society favourable to stable family life and the protection of children. In Wales, each diocesan association grew separately but the story of one mirrors that of others. In the Diocese of Llandaff, the bishop's wife convened a meeting in 1893 at the Bishop's Palace to bring existing Mothers' Union groups into a diocesan structure. In 1920 there were 5,190 members – but this dropped to 4,048 when the Diocese of Monmouth was formed from part of the Diocese of Llandaff in 1921. Through the Great Depression, groups in the diocese organised holidays for 'tired mothers' with other Mothers' Union members in Devon, but in 1926 a trip to London was cancelled due to the coal strike that grew into the General Strike. Until the early 1950s, the diocesan presidents, invited to take on the role, tended to be the bishop's wife or aristocratic women such as Mrs Cennydd Treharne. Though not a member, she was asked to become diocesan president by Bishop John Morgan of Llandaff in 1944. She was sent to see a former president, Mrs Llewellyn of Baglan Hall, and recalled: 'the only thing I can remember [Llewellyn] impressed upon my mind was, not to change anything, don't change anything, so as I had no idea what was happening anyway, I didn't feel frightfully keen to change it'.[15]

In the 1980s and 1990s, the Llandaff Diocesan Mothers' Union participated in a scheme to help teenage runaways send a message home, warned parents how to spot signs of drug misuse in their children, and provided caravan holidays for families under pressure. At the turn of the millennium, it was concerned with the commercialisation and sexualisation of childhood and keeping children safe online. Its sub-groups also ran prison crèches, providing supplies for women's shelters and knitting for premature babies. The first man to join in the Diocese of Llandaff was Peter Leonard, a cleric who joined in 1990. In 1993, its membership was bucking the general trend in church decline with 4,919 regular members in the diocese, and more in its sub-groups – 500 in the Young Families Department and 321 in the Indoor Prayer Circle.

Secondly, in 1943 the Governing Body appointed a Provincial Youth Council tasked with 'Binding young people together in a spiritual fellowship'.[16] Working with a scheme of the Government Board of

---

[15] C. Davies, *Mothers' Union Alive* (Cowbridge: D. Brown, 1993), 47.
[16] Church in Wales, Provincial Youth Council, *Cymry'r Groes 1951* (Church in Wales: Provincial Youth Council, 1951).

Education, the council created Cymry'r Groes (Welsh People of the Cross) for young people to 'play their rightful part in the Church's mission, first of all in Wales and then throughout the world'. It encouraged in its members a 'pride' in Welsh history and culture and the place of the Church in Wales in it, a 'proper regard' for the Welsh language, and a 'zeal for the Christianizing of Welsh life and for the regaining by the Church of the first place in the honour and affection of every Welsh man and woman'. The group also encouraged in members the discipline of daily prayer, regular public worship, Bible reading, study of the faith, and making Holy Communion 'the centre of my spiritual life'. Communicants under the age of twenty-five, after a six-month probation, were publicly enrolled by their parish priest and allowed to wear the badge: a Celtic cross with the Welsh dragon at its heart.

Cymry'r Groes was a strong influence in building a faithful generation within the Church in Wales. From its ranks came many of the lay and ordained leaders of the church in the years that followed. Stories from the bicycle pilgrimage to York and the St David's pilgrimage of 1955 were passed down in churches and families. The pilgrims decided that they would share everything equally on their journey. This meant, for example, the hilarious exercise of trying to divide one boiled sweet fairly between all those on the pilgrimage. On the way to St David's they slept in church halls and were given meals by the parishes they passed through. One former archdeacon of St David's was a small boy at the time of the 1955 pilgrimage, helping his mother feed the pilgrim group as it came through his parish. The sense of joy in the pilgrim group left a lasting, converting impression on his mind.[17]

It is possible that the hope and energy brought by Cymry'r Groes changed the nature of the Church in the post-war years.[18] The laity were so active in these years with various schemes and plans for social outreach that the new archbishop, John Morgan, called, unsuccessfully, for a 'Holy Year' in 1949 when there would be no new committees and work would be kept to a minimum so that every member of the church could put their energy into evangelism.

Thirdly, there is the group of deaconesses. There had been women serving in the lay role of deaconess at disestablishment. In June 1893, Sister Edith Thompson and Sister Alice Oswald had been appointed by

---

[17] These stories were passed down in my own family, my parents having met through Cymry'r Groes.

[18] D. D. Morgan, *The Span of the Cross: Christian Religion and Society in Wales, 1914–2000* (Cardiff: University of Wales Press, 2nd ed., 2011).

the bishop of Llandaff to set up the Llandaff Diocesan Deaconesses' Institution in Penarth. The deaconesses lived there and used it as a base for 'training ladies in all branches of church work', including parish work and rehabilitating 'fallen women' – the latter had previously been done by a former House of Mercy. Sister Alice was styled head deaconess, working there until the Penarth building was requisitioned for war work in 1941.

Records for the institution, and deaconess ministry in general, are scarce. Green's book on the Constitution only notes Lambeth Conference resolutions on the subject, and: 'the office of a Deaconess is primarily a Ministry of succour, bodily and spiritual, especially to women, and should follow the lines of the primitive rather than the modern Diaconate of men'.[19]

The first-recorded new deaconess after 1920 was set apart for her office in 1961. She was Irene Allen, in Llandaff, who was joined by Phoebe Willetts in 1966. Two other deaconesses transferred from England: Elsie Hedley went to St David's and Barbara John to Monmouth. In 1968, Margaret Harvey was licensed in St Asaph. But there were never many deaconesses. Records gathered by Peggy Jackson found only about twenty names in Wales from 1884, but they were important role models for women who sought ordained ministry when that became available. In 1980, the five deaconesses who remained in active ministry were ordained deacon along with four women coming out of training at that time. This then ceased to be a lay ministry in the terms of this chapter. The first female bishop of the Church in Wales, Joanna Penberthy, began in deaconess ministry, but in the Diocese of Durham.[20]

Fourthly, there are the Brothers and Sisters of the Church Army. This was founded in 1882 by Wilson Carlisle and in 1887 admitted women as well as men to 'reach those most in need with the Gospel'. It is predominantly and proudly a lay organisation working at the fringes of the Church. Until very recently, any Evangelist who was ordained had to resign his or her commission. In the 1920s, Church Army Evangelists were working in Caerau and Ely in the Diocese of Llandaff with a mission hall there that preceded the Church of the Resurrection. This work, now branded as 'pioneer ministry', still flourishes in the Church in Wales today at Centres of Mission in Merlin's Bridge (the Diocese of St

---

[19] Green, *The Setting of the Constitution of the Church in Wales*, 60.
[20] St Deiniol's Group, *Crossing Thresholds: The Licensed Ministry of Women in the Church in Wales: 1884–2014* (Cardiff: Church in Wales Publications, 2014).

David's), Caia Park, Wrexham (the Diocese of St Asaph) and Neath (the Diocese of Llandaff). Other work includes a long-running project with the young and homeless in Cardiff. Since 1984, this has helped more than 1,600 young people, many of whom 'have nowhere else to call home and no one else to look after them'.[21] In 2007 the Church Army's 'Solace', for city nightclubbers, was founded in a Cardiff bar.[22]

Fifthly, lay members have always had an important role in teaching the faith to children and young people. In 1961, Simon notes that there were 25,000 children on the books of Sunday Schools in the Diocese of Llandaff, and more than 17,000 regularly attended. Sadly, the 2017 Church in Wales membership and finance figures for attendance by under-eighteens records an average attendance of only 5,474 across the province, but this may not accurately capture the growth in other forms of children and families work, such as Messy Church.[23]

Praying

The prayer life of the average lay member of the Church in Wales changed gradually over the past century under the influence of the Liturgical Movement. This emphasised the centrality of the Eucharist to Christian worship and the participation of all in it, not just the president. The beginning of the movement is generally traced to a conference in Malines in Belgium in 1909 among Roman Catholics, and it spread geographically and ecumenically.[24] By the time Cymry'r Groes was founded in the 1940s, it was uncontroversial that young people should see Holy Communion as the centre of their spiritual life. That generation's eucharistic devotion led to the creation of liturgy that emphasised its centrality. Indeed, the normal funeral service in the Book of Common Prayer 1984 is notoriously titled 'The service in church if the Eucharist is not celebrated'.[25] The Bench of Bishops' decision in 2016 to allow Holy Communion to all the baptised, not just the confirmed, appears to be an outcome of the liturgical movement's influence.

---

[21] See www.churcharmy.org/Groups/245310/Church_Army/ms/Cardiff/Cardiff (accessed March 2016).

[22] See www.christiantoday.com/article/church
.army.evangelist.opens.night.club.church.in.wales/10263.htm?print=1.

[23] See, for example, https://monmouth.churchinwales.org.uk/old-pages/resources/messy-church.

[24] G. Wakefield, *An Outline of Christian Worship* (Edinburgh: T. & T. Clark, 1998), 152.

[25] The Book of Common Prayer 1984 provides that 'The Eucharist is the principal act of Christian worship' (3).

If the Eucharist is 'the Lord's family around the Lord's table, on the Lord's day', then to deny Holy Communion to the non-confirmed, particularly children, is to tell them they are not part of the family.[26]

Each successive liturgical change envisioned greater congregational lay participation. It is no longer acceptable that the priest says words on behalf of the people: we say them together. This has led to a strong expectation that the Eucharist will be the main act of Sunday worship, often the only regularly offered service. This, however, necessitates the presence of a priest who, in some areas, might have to dash to celebrate communion in three or four churches on Sunday. In some places it raises anxiety about how welcoming a communion service is to those on the fringes of faith. Certainly, it stretches ministerial resources. So some dioceses have experimented with communion by extension where a deaconess, reader or worship leader conducts the service using bread and wine already consecrated. These experiments have tended to be short-lived and are often stopped by the next diocesan bishop appointed.[27]

Churchwardens have always been able to lead worship in certain circumstances. In 1866 the Church of England had reintroduced the unpaid lay office of Reader, licensed to preach and lead worship. There is some evidence that initially the ministry was intended for the 'unchurched masses'. In 1901, four classes of Reader were recognised – stipendiary and non-stipendiary, diocesan (licensed to minister through-out the diocese), or parochial (licensed for only a particular parish). The use and understanding of Readers appears to have varied widely from diocese to diocese. In the Diocese of Norwich, for example, by 1903 Readers were allowed to speak in churches only in addition to a sermon from the cleric – and even then only after members of the congregation had been offered the opportunity to leave first.[28]

The Church in Wales inherited some of this confusion and appears to have licensed only a handful of Readers in 1930, 1952 and 1954.[29] Slowly, however, the ministry grew. In the early 1970s, women were admitted as Readers for

---

[26] See www.churchinwales.org.uk/faith/believe/admission-to-holy-communion-pastoral-letter.

[27] As in St David's, e.g., when Bishop Joanna revoked a practice common in Bishop Wyn's episcopacy.

[28] P. Garner, 'The Reader: An Exploration of the History and Present Place of Reader Ministry in the Church of England' (PhD Thesis, University of Leeds, 2010), 64, http://etheses.whiterose.ac.uk/1913/1/READER_ministry_THESIS_master.pdf.

[29] St Deiniol's Group, *Crossing Thresholds*.

the first time – though in the Diocese of St David's they were not allowed to wear cassocks but had to wear academic dress instead. This anomaly was resolved in 1983. In the Diocese of Swansea and Brecon, the long-serving secretary of the Readers' Association, Bill Mort, is remembered for his faithful and committed service. In 2018, there were 279 Readers across the dioceses – 59 in St David's, 57 in St Asaph, 49 in Bangor, 45 in Swansea and Brecon, 37 in Monmouth and 32 in Llandaff. Although St David's still has the largest figure, numbers have dropped considerably with the advent of a scheme to encourage non-stipendiary ordained local ministry. From its inception in 2013, to 2019, this scheme has trained forty-three ordinands for the diocese, twenty-three of whom were previously in Reader ministry.[30]

There are various tensions in understandings about Reader ministry. Are they the lay specialist teachers and preachers of the Church, or are they auxiliary ministers, like clergy but perceived as somehow lesser? This was complicated by the fact that, until very recently, 'Reader' was more or less the only designation to give highly active and competent lay workers in parish life, so a Reader might be encouraged for their pastoral gifts even if they were not a gifted preacher. There are also examples of Reader ministry being a place to 'park' people who feel they have a call to ordained ministry but are somehow deemed unsuitable, perhaps because of age or gender. So, in some places there are Readers in charge of parishes, and it is common for Readers to have extra training to take on funeral ministry.[31]

Since at least 2000, dioceses have also licensed lay worship leaders. Like 'parish readers' in 1903, worship leaders are commissioned to take services of the Word such as Morning and Evening Prayer, but not to preach. In the dioceses that responded to a recent enquiry this now is the largest category of lay ministers. There are 126 in Swansea and Brecon, around 150 in St Asaph and 169 in St David's.[32] In one rural church in Carmarthenshire all of the eight elderly regular worshippers have become worship leaders so that they can pray together and encourage one another regularly even when their cleric can only be with them infrequently.

Paying

As we see elsewhere in this book, disestablishment also brought disendowment. The fledgling Church in Wales had many of the same financial

---

[30] Figures supplied by the author.
[31] See below.
[32] Response to an email survey of ministry officers conducted by the author in the spring of 2019.

obligations in terms of the payment of clergy and maintenance of property, to say nothing of the need to engage in charity and mission work. Henry Gladstone of Hawarden gave £20,000 towards the appeal to raise a million pounds following disestablishment. But mostly it was raised by ordinary lay members against a background of severe financial hardship in the Great Depression. This went some way to offset the worst financial hardship. The Church in Wales also introduced the 'share' or 'Quota' that parishes would be expected (and, later, under a constitutional duty) to pay. It is now called the ministry share, but the financial realities continue. In 1923, the total levy stood at £45,000 divided as follows between the dioceses: Llandaff, £11,567.15s; St David's, £8,000; St Asaph, £7,500; Swansea and Brecon, £7,000; Monmouth, £5,932.5s and Bangor £5,000. In 2017, the dioceses together raised £16,456,000 in ministry share.[33]

In September 1949, a unique event took place. The lay members of the Governing Body met without the clergy present to discuss clergy stipends. These had fallen below inflation, and there was a worry that clergy would leave the Church in Wales for more remunerative posts in England. The Governing Body decided to hold a 'Layman's Appeal' for half a million pounds to fund increased stipends. The target had been exceeded by 1953.[34] In 1954, the Quota stood at £145,000 a year,[35] only £51,000 less than the entire Church of England had to raise. In that year the Representative Body was empowered to make more risky investments of the Church's money. The most spectacular of these was the purchase of an office block in London, Bush House, in 1955 at a cost of £2.5 million.[36] The property was sold in 1972 for £22 million. The architects of this financial policy were D. M. Vaughan, the chair of the Finance Committee of the Representative Body, and its accountant, W. R. Jones.[37]

Across the century, lay individuals have been very generous in their financial support. For example, in 1931 Frank Morgan, the first chair of the Representative Body, took a cut in his salary to help the Church's finances. In 1962, Sir David Jones offered to give the Church £204,000 over six years if it managed to raise an equivalent amount. It did. Lord

---

[33] Using the inflation calculator tool online – www.thisismoney.co.uk/money/bills/article-1633409/Historic-inflation-calculator-value-money-changed-1900.html – the £45,000 1923 levy would be £2,513,787.25 in today's money meaning that the current ministry share is six and a half times larger in real terms.

[34] The same calculator estimates that half a million in 1953 would be approximately £14,145,499 today.

[35] Approx. £3,978,850 today.

[36] Approx. £67,387,885 today.

[37] Approx. £305,974,438 today.

Tredegar provided land for a new cathedral and close in Newport. In 2013 Hazel Jones-Olszewski left £2.6 million to the Diocese of St David's for 'charitable church purposes' – the bulk was spent on reducing the ministry share and assisting with children, youth work and training. And, of course, each church building is a testament to the generous giving of the laity, not just in the running costs but in the donations of furniture, books and plate. These are often given as gifts in memory of a loved one and keep their names alive in their community.

Obeying

The discussions that formed the Constitution of the Church in Wales gave a high priority to lay participation in decision-making in the Church – or at least the participation of laymen. Each of the four dioceses sent sixty-six laymen to the Cardiff Convention of 1917 along with thirty-three clerics and its bishop. It was decided that the new Governing Body should contain fifty laymen from each diocese, twenty-five clerics and the bishop. Some debate was held over the inclusion of lay women and it was decided to co-opt twelve onto Governing Body.[38] Soon, however, lay representatives were being elected regardless of gender. But class and age remained harder issues. It was, and is, difficult for someone in work to give the time needed for church governance. Any advantage numbers might give to lay representation, though, is balanced by the way the Governing Body votes. If a bill is deemed 'non-controversial' it can pass by a simple majority – so the lay representatives have huge influence. If, however, it is deemed controversial, it must gain a two-thirds majority in each of the three orders of Governing Body, lay, clergy and bishops. So, the will of the lay representatives can be blocked by clergy, but equally the laity could block a move by both the clergy and bishops. This was seen in the votes concerning the ordination of women to the priesthood. In 1994, an overwhelming majority of laity and bishops was blocked by a narrow margin by the clergy.

Lay people were also hugely influential in forming church structures at disestablishment. As we see elsewhere in this book, John Sankey, assisted by Richard Atkin and John Bankes, drafted the Constitution. Frank Morgan was instrumental in shaping what was to become the Welsh Church (Temporalities) Act 1919. Nor were lay people afraid to challenge the exercise of authority by the bishops. For example, when

---

[38] Price, *History of the Church in Wales in the Twentieth Century*, 9–11.

Parliament debated the divorce bill 1937, in the House of Lords, Atkin (a Law Lord) opposed the clause for an absolute bar to divorce within five years of marriage as 'intolerable'. He also successfully moved an amendment to allow Church in Wales clergy to refuse to solemnise in church the marriages of a civilly divorced person whose former spouse was still living. This then appeared in the Act for 'the relief of conscience among the clergy'. But the Welsh bishops then forbade clergy to solemnise such marriages – marriage is dissolved only on the death of a spouse. The bishops also pronounced that, if a civil marriage after divorce had occurred, both parties must not receive Holy Communion unless allowed by the bishop. In an exchange with the archbishop, Atkin argued that the bishops had no right to impose such blanket prohibitions: while a parishioner had a right to marry in the parish church, the Matrimonial Causes Act 1937 relieved *individual* clergy by conferring a statutory right of conscientious refusal which could not be fettered by any blanket episcopal prohibition. And, as to Holy Communion, Atkin argued that the right to repel vested in the first instance in the cleric, not the bishop. The bishops rejected his position. In September 1938 at Governing Body, Atkin proposed a resolution on the issues but the matter was dropped due to the onset of the war. Atkin's position was later debated and adopted when the bishops lifted the ban in 1998.[39]

One of the most dramatic later instances of lay protest came when Edwin Morris, Bishop of Monmouth, became archbishop in 1958 and John Thomas became bishop of Swansea and Brecon shortly afterwards. Both were monolingual English-speakers, and some expressed their opinions that this showed a lessening of the Church's commitment to Welsh language and culture. The poet D. Gwenallt Jones left the Church in protest and returned to his roots in Calvinistic Methodism, claiming 'the Church in Wales has tied itself to royalty, the landowners and the Tories. Anglicanism is a middle way between Rome and Geneva, but it is the Englishman's Middle way.'[40] Magnificent as this protest was, it is atypical of the Church in Wales where dissent is more often expressed by absenting oneself or by stonewalling any unwelcome initiative. This is never clearer than in the lay attachment to church buildings. All the evidence points to the fact that to close a church building means that more than half the worshipping congregation will not find another

---

[39] G. Lewis, *Lord Atkin* (London: Butterworths, 1983), 34. See also Chapters 7 and 11.
[40] D. D. Morgan, *The Span of the Cross*, 2nd ed., 192.

church.[41] Even in 1961, Simon complained that even 'in the age of the motor car' congregations would not attend each other's buildings, which was a form of idolatry of the building.[42] A more sympathetic reading might be that the average congregation loves and is more loyal to the place which has formed much of their experiences of God than to the institutional Church.

Patterns of Ministry in the Church in Wales

By the time Governing Body met in 2010, it had become clear that the trends in church life noted above had become too serious to ignore. In both 2009 and 2010, the Governing Body had affirmed the parish struc-ture and the Anglican sense of ministry to the whole community but noted also 'the reality of aging congregations and declining resources'.[43] This was compounded by the fact that to support this system the Church used its historic resources to subsidise ministry by about 30 per cent. This subsidy was under severe pressure. And the ministry share was rapidly approaching an unpayable level, despite increases in lay generosity.

The dilemma comes from a combination of factors – falling clergy and lay numbers, an ageing laity, a reluctance to close church buildings, a strongly eucharistic spirituality and financial concerns. In 2010, Archbishop Barry Cennydd Morgan commissioned a report, stating: 'The Church is the Body of Christ [and] called to be: a channel of God's grace, renewal and pastoral concern for the individual, who is called to faith and fullness of life in Jesus Christ; a source of fellowship and community in our society, as the Church calls people into renewed relationships with one another; an agent of change in the world, as the Church is called to be open to the leading of the Holy Spirit and to bear witness to the justice and peace which are the marks of God's Kingdom.' It asked the commissioners to find out if the Church is '"fit for purpose" and able to respond to this vocation in the context of twenty-first century Wales'. Three particular concerns were noted, the challenges of structure, resources and leadership.[44]

The resultant Harries Report criticised the whole Church for holding onto a pattern of ministry that was no longer appropriate or practicable, one 'hindering people from making visible the Word of life'.

[41] B. Jackson, *Leading One Church at a Time* (Cambridge: Grove, 2018).
[42] Simon, *Then and Now*, 39.
[43] Ibid.
[44] Church in Wales, *Review* (July 2012), www.churchinwales.org.uk/review/, 42.

Furthermore, 'a number of people have said to us that the Church in Wales is still characterised by a culture of deference and dependence', which puts a brake on dynamism, especially for the laity. So, the report recommended a cultural shift from the Church being an organisation which mirrored a secular model, with clergy as providers of ministry and laity as recipients, to one in which all members are part of a fellowship in which all minister. It uses the Greek term *koinonia*, fellowship or common life to describe this – 'membership of the Christian community not only takes us into a *koinonia* with other human beings, it takes us into the very *koinonia* of God. The church as an institution, its structures and organisation, only have a purpose in so far as they serve and achieve that aim.' Without making explicit the connection of ideas, the report assumes that this *koinonia* is better served by ministry teams working over an area wider than a historic parish. In turn, the new Ministry Areas it recommended should have 'a small designated leadership team and designated leader for each congregation', the latter either 'a Non-Stipendiary Minister, Reader (Licensed Lay Minister) or other appropriately trained lay person' and 'part of the leadership team'.[45]

After receiving the report, the Governing Body authorised a 'period of experimentation', and dioceses began to consider how they might implement this cultural shift, rebranded as '2020 Vision', or 'Golwg 2020'. In implementing the report, however, each diocese drew heavily on work it had already been doing. All the dioceses were aware of the issues and had worked for some time to solve them. Different dioceses also saw differing levels of urgency in the task, and so moved at different speeds. In Bangor, St Asaph and St David's, the deaneries have become Ministry Areas (although St Asaph has renamed them Mission Areas and in Bangor they are constituted as United Parishes, an existing model under the Constitution). St Asaph stressed lay empowerment. Bangor radically flattened and changed its organisational structure. St David's experimented with a person or team to lead each congregation, and this led to the calling and training of local non-stipendiary ministers. Llandaff too has started to re-energise the laity. Monmouth began with re-educating the leaders as a way of changing culture. Swansea and Brecon began by trying to get clergy to work more closely together. There has been little consistency across the province.

These differences of emphasis began to trouble those charged with training people for ministry. How could the new St Padarn's Institute

---

[45] Ibid., 3, 4 and 7.

begin to prepare people for six different localised church polities? The provincial ministry officers tried to provide a framework by suggesting that there should be new recognised lay ministries within the Church. At the Ministry Area level there should be 'commissioned ministries', which the Diocese of Bangor calls 'team ministries', groups of lay people authorised to work on the Church's behalf in a particular area of its life – Readers to preach, worship leaders, pastoral assistants (sometimes called pastoral visitors), teachers (sometimes called catechists), pioneer workers, evangelistic workers and children, youth and families workers. No diocese has yet fully implemented this pattern. Some are working towards it. Others have reservations. In three dioceses responding to a recent enquiry, there are more than 657 lay people active in ministry on behalf of the Church at a time when there are 556 clerics in the whole province.[46] This suggests that as the Church moves into a second century the culture of a 'clerical church' is changing fast.

Conclusion

Recent ecumenical reports, such as *Baptism, Eucharist and Ministry* and *The Church: Towards a Common Vision*, stress that ministry is the task of all the baptised, whether or not some go on to ordination.[47] Although the Church in Wales has declined numerically over the past hundred years, it appears that many of the remaining laity have taken this ecumenical understanding to heart. In so doing, they are making a claim to a ministry which arises not by birth but by baptism. It is perhaps time, therefore, for the Church in Wales to reflect more fully on the role of the laity as this is set out in the principles of canon law common to the churches of the Anglican Communion: 'All persons are equal in dignity before God' with 'inherent rights and duties inseparable from their dignity as human beings created in the image and likeness of God and called to salvation through Jesus Christ'; and: 'Baptism is the foundation of Christian rights and duties'; as such: 'All the faithful, ordained and lay, enjoy in a church such rights to government, ministry, teaching, worship, sacraments, rites, and property as may flow from their human dignity, baptism, the duties of others, and

---

[46] Carried out by the author in the spring of 2019.

[47] See www.oikoumene.org/en/resources/documents/commissions/faith-and-order/i-unity-the-church-and-its-mission/.

the law of that church.' Above all: 'A church should provide for the affirmation and development of the ministry of all the baptized and should have, at the appropriate level, a commission or other body to promote these, the composition and functions of which may be prescribed by law.'[48]

---

[48] Anglican Communion Network of Legal Advisers, *The Principles of Canon Law Common to the Churches of the Anglican Communion* (London: Anglican Communion Office, 2008), Principle 26.

PART III

Doctrine, Liturgy, Rites and Other Faith
Communities

9

The Doctrine of the Church

PETER SEDGWICK

Anglicanism has no formal confession of faith, such as the Presbyterian *Westminster Confession*, or the Lutheran *Confessio Augustana*, to establish its doctrine. What is more, there are no founding theologians, such as John Calvin or Martin Luther, nor is there a central authority, such as the Roman Catholic *magisterium*, to appeal to for standards of doctrine. The foundations of Anglican doctrine are instead primarily the three major creeds of the early ecumenical councils (the Apostles', the Nicene and the Athanasian Creeds), the Thirty-Nine Articles, the Book of Common Prayer and the Ordinal. Secondly, Anglican churches have constitutions with canons which are legally binding. These can and do define doctrine. Thirdly, there are more recent expressions of liturgy, which have developed from the Book of Common Prayer. Canons and liturgy are formulated by synods, which include the episcopate.[1]

The Civil Law Basis of the Doctrine of the Church in Wales

It was prescribed by an Act of Parliament that the Church in Wales would accept the existing doctrines and rites of the Church of England.[2] The Governing Body, at its first meeting, held on 8 January 1918, reaffirmed this.[3] Here, then, is the legal basis of the doctrine of the Church in Wales. It rests on two pillars, an Act of Parliament, and a resolution four years later of the Governing Body. The power to change doctrine rests with the Governing Body. The Constitution states: 'The Governing Body shall

---

[1] I am grateful to many people who helped with this chapter. John Richfield and Julian Luke searched out files in the Representative Body. William Price did the same, and was a fount of knowledge. David Ceri Jones kindly sent me his article. I had excellent conversations, with many past and present members of the Doctrinal Commission: D. P. Davies, Rowan Williams, John Holdsworth, Jenny Wigley (who lent me past reports), John Rowlands, Jason Bray, Ainsley Griffiths and Mark Clavier, the current chair.
[2] Welsh Church Act 1914, s. 3(2).
[3] Constitution, Prefatory Note.

have power . . . to make new articles, doctrinal statements, rites, ceremonies and formularies and to alter those from time to time existing.'[4]

The Governing Body has since then very rarely debated doctrine. It has done so when there have been proposals to change the liturgy or the nature of ministry, or debates on the question of ecumenical relations with other churches, and when it has been asked to look at a few ethical questions, such as the nature of marriage, divorce and same-sex relationships. It was, of course, contentious that proposals to include women in the threefold order of ministry were held by its opponents to be changing the nature of ministry – whereas for those who wanted reform and the inclusion of women, the nature of ministry was not changing at all. Ordained ministry was simply becoming more inclusive – as though a fruit shop had started selling apples, or kiwi fruit, as well as oranges. Whether that claim was correct, given the doctrine of the Church in Wales, was where the argument was focussed. It was a hard-fought battle.

Across the century, the bishops have established and then abolished a standing Doctrinal Commission on several occasions. The Doctrinal Commission advises the bishops and can, with the consent of the bishops, produce reports for the Governing Body. Two recent examples are a report on the rite of confirmation and one on same-sex relations. It is unclear why the Doctrinal Commission has moved in and out of existence, although for the moment it has existed since 2008. There are few records in the archives of the Church in Wales which throw light on the decision to abolish, or restore, the commission. Nor is it clear if the Church in Wales would decide to enforce doctrinal discipline against any cleric, lay person or office-holder. The relevant norm in the Constitution provides, however, that 'teaching, preaching, publishing or professing, doctrine or belief incompatible with that of the Church in Wales' may be subject to disciplinary proceedings.[5] The possibility is there, but it has never been used.

The Theological Significance of Doctrinal Revision

This chapter will explore three topics, which are separate but deeply interrelated. One constant theme which runs through all three topics is the shifting balance within the Church in Wales between those who stand

---

[4] Constitution II.4.11.2: bill procedure must be used.
[5] Constitution IX.9 (b).

either in an evangelical, liberal or catholic tradition.[6] These terms refer to 'parties' inside Anglicanism. Such groups might meet to rally support, circulate papers and generally promote their identity. Liberals put a high stress on reason and adapting to the modern world. High-church, or catholic, proponents define themselves in relationship to Roman Catholicism or Orthodoxy, value tradition and also appeal to the doctrine of the church universal. Evangelicals, or low-church, see themselves as Protestant, would define themselves with reference to the Reformation and would stress the Bible, with a sense of being 'saved' or 'converted'.[7] These three parties often shade into each other, and some would reject party labels at all. Again and again in the last century Welsh Anglicans have divided between those who felt the desire to preserve the Church's tradition, or conversely the need to be open to new ideas. A common reality, especially among Welsh bishops and cathedral deans in the last forty years, has been the existence of those who greatly valued ecclesial tradition but sought to modernise it. They call themselves 'liberal catholics'.

The first topic to be treated is the doctrinal inheritance of the Church in Wales on disestablishment and during the succeeding century. Much of this inheritance is not consciously articulated in everyday church life. There is also a close relationship between the law of the Church (canon law) and church doctrine, as Norman Doe has shown in many publications.[8]

Secondly, however, the chapter considers the way in which the beliefs, implicit or explicit, of the Church in Wales come to be embodied in the work of the Doctrinal Commission, established in 1969. The Doctrinal Commission only advises the bishops, and the Governing Body, as to what the doctrinal understanding of the Church may be. Over a century there have been a number of changes, about the nature of ministry, gender and perhaps sexuality. The importance of this is very great. The question arises as to why a church might need a doctrine commission.

---

[6] D. D. Morgan, *The Span of the Cross: Christian Religion and Society in Wales, 1914–2000* (Cardiff: University of Wales Press, 1999); D. P. Davies, 'Welsh Anglicanism: A Renewed Church for a Reviving Nation', in N. Yates, ed., *Anglicanism: Essays in History, Belief and Practice* (Lampeter: Trivium Publications, 2008), 106; D. T. W. Price, *A History of the Church in Wales in the Twentieth Century* (Penarth: Church in Wales Publications, 1990).

[7] D. C. Jones, 'Evangelical Resurgence in the Church in Wales in the Mid-Twentieth Century', in A. Atherstone and J. Maiden, eds., *Evangelicals and the Church of England in the Twentieth Century: Reform, Resistance and Renewal* (Woodbridge: Boydell Press, 2014), 227–47.

[8] N. Doe, *Canon Law in the Anglican Communion* (Oxford: Clarendon Press, 1998).

Did the lack of controversy in the Church in Wales make such a body unnecessary until 1969, and why it was set up at all in 1969?

The third topic to be explored is the ecclesiology of the Church in Wales. In the definitive study volume, *The Study of Anglicanism*, there is a chapter titled 'Doctrine of the Church'.[9] This refers to the beliefs about the Church, as found in the Thirty-Nine Articles, and in the work of many theologians. It is no surprise that much of the work of the Doctrinal Commission of the Church in Wales has been about ecclesiology. Underlying debates about ecumenism, gender and sexuality, there has always been a continuous concern about the nature of lay and ordained ministry, the structure of the Church and its synodality, and the exercise of authority.

The Doctrine of the Church in Wales 1920–1969

The doctrinal inheritance of the Church in Wales in the first twenty years since disestablishment is summed up well by Densil Morgan in *The Span of the Cross*. He describes 'the progressive catholicization of the Welsh church' in 1914, which had begun thirty years earlier. St David's College, Lampeter, was the longstanding and pre-eminent theological training college, which is described by D. P. Davies as 'Prayer Book Anglican'.[10]

St David's College was low-church, not accepting catholic liturgy and ceremonial, but not strongly Protestant either. During the first half-century of the Church in Wales, the college supplied half its clergy.[11] It ceased training clergy through Bishop Burgess Hall in 1976, and its closure was part of the slow decline of the Church in Wales. Ordinands do, however, still continue to read theology at Lampeter. Furthermore, the Diocese of St David's, where St David's College was situated, was largely low-church. In spite of the influence of the college, the future doctrinal ethos of the Church in Wales did not lie there. D. C. Jones describes evangelicalism in the Church in Wales in the 1920s as 'invisible' or 'non-existent'.[12] Moreover, R. L. Brown talks of that party having 'virtually died out in the Church in Wales' by the 1950s.[13]

---

[9] P. E. Thomas, 'Doctrine of the Church', in S. W. Sykes and J. Booty, eds., *The Study of Anglicanism* (London: SPCK, 1988), 249–62.

[10] Personal email to author.

[11] D. D. Morgan, *The Span of the Cross*, 1st ed., 85.

[12] D. C. Jones, 'Evangelical Resurgence', 227–8.

[13] R. L. Brown, *The Welsh Evangelicals* (Welshpool: Tair Eglwys Press, 1986), and *Evangelicals in the Church in Wales* (Welshpool: Tair Eglwys Press, 2007); and D. D. Morgan, *The Span of the Cross*, 1st ed., 183.

Instead, from the 1920s the future lay with bodies such as St Michael's College, founded in 1892, which moved from Aberdare to Llandaff in 1905, where many future clergy were trained. This college was firmly Anglo-Catholic. Morgan notes that from the 1880s Evangelicals 'were being eclipsed by the influence of the Tractarians and their ritualist successors'.[14] A growing number of formerly evangelical parishes, such as Merthyr or Aberdare, called themselves both Anglican and catholic. Morgan writes that this doctrinal identity was shown by ever more advanced liturgical practices, the appointment of a strongly Anglo-Catholic bishop, Charles Green, as archbishop in 1934, and the growing role of St Michael's College. Yet it was a 'decidedly cautious, conservative and traditionalist' Catholicism.[15] It was far removed from employing biblical criticism or practising Christian Socialism. In 1936 in England, the brilliant young Anglo-Catholic theologian Michael Ramsey was reading Luther and Barth as he prepared his first book, *The Gospel and the Catholic Church*. Such a breadth of thought was completely unknown in Wales. Robert Paterson's article on Welsh liturgical revision confirms this judgment, describing its churchmanship for the first few decades after 1920 as 'conservative and moderately catholic in style'.[16]

The changes in the catholicism of the Church in Wales from the 1930s came through Glyn Simon. He became principal of St Michael's College in 1939. Although always austere, and theologically conservative, especially while a college principal, he had become by 1948 dean of Llandaff, and restored this bombed cathedral, using modern artists and architects, especially George Pace. He started to express what Rowan Williams has called 'a fresh vision for the Welsh church: confident, articulate, and culturally sophisticated'. Simon became a very well-known bishop, then archbishop, in the 1950s and 1960s. Williams describes his theology as remaining 'resolutely traditional', but his engagement with contemporary issues gained for the Church 'a new degree of confidence and public credibility'.[17] Densil Morgan describes 'a world-affirming catholicism [representing] central Welsh churchmanship'; he goes on:

---

[14] D. D. Morgan, *The Span of the Cross*, 1st ed., 25 and 28.

[15] Ibid., 87.

[16] R. Paterson, 'The Church in Wales', in C. Hefling and C. Shattuck, eds., *The Oxford Guide to the Book of Common Prayer: A Worldwide Survey* (Oxford: Oxford University Press, 2006), 426–430.

[17] R. Williams, 'Simon, (William) Glyn Hughes', *Oxford Dictionary of National Biography* (Oxford: Oxford University Press, 2004).

> Anglicanism, with its Prayer Book liturgy, sacramentalism and rounded doctrines of creation and incarnation, provided a very appealing version of Christian faith. Unencumbered by the negativities of sabbatarianism and teetotalism, it presented a viable spiritual alternative for those who were offended by nonconformity but chose not to succumb to secularism and irreligion.[18]

Yet all was not well doctrinally. In 1947, the bishops set up a Commission on Nation and Prayer Book, to examine both the life of the Church in the nation and possible liturgical revision. When it reported to the Governing Body in 1949, it said (quoting William Price's summary of its contents) that 'the Church in Wales had not been in the forefront of theological thinking for over a century, and a revival of theology was essential for the future health of Welsh Christianity'. The response was the creation of a Standing Liturgical Advisory Commission, but no Doctrinal Commission.[19] That had to wait until 1969. Individual leaders could set an attractive tone, but underneath there were deep issues, which meant that the new secular ethos from the late 1950s had few theologically astute clergy and laity to resist it.

Owen Geoffrey Rees, known as O.G., the principal of St Michael's College appointed in 1958, had studied with the great German liberal theologian Rudolf Bultmann, but his attempts to widen the curriculum of the college met with Simon's fierce disapproval as bishop of Llandaff. St Michael's College joined the Cardiff School of Theology, as part of University College, Cardiff, in the late 1950s: the South Wales Baptist College had always been part of that school. That move to be part of a secular university meant that staff had to teach their ordinands modern theology, as part of the Bachelor of Divinity degree from Cardiff, alongside secular and Baptist students. Simon replied to Rees that Protestantism 'sits lightly' to the doctrines of the Church, the ministry, and the sacraments, and that could never be acceptable in training ordinands for the Church in Wales. They had to have a fully catholic curriculum, liturgy and spiritual discipline. Rees persisted in widening the curriculum to include modern theology and liturgy, but it was a struggle to change the tone of Welsh Anglicanism.[20] Rees defied the

---

[18] D. D. Morgan, 'Christianity and National Identity in Twentieth-Century Wales', *Religion, State & Society*, 27(3/4) (1999), 337.

[19] Price, *History of the Church in Wales in the Twentieth Century*, 25–7; Paterson, 'The Church in Wales', 426.

[20] D. D. Morgan, *The Span of the Cross*, 1st ed., 225–6; see also O. W. Jones, *Saint Michael's College Llandaff 1892–1992* (Llandysul: Gomer Press, 1992), 97–104.

bishop's criticism, but it was not a good portent for the future. The 1960s saw much theological ferment across Britain, such as the uproar caused by the publication in 1963 of Bishop John Robinson's *Honest to God* – and Wales was no exception. Numbers attending Anglican churches began to decline, especially in baptism figures. Simon sought to set a politically radical tone, campaigning for nuclear disarmament, while remaining theologically and liturgically conservative.

Another evangelical straw in the wind was the encouragement of John Stott from London. Stott's influence was enormous. Although simply a parish priest in central London, he was rightly seen as the most important English Anglican Evangelical. Stott had a holiday home in Pembrokeshire, where he quietly began to foster Welsh Anglican Evangelicals from 1964. Stott lectured on evangelical doctrine and led Bible studies.[21] By 1967, the Evangelical Fellowship of the Church in Wales had come into existence. Though small, it published a journal, *Yr Eglwyswr Efengylaidd* ('The Evangelical Churchman') and held conferences and summer camps. The call in 1966–7 by Martyn Lloyd-Jones for Evangelicals to leave their denominations and form an evangelical group of their own cut no ice in Wales.

The Establishment of the Doctrinal Commission 1969–2000

Why was the commission set up in 1969? Partly, it was a request from the staff of the archbishop of Canterbury that year. So Simon persuaded his fellow bishops to set up a Doctrinal Commission. Its terms of reference were vague: 'It would be helpful if it kept the Bishops in touch with the current trend of doctrinal thinking.'[22] It was not, however, simply the request from Lambeth Palace that spurred on the Welsh Bench of Bishops. Three other factors were far more decisive. First, there was the new theological tone in Britain in the 1960s. This also allowed a much more exploratory style of ethical thinking, which encouraged change in behaviour, especially in personal morality, and attitudes to gender and sexuality. Secondly, after years of entrenched opposition to ecumenism, the Church in Wales was now being challenged to take part in the new ecumenical climate. Thirdly, the Church in Wales was now beginning to consider revising its liturgy. In all these areas, the new Doctrinal

---

[21] D. C. Jones, 'Evangelical Resurgence', 232.

[22] Church in Wales: Bench of Bishops, 'Minutes', 14 January 1969 (Cardiff: Church in Wales Representative Body, 1969), contained in file 'Standing Doctrinal Commission' (1969–2013) (hereafter SDC File).

Commission was seen as a way in which the Church in Wales should show its theological credibility. If the 1922 Church of England Doctrine Commission was an attempt to overcome longstanding ecclesial division in that church, the 1969 Welsh equivalent was a long-overdue response to a series of changes that would need a careful response. In an age of decline for the Church in Wales, and with the media becoming far more secular, the Church in Wales was proposing to tackle liturgical reform, give a credible response to issues of gender, and embrace new ecumenical partnerships. Yet most of its clergy had been trained in a conservative, catholic ethos, hostile to modern thought. It was a formidable task for the Church to undertake.

The initial response to the proposed liturgical reforms came from the Evangelicals, who were alarmed that the Book of Common Prayer was being abandoned. The Holy Communion text in that prayer book expressed for them the reality of sin and the once-for-all nature of Christ's saving death. In a pamphlet they spelled out their case.[23] Cledan Mears, a leading Evangelical and later bishop of Bangor, was concerned about the increased emphasis on eucharistic sacrifice, while others criticised the declining emphasis on sin, and the new prayers for the dead. Bishop Glyn Simon engaged in correspondence and discussion with this group, and with the English Evangelical John Stott. The Bench agreed to change the prayers for the dead as a result. Praying for the souls of the dead, anathema for Evangelicals, was not part of the new liturgy.

Six members of the new Doctrinal Commission were appointed by the bishops. Thomas Wood had been a professor at Lampeter since 1957 and served until 1985. He was an expert in moral theology, and his catholic voice provided caution on the commission, and sometimes a dissenting note. Herbert Lewis Clarke had also taught at Lampeter and St Michael's before becoming a parish priest. Raymond Renowden had taught philosophy at Lampeter for many years, and then became dean of St Asaph. The others were parish clergy: Elwyn Roberts, C. P. Willis and G. D. Yarnold. In 1973, the only lay person, Dr Keith Warren, a chemistry lecturer at University College, Cardiff, joined them. The retirement of Clarke in 1975 saw the name of Cledan Mears discussed by the Bench, but he was not appointed. Instead, David Thomas, Vice Principal of St Stephen's House, Oxford, and son of Bishop Jack Thomas of Swansea and Brecon, replaced Clarke. This theological college was

---

[23] *Revised Service of Holy Communion: Some Problems Considered*, cited in D. C. Jones. 'Evangelical Resurgence', 236–9.

firmly in the conservative, catholic wing of the Church. Thomas was an expert in liturgy, and ensured the catholic voice remained strong. There were no Evangelicals. In 1976, the bishops discussed the need to appoint someone 'representing the evangelical tradition', but took no action. In 1977–8, D. P. Davies from Lampeter and O. G. Rees, now a parish priest after leaving St Michael's College, joined the commission.[24]

The first Doctrinal Commission lasted from 1969 to 1978, when it ceased meeting. The reports had a mixed success. The topics it discussed were very wide-ranging. It produced a 1972 paper, *Women and the Ministry*, which was debated in Governing Body in 1975: 'The role of the Spirit in ordination is enabling therefore ... within the baptismal status, rather than creative of any new status', whereas 'baptism confers a status which is ontological, ordination a role which is functional'. Some high-church catholics were now the ones to be alarmed. In their view, ordination to the priesthood created a difference in kind from the laity. Further, the commission argued that the image of God depended on incorporation into the new humanity by baptism and the gift of the Spirit. There could then be the possibility of departure from tradition, so long as this was a development and not an abrogation. They argued: 'There were Gentile successors to the Jewish apostles; there could also be women successors.' Thomas Wood signed a dissenting note.[25] Governing Body agreed that there were no fundamental objections to the ordination of women.[26]

There were many reports on ecumenism both in Wales and internationally,[27] arguing about how much importance should be given to episcopacy and the idea of 'valid' ordinations. There was also a report in 1972 on *Christian Initiation* as a contribution to the reform of the liturgy. This report was seen as located in a wider discussion of the relationship of baptism to confirmation as part of the process of creating a new liturgy for the Church in Wales of Christian Initiation. Governing Body approved the services of baptism and confirmation in 1971, after thirteen years of trial use in some parishes, only to be faced with the Doctrinal Commission report of 1972 recommending abolition of

---

[24] SDC File, 1978.

[25] Church in Wales, *Women and the Ministry* (Penarth: Church in Wales Publications, 1972).

[26] Church in Wales, *The Ordination of Women to the Priesthood: The Record of the Debate during the April 1975 Governing Body Debate of the Church in Wales* (Penarth: Church in Wales Publications, 1975).

[27] See Chapter 12.

confirmation. In this, the Welsh report followed a similar report in the Church of England, the Ely Report of 1971, which argued that baptism is 'the one and complete sacrament of Christian initiation'. Governing Body rejected the Doctrinal Commission's report in 1974, since it believed in the reality of confirmation as part of liturgical tradition. Some did not want to end a liturgy which was pastorally valuable. Others felt on catholic grounds that the Spirit was given in this service to candidates by episcopal laying-on of hands. It was a major blow only five years after the Commission had come into existence. Finally, there was a report on *The Diaconate* as part of a discussion of ecclesiology. The commission was thinking about the possibility of a permanent diaconate. There was also the issue of whether women could become deacons. That report (undated) had an easier reception in Governing Body. This was surprising, given the catholic wish to preserve the tradition of male clergy.

Wood convened a separate working party on *The Remarriage of the Divorced,* which reported in 1976, but this was formally not a Doctrinal Commission report. It condemned divorce as contrary to Christ's teaching, and strongly disapproved of remarriage in church after civil divorce, but argued that those who did so should not be automatically barred from receiving Holy Communion. The issue of admission to Holy Communion was one of episcopal discretion and would be considered on a case-by-case basis. It was a deeply conservative report, although it balanced rigour with pastoral sensitivity.[28] In 1994, a new report from the commission on the subject came to the opposite conclusion, and advocated allowing the divorced to remarry in church.

In 1981, a new Doctrinal Commission was appointed. Archbishop G. O. Williams of Bangor sounded out David Thomas, who was by now moving back to a parish in Wales, both about members and about the role of a new commission. Thomas recommended that a moderate catholic should be appointed; he added: 'The catholic wing of the Church in Wales has tended of late to be conservative sometimes to the point of losing its credibility.' Thomas felt that the commission should stick to doctrine, and not move into ethical matters: 'It could find itself one day floundering about in the muddy waters of ethics (very muddy indeed, as far as I'm concerned).' He noted 'the debacle' on the *Christian Initiation*

---

[28] Interestingly, a similar proposal for the admission of the remarried to Holy Communion, in a papal apostolic exhortation, *Amoris Laetitia* in 2016, also divided the Roman Catholic Church.

report of 1972, saying that if the Standing Liturgical Advisory Commission of the Bench of Bishops and the Doctrinal Commission did not consult in future, great harm would ensue, as had happened in 1974.[29]

Thomas also recommended for appointment Barry Morgan and once again Cledan Mears. Mears was appointed, along with the first woman, Margaret Thrall, who lectured in the New Testament at University of Wales, Bangor. She was balanced by the presence of the strongly traditionalist John Hughes, the new principal of St Michael's College, who took the college back to its original, very catholic roots. Elwyn Roberts was the chair, and D. P. Davies the secretary. Mears, however, resigned the next year, when he was made bishop of Bangor in 1982. The representation of Evangelicals was once again in doubt. Barry Morgan, then warden of the Church Hostel in Bangor, replaced Mears. Much of the work of the new commission was on ecumenical matters, such as ecumenism in Wales, the reports of the Anglican–Roman Catholic International Commission (ARCIC), and dialogue with the Reformed Churches, Lutherans and the Orthodox. However, in 1983 Bishop Cledan asked the commission to look at the meaning of 'blessing' in marriage. Roman Catholic deacons were now empowered to bless marriages, and Mears felt that the Church in Wales should explore the idea. Mears had long been in dialogue with Roman Catholics on behalf of the Church in Wales. Morgan wrote a subsequent paper on the topic in 1984.[30]

D. P. Davies had become the chair in 1985, and John Rowlands, who was sub-warden at St Michael's College, eventually became secretary. It was as a result of his idea that the commission began to meet residentially at St Michael's College. A new tranche of members joined the commission. Donald Allchin and Rowan Williams were both at Oxford University, but that was not a problem. Another Welshman who was appointed, also teaching in England like Rowan Williams, this time at Trinity College, Bristol, was the Evangelical Gerry Angel. Hughes left, becoming bishop of Kensington. Cledan Mears took up the role of being the link bishop to the commission, and when D. P. Davies resigned, Morgan became the chair. He was by now archdeacon of Meirionnydd. Another Bangor theologian, Gareth Lloyd Jones, an Old Testament

---

[29] SDC File, 3 November 1980, Thomas to Williams.
[30] SDC File, 1984.

scholar, also joined.[31] Morgan wished to see the remarriage of divorced people in church.[32]

The Anglican Communion had produced a report, chaired by Archbishop Robert Eames of Ireland, on *Communion and Women in the Episcopate* (1989) and Angel and Allchin wrote a response. Allchin also wrote a paper justifying the remarriage of divorced in church, using a specially constructed service. The contrast with Wood's 1974 report, which ruled that out absolutely, was very stark. Davies convened a special group of doctors and theologians looking at the ministry of healing, including exorcism, for the bishops. Morgan wrote another paper on the sale of church buildings and schools at the request of the bishops, but the main underlying topic was again the ordination of women. In 1980, the Church in Wales had ordained a number of women deacons, some of whom were deaconesses, and some ordinands, but took no further action for a long while. Now the commission once again looked at the topic, with Thomas writing a minority report. However, after the debate in the Governing Body in 1990 on the ordination of women, where the commission's report was critically examined, the commission no longer met for three years. The time was not right for a re-examination of the nature of ordained ministry.[33]

The third commission began in 1993. Rowan Williams, by then bishop of Monmouth, chaired the body. Barry Morgan had by now become bishop of Bangor, succeeding Mears, and so left the commission. The archbishop of Wales, Alwyn Rice Jones, Bishop of St Asaph, had definite ideas about the role the new commission should have: 'It should take a more active stance in guiding the Bench on current problems relating to society, Church, Culture and the whole question of politics and morality – things that affected the life and work of the church in general.' Rowan Williams wrote the new terms of reference: 'to undertake theological work that will inform and stimulate reflection in the life of the province ... to provide theological comments on ecumenical agreed statements'.[34] Bishop Rowan intended the commission to lift the tone

---

[31] SDC File, 1988.

[32] 'In the 1970s, the Church in Wales used to refuse even the Sacrament to divorced and re-married people ... our views have evolved and changed on a subject which Jesus pronounced very clearly. He had nothing to say about same-sex relationships': Archbishop Barry Morgan, 'Presidential Address to Governing Body', April 2014, www.churchinwales.org.uk/structure/bishops/sermons-and-addresses-archbishop-barry-morgan/presidential-address-governing-body-april-2014.

[33] SDC File, 1990.

[34] SDC File, 1993.

of theological thinking across Wales, and not simply in the Church in Wales. A novel idea was to appoint a current theology student, Jason Bray, then studying in Cambridge. For the first time there were many women. Margaret Thrall had retired, but four women now became members, two deacons and two lay women. Roger Brown, the historian of the evangelical movement in Wales, was also appointed. The day-to-day chairing was done by Huw Jones, assistant bishop in Bangor, and later bishop of St David's. Jenny Wigley remembers that Bishop Rowan ran the body like a seminar. Again, the focus was primarily ecumenical, leading up to the proposal to create an ecumenical bishop in Wales. This was very much one of Bishop Rowan's ideas, but it was rejected by Governing Body in 2002. Some felt that it compromised the Anglican belief in the historic episcopate as the essence of the Church's ministry.[35]

The debates on the ordination of women – in which arguments for their ordination to the priesthood were rejected in 1994, but accepted in July 1996 – did not produce any new reports from the commission. It is unclear why the Doctrinal Commission did not produce any more reports. Instead, the literature came from a body called Women Priests for Wales. Their two reports, *Face the Facts: Women Who Wait,* and *Face the Facts: The Time Is Now*, were met by reports from the ultra-catholic wing of the Church in Wales, sometimes called the 'traditionalists' – but this time the momentum was with the reformers. There was great division as to whether the ordination of women to the priesthood would change the nature of this ministry, and the arguments on the New Testament and early church evidence were fiercely debated. By a single vote in the Order of Clergy, the two-thirds majority was reached to allow the bill to pass (85–40). David Thomas was appointed to be provincial assistant bishop to have pastoral oversight of those opposed to the change. Women were ordained to the priesthood in January 1997. Bishop Thomas saw his role as preserving the existence and integrity of those who remained fiercely opposed on doctrinal grounds.

Suspension and Rebirth of the Doctrinal Commission 2000–2018

In 2000, once again, the Doctrinal Commission was stood down, this time for nine years. There was no desire by the bishops for it to become

---

[35] R. Shortt, *Rowan's Rule: The Biography of the Archbishop* (London: Hodder and Stoughton, 2008), 202–3.

a permanent feature of the Church in Wales. During the period 2000–9, the Church in Wales produced reports on *The Ordination of Women to the Episcopate*, and *The Church and Homosexuality* under the series *Theology Wales*. These were not official Doctrinal Commission reports, but were produced by particular individuals, such as Jenny Wigley and Raymond Bailey, at the request of the bishops and sent to all members of Governing Body. They brought together different points of view. The one on homosexuality (2004), edited by Jenny Wigley, who had been a member of the 1993 Doctrinal Commission, had a wide range of articles. Archbishop Barry Morgan's September 2003 presidential address to Governing Body set the tone. D. P. Davies and Robert Paterson examined Scripture. Will Strange, as a conservative Evangelical, argued against any change, while other articles examined how Anglican identities, pastoral care and moral theology should be undertaken. It was published just before the Windsor Report of the Anglican Communion in 2004.

The report on women and the episcopate in 2006 was edited by Raymond Bayley, and contained two chapters by women – Mary Stallard and Joanna Penberthy (later to be the first woman bishop in Wales) – and two chapters which opposed the development. One was by Bishop David Thomas and the other by Peter Russell Jones. It was a response to the bishops' decision to bring a bill to the Governing Body to allow women to be ordained to the episcopate. That bill failed in the Order of Clergy in 2008, but a second attempt passed in 2013. There are now three women bishops in Wales, Joanna Penberthy, June Osborne and Cherry Vann.

The Doctrinal Commission was revived by the bishops in 2009, for the fourth time, nine years after the previous one had met. Simon Oliver was the chair, teaching at Lampeter. Matthew Hill was the secretary. All the members were new and included three women. Peter Sedgwick and John Holdsworth, as present and past principals of St Michael's College, were later appointed. Oliver was the only university academic, and he later moved to Nottingham. The main conservative Evangelical was Will Strange, although others would describe themselves as 'open Evangelicals'. In 2013 Oliver resigned as chair. Sedgwick chaired it for three more years, being succeeded as chair first by Ainsley Griffiths and then by Mark Clavier of Brecon Cathedral, who had taught at St Michael's College and St Stephen's House, Oxford. In 2016 St Michael's College closed, and was replaced by St Padarn's Institute. In 2018 Ainsley Griffiths became the first full-time director of faith, order and unity, responsible for all work relating to doctrine and theological reflection, liturgy, and ecumenical and interfaith relations.

As well as offering a response to ecumenical texts, there were three main topics which occupied the commission from 2009 to the present. One was a return to the issue of initiation, this time linking baptism to the reception of the Eucharist, without the need for confirmation. That became a rite on its own, and not a gateway to the Eucharist: 'Baptism is the complete rite of Christian initiation.'[36] Unlike the 1972 report, this one was both accepted by the bishops and implemented. It was not, however, received without criticism, which was expressed forcefully in Governing Body. This criticism was primarily for pastoral reasons, although some speakers from the catholic wing argued for the gift of the Holy Spirit explicitly in confirmation.

The second item was the issue of sexuality. There were two responses by the commission to this. The first in 2013 went to the bishops alone, and considered the issue of same-sex blessings. It rejected the idea of blessing civil partnerships, because the Church in Wales was not united on this matter, and civil partnerships were a legal and rights-based approach. The second response was the result of a year-long considera-tion of the issue. Papers discussing various views were presented and published on the Church in Wales' website. The final report in 2014, *The Church in Wales and Same-Sex Partnerships*, went to the bishops, and was debated in the Governing Body. It received wide publicity. It set out three options: the status quo; blessing of relationships; full and equal marriage. In the debate, there was no vote, but the report was well received. In 2018, a secret ballot in the Governing Body voted in favour of the pastoral need to make provision for those in such relationships. The bishops did not vote, but took note of the decision.

The third issue returns us to 'the doctrine of the Church'. From 2015 the commission was asked to look at ministry in its fullest expression, including all aspects of publicly recognised ministry. The bishops were implementing the policy of introducing Ministry Areas, whereby parishes were grouped together, and in which both lay and clerical ministry could be exercised. The bishops have requested a theological justification of the move away from the position where there was one priest in charge of a parish, to the new grouping of parishes. The doctrinal

---

[36] A consideration of issues relating to the regularisation of the admission of baptised children to Holy Communion before Confirmation in the Church in Wales by its Doctrinal Commission, 2014.

issue comes back again to the understanding of the ministry of the Church.

Conclusion

The doctrine of the Church in Wales has changed greatly since 1920, although the historic formularies have stayed in place. For the first fifty years it was a catholic, and fairly conservative, interpretation of the Anglican tradition it inherited in 1920. There were no intellectual giants, but when a Doctrinal Commission was established in 1969 there were enough Anglicans teaching theology at the university colleges at Lampeter and Bangor, along with St Michael's College, Llandaff, to make staffing it relatively straightforward. Other parish priests had studied and published doctrinal works on Christology and the ministry at a high level.

This chapter has shown how the resurgence of evangelicalism also began in the 1960s and has continued apace, to the point where many ordinands, perhaps even a majority, now come from that tradition.[37] This is a dramatic change, which will affect the doctrinal stance of the Church in Wales in decades to come. The evangelical tradition struggled, however, to produce those who were highly accomplished in theology. Cledan Mears was perhaps the only evangelical Anglican theologian living in Wales until the 1990s. However, the 1960s also saw the discovery of modern (essentially continental) theology in Wales, new patterns of behaviour and above all new attitudes to gender. By the end of the century, new attitudes to sexuality were also very evident. These changes were a challenge to the conservative, catholic inheritance of the Church in Wales, but also to the evangelical tradition. The controversies about the ordination of women to the priesthood and the episcopate are now largely a thing of the past. The controversy about sexuality, however, shows no sign of abating.

Nor is it clear how much the Church in Wales wishes to value its Anglican heritage, in terms of past theologians. Few clergy or laity would engage much with classical Anglican writers from the Reformation, English or Welsh. Archbishop Barry Morgan's presidential address to the September 2003 Governing Body, on the topic of same-sex relations, referred to 'The Nature of Anglicanism'. He said: 'The Anglican Church has from its inception been a broad and comprehensive church ...

---

[37] D. C. Jones, 'Evangelical Resurgence', 245.

a church which ... is not too anxious about pinning people down too precisely ... we have to live with differences of viewpoints on a whole range of moral issues.'[38] Morgan was arguing for a broad and loose definition of belief, which in turn would allow an equally broad toleration of different positions on moral issues. This appeal to historical relativism is now made by many bishops, and those in authority, and it has meant that it has become increasingly difficult in the Church in Wales to speak of an 'Anglican tradition' as guiding the mind of the Church. Anglicanism increasingly refers only to the empirical reality of a particular province of the Anglican Communion. The appeal to the historic formularies of the Church of England which the Governing Body reaffirmed in 1918 has now passed into history for many clergy and laity.

So, it is not surprising that the Doctrinal Commission has passed in and out of existence on many occasions in the fifty years of its short life. It has been welcomed for its comments on ecumenical texts, especially international bilateral and multilateral texts such as ARCIC, and those agreed with Protestant churches. It has found the going harder in other areas. The 1972 report on *Christian Initiation* and the reports on women had a mixed reception. Though the 1974 report on the remarriage of the divorced was not a Doctrinal Commission report, it was contradicted by a report written by Allchin twenty years later in 1994, which offered justification for a policy of remarrying divorced people in church. Sometimes the Bench of Bishops has preferred to commission its own series of reports on theology, especially on women and sexuality, independent of the commission. The relationship between the commission, the bishops and the rest of the Church is a theme which surfaces again and again in the minutes of the Bench, and there was no answer given. The brilliance of Rowan Williams and Donald Allchin as outstanding Anglican theologians, who knew the Anglican tradition well, could sustain the commission for only so long.

There are few Anglicans teaching now at Bangor, Lampeter and Cardiff, and the departments of theology are much smaller anyway. The residential theological colleges have all closed. The need for an articulation of the Anglican tradition, in dialogue with the modern world and contemporary theologians, and alert to the importance of

---

[38] Archbishop Barry Morgan, 'Presidential Address to the Governing Body', September 2003, www.churchinwales.org.uk/structure/representative-body/publications/down loads/theology-wales-back-issues/theology-wales-the-church-and-homosexuality/presi dential-address-archbishop-barry-morgan/.

pastoral and spiritual need, remains crucial. The alternative is ecclesial pragmatism or a form of episcopal managerialism. There does not have to be a Doctrinal Commission, except to guide the bishops as they respond to ecumenical texts, and for the first fifty years of the life of the Church in Wales it did not exist. Its existence thereafter has been episodic. Yet, at its best it can enable the Church in Wales to express its faith in response to new challenges, beliefs and events, and once again to proclaim the Gospel.

10

The Liturgy of the Church

GREGORY K. CAMERON

The centenary of the disestablishment of the Church of England in Wales corresponds with a period of one hundred years which encompasses probably the most dramatic changes in the liturgies of the Christian churches: only the Reformation period of the sixteenth and seventeenth centuries would be comparable in the scope of revision and change. The liturgical world in which the Church in Wales moves as it approaches the centenary would be unrecognisable to Archbishop Alfred Edwards, its first archbishop. Even the Roman Catholic Church, which began the twentieth century with the uniform Tridentine Latin Mass of the Counter-Reformation firmly ensconced, overturned its liturgical stasis at the Second Vatican Council. For Anglicanism, the devolution of an imperial Church of England into the separate provinces of the Anglican Communion[1] necessitated the invention of indigenous versions of a Book of Common Prayer. This unleashed a tidal wave of global liturgical creativity in the twentieth century, as each province sought to enculturate its sixteenth-century inheritance in a post-colonial world: a tidal wave of change which in truth has not subsided to the present time.[2]

If these internal factors were not enough, over the century, the world has changed around the Church, and the decline of religious life within

[1] The history of the Anglican Communion is the history of the evolution of two independent streams of Anglican/Episcopal church life which joined together to form the Anglican Communion in the nineteenth century. One stream derives from the overseas expansion of the Church of England alongside the expansion of empire, and the other from the Episcopal Church of the United States, which was responsible for the presence of Anglicanism in large parts of Latin America and South East Asia. Both streams contributed 'provinces' to the worldwide Anglican Communion. For a fuller account, see G. K. Cameron, 'Locating the Anglican Communion in the History of Anglicanism', in I. S. Markham, J. B. Hawkins, J. Terry and L. N. Steffensen, eds., *The Wiley-Blackwell Companion to the Anglican Communion* (Chichester: Wiley-Blackwell, 2013), 3–14.

[2] For further information on enculturation in the Anglican Communion, see M. D. Chapman, S. Clarke and M. Percy, eds., *The Oxford Handbook of Anglican Studies* (Oxford: Oxford University Press, 2016).

the context of Western civilisation has also generated a complete re-evaluation of what the Church tries to do in worship. There has been a shift in the nature of worship from liturgy – the public 'work'[3] of the Church – as the classical exposition of timeless truths in the worship of a praiseworthy deity to the desire to provide a liturgy prioritising accessibility and relevance as the vehicle for proclaiming Gospel truth and inviting access to God in a world which has largely lost touch with the idea of divine transcendence.

The Church in Wales has been as vulnerable to these wider changes as any other religious community, and the history of its liturgical life reflects a twofold movement: a desire to enculturate Anglican worship in the Welsh context, and a wish to find a mode of liturgical worship which can support effective evangelism to a nation which, in common with the Western developed world, has been moving decisively away from its Christian heritage, at least in terms of active participation.

However, it would not be true to say that the province of the Church in Wales was born into a liturgical ice age in which nothing was changing. At disestablishment, the liturgy that the Church in Wales inherited from the Church of England was already in the closing stages of receiving a major makeover which had started in the nineteenth century. This shift in liturgical worship did not arise from changes to the liturgical text, however – the Book of Common Prayer 1662 was still regarded as the gold standard of Anglican liturgy – but the ceremonial of the liturgy had altered substantially with the impact of the Oxford Movement and accompanying ritualist controversy.

The Liturgical Inheritance

The eighteenth century saw Anglicanism settle into a fairly consistent Protestant or 'low-church' style of worship, in which the pulpit held central place, and liturgical garb was limited, outside the cathedrals at any rate, to the intermittent use of the surplice for clergy. Although the growth in literacy among the general population in the nineteenth century meant that large parts of the prayer book of 1662 could now be recited in unison, and no longer merely repeated line by line after the parson, there was still a sense that Anglican liturgy was dominated by the Word, by which is meant not just the proclamation of Scripture and

---

[3] From *leit-ergos*, Greek for 'public work'.

the centrality of preaching, but that it was accompanied with little display of symbolism and ceremonial.

That had changed with the Oxford Movement, which had sought to emphasise the continuity of Anglicanism with the medieval Church in England. It was a movement which had begun in ecclesiology and an understanding of the Church Catholic as a divinely instituted society in its own right which had come to fruition in a desire to readopt the ceremonial of the Church as it was before the Reformation. This chapter is not the place to rehearse the history of controversy over surpliced quires and the use of 'lights', incense and vestments – except perhaps to note that, by the beginning of the twentieth century, in many parts of the four Welsh dioceses, particularly in the newly built parish churches of the late nineteenth century, a moderately Catholic climate of worship had become widely accepted and practised, and the leadership of the Welsh dioceses tended to be comfortable with newly adopted Catholic ritual.

The second archbishop of Wales, C. A. H. Green, made this abundantly clear in his magisterial survey of the canonical life of the new province, *The Setting of the Constitution of the Church in Wales*, published in 1937,[4] when he addressed the liturgy of the new province. Green describes the 1662 Book of Common Prayer as prescribing 'nothing . . . beyond the least required for decency and order'.[5] This may have been a straightforward statement of the situation which had prevailed in the eighteenth century, but Green offers a radical reinterpretation of this to signify the rubrics of the prayer book as setting a minimum standard (a 'no less than') rather than a maximalist (a 'no more than') position. Green was not slow in noting with approval several practices and vestures as natural additions to a 'baseline' of liturgical ceremonial,[6] which, he argued, was legitimately open to be enhanced in several ways, despite such practices having been at the heart of the ritualist controversies a few decades earlier.

The liturgical life of the Church in Wales in the century to come, therefore, opened with an inheritance which was already operating in a changed context, as layers of Catholic ceremonial were applied lacquerlike to the classical texts of the prayer book. Broadly speaking, however, disestablishment was met with conservatism. Disestablishment had been

---

[4] C. A. H. Green, *The Setting of the Constitution of the Church in Wales* (London: Sweet & Maxwell, 1937).

[5] Ibid., 291, quoting Edmund Bishop in *Liturgica Historica* (Oxford: Oxford University Press, 1918) and 1 Cor. 14.40.

[6] Green, *The Setting of the Constitution of the Church in Wales*, 291ff.

unwelcome to the Welsh dioceses, and the early spirit of the newly minted province was largely to conserve its heritage from the Church of England. There was no desire to create a new Book of Common Prayer, beyond inserting those liturgical changes in texts which were required to conform to the provisions of the Welsh Church Act 1914, such as the removal of references to the monarch as supreme governor. If anything, it might be said that, while disestablishment had taken place, the liturgy was largely an assertion of establishment life, of business as usual. This attitude prevailed for much of the first half of the twentieth century and, even when liturgical reform began, the overall tone of worship was of an establishment kind – a fact distinctly asserted in the live television broadcast of the enthronement of John Morgan as archbishop of Wales in 1949,[7] in a ceremonial which had scarcely changed from that captured by the newsreels of Archbishop Edwards' enthronement in 1920.[8]

At disestablishment, the Church in Wales simply inherited the worship of the Church of England, as expressed in 1920. The new Constitution of the Church in Wales (Chapter II, section 30) 'required the Governing Body at its creation to accept the Rites, Ceremonies, and Formularies of the Church of England, as set forth in, or appended to, the Book of Common Prayer of the Church of England, save in so far as those Formularies were necessarily varied by the Passing of the Welsh Church Act 1914'.[9] The Church in Wales therefore inherited the Book of Common Prayer 1662 as its collected authoritative liturgical texts, together with their definitive Welsh translation of 1664. Given that disestablishment had been such an unwelcome development, it is not surprising that the first generation of leaders in the new province were keen to maintain the Book of Common Prayer as a mark of their Anglican identity,[10] and the same uniformity of use that had been required of clergy of the Church of England was now required by the Constitution of the Church in Wales.[11]

---

[7] See www.youtube.com/watch?v=M0FyVK2q3Qw.

[8] See www.library.wales/digital-exhibitions-space/digital-exhibitions/david-lloyd-george-film-clips/enthronement-of-the-first-archbishop-of-wales-1920/.

[9] Green, *The Setting of the Constitution of the Church in Wales*, 287.

[10] In September 1927, for example, a motion was actually passed in Governing Body proposing that the bishops consider revision of the prayer book. The bishops, however, took no action whatsoever on the motion.

[11] Constitution VII.61, and schedule: 'in Public Prayer and Administration of the Sacraments I will use the Form in the said Book prescribed, and none other, except so far as shall be ordered by lawful authority'.

Green, who had become first bishop of the newly created Diocese of Monmouth, foresaw minimal ongoing change in the liturgical provision of the Church in Wales, and described three areas in which this might occur. First, there might be need for 'improving the language or phraseology of any Ecclesiastical Rule or Formulary, whenever the strict or literal construction or interpretation thereof has created a situation or state of affairs incongruous with the general mind of the Church'.[12] The most obvious of these changes was the acknowledgment that the Welsh Church Act had effectively ended the royal supremacy, and this meant the slight reordering of the liturgy to reflect that fact. In Morning and Evening Prayer, the petitions for the monarch were placed later in the suffrages, and references to the monarch as supreme governor were excised. Secondly, Green also acknowledged that the variations introduced in the ecclesiastical law in the latter half of the nineteenth century had been received by the new province. Thus, the limited liturgical revision effected by the Act of Uniformity Amendment Act 1872, which allowed for shortened forms of Morning and Evening Prayer during the week, carried over into Welsh church law. Thirdly, but importantly, and arising from a very high view of episcopal authority, Green asserted the *ius liturgicum* of the bishop, which he defined as the authorisation of 'special services for special occasions'. Such services might include the consecration of buildings for worship, inductions and the like, while it fell to the archbishop of Wales, as successor to the archbishop of Canterbury in the province of Wales, to design services for 'National Occasions'.[13]

Nevertheless, the possibility of change to the rites of the Church in Wales was recognised by the Welsh Church Act itself.[14] As with everything else, the new province was empowered to do what it wished in the future. The first Constitution of the Church in Wales recognised that change might be necessary, and wisely included mechanisms for change, even while it adopted a conservative attitude.[15] The rites and ceremonies of the Church were placed in a special category, which required all bills to be introduced in the Governing Body by the bishops, and which were subject to the full rigours of bill procedure. This distinctive status in the legislative process is a complication which has not always been greeted with enthusiasm, given the extensive mechanisms which attach

---

[12] Green, *The Setting of the Constitution of the Church in Wales*, 288–9.
[13] Ibid., 14, 113–14.
[14] Welsh Church Act 1914, s. 3(2).
[15] Constitution II.34.

themselves in the Constitution to any such changes, making them long, laborious and time-consuming – but it does illustrate the seriousness and prominence with which the new Church in Wales regarded its liturgical provision.

At first, changes were slow. In 1922, when the Church of England adopted a new lectionary, the Church in Wales followed suit, mimicking English provision.[16] Where England led, Wales was still following. Indeed, so closely did the Church in Wales intend to tie itself to the traditions of establishment that it sought, and got, legislation to maintain its established position with regard to marriages and funerals.[17] Apart from obvious adjustment, it was, as far as possible, business as usual. More radical changes, such as a motion in the Governing Body in 1927 asking for a more thorough revision of the prayer book, were not well received.[18]

As the United Kingdom emerged from the Second World War, there was a feeling throughout society that a new world order was being established, and all institutions came in for an intense amount of self-scrutiny, measuring themselves against the brave new world to which those coming out from war aspired. The first major wave of liturgical reform was about to overtake the rites of the Welsh Church. The beginnings were tentative. In 1944, the Church in Wales began to assert its distinctive character and voice – and liturgical reform oriented towards celebrating its distinctly Welsh character began with the introduction of a supplement to the Calendar, which acknowledged Welsh saints: David, Asaph, Cadoc and Illtud were all given commemorations. These changes were so positively received that the possibilities of a more thorough liturgical reform began to take hold, and the Bench of Bishops appointed a Nation and Prayer Book Commission. This commission reported in 1949, recommending the appointment of a new Standing Liturgical Advisory Commission which came into being at the beginning of 1951: it was intended to oversee what became a first wave of liturgical reform. If liturgical change in the new province had begun conservatively following disestablishment, then, since the Second World War, it is possible to identify two major waves of liturgical reform: one which lasted from the

---

[16] E. Lewis, *Prayer Book Revision in the Church in Wales* (Penarth: Church in Wales Publications, 1958), 24.

[17] Welsh Church (Temporalities) Act 1919 and Welsh Church (Burial Grounds) Act 1945: see Chapter 11.

[18] E. Lewis, *Prayer Book Revision*, 25.

end of the war to the publication of the 1984 prayer book; and another from 1984 to the present day.[19]

Towards the 1984 Book of Common Prayer

As in so much of our history, what happens in the Church in Wales cannot be divorced from what is happening to its sister Church in England. As the Church of England moved out of the war, an emphasis on renewal tended to go hand in hand with a reconsideration of the claims of the Holy Eucharist to be at the heart of church life. The parish communion movement can probably be dated to the early decades of the twentieth century, but it received renewed impetus and force in the organised 'Parish and People Movement' which emerged after the war. It is not surprising that one of the first tasks that the new Standing Liturgical Advisory Commission was directed to tackle was the Holy Eucharist. With a process of revision for the liturgical texts came permission to experiment, and a new canon in 1956 prepared the way for recommended changes to be enacted in the Governing Body. This proposed experimental periods for new liturgies of up to ten years, to be authorised by any bishop within his diocese, during which the products of the Liturgical Commission could be put through their paces.

In 1966, the Bench of Bishops authorised the Liturgical Commission's proposals for a revised rite for the Holy Eucharist for experimental use, the so-called blue book.[20] The overall feel of the liturgical changes proposed was in line with a broadly Catholic character which now suited the temperament of the majority of clergy in the Church in Wales. The Cranmerian order of the 1662 Holy Communion liturgy was replaced by something which returned to the medieval ordering with an Introductory Rite, Confession and Gloria in Excelsis, followed by a Ministry of the Word, intercessions and Ministry of the Sacrament. In adopting such a model, the Church in Wales was at the forefront of liturgical revision in the Anglican Communion, going further than the changes which were

---

[19] For a brief overview of revisions to the Book of Common Prayer 1662, see R. Paterson, 'The Church in Wales', in C. Hefling and C. Shattuck, eds., *The Oxford Guide to the Book of Common Prayer: A Worldwide Survey* (Oxford: Oxford University Press, 2006), 426–30.

[20] This is an instance of a continuing convention in popular culture in the Church in Wales of naming its rites according to the colour of the cover of the published text. Hence, the first revision was the 'blue book', and the new Book of Common Prayer 1984 the 'green book'. The 'orange book', 'gold book' and 'red book' followed.

proposed in the Church of England's 'Series 2' which was promoted about the same time.[21]

The changes were not entirely well received by the Evangelicals of the province, who objected to the abbreviation of the confession, prayers for the dead in the intercessions, and a form of words included in the eucharistic prayer which implied eucharistic oblation. However, by and large, the blue book became an accepted feature of the life of the Church in Wales, and quickly established itself in the hearts of the worshippers, effectively becoming the standard rite until and beyond the time when it was incorporated into the Book of Common Prayer in 1984. Part of the reason for this is the care with which the rite was introduced, holding back from radical change in the use of language, and supporting its introduction with a national Liturgical Congress, and the brave decision to make pioneering use of new technology to introduce the new liturgy: film strips were produced to introduce and explain the new rite – in both high-church and low-church editions. A further factor was undoubtedly the user-friendly nature of the blue book: it was printed in a convenient and small-sized volume, which included the rite and the collects and readings under one cover.

The new eucharistic rite was supported by other work on initiation and burial, on the daily offices and the Ordinal, all taking their lead from revision in a moderately Catholic direction, but early enthusiasm seemed to turn into caution, as the ten-year experimental period extended to three decades. It is a pattern all too familiar in the Church in Wales, which is capable of taking great strides forward, and then holding its breath, while other Anglican provinces catch up and overtake.[22]

By the beginning of the 1980s, there was a feeling across the province sensing completion to all this liturgical reform, and a desire to consolidate the work of revision. The publication in the Church of England in 1980 of the Alternative Service Book was looked at with envious eyes

---

[21] Published from 1966 by the same consortium which has the right to publish the 1662 Book of Common Prayer, namely the Oxford and Cambridge University Presses, Eyre & Spottiswoode and the SPCK.

[22] It was a pattern replicated, for example, in the recognition of the ministry of women. The Church in Wales led the way among the Anglican Churches in Britain in ordaining women to the diaconate in 1980 (the third province in the Anglican Communion to do so), and then dallied until 1997 in permitting their ordination to the priesthood (see Chapter 7). Equally, it signed a Covenant for Union with four other denominations in Wales in 1975, placing itself at the forefront of ecumenical co-operation, but the United Church confidently anticipated before the end of the twentieth century remains a neglected aspiration (see Chapter 12).

since it offered a comprehensive suite of liturgies, even if the state of Welsh liturgical reform was, by this stage, beginning to look distinctly behind the times. The aim now was to bring all the fruits of experimentation together in the publication of a new set of definitive liturgies, and some senior clergy, including Frank Jenkins, Dean of Monmouth and then chair of the Liturgical Commission, particularly argued for a new single-volume Book of Common Prayer, in which all the rites and worship of the Church would be brought together under one cover.

Alas, it was not to be. The sheer exigencies of bringing together so many rites in bilingual format prohibited a one-volume format: the propers (those parts of the liturgy which relate to particular Sundays or saints' days) and the psalter alone ran to 600 pages. Eventually, the 1984 Book of Common Prayer was published in a series of four volumes: an English-only volume I, which contained those services and liturgical material which any parish church might expect to use in English on a Sunday (Holy Eucharist and Morning and Evening Prayer, together with the Calendar, framework lectionary, the propers and a psalter); a second volume containing the eucharistic rite, Calendar and propers bilingually; a third volume containing Morning and Evening Prayer, Calendar, lectionary, collects and the psalter bilingually; and finally a volume II, containing all the occasional rites and related material in bilingual format together with the Eucharistic Rite (Public and Private Baptism, Thanksgiving for the Birth or Adoption of a Child, the Catechism, Confirmation, Ordination, a table of Kindred and Affinity, Matrimony, Blessing of a Civil Marriage, a rite for the Ministry of Healing, and Burial).

However, even as the Governing Body exhausted itself between 1980 and 1984 with a line-by-line revision process, consigning the 1662/1664 Book of Common Prayer to the grave,[23] and replacing it with a new definitive prayer book, the writing was on the wall for the new publication. There had been little movement in the liturgical revisions proposed in thirty years: the liturgical world, if not the parishes, had moved on. No sooner had the new volumes been privately published (no commercial publisher could be persuaded to take the risk) than the inadequacies of the liturgies were exposed by clerics who demanded something more accessible, by liturgical scholars who were becoming more radical and

---

[23] As a liturgical text, the 1662/1664 Book of Common Prayer remains enshrined in the Constitution as one of the 'historic formularies' which constitute the doctrinal standards of Anglican faith for the Church in Wales.

creative in their approach, by congregations who expressed dissatisfaction at the lack of variety and, not least, by Welsh-speakers, for whom the Welsh language of the 1664 prayer book was even more outmoded than Cranmerian English.

Almost immediately the dam broke, and the Liturgical Commission and Bench of Bishops rushed out the publication of the 'orange book', authorised by the Governing Body in April 1984 as a further revision, *The Holy Eucharist in Modern Language*.[24] This proved to be an ill-conceived attempt to provide radically modern alternatives to meet the criticism that the 1984 eucharistic rite was already provoking. The orange book (now a rare collectors' edition) even contained a form for the celebration of the Holy Eucharist which was little more than seven headings, providing stage directions to the seven elements deemed integral to a proper celebration of the Eucharist.[25] Although the preface to the 1984 prayer book proclaimed that 'it remains the intention of the Church in Wales that there be one Use in this Province',[26] the cat was out of the bag, and pressure was building for a new wave of revisions.

Towards a Multiplicity of Forms of Service

It was also clear that the existing procedures for liturgical revision were not fit for use. Revision started with an overhaul of the legislative processes required, and a new set of protocols for liturgical revision was agreed by the Bench of Bishops in 1996. First of all, while bishops continued to authorise experimental periods for new liturgical material, these would be varied to include shorter periods. Secondly, an abbreviated legislative process was adopted which did not require the whole Governing Body to approve every comma of any new liturgy. Although this provision has not been uniformly applied since 1996, some liturgical legislation did not require a select committee or committee stage in the legislative process. Rather, there could be a continuous process of experimentation and revision, which would culminate in the presentation of a complete text to Governing Body for authorisation. Thirdly, future authorised liturgies would not replace existing provision, nor be incorporated into an Alternative Service Book, the route taken in England, but

---

[24] Church in Wales, *The Holy Eucharist in Modern Language* (Penarth: Church in Wales Publications, 1984).
[25] It survives in a little-used section of the 2004 'red book' publication: Church in Wales, *An Order for the Holy Eucharist* (Norwich: Canterbury Press, 2004), 145ff.
[26] BCP (1984), v.

would be additional rites added to the Book of Common Prayer,[27] providing the Church with a choice of traditional and contemporary language liturgies. By a strange quirk of compromise, even the 1662 Holy Communion rite was rescued from oblivion and allowed to be used.[28] Finally, implicit consent was given acknowledging that the bishops retained sufficient of the *ius liturgicum* to be able to issue supplementary material on their own authority, not only issuing experimental rites, but also authorising the production of seasonal and occasional material. This new climate bore fruit in 1990 with the approval of a new rite of initiation, a new lectionary based on the idea of a three-year cycle of readings, complemented by a new Calendar, and set of collects (or prayers for the day). This was quickly followed by a Service of Compline (or Night Prayer) and a rite for Holy Communion outside the Celebration of the Eucharist.

A major initiative was to produce a modern eucharistic rite which incorporated the best of recent liturgical scholarship and creativity, and which had a more contemporary feel. In 1994, as the ten-year period for the orange book finally expired, a new experimental rite developed by the Liturgical Commission – the 'gold book' – was published, which evolved in time into the 2004 'red book', incorporating an enriched version of eucharistic liturgy into the Book of Common Prayer.[29] In a nod to entrenched parish liturgical conservatism, the red book also included the 1984 rite, even though there remain to this day redoubtable church fortresses where the 1984 'green books' have not yet cracked their spines or dog-eared their pages sufficiently for church councils to invest in new liturgical volumes.

The 2004 rite took seriously the need for diversity and for the introduction of the congregation to the wider aspects of faith by offering differing emphases for the liturgical seasons. The rite incorporated a number of alternatives, such as allowing the penitential rite to take place at the opening of the service or before the Ministry of the Sacrament, together with enhanced alternatives in the appendices. No fewer than seven eucharistic prayers are included, one drawing on the

---

[27] Today, the phrase 'the 1984 Book of Common Prayer' refers only to the texts incorporated in that volume; the 'Book of Common Prayer' is no longer dated, as it is presently a compilation of texts of different vintages.

[28] Canon 17-9-1981: it is not unlawful to use the 1662 service of Holy Communion and its Welsh versions with such variations permitted by the Ordinary as have been customary in the Church in Wales.

[29] Church in Wales, *An Order for the Holy Eucharist*.

liturgy of the Scottish Episcopal Church, and others contrasting in their use of congregational responses, and in the placing of the Sanctus and Epiclesis. In terms of theology, the Liturgical Commission was firmly of the view that the whole of the eucharistic prayer is consecratory, and not just the anaphora or epiclesis.[30] There was also a conscious seeking of a more poetic style, so that modern language could not be accused of being pedestrian, and two of the eucharistic prayers were deliberately designed to be open to varying age ranges of children. These prayers have come into increasing significance in recent years, given the 2016 decision of the Bench of Bishops to admit all the baptised, regardless of age, to Holy Communion (see Chapter 11).

If there is to be any criticism, it is that, although the rite is fully bilingual, little if any of the rite was composed in Welsh and then translated into English. This results in translations into Welsh which are less authentically idiomatic, although the Church in Wales was blessed during this period with an outstanding liturgical and Welsh-language scholar in the Revd Gwynn ap Gwilym, a chaired bard[31] who staffed the Liturgical Commission, and who undertook much of the liturgical translation until his untimely death in 2016. One of his outstanding achievements was the composition of a modern Welsh metrical translation of the Psalms, *Salmau Cân Newydd*. With the 2004 rite, a new measure of liturgical stability was introduced, and the rite, in Welsh and English, seems to be well established and received.

In 1992, a modern form of Morning and Evening Prayer was authorised for experimental use, coming to fruition in 2009, when it was incorporated into the ever-expanding Book of Common Prayer. However, if the 1984 prayer book had been overtaken by liturgical advancement at its publication, this time round, the liturgy of the Church in Wales was in danger of being overtaken once again, not by liturgical innovation, but by the technology through which it was communicated.

Growing Diversity in a Technological Age

The vast array of alternative and seasonal material put into the expanded Morning and Evening Prayer resources with the intention of enlivening and

---

[30] The anaphora is that part of the eucharistic prayer which includes the recital of the actions of Christ at the Last Supper, and the epiclesis is that part of it which invokes the action of the Holy Spirit in sanctifying the gifts.

[31] The Chair is the highest prize at the National Eisteddfod (an annual competitive Festival of the Arts) for the best poem in traditional strict metres.

enriching worship, generated a single published volume which was inoperable without a large arsenal of ribbons and bookmarks, and almost certainly inaccessible to the average lay user. At the same time, the advent of smartphones and apps meant that fully customised liturgies of prayer for the day were now available for instant download from the Church of England. The sheer accessibility of this resource from another province has probably eclipsed any hope that the Church in Wales' own *Daily Prayer*,[32] which retails at a weighty price, could take root as the staple diet of weekday, or even Sunday, prayer among the majority of clergy and laity. The Church in Wales is fighting back with the development of downloadable seasonal booklets, which are tailored towards congregational use, and which are likely to become available in the course of 2019.[33]

If the printing press had enabled liturgical books of common prayer to be placed into the hands of congregations in the sixteenth century, then technology now introduced a multitude of ways of presenting and displaying liturgy in the twenty-first. The Church in Wales is still coming to terms with the revolution that the internet and wi-fi technology will impose upon the worship of the Church. Many of those ordained in the 1980s will remember with nostalgia, but without regret, the difficulty of typing up and reproducing orders of service when they were newly ordained. Now, after forty minutes on the internet and with the use of a word processor, fully customised and beautifully presented liturgies can be produced and photocopied to the highest standards of full-colour printed material and placed in the hands of the average Sunday congregation. Even so, the tide of change is forever quickening, and environmental concerns may yet put paid to all forms of paper-based liturgies. The ability to present a liturgy in the form of a computerised projection of slides gives total flexibility, so that each occasion of worship can be resourced by liturgy tailored to that specific event without the need for any printing at all.

The impact of these changes is yet to be absorbed by the Church in Wales. At the beginning of its first disestablished century, the Church in Wales required a standard printed volume that could be put into the hands of every single one of its worshippers. Such simple standardisation and uniformity are profoundly challenged in a world where every cleric has the technical resources to produce a different liturgy for every service and every possible combination of worshippers in church.

---

[32] Church in Wales, *Daily Prayer* (Norwich: Canterbury Press, 2010).
[33] Work is currently being done to provide the material online.

For its part, the Bench of Bishops appears to have recognised this need and extended its use of the *ius liturgicum* to authorise a wide variety of supplemental texts. In the first two decades of this century, the Liturgical Commission has undertaken at the request of the Bench the development of three sets of material for 'Times and Seasons'. This material aims to supplement the main eucharistic or Morning and Evening Prayer services with a wealth of material that can enhance and extend the main Sunday liturgy by introducing short ceremonial material such as the lighting and blessing of candles, specific penitential rites, and special prefaces and prayers which acknowledge the specific nature of the season, whether Advent, Lent or Easter.

The first cycle of material covers the period Advent to Candlemas, that is, from the preparation for Christmas to the presentation of Christ in the Temple on the fortieth day after his birth – what might be termed the Nativity cycle. This includes ceremonies probably already familiar to Church in Wales worshippers from other sources, such as the lighting of special candles for the four Sundays of Advent, attached to specific Advent themes, culminating with the blessing of the fifth candle and the Christmas crib on Christmas Day. There follows material for the Epiphany, mainly as part of Church ceremonial, but also some material (such as the Epiphany blessing of the lintel of a home) which is oriented towards family and domestic liturgy and prayer. These ceremonies are intended to emphasise by liturgical action the meaning and symbolism of the season for which they have been prepared, and so to call people into a closer relationship with the Christ who stands at the centre of our liturgy.

The second cycle of material covers the period from Lent until Pentecost, namely the Passion cycle. While the first half of this material calls people to a deeper observance of Lenten discipline as a means of deepening faith, the second half of the material concentrates on the celebration of the Resurrection and the living Christ as Saviour and Lord. A third cycle is in preparation, as of February 2019, to complete the Church year by addressing the Trinity to Kingdom seasons, while a fourth may go on to tackle the various feast and saints' days worthy of material, but not included in the main three liturgical cycles of liturgical provision.

Ancient and Modern: The Shape of Things to Come

As it approaches its centenary, the Church in Wales faces the future with a number of cross-currents playing around its feet. On the one hand, it has faced enormous decline, and the Church today regularly attracts only about 2 per cent of the population of Wales to worship on any given Sunday. On the other hand, it has become Wales' most significant single Christian church, with more ordained ministers than every other Christian denomination in Wales put together. It retains more than 1,400 churches, some of which are located in Wales' smallest communities – from places such as Bala, where the local population are more than 80 per cent first-language Welsh-speakers, to places in the same diocese (of St Asaph), such as Hanmer near Wrexham, where Welsh would be regarded as a foreign language.

The context of worship in the twenty-first century is therefore very different from that at disestablishment, a context shaped by societal attitudes as much as by geographical or demographical factors. The learned hierarchies to which the members of the Church deferred in the first half of the twentieth century have been replaced by congregations used to participation. Congregations come to church already familiar with sophisticated channels for the delivery of variegated and personalised forms of news, education and entertainment. A single authoritative liturgical text is almost otiose amidst so much variety. The readiness of a congregation to remain passive recipients and auditors of liturgy is confined to those places, such as cathedrals, where highly professional and resourced worship can produce liturgy of a kind which competes with the musical and literary fare offered in the media and the arts.

Nonetheless, the Church in Wales has a duty to set before the people of Wales, Christianised or not, the transformative claims of faith and the place of liturgy in forming and sustaining faith. Liturgy is of vital importance to the life of a church. Classical Anglican theological exposition is to begin with Scripture and by quoting the Church Fathers. Not only does Scripture in many places exhort people to experience the life-giving exchange that results from the encounter with God in worship,[34] but the earliest teachers of the church were unanimous in their opinion that 'the glory of God is a human being who is fully alive, and the life of mankind is contained in the vision of God'.[35] This statement by the second-century saint, Irenaeus, summarises the intimate connection between salvation and a living relationship with God which is at the heart of Christian faith. Christians believe that in liturgy we are drawn into a relationship with the divine who transfigures and

---

[34] This chapter is not the place to make the scriptural argument for worship, but a good place to begin might be with the entire Book of Psalms. This ancient compilation of prayer and liturgy provides ample demonstration of the value the worshipper derives from entering into an active relationship with God based on worship.

[35] Irenaeus, *Against Heresies*, Book 4, Chapter 34.7.

empowers. Without a clear grasp of this fundamental dimension to Christian religion, worship cannot be understood. Since liturgy is the vehicle of public worship, it is therefore rightly at the centre of any church's life.

Not only this: the historic aphorism on which Anglicans draw to describe their worship is *lex orandi, lex credendi* – the law of what is to be prayed is the law of what is to be believed. This maxim, attributed to the fifth-century saint, Prosper of Aquitaine, has achieved almost dogmatic status to describe the significance Anglicans place upon their liturgy, not only as a vehicle for encountering God, but as the primary way in which our faith is articulated. To discuss the liturgy of the Church is therefore a discussion of the central dynamic of forming Christian discipleship in the Church, both by living encounter and didactic intent.

As every theological student has been taught, the liturgy is the public work of the Church, and the practical expression of the duty of each Christian. The Church in Wales is nothing if it is not the heir to this liturgical and worshipping tradition. Although the text of the Catechism of the Church in Wales[36] could be viewed as rather pedestrian (which actually befits its original purpose as instruction for young Christians), it clearly sets out for members of the Church in Wales this emphasis on the fundamental relationships between discipleship, worship, and the public liturgy of the Church:

> My duty to God is:
>
> i. to worship him as the only true God, to love, trust and obey;
> ii. to put nothing in the place of God;
> iii. to show God respect in thought, word and deed;
> iv. to keep Sunday as a time for corporate worship, learning and fellowship.[37]

This answer is further elaborated in the answers to two later questions (36 and 37):

What do you mean by worship?

> Worship is my response to God's love: first, by joining with others in the Church's corporate offering of prayer, celebration of the Sacraments and reading his holy Word; secondly, by acknowledging him as the Lord of my life, and by doing my work for his honour and glory.

---

[36] Church in Wales, *The Catechism: An Outline of the Faith, Church in Wales*; it is accessible at https://s3.amazonaws.com/cinw/wp-content/uploads/2013/07/Catechism-English-Text-A4.pdf.

[37] Question 30, as published ibid.

Why do we keep Sunday as the chief day of public worship?

> We keep Sunday as the chief day of public worship and as a weekly celebration of Easter Day, the day on which our Lord Jesus Christ rose from the dead.

The liturgy of the Church in Wales is therefore at the heart of what members are taught about the fundamentals of Christian discipleship. Liturgy is at the heart of its life and doctrine. It must retain a place, therefore, at the very centre of the Church's mission as it embarks upon its second hundred years.

Conclusion

The history outlined here illustrates quite clearly a journey from uniformity towards diversity. At disestablishment, there appears to have been no desire except that the liturgy as defined by the 1662/ 1664 Book of Common Prayer should continue as far as possible unaffected by disestablishment. In the years following the Second World War, the revision that was undertaken was largely conservative, and still aimed to maintain a single usage throughout the province. The year 1984 was both the apogee and the culmination of such a process, but almost as soon as the Welsh Church had a new Book of Common Prayer in that year, it decided against maintaining it as a single use, that is, as the use of only one liturgical text throughout the province. Today, it is believed that a rich and varied diet of liturgical observance is more likely to sustain faith and to teach it – and so variety is positively encouraged. Technology supports the ability of each church to have its own tailor-made liturgy, especially in the seasons and at festivals, and this is seen as a positive benefit. The old declaration 'to use only the forms of service authorised by lawful authority and none other' should not imply a rigid observance of a single use, but the ability to draw on an increasing body of varied liturgical material. Not only does the prayer book of the Church in Wales offer at least two different liturgies – a traditional and a contemporary – for each of the major acts of worship of the Church, but those acts are supplemented and enriched by a multiplicity of further optional texts and ceremonies.

At the same time, the 'tribal' nature into which Anglican worship can break down is beginning to blur. Evangelicals will maintain an emphasis on the proclamation of the Word of the Gospel, and of simplicity in ritual – but that does not preclude them calling upon and utilising the material produced in Times and Seasons. Catholic worship has altered, with more traditional forms of observance coexisting alongside modern Catholic and modified liturgical worship.

There is a danger in this that it can become a free-for-all, a pick-and-mix approach to liturgy – but such a movement itself is in keeping with the times, where context is privileged, and worshippers' needs prioritised. For such diversity to succeed, it must be balanced by a high degree of liturgical formation through the training of ministers, so that flexibility is marshalled by the discipline of good preparation, high standards of execution, and a clear orientation towards teaching and communicating the underlying message of new life in Christ. The emphasis should be on professionalism in balance with an acknowledgment that the liturgy is encounter, not performance, oriented towards God and not entertainment.

In part, variety also represents a growing realisation that the spirit of evangelism and worship does not consist in the words of the text, but in the vibrant interplay of text and action. The congregation is increasingly invited to take part in liturgy, by extending the use of versicle and response, by question and answer, by being invited to take the lead in some of the newer and less restricted liturgical actions. The century has, therefore, seen a movement from passivity to participation.

There is a third movement, which takes all that has been said above one step further, although it is probably the hardest to describe. Society at the time of disestablishment was, in the aftermath of the First World War, still highly stratified and regimented. A liturgy which was primarily led from the front and confined within strict criteria therefore met the spirit of the age. As the Church has become less representative of society as a whole, however, there is the need to affirm the Church as the place of the family of God, where all are gathered around the Lord's Table. It is a shift from formality to informality. Café Church and Messy Church are liturgical, but not in a way which the bishops of disestablishment would recognise. These forms of worship place the emphasis on the family of God being gathered together, with the liberty to relax into worship.

Some might argue that all this might lead to the danger that the baby is thrown out with the bathwater. A church which entertains is not necessarily a church which worships. While the Church in Wales has changed a great deal in its first century, it still exists in order to proclaim repentance and new life for those who turn to the fullness of redemption for those who believe and follow Jesus Christ. Familiarity must not eclipse mystery, and we need a liturgical economy in which old and new can coexist, everything done is done to approach the throne of God and communicate the Gospel, and in which the formula *lex orandi, lex credendi* still applies.

11

The Rites of Passage

CHARLOTTE WRIGHT

The so-called rites of passage – baptism, confirmation, Holy Communion, marriage and burial – are rarely addressed in the two volumes of the Constitution of the Church in Wales, including the canons.[1] Therefore, to find norms regulating the administration of these rites, it is necessary to turn to liturgical rubrics and other regulatory forms in the service books, to ecclesiastical soft law (in the forms of guidance and the like) and to the substantial body of pre-1920 ecclesiastical law which continues to apply to the Church in Wales unless and until altered by it.[2] Whilst baptism, confirmation and Holy Communion are not governed by state law, there is a significant body of civil law on marriage and burial. This is due to the fact that the Church in Wales has retained several vestiges of the established Church of England in relation to marriage and burial, rules which continue to apply to the Church in Wales as part of the law of the land. Accordingly, the State retains a hold over governance of these rites.

The Rite of Baptism

There have been very few changes to the regulation of baptism since disestablishment, and in particular to the requirements for an individual to qualify for baptism, and to those for a baptism to be validly administered. These requirements can be found in the Thirty-Nine Articles, the rubrics in liturgical texts, and case law. Baptism is treated in the Thirty-Nine Articles as a dominical sacrament. The Articles set out the traditional doctrine of the Church in Wales and were inherited by the Church at disestablishment. By baptism, 'the promises of forgiveness of sin, and of adoption to be the sons of God by the Holy Ghost, are visibly signed and sealed; Faith is confirmed,

---

[1] See www.churchinwales.org.uk/resources/constitution-handbooks/constitution-of-church-in-wales/.
[2] N. Doe, *The Law of the Church in Wales* (Cardiff: University of Wales Press, 2002), 232.

and Grace increased by virtue of prayer unto God' (Article 27). Historically, the Church in Wales taught that baptism was necessary for salvation.[3] The canon law of the Church recognises that all its members are 'members of Christ in virtue of their ... baptism'.[4] Thus baptism can be seen as the gateway to the Church.

There are three forms for the liturgical celebration of baptism: the public baptism of infants; the private baptism of infants; and the baptism of adults.[5] Furthermore, in order to be valid, baptism must be administered with water invoking the Trinity.[6] Case law has also determined that this is the essence of baptism.[7] The Book of Common Prayer 1984 provides, as to the administration of the water, that 'the priest pours water three times on [the candidate] or dips him three times in the water'.[8] However, in the General Notes to Services for Christian Initiation 2006, General Note 5 additionally states that 'a single administration is, however, lawful and valid'.[9] The priest also makes the sign of the cross on the candidate's forehead, although legally this does not add to the substance of the sacrament. If there is any doubt about the administration of baptism, this must be referred to the bishop for determination, who may refer the case to the archbishop if there is still any doubt.[10] Moreover, no minister may refuse or delay to baptise any child brought to the church after convenient warning.[11] These principles on the rite of baptism are much the same as they applied before 1920 to the Church of England in Wales,[12] and they are wholly consistent with the principles of canon law common to Anglican churches.[13]

---

[3] BCP (1984), 654, 660: 'No one can enter into the kingdom of God unless he is born again of water and of the Holy Spirit.'

[4] See Canon 1-5-1974, First Schedule, 4(a).

[5] BCP (1984), 653; Services for Christian Initiation (2006), 15, 45, and 59: however, in this service the final version is headed 'An order for baptism with confirmation'.

[6] BCP (1984), 661: 'N, I baptize you in the Name of the Father, and of the Son, and of the Holy Spirit, Amen'; Services for Christian Initiation (2006), 9 General Note 5, and 33.

[7] *Kemp v Wickes* (1809) 3 Phillim. 264.

[8] BCP (1984), 661: infants; 677: adults.

[9] Christian Initiation (2006), 9, General Note 5.

[10] BCP (1984), vi.

[11] Canons Ecclesiastical 1603, Canon 68: this still applies to the Church in Wales.

[12] Compare e.g. R. Phillimore, *Ecclesiastical Law* (London: Sweet & Maxwell, 2nd ed., 1895), 486–509, and C. A. H. Green, *The Setting of the Constitution of the Church in Wales* (London: Sweet & Maxwell, 1937), 65f.

[13] Anglican Communion Legal Advisers Network, *The Principles of Canon Law Common to the Churches of the Anglican Communion* (London: Anglican Communion Office, 2008), Principles 61–4.

The Rite of Confirmation

The regulation of confirmation and the requirements for candidates presented for confirmation have changed relatively little since disestablishment. In accordance with the doctrine of the Church in Wales, as received at disestablishment, confirmation is 'not to be counted for [a sacrament] of the Gospel' because it has 'not any visible sign or ceremony ordained of God'.[14] Under the teaching of the Church in Wales, confirmation is 'the rite by which we make a mature expression of the commitment to Christ made at Baptism, and receive the strength of the Holy Spirit through prayer and the laying on of hands by a bishop'; confirmation seals baptism, and is considered sacramental.[15] Thus, historically, it was following confirmation that an individual was entitled to receive Holy Communion. However, as a result of a 2016 decision of the Bench of Bishops, this requirement has changed – potentially, this alters the status of confirmation in the future (see below).

Canonically, confirmation is administered by the bishop laying hands on, praying over and blessing the candidate.[16] Only a bishop may confirm. There are two approaches to the requirements of candidates wishing to be confirmed.[17] According to the Catechism, to be confirmed a candidate must be baptised, sufficiently instructed in the Christian faith, penitent for their sins, and ready to confess Christ as Saviour and obey him as Lord.[18] However, under norms in the Book of Common Prayer 1984, to be confirmed, an individual must have been baptised, have worshipped regularly with the Church, have been instructed in the Catechism and be able to say the Creed, the Lord's Prayer and the Ten Commandments.[19] It is the second approach which most resembles the pre-1920 position.[20] Nevertheless, both seem consistent with the principles of Anglican canon law.[21]

---

[14] Thirty-Nine Articles, Article 25.
[15] BCP (1984), 698 (Catechism).
[16] Canons Ecclesiastical 1603, Canon 60.
[17] See Doe, *The Law of the Church in Wales*, 242.
[18] BCP (1984), 699 (Catechism).
[19] BCP (1984), 704 (Confirmation).
[20] See introduction to the confirmation service in the BCP 1662: 'none hereafter shall be confirmed but such as can say the Creed, the Lord's Prayer, and the Ten Commandments; and can also answer to such other Questions, as in the short Catechism are contained'.
[21] Anglican Communion Legal Advisers Network, *The Principles of Canon Law Common to the Churches of the Anglican Communion* (2008), Principle 65.

The Rite of Holy Communion

According to the doctrine of the Church in Wales, Holy Communion is a sacrament instituted by Christ.[22] At present, an individual must have communicant status to be eligible for ordination and for various offices in the Church.[23] In 1920, the Church in Wales inherited the rule in the Book of Common Prayer 1662 on admission to Holy Communion.[24] As a mark of its commitment to continuity, the Book of Common Prayer 1984 provided, similarly, that: 'except with the permission of the Bishop, no one shall receive Holy Communion until he is confirmed, or is ready and desirous to be confirmed'.[25] Nevertheless, sixteen years later, in 2001, the Bench of Bishops issued guidelines for a 'new practice' of admitting unconfirmed baptised children to Holy Communion, if a proposal to do so had 'received appropriate support from the clergy, [Parochial Church Council], and parishioners'. Their admission should be seen as part of the parish's 'whole programme for nurture in the Christian faith', and an appropriate period of preparation for the children and parents/sponsors should precede it. Also, children were to be admitted in the expectation that they would wish to seek confirmation in due course. Before a scheme could be introduced in a parish, it was desirable that as many parishioners as possible understood the reasons for this new practice. If a child communicant moved to a new area, then the child 'should be received as a communicant in the new parish and communicant status should not be withdrawn'.[26] This was the regulatory response to the position of the Doctrinal Commission in 1972.[27]

Then, in September 2016, the Bench of Bishops issued a pastoral letter. It stated that from the First Sunday of Advent, 27 November 2016, the bishops permitted 'all those who are baptised in water and in the name of the Holy Trinity, to receive Holy Communion at the Celebration of the Holy Eucharist within their dioceses and jurisdictions'. Moreover: 'None is required to receive, but no barrier should be erected to prevent all the

---

[22] Thirty-Nine Articles, Articles 25, 28.

[23] Constitution I.II.7, Definitions: 'communicant' means 'a person who has lawfully received Holy Communion in the Church in Wales or some Church in Communion with it and is entitled to receive communion in the Church in Wales'. But see below for changes.

[24] BCP 1662 (300): 'there shall none be admitted to the Holy Communion, until such time as he be confirmed, or ready and desirous to be confirmed'.

[25] BCP (1984), 704; 6.

[26] Church in Wales, Bench of Bishops, 'Children and Holy Communion: Guidelines and Resources for Parishes' (2001), 5.

[27] See Chapter 9.

baptised from making their Communion, other than that which is required by civil law.'[28] This was to be implemented in all parishes by Advent 2017, but this was extended to Advent 2018 following concerns expressed in Governing Body. In terms of theology, the pastoral letter states: 'In the Church today, there are many who believe that the witness of the Church to Jesus Christ, and the process of nurturing children and young people in the Christian faith, would be immeasurably strengthened by recovering this earliest symbolism. Baptism alone should be seen as the gateway into participation in the life of the Church, including admission to the Sacrament of Holy Communion.' Also: 'in conjunction with advice from the Doctrinal Commission of the Church in Wales, and from the Governing Body, the Bench of Bishops wishes now to readopt the practice of the early Church with respect to admission to Holy Communion. It is our conviction that all the baptised, *by virtue of their Baptism alone* [italics added], are full members of the Body of Christ and qualified to receive Holy Communion.'[29]

It appears that the driving force behind the initiative was the desire to 'strengthen ministry to children and young people in particular'.[30] In turn, confirmation will become 'the service for those who wish to affirm their commitment to the Church or be commissioned for service within it'.[31] Indeed, the bishops have commented that this policy will lead to a strengthened understanding of confirmation: 'it will be no longer the gateway to Communion, but take its proper place in the sacramental acts of the Church as a channel of God's grace, affirming disciples of their place in the fellowship of the Church and commissioning them for service in the Church and world'. Whilst the bishops state that confirmation will remain within the rites of passage, will continue to provide the opportunity to affirm the faith, and will remain a requirement for those wishing to be ordained or hold certain offices in the Church, as yet it is unclear what impact this change will have on the number of people seeking to be confirmed, the preparation of confirmation candidates, the requirements for those taking up certain offices in the Church (such as members of

---

[28] Church in Wales, Bench of Bishops, 'A Pastoral Letter from the Bishops of the Church in Wales to All the Faithful Concerning Admission to Holy Communion' (September 2016), www.churchinwales.org.uk/news/2016/09/confirmation-no-longer-required-for-holy-communion-bishops-letter/.

[29] See ibid.

[30] Ibid.

[31] L. Chandler, 'Governing Body of the Church in Wales: April and September 2016', *Ecclesiastical Law Journal*, 19 (2017), 76.

CHAPTER 91.

An Act to terminate the establishment of the Church of England in Wales and Monmouthshire, and to make provision in respect of the Temporalities thereof, and for other purposes in connection with the matters aforesaid. [18th September 1914.]

BE it enacted by the King's most Excellent Majesty, by and with the advice and consent of the Commons, in this present Parliament assembled, in accordance with the provisions of the Parliament Act, 1911, and by authority of the same, as follows :

1 Welsh Church Act 1914 (4 & 5 Geo. V, c. 91): the Act which disestablished the Church of England in Wales and led to the foundation of the Church in Wales. Reproduced from Public General Acts 4 & 5 Geo. V, 1914, Eyre and Spottiswoode, Ltd., for Frederick Atterbury, Esq., C.B., King's Printer of Acts of Parliament.

Photo. H. J. Whitlock & Sons, Ltd.

2 The Convention of members of the Church of England in Wales, Cardiff, October 1917.
Reproduced from a photograph by H. J. Whitlock and Sons Ltd., published in the *Official Report of the Proceedings of the Convention of the Church in Wales Held at Cardiff*, 2–5 October 1917, Cardiff (Western Mail, 1917), with permission from the Western Mail.

3   The Royal Charter of the Representative Body of the Church in Wales, as reissued in 1954.
Reproduced, from its photograph archive, with the permission of the Representative Body of the Church in Wales.

4   John Sankey (1866–1948), brought up in Roath, Cardiff, the judge who drafted the Constitution of the Church in Wales and later became Lord Chancellor.
Reproduced with permission from D. T. W. Price, *A History of the Church in Wales in the Twentieth Century* (Penarth: Church in Wales Publications, 1990).

5 The Enthronement of the first Archbishop of Wales, Alfred George Edwards, on 1 June 1920 at St Asaph Cathedral.
Reproduced, from *The Church in Wales Today* (Penarth: Church in Wales Publications, 1990), with permission of the Representative Body of the Church in Wales.

6 Llandaff Cathedral is devastated by a bomb dropped during a Blitz raid which killed 167 people in Cardiff on the night of 2 January 1941.
Reproduced with the permission of Western Mail–Media Wales.

7   Cymry'r Groes (Welsh People of the Cross), National Pilgrimage to St David's in 1955, 'The Procession Assembles'.
Reproduced, with permission, from *The Church in Wales Quarterly* (Autumn 1955), the Youth and Adult Committee of the Provincial Council for Education of the Church in Wales, published by Llan and Welsh Church Press Co. Ltd., 1955.

8   New church building projects: St George's Church, Rhos-on-Sea, Diocese of St Asaph, opened in 1913 with a new tower completed, 1965.
Reproduced with permission from D. T. W. Price, *A History of the Church in Wales in the Twentieth Century* (Penarth: Church in Wales Publications, 1990).

Back Row, L-R   D.Neale, C.K.Clawson, J.T.Hughes, P.C.Titcombe, D.J.Lodge, J.D.E.Davies, W.D.A.Griffiths, *The Revd.* N.F.Gillman, R.A.Gordon, F.S.St.Amour, I.M.Liversuch, P.M.Winchester, L.D.Homer, B.P.Luck.
Middle Row, L-R M.V.Jones, C.L.Bolton, R.N.Parry, D.Prys, C.H.Gibbs, J.F.Ward, M.Davies, R.E.Pain, M.J.Gollop, G.K.Cameron, R.Lloyd, H.S.Pennington, B.J.Lloyd.
Front Row, L-R   D.R.Rees, D.Roberts, V.F.Millgate, S.J.Bodycombe, J.H.L.Rowlands, *The Revd.* Dr.J.G.Hughes, *The Revd Canon* G.H.Watts, *The Revd.* R.Bewley, *The Revd.* B.D.Witt, R.A.Hemmings, M.J.Gill, K.P.Vinsel.
                 Senior Student *Director of Academic Studies* *Warden* *Old Testament Tutor* *Director of Pastoral Studies*

9 St Michael's College, Llandaff, students and staff, 1982–3, including three future bishops: back row, 6th from left, John D. E. Davies (Swansea and Brecon 2008–, and Archbishop of Wales 2017–); 2nd row, 4th from the right, Gregory K. Cameron (St Asaph 2009–); 2nd row, 6th from the right, Richard Pain (Monmouth 2013–9). Reproduced with permission of the Representative Body of the Church in Wales on behalf of St Michael's Theological College, Llandaff.

10 The Anglican Consultative Council of the worldwide Anglican Communion (ACC-8) is hosted for the first time by the Church in Wales, at Dyffryn Gardens, near Cardiff, in 1990.
Reproduced with permission of the Anglican Communion Office.

11 Bangor Cathedral, 11 January 1997, the ordination of the first women priests. Reproduced with permission from *Y Ddolen / Link Bangor Diocesan Magazine*.

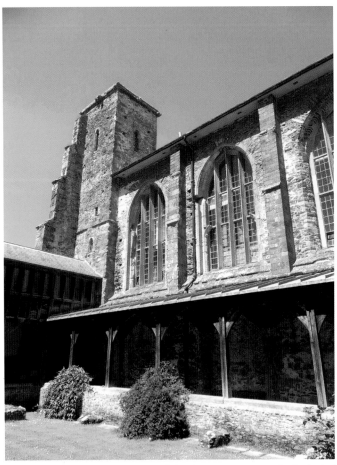

12 The reconstruction in 1998 of the cloisters at St David's Cathedral with its visitor centre, education suite and refectory, in continuity with the ancient monastic complex. Reproduced with the permission of Very Revd Dr Sarah Rowland Jones, Dean of St David's Cathedral.

13　Dr Rowan Williams, the Archbishop of Wales before his appointment as the 104th Archbishop of Canterbury in 2002.
Reproduced with the permission of the Representative Body of the Church in Wales.

14　2020 Vision/Golwg 2020, logo used at the time of the Church in Wales' *Review* (2012) - 'Serving community, inspiring people, transforming church'.
Reproduced with the permission of the Representative Body of the Church in Wales.

15   Presenting the Church in Wales' *Review* to Governing Body in 2012, Lord Richard
Harries of Pentregarth, former bishop of Oxford, chair (second from left), Professor
Charles Handy, formerly at the London Business School (far right), and Professor
Patricia Peattie (far left), former Chair of the Standing Committee of the Scottish
Episcopal Church, with the Archbishop of Wales, Barry Morgan.
Reproduced, from a photograph taken by the Venerable Philip Morris for Governing
Body *Highlights*, with permission of the Representative Body of the Church in Wales.

16   June Osborne is consecrated as the 72nd Bishop of Llandaff, the first woman to
hold the office, at Brecon Cathedral, 15 July 2017, pictured with Joanna Penberthy, the
first woman to be consecrated as a bishop (St David's) in the Church in Wales.
Left to right: Sarah Mullally (London); Karen Gorham (Sherborne); Kay Goldsworthy
(Archbishop of Perth, Province of Western Australia); June Osborne (Llandaff);
Katharine Jefferts Schori (former Presiding Bishop of The Episcopal Church (USA));
Joanna Penberthy (St Davids); Mary Gray-Reeves (El Camino Real, California).
Reproduced, from a photograph by Ritchie Craven, Church in Wales Publications
Manager, with permission of the Representative Body of the Church in Wales.

Governing Body) where eligibility is conferred from the individual's status as a communicant, or on the rite itself.

The bishops' pastoral letter also provides that although even the youngest of children are permitted to receive Holy Communion, restrictions imposed by civil law regarding receiving in both kinds (bread and wine) must be adhered to: therefore, giving alcohol to children under the age of five is not permitted, and parental permission is required before children over the age of five may receive in both kinds. The letter also requires parishes and clergy to establish records of what permissions are given, and communion in other cases has to be in one kind.[32]

Admitting children and young people to Holy Communion has been much debated elsewhere recently. For example, some Church of England dioceses also allow baptised but unconfirmed children, not yet ready and desirous to be confirmed, to be admitted.[33] Parishes wishing to adopt this approach must make an application to the bishop, to be considered on a case-by-case basis. Furthermore, before allowing a parish to take such steps, the bishop must be satisfied that the parish has made adequate provision for preparation and continuing nurture in the Christian life and will encourage any children admitted to Holy Communion to be confirmed at the appropriate time. In comparison, the policy adopted by the Church in Wales is such that admission to Holy Communion after baptism is to be offered by all churches throughout the province – and it appears that there are no checks in place to ensure adequate provision is in place in all parishes to nurture youngsters who wish to receive Holy Communion in the Christian life.[34] However, the new position in the Church in Wales is mirrored in the principles of canon law common to Anglican churches.[35]

The Rite of Confession

Whilst not commonly listed as a rite of passage, it is worth noting the development of norms on confession. The regulation of confession in the

---

[32] Church in Wales, Bench of Bishops, 'A Pastoral Letter'.

[33] Admission of Baptised Children to Holy Communion Regulations 2006.

[34] The bishops' pastoral letter states that there is no need to change the Constitution to bring about the changes. Furthermore, in stating that 'no barrier should be erected to prevent all the baptised from making their Communion, other than that which is required by civil law', the Bench imply that the 2001 guidelines have been superseded and no longer apply, but this is not made explicit in the pastoral letter.

[35] Anglican Communion Legal Advisers Network, *The Principles of Canon Law Common to the Churches of the Anglican Communion* (2008), Principle 68.

Church in Wales is minimal. The Church in Wales teaches that, through confession, those who are truly sorry for their sins and determined to renounce them for the future, having confessed their sins to God freely and fully in the presence of a priest, receive through the ministry of the priest the forgiveness of God.[36] Thus, the ministry of absolution can be exercised only by a priest or bishop, and it may be given generally, as in services at public worship,[37] or individually and privately.[38]

Some Anglican churches have an absolute prohibition against a priest disclosing information given during confession.[39] In some, this prohibition continues after the death of the penitent,[40] but in others disclosure is allowed with the consent of the penitent[41] or if, in the case of a 'grave offence', the minister is not satisfied that the penitent has reported the crime to the police.[42] In the Church in Wales, liturgical provisions state that the practice of confession operates 'under the seal of secrecy'.[43] In accordance with the pre-1920 ecclesiastical law (which continues to apply in the Church, unless amended): 'if any confess his secret and hidden sins to the Minister, for the unburdening of his conscience, and to receive spiritual consolation and ease of mind from him; we do not in any way bind the said Minister by this our Constitution, but do straitly charge and admonish him, that he do not at any time reveal and make known to any person whatsoever crime or offence so committed to his trust and secrecy (except they be such crimes as by the laws of this realm his own life may be called into question for concealing the same), under pain of irregularity'.[44] Norman Doe suggests, thus, that in the Welsh Church, the prohibition against disclosure is not absolute.[45] However, as no

---

[36] BCP (1984), 699 (Catechism), cf. opening notes of Holy Eucharist (2004), appendix ix.

[37] See BCP (1984), 5–6 (Holy Eucharist); 392 (Morning Prayer); 404 (Evening Prayer); and Holy Eucharist (2004), 24–5 (Holy Eucharist); Daily Prayer (2009), 20–1 (Morning Prayer – introduction option A); 46–7 (Evening Prayer).

[38] Holy Eucharist (2004), notes to appendix ix, 'The practice of private confession, made under the seal of secrecy . . . is open to all.'

[39] See, for example, the Episcopal Church (USA), Canon IV.19.27: 'no waiver by a penitent of the privilege which attaches to communications or disclosures made within the Rite of Reconciliation of a Penitent shall work to require any confessor to divulge anything pertaining to any such communications or disclosures, the secrecy of a confession being morally absolute as provided in the Book of Common Prayer'.

[40] Scottish Episcopal Church, Canon 29.2.

[41] Anglican Church of Australia, Canon 10 1992, 2 as amended by Canon 16, 2017.

[42] Anglican Church of Australia, Canon 10 1992, 2A(2) as amended by Canon 17, 2017.

[43] BCP (1984), 23.

[44] Canons Ecclesiastical 1603, Can 113.

[45] See Doe, The Law of the Church in Wales, 271.

crimes now carry the death penalty, the norm would seem to be redundant.

Today, however, the Clergy Handbook provides guidance on the seal of the confessional. As a general principle: 'there should be no disclosure of what is revealed when a person confesses to God in the presence of a priest ... This principle holds even after the death of the penitent. The priest may not refer to what has been learnt in confession, even to the penitent, unless explicitly permitted by the penitent. Some appropriate action of contrition and reparation may be required before absolution is given.'[46] Furthermore, a priest may withhold absolution. The Handbook continues that guidelines can be found in the forms of reconciliation appended to the two Orders for the Holy Eucharist, 1984 and 2004. However, there are two exceptions to the 'seal of the confessional'. The first is where abuse of children or vulnerable adults is admitted in the context of confession. In these circumstances, the priest should urge the person to admit his or her behaviour to the social services, 'and should also make this a condition of absolution, or withhold absolution until this evidence of repentance has been demonstrated'.[47] The second is that 'if a penitent's behaviour gravely threatens his or her own well-being or that of others, particularly children or vulnerable adults, the priest should insist upon action on the penitent's part'.[48]

Moreover, the Clergy Handbook notes that in civil law there is no absolute duty of confidentiality, and a court or the police may require disclosure. Furthermore, it states that there may be an 'over-riding duty to break confidence' where the safety of children or vulnerable adults is concerned. If a priest believes a penitent will give such information, 'it should be made clear to the penitent in advance, that disclosure may be necessary'.[49] What this implies is that, if the penitent refuses to disclose his/her actions (under the two exceptions) to the social services or police, the priest has a duty to break the confidence and to report the penitent to them. But in those circumstances the priest should inform the penitent beforehand. However, what the Handbook does not provide is an ability for the priest to seek the advice of the bishop before taking any action. It is submitted that

---

[46] Church in Wales, 'Clergy Handbook' (hereafter Clergy Handbook), Section 2, par. 7.2: www.churchinwales.org.uk/resources/constitution-handbooks/clergy-handbook/sec tion-2/section-2-professional-ministerial-guidelines/.

[47] Clergy Handbook, Section 2, par. 7.3.

[48] Clergy Handbook, Section 2, par. 7.4.

[49] Clergy Handbook, Section 2, par. 7.4.

the Handbook should so provide to enable episcopal support for clergy in these very difficult circumstances. Nevertheless, once again, Welsh norms on confession are broadly consistent with the principles of Anglican canon law.[50]

The Rite of Holy Matrimony

What follows develops some of the themes introduced in Chapter 7, treating them from a legal perspective. Commentators suggest that there are two areas in particular where it can be argued that the State has not fully disestablished the Church, and that the Church in Wales is subject to laws made for the Church by the State: these areas are in relation to marriage and burial.[51] The most extensive consideration of this argument in relation to marriage can be found in a 1992 study by Thomas Glyn Watkin;[52] this section draws on Watkin's argument.

First, the Church of England long enjoyed certain privileges in relation to the solemnisation of Holy Matrimony due to its position as an established church. Whilst other religious denominations are permitted to hold marriage ceremonies in their places of worship, in civil law these are treated as civil ceremonies which take place outside a registration office. If the officiating minister is not an 'authorised person' then a separate ceremony is required, conducted by a civil registrar. In comparison, for the Church of England, banns of marriage are published prior to the ceremony, and from a legal perspective the ceremony is not a civil ceremony in a registered religious building, but an ecclesiastical ceremony of equal validity.[53]

Following Lord Hardwicke's Marriage Act 1753, the ecclesiastical ceremony became essential for a valid marriage. And, as an ecclesiastical ceremony was essential for a valid marriage, so it followed that there was a duty upon the established English Church to solemnise the marriages of all subjects in the realm, regardless of their religious persuasion or lack thereof. Accordingly, the courts held that a clergyman who unreasonably

---

[50] Anglican Communion Legal Advisers Network, *The Principles of Canon Law Common to the Churches of the Anglican Communion* (2008), Principles 76–7.

[51] See T. G. Watkin, 'Vestiges of Establishment', *Ecclesiastical Law Journal*, 2 (1990), 110–15.

[52] T. G. Watkin, 'Disestablishment, Self-Determination and the Constitutional Development of the Church in Wales', in N. Doe, *Essays in Canon Law: A Study of the Law of the Church in Wales* (Cardiff: University of Wales Press, 1992), 35.

[53] Ibid., 33–4. There are also marriages by common licence and special licence.

refused to solemnise the marriage of a duly qualified person committed an ecclesiastical offence (although he was liable to an action for damages, not to a criminal prosecution).[54]

However, the framers of the Welsh Church Act 1914 intended to end the recognition of ecclesiastical marriage in the Church in Wales, and place it on an equal footing with other denominations in Wales. Section 23 originally stated that from the date of disestablishment:

> The law relating to marriages in churches of the Church of England (including any law conferring any right to be married in such a church) shall cease to be in force in Wales and Monmouthshire, and the provisions of the Marriage Acts, 1811 and 1898, relating to marriages in registered buildings, shall apply to marriages in churches of the Church in Wales.

If this provision had actually become effective, then marriage by banns, common licence or special licence (as is also the case today) would have ceased in Wales in 1920,[55] and there would have been no difference between the Church in Wales and other Welsh denominations.

However, section 23 was repealed by section 6 of the Welsh Church (Temporalities) Act 1919 (prior to disestablishment). This provided that nothing in the 1914 Act or the 1919 Act should affect the civil law as to marriages in Wales and Monmouthshire – thus, argues Watkin: 'despite having been disestablished, the Church in Wales continues to enjoy a privileged position with regard to the solemnizing of marriages and remains subject to the powers of the Archbishop of Canterbury, and the Archbishop of Wales, with regard to the issue of special licences'.[56]

This leads Watkin to question the extent to which Church in Wales clergy remain obliged to solemnise marriages for parishioners who are not communicants of the Church and who are unbaptised. Refusal to officiate a marriage of a duly qualified person is an offence under ecclesiastical law. However, as Watkin points out, by section 3 of the Welsh Church Act 1914, the ecclesiastical law has ceased to exist as the law of the land in Wales but continues as terms of a contract binding on members of the Church. Therefore, to the extent that the courts will intervene, the only persons who can complain of such terms of the contract being broken are those party to it – that is, church members (who are unlikely to include the unbaptised). In turn, the only way such

---

[54] *Argar v Holdsworth* (1758) 2 Lee 515; *Davis v Black* (1841) 1 QB 900; *R v James* (1850) 3 Car & Kir.

[55] Watkin, 'Disestablishment', 35.

[56] Ibid.

a person can bring a claim against a cleric refusing to solemnise their marriage is by finding a church member to bring the claim.[57]

The right to be married in the parish church vests in those persons who: reside in the parish where the wedding is to take place; are regular worshippers in the parish and have their name on the church electoral roll; or have a 'qualifying connection' to the church. A 'qualifying connection' is set out in the Marriage (Wales) Act 2010, a private Act of Parliament designed 'to enable persons to be married in a place of worship in the Church in Wales with which they have a qualifying connection'. A person has a 'qualifying connection' if that person: was baptised or confirmed in that parish; has at any time had his/her usual place of residence in that parish for a period of not less than six months; has at any time habitually attended public worship in that parish for a period of not less than six months; has a parent who has (during the person's lifetime) lived in the parish or habitually attended public worship in the parish for a period of not less than six months; or has a parent or grandparent who has been married in that parish. It is clear that the 'qualifying connections' are extremely broad.[58]

The 2010 Act is another example of the vestiges of establishment. However, one question is how the introduction of Ministry Areas in many dioceses will affect the application of this 'qualifying connection' to a specific church. It is possible that couples attending Church A in a Ministry Area could thereby gain a qualifying connection to have their marriage solemnised in (more desirable) Church B in the same Ministry Area.

Secondly, while the Church in Wales teaches that a marriage 'is dissolved only by the death of either party',[59] the remarriage of divorced persons, whose former marriages have been civilly dissolved, is regulated by parliamentary statute and by episcopal guidance. The Matrimonial Causes Act 1965, which also applies to the Church in Wales, specifically states that 'no clergyman of the . . . Church in Wales shall be compelled (a) to solemnise the marriage of any person whose former marriage has been dissolved and whose former spouse is still living; or (b) to permit the marriage of such a person to be solemnised in the church or chapel of which he is the minister'.[60] Whilst the Matrimonial Causes Act 1937

[57] Watkin, 'Vestiges of Establishment', 113.
[58] Marriage (Wales) Act 2010, s. 2(3)(a)–(e).
[59] BCP (1984), 736; Marriage Services (2010), 5: 'God joins husband and wife in life-long union.'
[60] Matrimonial Causes Act 1965, s. 8(2).

contained much the same rule, the bishops in that year forbade clergy from solemnising such marriages. But they lifted this ban in 1998.[61] So, the ability of divorced people to marry in a particular parish church is dependent upon the conscience of the minister concerned, and this cannot be restricted by episcopal prohibition. Accordingly, the right to be married in the parish church (or of a church with which the individual has a qualifying connection) does not extend to divorced people if the cleric has a conscientious objection to it. If the cleric does not have any conscientious objection to the remarriage of those divorced, then the ordinary duty to marry is applicable.[62]

Under guidelines issued by the Bench of Bishops in 1998, when approached by divorced persons seeking marriage in church, it is recommended that clergy talk to the parties in the first place without a commitment to solemnise it. This enables the minister to explore the appropriateness of the marriage in the context of the teaching that 'marriage' is 'a life-long union'. In some circumstances, the bishop's guidance may be sought, particularly if: the collapse of the previous marriage was the subject of public scandal; the failure of that marriage was directly as a result of the proposed partner; there are concerns over children of a former marriage; or a third or subsequent marriage is in view.[63] It is also recommended that clergy exercise their discretion in each and every case and insist on seeing the decree(s) absolute;[64] but they have no discretion in calling of banns or issuing certificates.[65] This change is also reflected in the principles of canon law common to Anglican churches.[66]

Thirdly, one area much debated over recent years is in relation to same-sex partnerships and whether the Church should extend marriage to same-sex couples. Some argue the traditional line that marriage should be between a man and a woman, and church marriage should therefore not extend to those in a same-sex relationship. For others, marriage should be so extended. The debate has been stimulated by two parliamentary statutes. Under the Civil Partnership Act 2004, two people of the same sex may enter a civil partnership, which, if registered, provides the parties to the partnership with similar rights and obligations to those in a civil marriage.

---

[61] See Chapter 7 and, for Lord Atkin opposing the bishops, Chapter 8.

[62] Doe, *Law of the Church in Wales*, 268, n. 116.

[63] Church in Wales, Bench of Bishops, 'Marriage and Divorce: Guidelines' (1998), para. 2.

[64] Doe, *The Law of the Church in Wales*, 268.

[65] Church in Wales, Bench of Bishops, 'Marriage and Divorce: Guidelines' (1998), para. 3.

[66] Anglican Communion Legal Advisers Network, *The Principles of Canon Law Common to the Churches of the Anglican Communion* (2008), Principle 75.

For example, civil partners are entitled to the same property rights as married opposite-sex couples, the same enjoyment as married couples of social security and pension benefits, the ability to gain parental responsibility for a partner's children, responsibility for reasonable maintenance of one's partner and their children, and tenancy and other rights and duties. The Act also sets out a formal process to dissolve partnerships similar to those for the divorce of opposite-sex marriages. Under the Equality Act 2010, religious premises may be registered for civil partnerships. However, nothing in the 2004 Act places a duty on religious organisations to host civil partnerships in their places of worship.[67] This legislation did not make any change in the law in relation to marriage of same-sex couples. The Church in Wales' website provides guidance for clergy and sets out a statement on marriage between same-sex couples issued by the Bench of Bishops in 2012: 'We abide by the Christian doctrine of marriage as the union of one man with one woman freely entered into for life. We acknowledge that whilst issues of human sexuality are not resolved, there are couples living in other life-long committed relationships who deserve the welcome, pastoral care and support of the Church. We are committed to further listening, prayerful reflection and discernment regarding same-sex relationships.'[68]

The Marriage (Same Sex Couples) Act 2013 now permits marriage of same-sex couples. However, any duty of clergy to solemnise marriage (and any corresponding right to have a marriage so solemnised) does not extend to the marriages of same-sex couples; 'clergy' includes a clerk in Holy Orders of the Church in Wales (section 1). The statute amends the Marriage Act 1949 and allows religious organisations to opt in to conduct same-sex marriages if they so wish, except specifically the Church in Wales and the Church of England (section 4). Accordingly, clergy of the Church in Wales still cannot solemnise marriages of same-sex couples. Section 8 then enables the Church in Wales to decide in the future to allow for marriage of same-sex couples. If its Governing Body does so, the Lord Chancellor must make such order as he considers appropriate to allow for the marriage of same-sex couples according to the rites of the Church in Wales.[69] This is a further vestige of establishment.

---

[67] See M. Hill, R. Sandberg and N. Doe, *Religion and Law in the United Kingdom* (Alphen aan den Rijn: Wolters Kluwer, 2nd ed., 2014), 208–11.

[68] See www.churchinwales.org.uk/faith/believe/bench_samesexmarriage/.

[69] This obviates the need for the Church to seek from Parliament a private act on the matter. The bill originally gave the Lord Chancellor a discretion to make the order – this was changed into a duty: see Chapter 7.

A consultation on the matter was instituted across the Church in Wales, and on 6 April 2016 the Bench of Bishops issued a pastoral letter in response to it and to a statement from the Primates of the Anglican Communion in January 2016. The letter states: 'we, as Bishops of the Anglican Communion, mindful of the results of our consultation and the Statement of the Primates of the Anglican Communion, and of all our members, including those who are gay and lesbian, do not feel that we can support at this time a move to change the discipline of the Church in Wales with respect to the teaching on marriage, nor can we permit the celebration of public liturgies of blessing for same sex unions'.[70] Instead, the Bench of Bishops provided prayers it considered suitable for those marking a committed relationship. More recently, in September 2018, Governing Body agreed that it was pastorally unsustainable for the Church to make no formal provision for those in same-sex relationships, and it voted in favour of the bishops exploring such formal provision, to be brought back before Governing Body at a later date.[71] This vote does not change the present doctrine or practice of the Church in Wales, but clearly opens the way to changes being introduced in the future. In the meantime, the position of the Church is as follows: 'As the law stands, same-sex marriages may not be solemnised by the Church in Wales. Such marriages are also at variance with the church's doctrine of marriage which states that marriage is a lifelong and faithful union between a man and a woman. The church, however, has to recognise the legality of same-sex marriages but also has to recognise that there is now a dissonance between it and the State's view.'[72]

Funeral Rites and Burial

As today in the Church of England, before 1920, residents and those dying in a parish were entitled to burial in its churchyard. Disestablishment was not intended to affect this right. The Welsh Church Act 1914 provided that when the incumbent died, retired or moved, ownership of the churchyard or burial ground would automatically be transferred to the local authority. This transfer was postponed until there was a change of incumbent because the freehold in the churchyard continued to vest in the incumbent. After the transfer, parishioners had rights of way over the churchyard to attend the church for worship. And the right of the public to burial in local

---

[70] See www.churchinwales.org.uk/news/2016/04/same-sex-marriage-statement/.
[71] See www.churchinwales.org.uk/news/2018/09/church-to-explore-formal-provision-for-same-sex-couples/.
[72] See www.churchinwales.org.uk/faith/believe/bench_samesexmarriage/.

authority-owned churchyards continued.[73] Many churchyards were passed to local authorities in the decades after 1920. However, the arrangement proved problematic, particularly with regard to the maintenance of churchyards.[74] As a result, the Welsh Church (Burial Grounds Act) 1945 was passed: it ended automatic transfers and allowed the Church to reclaim churchyards already transferred. Churchyards and burial grounds retransferred would be held on trust by the Representative Body, like those remaining in church ownership. Some churchyards which had passed into local authority control were reclaimed. The 1945 Act also empowered the Church to make rules about public rights of burial and the charges for this. To ensure that members of the public who were (and are) not members of the Church were not discriminated against, these rules had to be approved by the Secretary of State – and later, after devolution, by the National Assembly for Wales, and now by the Welsh Ministers. And so the residents in each parish retain the right to burial there whether or not the burial ground had been transferred to a local authority.[75] This remains a further vestige of establishment.[76]

Finally, the Church in Wales' position in relation to the burial of those who die unbaptised or excommunicate, or who commit suicide, appears to have developed in line with changes in current thinking about the subject much more quickly than that in the Church of England. At disestablishment, rules relating to the burial service[77] in the Church in Wales were the same as in the Church of England. The rubric in the Order for the Burial of the Dead in the 1662 Book of Common Prayer (which was the authorised office at the time of disestablishment) prohibited the use of the Burial Office, with its assurances of salvation, for 'any that die unbaptized, or excommunicate, or have laid violent hands upon themselves'. There has been some debate among commentators as to whether this applied to all who committed suicide, or whether it only applied to those who had taken their own life whilst of 'sound mind'.[78]

---

[73] Welsh Church Act 1914, ss. 8(1)(b) and 24(3).

[74] See S. White, *The Churchyards of the Church in Wales* (Bangor: Welsh Legal History Society, 2018).

[75] See law.gov.wales/constitution-government/intro-to-constitution/ecclesiastical-church-in-wales/?lang=en#/constitution-government/intro-to-constitution/ecclesiastical-church-in-wales/?tab=overview&lang=en.

[76] Watkin, 'Vestiges of Establishment', 114.

[77] The term 'burial service' is used throughout this section to denote the title 'Order for the Burial of the Dead'.

[78] For a more detailed commentary on the history of burial law relating to suicide victims, see C. Wright, 'The English Canon Law Relating to Suicide Victims', *Ecclesiastical Law Journal*, 19 (2017), 193–211.

Further, under the Burial Laws Amendment Act 1880, it was permitted, in circumstances where the Church of England burial service (and that of the later Church in Wales) could not be used, for any cleric to use prayers taken from the Book of Common Prayer 1662 or extracts from Holy Scripture at the burial service if this was permitted by the Ordinary.[79] By way of contrast, the Canons Ecclesiastical 1603 permit a minister to refuse to bury, in accordance with the 1662 prayer book, only if 'the party deceased were denounced Excommunicated *majori excommunicatione*, for some grievous and notorious crime, and no man [is] able to testify of his repentance'.[80]

The Church in Wales then underwent a liturgical revision in the 1960s and 1970s. Initially, a revised funeral service was authorised for experimental use for ten years. During this period, the Book of Common Prayer 1662 form of service was also permitted for use. A further draft was prepared by the Standing Liturgical Advisory Commission, and this new funeral service was approved by Governing Body in 1974. Once this new service had been authorised, it became part of the Book of Common Prayer, and the 1662 Order for the Burial of the Dead was no longer permitted for use at burials in the Church in Wales.[81]

In this new burial service, the norm prohibiting use of the service for those who have died unbaptised or excommunicate, or who have laid violent hands upon themselves, was omitted. This norm is also absent from later revisions of the office for the burial of the dead. The implication of the removal of the explicit prohibition of the use of the burial service for those who die unbaptised or excommunicate or who have committed suicide is that the service may now be used for individuals who fall into those categories. However, it is not clear whether the removal of this norm was a deliberate move to allow the burial service to be used for those who fall into these categories, or whether it has simply slipped under the radar. One of the problems with bringing about this change by simply omitting the rubric in the 1662 Book of Common Prayer, rather than by a positive amendment, is that it creates uncertainty over whether the use of the burial service for those who die unbaptised or excommunicate or who have committed suicide is now permissible. This is particularly the case in circumstances where some of the prayers included in the burial service are not appropriate for individuals otherwise falling into these categories.

---

[79] Burial Laws Amendment Act 1880, s. 1.
[80] See Canons Ecclesiastical 1603, Canon 68.
[81] See D. Thomas, 'Liturgical Revision in the Church of Wales' (1977), www .churchservicesociety.org/journals/volume-07-number-02-nov-1977/liturgical-revision-church-wales.

If this analysis is correct, it appears that the Church in Wales has been much more progressive than a number of other churches in the Anglican Communion. For example, it was not until 2017 that the Church of England amended its canons to enable the standard burial service to be used for those who die unbaptised or excommunicate, or who have committed suicide whilst of sound mind (although the canon does insert a conscience clause).[82] It appears that the Church of England effected this change some forty-five years later than the Church in Wales. The Church in Wales is also currently undergoing further additions to the funeral services. A canon to incorporate further Alternative Funeral Services into the Book of Common Prayer was promulgated at the Governing Body in the May 2019 session. If this bill is accepted, it will authorise the draft Alternative Funeral Services to be used in the Church in Wales, and they will become part of its Book of Common Prayer.

Conclusion

Over the past century, there have been several changes in relation to norms applicable to the administration of the rites of passage in the Church in Wales. In some respects, the Church in Wales can be seen as progressive, adopting changes in advance of many of the other churches in the Anglican Communion. For example, the changes to the norms of the burial service during the 1970s appear to have removed the prohibition for using the standard service for those who die unbaptised or excommunicate or who commit suicide. This is some forty-five years before such changes were made in the Church of England. Similarly, the Church in Wales is only the fourth church in the Anglican Communion to introduce across the province admission to Holy Communion for all those who have been baptised. Moreover, there are proposed changes afoot in relation to solemnising same-sex marriages. However, the way in which these changes have been implemented has, in some respects, led to a degree of uncertainty – as in the case of funeral services – and it remains to be seen what impact some of the changes (such as in the case of confirmation) will have on the rites in the future.

---

[82] For further information, see Wright, 'The English Canon Law Relating to Suicide Victims', 206–9.

12

The Church and Other Communities of Faith

AINSLEY GRIFFITHS

The very name bestowed upon the fledgling Anglican Province of Wales even before 1920 – an appellation received ostensibly by legislative accident – might be deemed to constellate a certain ecclesiastical identity.[1] Whilst no longer yoked to the British Crown and State – and thus deprived of any lingering pretensions of still being Wales' 'default' religion – being branded '*the* Church in Wales' seems anachronous, particularly as it eschews the qualifying prefix 'Anglican' which many other provinces attach. To maintain the definite article might bolster those who emphasised its ancient, saintly, pre-eminent foundations as *yr hen fam* ('the old mother') to whom its separated children would return, even though some such 'children' – those long-disaffected Nonconformists who, together, formed the bulk of Welsh Christians – sometimes regarded her as *yr hen estrones* ('the old foreigner'), emblematic of English subjugation. Moreover, as 'the Church *in* Wales' was it simply another contextual instantiation of the all-encompassing Catholic Church, universal in time and space, or else (to Roman Catholics) a schismatic sect, or (to Nonconformists) an imperious alien? Did being '*in* Wales' rather than '*of* Wales' reveal a certain self-understanding?

Ambiguity concerning commitment to Welshness riddled the Church's pre-disestablishment history. The Church in Wales' precursor had been responsible for the translation of the New Testament and prayer book (both published in 1567), followed by the entire Bible (1588) whose scholarly architect, Bishop William Morgan, is described in a commemoratory plaque at his birthplace as 'achubwr yr iaith Gymraeg . . . the saviour of the Welsh language'. The Church had nurtured the likes of Griffith Jones (1683–1761),

---

[1] Sincere thanks are due to friends and colleagues who have contributed in some way to this chapter, among them Dean Atkins, Gregory Cameron, Noel Davies, Mark Dimond, Aled Edwards, John Evans, Peredur Owen Griffiths, Rhian Linecar, Barry Morgan, Densil Morgan, Enid Morgan, Gwendraeth Morgan, Anna Morrell, Sasha Perriam, William Price, Gethin Rhys, John Richfield, Stephen Roberts, Sarah Rowland Jones, Peter Sedgwick and Sally Thomas. Nevertheless, any error remains mine.

the Carmarthenshire clergyman whose innovative circulating schools enabled previously illiterate children and adults to read the Bible and Catechism in Welsh and *yr hen bersoniaid llengar* ('the old literary parsons') who strove to revive ancient eisteddfodic traditions. Yet, between 1715 and 1870 no native Welsh-speakers became bishops, whilst those Englishmen who were appointed were often absent from their dioceses but nevertheless derived financial benefit from the tithes paid by a more radically reformed – and increasingly vociferous – free-church majority. Moreover, Welsh Anglicans were perilously implicated in the 1847 review of Welsh education which castigated the native tongue as 'a vast drawback to Wales ... a manifold barrier to ... moral progress and commercial prosperity',[2] and derided the Nonconformist faith which most Welsh-speakers professed as responsible for 'dissolute habits ... recklessness of living ... contempt for authority ... turbulent insubordination ... [and] haughty independence'.[3] Serving, somewhat paradoxically, to inculcate both a perceived sense of national inferiority and furious religio-nationalistic outrage, this so-called *Brâd y Llyfrau Gleision* – the 'Treachery of the Blue Books' – proved devastating, being 'handed down in oral tradition as the censure of a nation, the Glencoe and the Amritsar of Welsh history',[4] whilst Anglicans became 'treated as a kind of pariah people, like "black sheep"',[5] practising *crefydd y Sais* ('the religion of the English'). Such scholarly assessments may appear alarmist and far-removed from subsequent ecumenical warmth, but they do delineate the rather barren contours of inter-church relations at disestablishment.

Whilst this chapter focusses largely on ecumenical relationships, implicit linguistic and cultural sensitivities seem ever present, raising questions of how this once state-bound church might speak to and for the nation, engaging in missional encounter alongside cultivating a decidedly Welsh, autonomous, self-distinguishing identity.[6] Having clear theological, ecclesiological, liturgical and ethical foundations is essential, moreover, in relation to other Anglican provinces as well as

[2] Commission of Enquiry into the State of Education in Wales, *Report* (London: HMSO, 1848), 309.

[3] Ibid., 400.

[4] K. O. Morgan, *Wales in British Politics, 1868–1922* (Cardiff: University of Wales Press, rev. ed., 1980), 16. See also G. T. Roberts, *The Language of the Blue Books: The Perfect Instrument of Empire* (Cardiff: University of Wales Press, 1998).

[5] J. Morris, 'Anglicanism in Britain and Ireland', in J. Morris, ed., *The Oxford History of Anglicanism, Volume IV: Global Western Anglicanism, c. 1910–Present* (Oxford: Oxford University Press, 2017), 402.

[6] See, further, Enid Morgan's critical analysis of linguistic and cultural stances in Chapter 15.

other faiths. This survey of the Church in Wales' relations with other communities of faith since disestablishment therefore demands (at least) three dimensions, and these structure this chapter's three principal sections. The first considers the Church in Wales' identity as a self-governing province within the Anglican Communion (including relations with the Church of England); the second recounts the significant ecumenical journey from ignorance, indifference and mild hostility regarding other denominations towards more generous hospitality and collaboration, both within Wales and beyond; and the third explores the Church's relationship with non-Christian faiths within an increasingly diverse nation.

This necessarily succinct overview of this multifaceted story inevitably precludes much substantiating detail, reading history through high-level decisions and pronouncements (often from bishops) rather than the attitudes, experiences and actions of ordinary Welsh Anglicans. Counterbalancing that manifest weakness will, I trust, stimulate much-needed future research concerning Wales' social and cultural history.

Reforming Allegiances: A New Province Within the Anglican Communion

Freed from former oaths of obedience to the archbishop of Canterbury during Holy Week 1920 and having relinquished their membership of Convocation, their seats in the House of Lords and oversight for several anomalous border-straddling parishes, the Welsh bishops met on Easter Wednesday to elect the fledgling province's first archbishop. Deliberating within the evocative liturgical setting of the Church's annual celebration of Christ's death and resurrection heightened the theological significance of their momentous task. Notwithstanding this innovative appointment, profoundly symbolic of newfound autonomy, long-established allegiances faded slowly even though the Church of England's pre-disestablishment promises of financial assistance came to little. Moreover, despite some early enthusiasm for innovative liturgy, it took until 1944 for a new Calendar, which included celebrations of the Welsh saints, to be adopted, and Church in Wales worship remained decidedly bound to the 1662 norm until new, experimental rites appeared during the 1960s. According to the distinguished convert from Nonconformity, Aneirin Talfan Davies, 1950s Welsh Anglicans still resembled 'a people who have been left in an open boat, casting longing eyes at the liner which [they had] just left, feeling a little despondent in the desert of sea around [them]'.[7]

Such a boat might, however, become a vehicle for intrepid, international adventures. Welsh Anglicans found themselves refashioning relations with the Church of England as part of a global communion undergoing enormous changes triggered by colonialism's gradual demise and as unprecedented growth in newly formed autonomous provinces transposed Anglicanism's centre of gravity to non-Western nations. As regions once regarded as 'dependent and secondary' were discovering 'new and breathtaking independence and self-reliance' so 'the Anglican Communion [had] come of age . . . the keynotes . . . [being] equality, interdependence, mutual responsibility', an intensifying relationality expressed in consultation and the sharing of resources, both human and financial.[8] Several Welsh bishops would understand this shift through their former service overseas: John Charles Jones (Bangor, 1949–56) with the Church Missionary Society in Uganda (1934–45); John Richards (St David's, 1956–71) in Iran (1927–45); John Poole-Hughes (Llandaff, 1975–85) as bishop of South-West Tanganyika (1962–74); and Benjamin Vaughan (Swansea and Brecon, 1976–87) as dean of Trinidad (1955–61), bishop suffragan of Mandeville (1961–7) and bishop of Belize (1967–71). All of them gave the Church in Wales necessary international perspectives and energy to form diocesan links and exchanges.

Welsh Anglicans became embedded within a global fellowship of self-governing provinces in communion with Canterbury, sharing 'bonds of affection' shaped by Scripture, creeds, the dominical sacraments and the historic episcopate and constituted by the global instruments of communion, namely the archbishop of Canterbury, the Lambeth Conference, the Anglican Consultative Council (established in 1967 and hosted in Cardiff in 1990) and the Primates' Meeting (established following Lambeth 1978).[9] Certain Welsh Anglicans have played key roles in the Communion. Gregory Cameron (now bishop of St Asaph) was appointed director of ecumenical affairs of the Anglican

---

[7] Quoted by D. T. W. Price in *A History of the Church in Wales in the Twentieth Century* (Penarth: Church in Wales Publications, 1990), 23.

[8] The statement 'Mutual Responsibility and Interdependence in the Body of Christ' arising from the 1963 Toronto Anglican Congress, section I.

[9] See, further, Norman Doe, 'The Instruments of Unity and Communion in Global Anglicanism', in I. S. Markham, J. B. Hawkins, J. Terry and L. N. Steffensen, eds., *The Wiley-Blackwell Companion to the Anglican Communion* (Chichester: Wiley-Blackwell, 2013), 47–66.

Communion in 2003, and became deputy secretary general in 2004. He also served as secretary to the Lambeth Commission. Its Windsor Report (2004) sought to address tensions arising from certain provinces' contentious innovations concerning same-sex relationships, and its 'Anglican Covenant' was proposed and drafted initially by a lay member of the Church in Wales, Norman Doe of Cardiff Law School, also a commission member.[10] In 2009, the Anglican Consultative Council commended the final version of the 'Anglican Communion Covenant' to the provinces, but Wales' Governing Body in 2012 deferred ratification, following its rejection by the Church of England. Gregory Cameron also acted as Anglican co-secretary during numerous international dialogues with other traditions such as the Orthodox, Eastern Orthodox, Roman Catholic, Lutheran and Methodist. Sarah Rowland Jones (now dean of St David's) was a British diplomat before ordination, subsequently ministering in both Wales and South Africa. Drawing on her international, cross-cultural experience she has served on a wide range of Anglican and ecumenical bodies since 1999 and, as a well-established member of the Inter-Anglican Standing Commission for Unity, Faith and Order, she now convenes its ecumenical work.

Furthermore, the Anglican–Roman Catholic International Commission (ARCIC) has benefited from Welsh insights, including from Peter Sedgwick (former principal of St Michael's Theological College, Llandaff) who serves on ARCIC-III. Both Patrick Thomas (vicar of Christchurch, Carmarthen) and Gregory Cameron currently serve on the Anglican–Oriental Orthodox International Commission, the former having nurtured remarkable interest in Armenian Christianity and the latter acting as co-chair for the recent phase which produced a shared doctrinal statement on pneumatology (2017).

Both as a distinguished academic and as bishop and archbishop, Rowan Williams' contribution to doctrinal dialogue and ecumenical exchange has been outstanding. His translation from Wales to Canterbury in 2002 bestowed a self-effacing spiritual and intellectual master to lead the global communion during turbulent times, suffused with exceptional theological scholarship. His successor as archbishop of Wales, Barry Morgan, subsequently undertook significant roles within

---

[10] Lambeth Commission on Communion, *The Windsor Report* (London: Anglican Communion Office, 2004), 81, Appendix; see also n. 61, using the Church in Wales as an example of how the Covenant might be ratified by each province.

the Communion; as well as being on the Primates' Meeting, he was a primate representative on the Joint Standing Committee of the Anglican Consultative Council.

However, the thorny path to be negotiated globally concerning same-sex relationships made the sometimes liberal Welsh stance somewhat delicate, particularly given the contentious 1998 Lambeth Resolution 1.10 which, despite instigating a 'listening process' nevertheless '[rejected] homosexual practice as incompatible with Scripture'.[11] Undeterred, Archbishop Morgan used his first address as Governing Body president to address five debatable issues, advocating (i) a non-literalistic, reason-informed interpretation of Scripture; (ii) Anglicanism's capacity simultaneously to hold diverse viewpoints on certain issues; (iii) respect for the self-governance of the Communion's provinces; (iv) the non-binding nature of Lambeth resolutions; and (v) the need for non-legislative face-to-face conversations regarding sexuality across the Communion.[12] Some of the 200 or so bishops who chose to attend the Global Anglican Future Conference in Jerusalem rather than Lambeth 2008 might question Morgan's reading; yet such principles reflect enduring Welsh episcopal teaching concerning Anglican polity. These same principles, and many others, also appeared in *The Principles of Canon Law Common to the Churches of the Anglican Communion*, proposed and drafted in Wales by Norman Doe, adopted by the Anglican Communion Legal Advisers Network, launched at the Lambeth Conference in 2008, commended by the Anglican Consultative Council in 2009, and fed into the work of ARCIC-III in 2018.[13]

Nevertheless, sexuality still divides Welsh Anglicans. When the Doctrinal Commission's 2014 report presented three possible paths – (i) maintaining the status quo; (ii) offering blessings of same-sex partnerships;

---

[11] See www.anglicancommunion.org/media/76650/1998.pdf.
[12] 'Presidential Address to Governing Body', September 2003. See www.churchinwales.org .uk/structure/representative-body/publications/downloads/theology-wales-back-issues/ theology-wales-the-church-and-homosexuality/presidential-address-archbishop-barry-morgan/.
[13] Anglican Communion Legal Advisers Network, *The Principles of Canon Law Common to the Churches of the Anglican Communion* (London: Anglican Communion Office, 2008), 13 (Preface) and, at 97–124, N. Doe, 'The Contribution of Common Principles of Canon Law to Ecclesial Communion in Anglicanism'; ACC-14, Resolution 14.20 (5 May 2009); and Anglican–Roman Catholic International Commission, 'Walking Together on the Way: Learning to be the Church – Local, Regional and Universal. An Agreed Statement of the Third Anglican–Roman Catholic Commission' (ARCIC-III) (2018) para 145, recommendation VI.C.

(iii) permitting same-sex marriage – considerable numbers espoused some change. Moreover, when the bishops, under the leadership of Morgan's successor, Archbishop John Davies, declared in September 2018 that they were 'united in the belief that it is pastorally unsustainable and unjust for the Church to continue to make no formal provision for those in committed same-sex relationships', the Governing Body indicated substantial support (76–21). Concerned that such views might provoke a departure from traditional teaching on marriage, a new movement – Anglican Essentials Wales – has emerged to 'provide a forum, a rallying point, and an identity for all "orthodox Anglicans" in the Church in Wales' and 'a voice for this constituency to the leadership of the Church in Wales, to other Anglican constituencies, and to the world'.[14] Despite being episcopally steered towards some change by its bishops, Welsh Anglicans' final verdict on sexuality is as yet undetermined. Wales provides a microcosm of the Communion's divergent convictions, recognising that any shift will elicit simultaneous elation and consternation, nationally and globally. Moreover, in a more generic sense, Archbishop Morgan's sincerely held perceptions concerning the very character of Anglicanism provide litmus tests for how the Communion's unity-amid-diversity might – or might not – endure during the decades and centuries to come.

Ecumenism: From Resentment to Receptivity

Nevertheless, whilst becoming immersed in a global Anglican context, cultivating an enhanced Welsh identity served to overcome long-held (self-)perceptions of being merely the Cambrian branch of the Church of England. Authenticated by evidence of Welsh Christianity long predating Augustine of Canterbury's mission to England – a faith enduring in Celtic lands despite its demise in areas overrun by Angles, Saxons and Jutes – the decades following disestablishment witnessed bishops vaunting the Welsh Church's foundational credentials. Evangelised by sixth-century saints profoundly shaped by Eastern eremitism and monasticism received via Gaul – those such as Dyfrig, Illtud, Dewi (David), Non, Teilo, Padarn and Cadog in the south and Deiniol, Asaph and Beuno in the north – Wales had embedded these blessed forebears in place names which survive across the country – Llanilltud, Llanddewi, Llannon, Llandeilo, Llanbadarn, Llangadog, Llanddeiniol, Llanasa and so on – and these

---

[14] See www.anglicanessentialswales.org.uk.

venerable mission settlements secured the ancient pedigree of the new province.[15]

The little-remembered visit of numerous Orthodox patriarchs to St David's Cathedral in July 1925, to commemorate the 1600th anniversary of the Nicene Creed, accorded Archbishop A. G. Edwards an imposing international forum to champion the pure doctrinal and ecclesiological ancestry of the Church in Wales. This theologically motivated liturgical celebration, during which the creed was proclaimed in Welsh, English, Greek and Russian, nevertheless became 'overlaid by . . . ecclesio-political pragmatism'.[16] According to Rhygyfarch's eleventh-century hagiography, Dewi Sant (St David) had been consecrated archbishop during a pilgrimage to Jerusalem and so 'the presence of the reigning Patriarch of Jerusalem at St David's was, therefore, something of a godsend to those struggling to find an identity for the nascent Church in Wales',[17] fortifying a saintly ecclesiology neither English nor Roman (and certainly not Nonconformist) but fundamentally *Eastern*, notwithstanding Wales' eventual assimilation into medieval Western Catholicism.[18] A specially composed hymn, 'Lord, Who in Thy Perfect Wisdom', by the mission-hearted Mirfield Father Timothy Rees CR (himself a convert from Welsh-speaking Nonconformity and later to become bishop of Llandaff) honoured 'all the gallant saintly band, who of old by prayer and labour hallowed all our native land'. So here was a native church which had merely secondary historical allegiance to Rome and Canterbury, whilst professing little empathy with the Dissenting faith which commanded widespread allegiance across Wales.

Indeed, on that occasion the dean of St David's waxed lyrical 'that the Welsh people should return to their ancient Mother, and win the world for the Christ of the Incarnation', whilst the sight of the Jerusalem

---

[15] B. Morgan, 'The Church in Wales', in Markham, Hawkins, Terry and Steffensen, eds., *The Wiley-Blackwell Companion to the Anglican Communion*, 452–63. See further D. Llywelyn, *Sacred Place, Chosen People: Land and National Identity in Welsh Spirituality* (Cardiff: University of Wales Press, 1999).

[16] J. Morgan-Guy, 'The Visit of the Eastern Metropolitans and Patriarchs to St Davids Cathedral in 1925, a Lecture Given to the Cathedral Friends, September 2014', in *Friends of St David's Cathedral: Annual Report 2015* (St David's: St David's Cathedral, 2015), 17.

[17] Ibid.

[18] In contrast, Catherine Daniel's 'Wales: Catholic and Nonconformist', *Blackfriars*, 38(444) (1957) 100–11, posits a *Roman*-Welsh identity forged during earliest Christianity, thereby defying Anglican posturing. See, further, T. O. Hughes, *Winds of Change: The Roman Catholic Church and Society in Wales, 1916–1962* (Cardiff: University of Wales Press, 1999).

patriarch kissing the cathedral altar stone allegedly given to Dewi by his episcopal consecrator was interpreted by a *Church Times* journalist as being 'assuredly symbolic of the speedy reunion of the Orthodox and Welsh Churches'.[19] The episode speaks of a church magnifying strands of romanticised history/legend to configure an ecclesial identity geographically, linguistically, culturally, liturgically and theologically remote from ordinary Welsh Anglicans whilst alienating their immediate neighbours – Nonconformist and Roman alike – imagining future Christian unity solely through their absorption into the true Church of the ancient saintly founders: namely, the Church in Wales.

In one sense, this 'Eastern turn' might be interpreted as wholehearted approval of global Anglicanism's newfound ecumenical commitments which the bishops of the newly disestablished Welsh Church had helped to craft through the 1920 Lambeth Conference's celebrated *Appeal to all Christian People*. Recognising non-Anglican Christian believers baptised in the trinitarian faith as members of Christ's body, called together to divinely willed fellowship, gathered bishops contritely acknowledged that 'self-will, ambition, and lack of charity' and 'blindness to the sin of disunion' had perpetuated 'the guilt of . . . crippling the Body of Christ and hindering the activity of his Spirit'.[20] Nevertheless, Welsh Anglicans initially made no structural interdenominational efforts with Presbyterians, Independents, Baptists, Wesleyans and Roman Catholics living alongside them – and whilst their constitution implied growing ecumenical warmth, it radiated towards Christians far away.

Thus, as the Anglican Communion established inter-communion with Old Catholics of the Union of Utrecht in 1931, so the Church in Wales promulgated a corresponding canon in 1937 to extend this specifically to Wales. Subsequently, it legislated for full communion with the Philippine Independent Church (1966) and the Mar Thoma Syrian Church of Malabar (1975), as well as churches now members of the Anglican Communion, namely the Lusitanian Church and the Reformed Episcopal Church of Spain (both 1966) and the Churches of South India, North India and Pakistan (all 1973), as well as the Church of Bangladesh (1976). Whilst theologically and ecclesiologically significant, such ecumenism appeared somewhat remote, abstract and theoretical until matched by a fervent Wales-wide quest for reconciliation with

---

[19] That is, by the author of the report in the *Church Times* of 17 July 1925.
[20] 1920 Lambeth Conference, Resolution 9.III: www.anglicancommunion.org/media/127731/1920.pdf.

estranged Christian neighbours at home. Several decades would elapse following the *Appeal* before that vision became realisable, for unity rooted in a common identity 'in Christ' seemed perennially eclipsed by memory of the rancorous disestablishment campaign and counter-campaign which had intensified inter-church prejudice, suspicion and rivalry whilst keeping denominational loyalties stubbornly resilient. Disestablishment feuding had been largely disengaged from genuine theological concerns and did little to enhance Christ's reputation in Welsh society or witness to the unconditional, all-encompassing, extravagant love of God.

With clerics perceived as being detached and self-important, friendly relations between priests and ministers were rare,[21] such social superiority reinforcing the ecclesiological pre-eminence paraded before the Orthodox at St David's. Long before disestablishment, Bishop (later Archbishop) A. G. Edwards emphasised that revered, unbroken lineage which pre-dated Saxon and Norman influences yet which had merged perfectly during the medieval period with the Church of Augustine of Canterbury, maintaining immaculate doctrinal and ecclesiastical heritage. For Edwards, the Church in Wales could claim therefore to be older than the State itself and therefore the only truly national organisation even though he, a native Welsh-speaker, scorned its ancient language and distinguished indigenous culture, fostering instead a bizarre, self-contradicting Anglocentrism.

Such contempt distanced the Church from Nonconformists as did its gradual 'catholicisation', shifting worshippers' gaze from pulpit to altar, embellishing church buildings with visual imagery, and enriching liturgy with elaborate ceremonial. J. E. Jones, vicar of Brymbo, near Wrexham, declared that Church–Chapel dissimilarities were 'too great to admit of anything in the way of religious co-operation',[22] whilst Edward Latham Bevan, vicar of Brecon, fortified resistance, alleging that Anglicans '[regarded] the orders and sacraments of the Nonconformists as invalid'.[23] Such negativity, coupled with chapels' spiralling demise, enabled Anglicans to transform their pre-disestablishment anxieties into self-differentiating, mission-minded optimism. William Morgan, vicar of Bethesda, spoke of the vocation to 'popularise, democratise, and nationalise the old Church of our

---

[21] D. D. Morgan, *The Span of the Cross: Christian Religion and Society in Wales, 1914–2000* (Cardiff: University of Wales Press, 2nd ed., 2011).
[22] Quoted ibid., 29.
[23] Ibid.

Fathers'[24] and, whilst advocating greater evangelistic connectedness, imagined a spiritual revival accomplished through receiving estranged children back into the Anglican fold rather than subsequent, more radical and egalitarian, ecumenism. Even though the Church in Wales, along with the Annibynwyr (Union of Welsh Independents), Calvinistic Methodists, Baptists and Wesleyans, had formed the 'General Committee on Mutual Understanding and Co-operation' in 1933, with Bishop David Prosser of St David's as its chair, there is meagre evidence of widespread ecumenical interest amongst Anglicans whilst, as observed below, examples of glaringly undiplomatic episcopal rhetoric survive. Bishops, nevertheless, remained hierarchical and authoritarian whilst the Governing Body maintained disproportionately high numbers of monied gentry and higher-ranking military personnel.[25] Thus, even as the Great Depression engulfed Wales and fascist regimes plunged Europe towards another global conflict, the Church in Wales remained largely self-enthralled and less inclined towards the Gospel-based social vision emerging in Nonconformity, despite certain illustrious exceptions such as Bishop Timothy Rees of Llandaff (1931–9).

Notwithstanding growing sacramentalism, ceremonialism and sacerdotalism, rapprochement with Rome appeared fanciful. This once-outlawed and -persecuted communion began to flourish anew, enjoying unprecedented, inconceivable growth, making new adherents through both marriage and heartfelt conversion to the rock-like unchangeability and exotic magnetism of the Petrine Church. Francis Mostyn, enthroned as archbishop and metropolitan Cardiff in 1921, maintained an unyielding ultramontanist stance, dashing Anglo-Catholic pretensions when he declared in 1929 that Wales' ancient cathedrals 'stood as cold and empty shells awaiting the time when new life will be infused into them, and they will once more be used for the purpose for which they were erected'.[26] Anglicans were deemed heretical schismatics making groundless claims about their apostolic foundation and saintly credentials, enmeshed, like Nonconformists, within a humanly devised Protestant forgery riven by disunity, a pale imitation of the one, divine-created, holy, catholic and apostolic communion subsisting in the Church of Rome.[27]

[24] Quoted ibid., 78.
[25] Ibid., 85.
[26] Quoted ibid., 98.
[27] Ibid.

Even so, Anglican confidence remained undented, spawning a certain triumphalism that resisted Roman Catholic claims for sole legitimacy. Edwin Morris, Bishop of Monmouth (1945–67) and Archbishop of Wales (1957–67), avowed unflinchingly that 'the Church in Wales is the Catholic Church in this land ... we cannot, without denying our very nature, yield one iota of this claim'.[28] Furthermore, Morris believed that, unlike Nonconformity, Anglicanism preserved fidelity to the catholic creeds and threefold ministry whilst avoiding Rome's propensity for theological error. Eluding post-war Europe's ecumenical optimism, Morris forbade his clergy from evangelistic collaboration with Nonconformists, believing that missional endeavour entailed more than merely preaching and hearing the Gospel: it required sacramental incorporation into Christ's ecclesial body, equated, unsurprisingly, with the Church in Wales. Moreover, despite Leo XIII's 1896 papal bull – denouncing Anglican ordinations as defective in intention and form and therefore 'absolutely null and utterly void'[29] – Morris asserted that 'both the Roman clergy and Nonconformist ministers are, strictly speaking, intruders. There may be historical reason for their being here, but we cannot recognise their right to be here.'[30]

Whilst less stridently antagonistic, Morris' fellow bishops shared these elevated perceptions of Anglican pre-eminence and the necessary reincorporation of other traditions – that is, until Gwilym Owen Williams – universally known as simply 'G.O.' – was elected bishop of Bangor in 1956. This brilliant, Oxford-educated, fervent Welsh-speaker had converted from Calvinistic Methodism to Anglicanism in 1936, taking the opposite path to celebrated eighteenth-century Revivalists such as Howel Harris, Daniel Rowland and William Williams whom the Church had failed to contain. Whilst discerning within Anglicanism evidence of oneness, holiness, catholicity and apostolicity, he nevertheless imagined a pilgrimage towards unity alongside all Christians sharing a common baptism. Unlike Morris' anti-ecumenical sentiment delivered through sermons, addresses and public letters, G.O. believed in charitable, trust-building, face-to-face encounter as the necessary precursor to formal unity-building dialogue. Convinced that 'divisions are a sad offence to God as well as

---

[28] From Morris' 1946 Visitation Charge, quoted in J. S. Binns, *Alfred Edwin Morris: Archbishop of Wales* (Llandysul: Gomer Press, 1990), 81.

[29] *Apostolicae curae* (1896).

[30] A. E. Morris, *The Church in Wales and Nonconformity: Being the Second Visitation Charge of Edwin, Lord Bishop of Monmouth* (Newport: A. T. W. James, 1949).

injurious to the Church's mission',[31] he nevertheless remained resolute in upholding Anglicanism's episcopal, doctrinally orthodox, core and agreed eucharistic discipline.

G.O. welcomed the formation of the Council of Churches in Wales in 1955 and the emphasis of the Third Assembly of the World Council of Churches (New Delhi, 1961) concerning the interdependence of unity and mission. He discerned similar priorities emerging from the WCC Faith and Order Conference (Montreal, 1963) whilst the Anglican Congress in Toronto a month later reinforced this through the celebrated concept of mutual responsibility and interdependence in the Body of Christ. These global pronouncements inspired Wales' own faith and order conference, held at Trinity College, Carmarthen, the following month, at which, to G.O.'s delight, Roman Catholic delegates were present, 'entering in an unprecedented way into living encounter with other churches'.[32] However, whilst he rejoiced as the British Council of Churches' Faith and Order Conference in Nottingham (1964) set Easter 1980 as the deadline for achieving visible unity between participating churches, Archbishop Morris dissented, the lingering, yet waning, voice of Anglican intransigence.

Indeed, that Bangor's ecumenical enthusiast was elected archbishop in 1971 signified a Church refashioning its attitudes to other Christian traditions, relinquishing cold, self-important disdain for warmer, more self-effacing, receptivity. Many church people remained sceptical,[33] and some non-Anglicans feared an inexorable drift towards accepting the catholic creeds as sufficient statements of faith, the imposition of hierarchical governance, and an objectivised understanding of sacraments as mediating grace in a quasi-magical manner.[34] Nevertheless, G.O. emerged as architect of an ecumenically engaged Wales taking cautious but decisive steps towards organic unity through the 1975 Welsh Covenant, involving Anglicans, Methodists (Wesleyans), Presbyterians (Calvinistic Methodists), the United Reformed Church and (from 1978) certain Baptist churches.

---

[31] D. T. W. Price, *Archbishop Gwilym Owen Williams 'G.O.': His Life and Opinions* (Cardiff: Church in Wales Publications, 2017), 49.

[32] Ibid., 55.

[33] Christopher Harris and Richard Startup's *The Church in Wales: The Sociology of a Traditional Institution* (Cardiff: University of Wales Press, 1999) showed that Anglicans' ecumenical ambivalence persisted.

[34] See N. A. Davies, *A History of Ecumenism in Wales, 1956–1990* (Cardiff: University of Wales Press, 2008), 18.

At the Governing Body debate in 1973, the archbishop had recalled the 'tremendous theological revolution' witnessed at Montreal, transforming 'entrenched positions' through refusing to nurse past divisions but rather gaze upwards to the glorified enthroned Christ, for 'unity is God's gift to the Church in Jesus'.[35] At the Covenant's inaugural thanksgiving service held in Seilo, Aberystwyth, G. O. preached on Romans 15:7 –'accept one another, as Christ accepted you, to the glory of God' – reflecting both the Church in Wales' ecumenical *volte-face* and the free churches' growing openness to Anglican perspectives.

However, such receptivity did not involve compromising theological and ecclesiological convictions, among them the threefold ordained ministry, which for Anglicans – G.O. included – constituted a God-given axiom. That the Governing Body subscribed to the Covenant, 'provided that nothing ... shall affect or be deemed to affect the faith, discipline, articles, doctrinal statements, rites, ceremonies or formularies of the Church in Wales',[36] might, for some, echo longstanding, pompous, obdurate narrow-mindedness or, otherwise, confirm heartfelt faithfulness to well-established, mission-enhancing Anglican ecclesiology. In subsequent ecumenical discussions in Wales, it became clear that, despite the Covenant's wholehearted mutual affirmation of ministries, Anglicans regarded episcopal oversight as intrinsic to any truly catholic and apostolic united church. Orthodox faith required Catholic order exercised through episcopacy – personal, collegiate and conciliar – thereby delineating Anglican ecumenical limits – what we might designate an unbreachable 'purple line'. Implementing the Porvoo Declaration (1995) concerning mutual recognition between Anglicans of the British Isles and Lutherans of Scandinavia and the Baltic meant that the Church in Wales would enter into full communion with certain churches whose exercise of the historic episcopate had temporarily lapsed; hence solving the Welsh 'episcopal conundrum' might become less impenetrable.[37]

---

[35] Quoted by Price, *Archbishop*, 63.
[36] Canon 'For Covenanting between the Church in Wales and Other Churches for Union in Wales' (promulgated, 1 May 1974).
[37] See E. Eckerdal, 'Apostolic Succession in the Porvoo Common Statement: Unity through a Deeper Sense of Apostolicity' (PhD Thesis, Uppsala University, 2017), http://uu.diva-portal.org/smash/record.jsf?pid=diva2%3A1129750&dswid=-9729.

Space does not permit full analysis of the Covenant's ramifications or of the impact of the national ecumenical instrument, Cytûn: Churches Together in Wales, but three developments stand out. The first involved a canon (promulgated in 1991) to allow informal ecumenical co-operation to be recognised as local ecumenical projects (LEPs) under the auspices of the diocesan bishop. Such legislation inspired Wales-wide grass-roots initiatives, from the remote, Welsh-speaking, deeply rural area of Llŷn, around Botwnnog, to the burgeoning commuter belts of the anglicised south-east. One of these urban experiments – the East Cardiff LEP – sparked the second consideration, namely the ordination of an ecumenical bishop, satisfying Anglican episcopal polity, to exercise pastoral leadership in collaboration with the bishop of Monmouth and participant free-church covenanting traditions. That Gethin Abraham-Williams, the provincial ecumenical officer co-ordinating the proposals, was himself an ordained Baptist minister indicated considerable movement from previous generations' corrosive rhetoric.[38] Nevertheless, in 2002, despite unanimous episcopal support, the Governing Body's clerics and lay people refused the two-thirds majority needed to proceed. Whilst this did stimulate a new, more permissive 'ecumenical canon' on LEPs in 2005, many became frustrated that substantial progress on oversight still eluded the churches.

The third significant effort again reimagined episcopal ministry, this time within a broader context. *The Gathering* proposed in 2012 that alongside the six Anglican dioceses of Wales three new jurisdictions be formed, representing the Methodist, Presbyterian and United Reformed Church/Covenanting Baptist traditions, each appointing its own bishop who would be consecrated into the historic episcopate, assuming responsibility for presiding at all ordinations within the jurisdiction.[39] Furthermore, 'all existing ministers [would] agree to the laying on of hands by at least one Anglican bishop and at least one other bishop representing the other traditions'.[40] However, for some such an 'act of reconciliation' implied rejection of non-Anglican ministerial orders and

---

[38] For detailed preparatory analysis, see G. Abraham-Williams, ed., *Towards the Making of an Ecumenical Bishop in Wales / Tuag at Benodi Esgob Ecwmenaidd yng Nghymru* (Penarth: Enfys – The Covenanted Churches in Wales, 1997), and S. Rowland Jones, ed., *An Ecumenical Bishop for Wales?* (Cardiff: Church in Wales Publications, 2002).

[39] Covenanted Churches of Wales, 'The Gathering: Summary of Recommendations' (Cardiff: Covenanted Churches of Wales, 2012), recommendation 2; see www.cydgynulliad.org.uk/.

[40] Ibid.

imposed quasi reordination, whilst others openly struggled to embrace an ostensibly 'Anglican-shaped' episcopally focussed model. The remarkable enthusiasm afforded by the Church in Wales differed markedly from former indifference and hostility. However, the episcopal polity espoused demanded little from Anglicans whilst expecting widespread – and ultimately unacceptable – ecclesiological adaptations for Nonconformists.

To enact such imaginative schemes would necessitate legislative procedures for the participating denominations, and another Welsh initiative, this time in the international ecumenical sphere, would be instructive. *A Statement of Principles of Christian Law*, proposed and drafted by Norman Doe, Diocesan Chancellor of Bangor, was issued in 2016 by an ecumenical panel meeting in Rome (2013–16). The panel at Geneva 2017 formed a partnership with the World Council of Churches Faith and Order Commission, feeding the statement into its work – the statement is being discussed at national events globally prior to its presentation at the World Council of Churches Assembly in 2021.[41]

Nevertheless, as the centenary of disestablishment approaches, Welsh Anglicans' appetite for ecumenical innovation remains subdued. The Church in Wales' *Review* of 2012 recommended far-reaching change for Anglicans with dioceses reshaping existing benefices into geographically larger local Ministry/Mission Areas, sometimes equivalent to former deaneries.[42] Whilst the review mentions ecumenical potential, there is scant evidence of other traditions actually becoming embedded in these Areas despite the significant freedom that the Constitution permits. Moreover, whilst certain independent, evangelical community-focussed, family-friendly churches, bearing few denominational allegiances, enjoy remarkable growth, the Church in Wales seemingly inhabits a distinct, parallel ecclesiological plane, simultaneously fettered by historical infrastructural commitments, yet blessed with exceptional resources – spiritual, human and material – to enliven its extensive network of ancient churches. By recovering the missionary zeal of the earliest saints associated with these *llannau* and so prized at disestablishment – a self-initiating passion unencumbered by sensitivities of tradition – the Church might renew its fidelity to Christ's great commission and become most fully ecumenical, sent out

---

[41] M. Hill and N. Doe, 'Principles of Christian Law', *Ecclesiastical Law Journal*, 19 (2017), 138–53.

[42] See www.churchinwales.org.uk/structure/representative-body/publications/downloads/review/.

with gospel joy into the whole inhabited world – or at least this land 'built on the foundation of the cradle, the cross and empty tomb'.[43]

Interfaith Relations: Inhabiting a Hopeful Counter-Narrative

Despite earlier evidence of fruitful interfaith discourse,[44] it was the 9/11 terrorist atrocities that prompted people of faith in Wales to co-ordinated, intentional collaboration. Initiated in 2002 by the then First Minister, Rhodri Morgan, the Faith Communities Forum meets twice-yearly to 'facilitate dialogue between the Welsh Government and the major faith communities on any matters affecting the economic, social and cultural life in Wales'.[45] It involves high-level delegations from Wales' religious groups, with the Church in Wales represented by the archbishop. These mutually beneficial encounters provide channels for religious concerns to be voiced to government whilst allowing politicians to receive advice on particular issues.

Paralleling such sophisticated engagement, the Interfaith Council for Wales, founded in 2003, specifically exists 'to advance public knowledge and mutual understanding of the teaching, traditions and practices of the different Faith communities in Wales . . . mutual awareness of the distinctive features, and of the common ground of the different Faith communities in Wales . . . to promote good relations between persons of different Faiths and to be of service to the people of Wales'.[46] Alongside other Christian traditions, the Church in Wales was a founding member and two of its priests have served in key roles, with Alan Bayes acting as chair and Aled Edwards (whilst chief executive of Cytûn) its secretary. The council co-ordinates regional awareness-raising during National Interfaith Week, participates in momentous national events and contributes faith-related perspectives on diverse ethical and social issues. Through the Council 'faith communities . . . have a presence in the public sphere of Welsh politics that was inconceivable in 1999' whilst promoting 'a counter-narrative . . . that sees diversity as an opportunity rather than

---

[43] From 'Dewi Sant' by the Anglican/Nonconformist poet Gwenallt: D. Gwenallt Jones, *Cerddi Gwenallt: Y Casgliad Cyflawn*, ed. C. James (Llandysul: Gomer Press, 2001), 182–3.

[44] The poet-academic Grahame Davies (himself a Welsh-speaking Anglican) offers comprehensive historical perspectives in his *The Chosen People: Wales and the Jews* (Bridgend: Seren, 2002) and *The Dragon and the Crescent: Nine Centuries of Welsh Contact with Islam* (Bridgend: Seren, 2011).

[45] Faith Communities Forum, 'Terms of Reference': https://gov.wales/faith-communities-forum/terms-of-reference.

[46] Constitution for the Interfaith Council for Wales, revised and adopted July 2018.

a threat . . . driving communities towards their aspirations rather than their fears'.[47]

Whilst archbishop, Barry Morgan shaped Welsh Anglicans' desire to inscribe this hopeful counter-narrative through close collaboration with the Muslim Council of Wales. Having hosted a delegation of Syrian church leaders in 2007, the council's secretary general, Saleem Kidwai, worked with Robin Morrison, the Church in Wales' Church and Society advisor, to establish a series of interfaith dialogues called 'Finding A Common Voice', seeking to respond creatively to contentious issues such as terrorism, the role of women, stereotyping, tackling prejudice in schools, citizenship, community cohesion and environmental challenges. Morrison described this work as 'much more than interfaith dialogue' but 'a search for a "common humanity in and under God" which goes far deeper than our religious differences'.[48]

At a dinner in 2010 hosted jointly by the Church in Wales and the Muslim Council to celebrate Common Voice's contribution, the then First Minister Carwyn Jones observed that it was 'important to build a bridge between the world of politics and faith communities and work together in a spirit of unity and co-operation to ensure that people in Wales can lead their daily lives without fear of abuse and violence. Through these events, we can show the world and our own citizens that we have laid the foundations for a modern, culturally diverse and more tolerant Wales.'[49]

On the tenth anniversary of 9/11, Kidwai and Morgan declared jointly that 'working together has broken down barriers, built positive relationships, and underlined a passionate commitment to create a more harmonious society ... [remembering] and [praying] for the victims of terrorism, [denouncing] the use of religion to justify violence and [urging] people of all faiths and cultures to continue working together so that we can live as God intends ... side-by-side in mutual understanding and respect'.[50] They also issued a joint statement against demonstrations organised by the English/Welsh Defence League and welcomed the Interfaith Council's peace vigil the previous evening. The archbishop also joined other faith leaders in calling for cessation of religiously motivated hostilities in the Middle East (2014), an end to

---

[47] Aled Edwards' 'Introduction' to *Inter-Faith Wales: Building Trust and Respect between People of All Faiths throughout Wales* (Cardiff: Interfaith Council for Wales, 2008).
[48] News release, 11 June 2010.
[49] News release, 24 May 2010.
[50] Shared news release, 9 September 2011.

nuclear deterrence (2015) and, in support of the Lambeth Declaration on climate change, the development of spiritual and theological resources across faith traditions to aid urgent transitions towards low-carbon economies (2015). Concurring with the archbishop of Canterbury's appeal to 'support one another in defiance of those who wish to divide us', they inhabited a counter-narrative 'so exciting and so beautiful that it defeats the radicalisers, with their message of hate and despair'.[51]

High-level interreligious dialogue can nevertheless be prone to over-looking community-based initiatives. Chaired by Archbishop Morgan's then chaplain, Mark Dimond, the South Cardiff Interfaith Network published a booklet, titled 'Our Faith', outlining perspectives of local Buddhists, Baha'i, Christians, Hindus, Jews, Muslims and Sikhs, thereby raising public awareness by demonstrating religions 'striving for the same end: to be kinder and more compassionate human beings'.[52] That desire to transform hostility into hospitality lay behind Welsh Third Order Franciscans' decision gratefully to mirror the benevolence shown to St Francis of Assisi in 1219 by Sultan Malik al-Kamil during the Fifth Crusade in Egypt. Through inviting Christians and Muslims to a shared halal meal in September 2019 the Franciscans commemorated, 800 years later, the Christlikeness of the encounter as both men crossed spiritual, cultural and linguistic frontiers to enact a courageous alternative to the savage, religiously motivated barbarity blazing around them.

Multiplying such face-to-face peaceability – thankfully in less alarming circumstances – might become Welsh Anglicans' lasting contribution to interreligious encounter. Whereas much of Wales lacks religious variety – thus making dialogue more theoretical than practical – Butetown, south of Cardiff city centre, has embodied diversity ever since the docks were built in the mid-nineteenth century to transport Welsh goods worldwide whilst thereby attracting seafarers from Yemen, Somalia, Greece, the Caribbean and elsewhere, with more than fifty nationalities represented by the 1950s. Clearly visible from the Church in Wales' provincial office, St Mary's Church – originally evangelical but since the 1870s decidedly Anglo-Catholic – has served the community since 1843, and at Sunday Mass welcomes children of religiously mixed marriages who may also worship at the mosque on Fridays. The church school, 85 per cent of whose pupils are Muslims, seeks to nurture all pupils in their chosen

---

[51] Speech by Justin Welby delivered at the Muslim Council of Wales' interfaith dinner on 2 October 2015; see www.archbishopofcanterbury.org/speaking-and-writing/speeches/archbishop-justin-addresses-muslim-council-wales.

[52] News release, 15 October 2015.

faith, with core values of appreciation, equality, unity, friendship, love, happiness, perseverance, trust, respect, honesty, tolerance and hope. Together with St Paul's School in nearby Grangetown, it has established a pen-pal scheme with two schools in Caerphilly, some eight miles north, in order to foster appreciation of religious difference in a less diverse area. Whilst Butetown is not immune to religious and racial tension, faith leaders are committed to promoting mutual understanding and peaceful coexistence, an attitude echoed in the church's motto for its 175th anniversary: 'that in its beauty Cardiff may rejoice'. Life-changing co-operation between St Mary's, Tabernacl Baptist chapel and the Islamic Centre is shown in an ongoing scheme called 'Croeso Butetown' to resettle a Syrian refugee family locally, under the strapline 'we are no strangers to strangers'. In close partnership, Butetown Anglicans seek to be involved in building God's kingdom through consistent commitment to peace, justice and reconciliation, learning to recognise and cherish those who are 'other' in the generous light of the divine Other.

Conclusion

Much has been written recently of the practice – conscious or other-wise – of 'othering', that tendency to categorise those who are different – in terms of nationality, race, religion, sexuality, power, political outlook etc. – under a single, unnuanced, characterising label, with the intention of denigrating or even demonising. The presenting issues might include immigration, asylum, security, economics, isolationism and many others, but each regards the 'othered' as profoundly menacing, poten-tially triggering diminishment, suffering or even destruction. To be 'othered' might lead to scapegoating, as societies load upon the alleged threat their own conflicted desires and frustrations, potentially with violent (yet momentarily cathartic) consequences.[53] Brexit's tortured debates have exposed such structures deep within British democratic structures.

The history outlined in this chapter has shown the Church in Wales engaged in othering, at worst maligning other Christians whilst arrogat-ing a theological, ecclesiological and social self-importance. As such superciliousness yielded to greater humility, generosity and maturity, other Christians became appreciated as potential wellsprings of

---

[53] This is described classically by René Girard in his *Violence and the Sacred*, trans. P. Gregory (Baltimore: Johns Hopkins University Press, 1977).

enrichment, augmenting Anglicanism and promoting a shared vocation to witness within an increasingly secularised nation. That shift is to be welcomed both as fulfilling Christ's call for unity in mission (John 17:21–6) and also as spiritual growth in divine love, desiring transformation by the One whose triune relations of perfectly transparent reciprocity represent not some 'added extra' but the very divine essence.[54] Through such 'kenoticism' – a self-forgetful openness to the awesome mystery of difference 'othering' takes on quite different, immensely creative possibilities achieved through costly nurture of the other, desiring their full flourishing in their very alterity. The church 'most truly witnesses to the Gospel when it tries to serve Christ in the other person', offering 'selfless attention to the other because of God's selfless attention toward us'.[55]

Such noble othering resists smothering, seeking Christians' reabsorption into an undifferentiated sameness as certain Welsh Anglicans sometimes fancied. Rather, it rejoices in Christ's presence and the Spirit's activity in hitherto unexperienced, unimagined ways, believing that encountering otherness can be *mutually* enhancing rather than self-draining and ultimately annihilative; thus self-giving becomes self-reception. In response to Christ's high-priestly prayer for unity-in-mission – a 'co-mission' exceeding the most laudable ecumenical commission – it purposefully lays flawed human effort before the excess of God whose paschal paradigm reveals a way of being which may appear reckless within the old creation yet emerges as constitutive of the new.

Ecumenically speaking, this means that non-Anglicans might enjoy a relationship with *yr hen fam* which transforms Anglicans' unredeemed 'othering' into outstanding 'mothering', not some condescending maternalism but the joyful desire to see all reach maturity in the shared trinitarian faith of perfect unity-within-diversity. Such oneness – found in Christ rather than in institutionalism – desires both independence and interdependence, fullness, creativity and genuine reciprocity so that horizons of unity are not merely the creaking parameters of finance, infrastructure and past prejudices but infinite divine resourcefulness.

[54] See St Thomas Aquinas' doctrine of divine relations, e.g., *Summa Theologica* Ia.28.2, *responsio*.

[55] Archbishop Barry Morgan in his first 'Presidential Address to Governing Body', September 2003, www.churchinwales.org.uk/structure/representative-body/publica tions/downloads/theology-wales-back-issues/theology-wales-the-church-and-homosexuality/presidential-address-archbishop-barry-morgan/.

Amidst its strained wrangling concerning sexuality, it remains to see whether the Anglican Communion might preserve, or even intensify, its long-held unity, discovering its divergent ethical outlooks to be complementary rather than incompatible. Whilst interfaith dialogue lacks the explicitly trinitarian depths of Christian communion, seeking peaceful and respectful mutual flourishing across faith divides demands more than mere conflict-avoidance or indifferent coexistence but rather recognising that we ourselves are 'mothered by our others', thereby 'birthing forth a better world'.[56] Speaking in the wake of the atrocious New Zealand mosque attacks of March 2019, former archbishop Rowan Williams stated that it is imperative that we recognise the depth and mystery of our neighbour, acknowledging that 'God has made us so that we may recognise each other' (Qur'an 49:13), that 'deep calls to deep' (Psalm 42:7).[57] Thus believers – Welsh Anglicans included – are called intentionally to shape a reality radically different from the hateful brutality of extremists, 'summoned to witness' to the 'inalienable dignity' of the other.[58] In realising such a vision, suspicion, hatred and intolerance may become fuel for compassion, justice, creativity and love to be fired.

---

[56] These phrases derive from Jeannine Hill Fletcher's *Motherhood as Metaphor: Engendering Interreligious Dialogue* (New York: Fordham University Press, 2013), 205, 210.

[57] Rowan Williams, Address to the Muslim Council of Wales Interfaith Dinner, 26 March 2019 (unpublished).

[58] Ibid.

PART IV

The Church and Society

13

Welsh Anglicans and Cultural Debate

ROWAN WILLIAMS

The story of the Church in Wales might be seen as a story of battles won and wars lost: the lost battle over disestablishment, which cost the largest Nonconformist churches dearly in the long run, was offset in the minds of many by the renewed theological self-confidence of an autonomous Anglican province, strongly marked by a Tractarian identity. As elsewhere in the Christian world, there was a further round in that process of 'inventing tradition' that has been so marked a feature of modern societies at certain points of crisis and change. Anglicans and Nonconformists continued well into the late twentieth century to construct and deploy sophisticated and slanted versions of 'historic' Welsh Christian identity. In this chapter, I shall be looking at aspects of this process – but also asking whether the energy devoted to these ongoing battles had the effect of limiting the depth at which Welsh Christians of all backgrounds were able to imagine the challenges of contemporary Wales.

Anglican Victories

Moelwyn Merchant's autobiography, *Fragments of a Life*,[1] refers briefly to a period in the history of the Church in Wales after the Second World War which saw the flourishing of 'a very vigorous group of young clerics, all friends and of a similar age, and determined to establish a thoroughly Welsh and Catholic Anglicanism in a tradition which we knew united us with the rich literary, artistic and liturgical tradition of mediaeval Wales'. Merchant was at this time still teaching in University College, Cardiff, before his move in 1961 to Exeter University, where for many years he led an unusually creative and distinguished Department of English and consolidated his international reputation as a Shakespeare scholar, as well as beginning what was to be a notable late career as a sculptor under the tutelage of Barbara

---

[1] M. Merchant, *Fragments of a Life* (Llandysul: Gomer Press, 1990), 56.

Hepworth. His career certainly bears out Densil Morgan's judgment of the 'exceptional quality' of this group,[2] which included the future archbishop, Gwilym Williams, two other future bishops and Gwynno James, whose death in 1967 after a short tenure as dean of Brecon deprived the Church in Wales of one of its most gifted teachers and preachers. Nearly all of them were native Welsh-speakers, fluent and lively communicators with a degree of curiosity and enthusiasm about the culture of their time. They were theologically quite traditional (none of them was to show any marked excitement about the new theology of the early to mid-1960s), but willing to spend time and energy exploring the frontiers of theology and culture.

The example of the slightly older Glyn Simon, dean of Llandaff (1948–53), later bishop of Llandaff (1957–71) and then archbishop of Wales (1968–71), was very clearly a significant element in the background of this group: Simon's supervision of the post-war reconstruction of Llandaff Cathedral had brought him into contact with a range of influential contemporary figures in the arts, not least Jacob Epstein, whose monumental *Majestas* was commissioned for the new central pulpitum arch in the restored cathedral, and John Piper, who designed a number of features, including the east window.[3] Simon's mixture of firmly traditional Anglo-Catholic theology and spirituality with a strong and articulate commitment to the needs of the industrial working population, to international struggles against nuclear armaments and racism, and, increasingly, to the cause of the Welsh language provided many younger clergy and ordinands in Wales with inspiration for their ministry. But part of his charismatic influence also had to do with his capacity to show that the Catholic faith as he understood it could afford to be hospitable to contemporary art of various sorts. Densil Morgan notes Simon's 'sensitivity to the changing cultural patterns of post-war Wales' as the major factor in his influence as a 'modernising' presence in the province during the 1960s.[4] And it is true that, between roughly 1950 and 1970, it was possible to claim that Welsh Anglicanism was clearly in the ascendant, both culturally and numerically, attuned to many aspects of contemporary society: a steady rise in attendance figures through the

[2] D. D. Morgan, *The Span of the Cross: Christian Religion and Society in Wales, 1914–2000* (Cardiff: University of Wales Press, 2nd ed., 2011) – this is a notably comprehensive and sensitive survey of church life in twentieth-century Wales – 182, connecting this with what was then the fairly new Anglican youth movement, Cymry'r Groes, and its monthly journal of the same name, founded by Merchant.

[3] See O. W. Jones, *Glyn Simon: His Life and Opinions* (Llandysul: Gomer Press, 1981), ch. 4.

[4] D. D. Morgan, *The Span of the Cross*, 2nd ed., 194.

1950s reached a plateau around the early 1960s, while membership of the historic Nonconformist bodies was declining rapidly.[5] Also, for those who noticed such things, it was significant that two of the foremost literary figures in Wales in the 1960s and early 1970s, R. S. Thomas and Euros Bowen, were both Anglican parish clergy.

Yet that apparent moment of success or even 'victory' did not prove durable. From the plateau of the early 1960s, and a few years of more or less holding steady, the numbers of Anglican worshippers began to fall from around 1970 at a rate that has generally accelerated in the half-century or so since. Wales in general, once statistically one of the more religiously observant parts of the United Kingdom, has become one of the most conspicuously unchurched, and the cautiously but unmistakeably triumphant Anglican narrative of fifty years ago now seems very remote indeed. That narrative – still audible as recently as the 1990s – might be summed up in something like these terms. The disestablishment of the four Welsh dioceses in 1920, the result of relentless and (in the eyes of some indignant Anglicans) unscrupulous campaigning in the decades leading up to the First World War, proved a *felix culpa*. Liberated from the messy and lazy compromises of Victorian establishment, Welsh Anglicans were free to determine the sort of Christians they wanted to be, and to organise their corporate life accordingly. The Constitution of the new province – and even more, Archbishop C. A. H. Green's monumental commentary[6] – defined a church polity firmly grounded in a Tractarian commitment to the independent spiritual authority of an ecclesial body convened and governed by bishops in the historic apostolic succession. But this Tractarian skeleton needed to be clothed with missionary energy, spiritual discipline and creative flair; it needed also itself to be liberated from the aristocratic Toryism and paternalism that had coloured the ethos of Welsh Anglicanism before and after disestablishment. Archbishop Green was a Tory paternalist of plain colour in his politics; but this was combined with a very visible and serious sacramental spirituality, a deep conviction of the evils of Erastianism, and a cautious willingness to make room for the social as well as the liturgical concerns of post-Tractarian Anglo-Catholics – as shown in his

---

[5] See the statistics ibid., 189, 252 and 254.

[6] C. A. H. Green, *The Setting of the Constitution of the Church in Wales* (London: Sweet & Maxwell, 1937). On the contents and reception of this work, see Arthur Edwards' excellent biographical study, *Archbishop Green: His Life and Opinions* (Llandysul: Gomer Press, 1986), 90–8.

promotion of a former colleague, Timothy Rees, as a candidate for the bishopric of Llandaff in 1931.[7]

Rees had been since 1906 a member of the Community of the Resurrection at Mirfield, and had distinguished himself as a military chaplain in the Great War and as a mission preacher of extraordinary power. He had also assimilated the Christian Socialist ethos of the early generations of Mirfield brethren and was to bring to his episcopal ministry a consistent and selfless advocacy for the victims of the desperate hardships of the 1930s in industrial south Wales. Not until Glyn Simon's episcopate was there any similarly forceful engagement with the social and political realities of industrial and post-industrial society; nor, as Morgan puts it, was there any comparably 'robust Welshness' in evidence on the Welsh Bench of Bishops for a good many years.[8] But Rees had shown how an Anglican Catholicism purged of any High Tory legacy (such as had become widespread in so many deprived urban areas of England and already had a footing in some south Wales parishes) could inspire a renewed Welsh Christian identity, fully in touch with the realities of the day; and his story was an important part of the narrative current in the high tide of Catholic confidence in the 1960s.

Unfinished Conflicts

One aspect of this version of Welsh Anglican history was, of course, the belief that Welsh Nonconformity, in successfully agitating for disestablishment, had won the battle but lost the war. The shrillness of the campaign and the sheer amount of energy devoted to it, along with the nakedly partisan politics that bound the fortunes of Welsh Nonconformity almost without reservation to those of the Liberal Party, all contributed to a certain sense that the world of Welsh Dissent was spiritually exhausted or worse.[9] Once disestablishment had been won, there was, you could say, nothing left for Nonconformity to do: the 'war' was being gradually won by Anglicans. This is not to say that such bluntly military language would have been used or endorsed by the leading figures of mid-century Welsh Anglicanism; but this subtext of

---

[7] D. D. Morgan, *Cedyrn Canrif: Crefydd a Chymdeithas yng Nghymru'r Ugeinfed Ganrif* (Cardiff: University of Wales Press, 2001), has a very full and sympathetic account and assessment of Rees' life (28–67).

[8] 'Ni chai Cymreictod cyhyrog ei adfer i'r fainc am flynyddoedd lawer': ibid., 66.

[9] Cf. ibid., 28, quoting Tudur Jones; though the point Jones makes is really about the entire spectrum of Welsh religious institutions, Anglicans very much included.

a kind of Anglican 'supersessionism' helps to explain why there was so persistent a sense in many circles in the Church in Wales that ecumenical co-operation was not a particularly powerful or meaningful imperative, and why there is so little evidence in much of the twentieth century of regular and serious critical conversation between Anglicans and others in Wales about theology.

This should not be overstated: a periodical like *Diwinyddiaeth*, the organ of the theological section of the Guild of Graduates of the University of Wales, carried contributions from Anglicans as well as Nonconformists, and even had an Anglican editor (O. G. Rees of St Michael's Theological College, Llandaff) in the 1960s and early 1970s. But it is striking if we look at biographies of distinguished non-Anglican Christians of the twentieth century how little the presence of the Church in Wales is noted. The great Welsh Independent theologian and poet, Pennar Davies, seems to have had no contact to speak of with local Anglicans during a long and nationally significant ministry;[10] and it must be said that there is as deafening a silence on the other side, from Welsh Anglican voices. To take a rather different case of Welsh 'Nonconformity', the biographer of Wales' foremost modern Roman Catholic writer gives little evidence of any awareness of Anglicanism, though the book contains a photograph of Saunders Lewis broadcasting alongside Gwilym Williams.[11] The only mention of interest is in an article of 1946, in which Saunders Lewis discusses the conversion of the poet David Gwenallt Jones from Calvinistic Methodism to the Church in Wales as 'the only Church that presented to him a Welsh Catholicism' (in contrast to the Roman Catholic Church in Wales at that time).[12] It is an ironic sidelong tribute to the success of the Welsh Anglican narrative we

---

[10] He is not unaware of Anglican tradition. An unenthusiastic comment on an 'old Anglo-Catholic book which contains a list of sins' can be found in P. Davies, *Diary of a Soul*, tr. H. Hughes (Talybont: Y Lolfa, 2011), 90; cf. his mixed reaction to Lancelot Andrewes, ibid., 95, and his notes on Anglican reluctance to communicate at an ecumenical event abroad, 139–40. But of local relations with the Church in Wales there is no trace, and the personal recollections printed in Ivor Thomas Rees' brief biography, *Saintly Enigma: A Biography of Pennar Davies* (Talybont: Y Lolfa, 2011), 105–13, do not include any Anglican (or, for that matter, Calvinistic Methodist!) names. D. D. Morgan, *Pennar Davies* (Cardiff: University of Wales Press, 2003), 67, intriguingly notes that Pennar Davies and Moelwyn Merchant were each awarded a first-class honours degree in English at University College, Cardiff, in the same year, but I have found no trace of any further connection.

[11] T. R. Chapman, *Un Bywyd o Blith Nifer: Cofiant Saunders Lewis* (Llandysul: Gomer Press, 2006).

[12] Ibid., 272.

have been exploring; but there is no suggestion that Saunders Lewis himself took that story seriously enough to engage with it. His purpose is to make a polemical point to his fellow Roman Catholics.

The issue is not just the familiar one about the relative sluggishness and lukewarmness of much of the ecumenical scene in Wales in the middle and later periods of the twentieth century. It is more fundamentally to do with the way in which both Anglican and Nonconformist histories, by casting their narrative in terms of struggle and victory, increasingly made it hard to construct a sense of common Christian purpose in a rapidly changing Wales. If Nonconformists were liable to see the disestablishment saga as the final blow to the credibility of a foreign (and oppressive) body, with post-disestablishment Anglo-Catholicism simply another piece of evidence for the alien character of the Church in Wales, Anglicans were readily inclined to see disestablishment as a providential moment allowing them to appear unequivocally as 'the ancient Catholic Church of the land' (a favourite phrase of Anglican apologists in Wales as in England), in a way that legitimised the air-brushing of Protestant Dissent from Welsh history and absolved Anglicans from any attempt to relate constructively to bodies whose day had manifestly passed. The most egregious expression of this came in a notorious sermon of Edwin Morris, at that time bishop of Monmouth, later archbishop of Wales, delivered in 1951, which categorised both Dissenters and Roman Catholics as 'intruders' in the canonical territory of the Church in Wales.[13] This was to revive with a vengeance the rhetoric of the great anti-disestablishment campaigners of the late nineteenth century, pre-eminently A. G. Edwards, Bishop of St Asaph from 1889 and first archbishop of Wales; and it aimed to turn the tables on the routine Nonconformist charge that *Anglicanism* was the 'intruding' presence. The fact is that the mid-twentieth century was a period when each of the main Christian bodies of Wales sincerely believed itself to embody the 'natural' historic Christian identity of the Welsh people. All in one way or another looked to the Age of the Saints, the almost mythical generation of holy and charismatic figures who preserved and spread the Gospel in the dark times following the end of Roman rule in Britain. Anglicans saw this period as an age of integral, sacramental Catholic Christianity prior to the imposition of Roman centralisation in the wake of Augustine's mission in 597; Roman

---

[13] J. Peart-Binns, *Edwin Morris, Archbishop of Wales* (Llandysul: Gomer Press, 1990), 81; see D. D. Morgan, *The Span of the Cross*, 2nd ed., 185–6, on the effects of this utterance.

Catholics could point to the unbroken continuity between that era and the Church of the early and high Middle Ages; and some Nonconformists argued on the basis not only of the glories of Reformation and Revival but of a continuity between their pattern of life and teaching and a supposedly 'radical' Celtic Christian world.[14]

In short, Anglicans and Nonconformists alike tended to regard each other as representing *both* a corruption or a distortion of true historic Welsh Christianity *and* a now decisively superseded recent history. Both appealed for legitimation to a 'deep history' beyond the contemporary scene; but, in the nature of the case, this implied that one narrative was going to be radically at odds with the other, as both claimed a natural right over Welsh territory – imaginatively as well as literally. And the conflict was sharpened by the number of very influential figures throughout the twentieth century who had moved their allegiance from Nonconformity to Anglicanism – from Bishop John Owen of St David's, who had led the resistance to disestablishment alongside A. G. Edwards, to Bishop J. C. Jones of Bangor (another figure whose early death in 1956 was a great blow to the Church),[15] and some of the younger group mentioned at the beginning of this chapter, including Gwilym Williams and Moelwyn Merchant himself – though Williams, in fairness, showed more ecumenical initiative than many of his contemporaries. Nonconformity, in other words, was temptingly easy to understand as a phase that had passed in national as in individual experience. The impulse to serious dialogue was not likely to be strong in such circumstances.

But the price was a mutual isolation damaging to all: as the Christian world in general gradually began in the second half of the twentieth century to work at what a shared language about the nature of the

---

[14] 'That free and responsible Christian world which had been fashioned by the great saints of the fifth and sixth centuries': Pennar Davies, quoted in D. D. Morgan, *Pennar Davies*, 69. Davies would have included Pelagius among these 'great saints', anticipating the mythology of more recent accounts of 'Celtic' Christianity; most of his fellow Nonconformists would not have agreed.

[15] See the vivid and affectionate biography by his brother-in-law, E. Lewis, *John Bangor – The People's Bishop: The Life and Work of John Charles Jones, Bishop of Bangor 1949–1956* (London: SPCK, 1962). Densil Morgan, in *The Span of the Cross*, 2nd ed., 184, rather unexpectedly describes him as an Anglo-Catholic; he is more accurately viewed, despite his relative rigorism about denominational boundaries, as a mildly liberal Evangelical – and as such a somewhat unusual figure in the mid-century Church in Wales. He would certainly have counted as exhibiting a 'Cymreictod cyhyrog' (above, n. 8) to match that of Timothy Rees.

Church might entail, as even the Roman Catholic Church began to reconfigure its understanding of other Christian bodies, the distinctive history of denominational tension in Wales made it harder to cooperate in such work. As late as the 1990s, the attempt to create a shared episcopal ministry jointly commissioned by the Covenanting Churches in Wales (the Church in Wales, the Presbyterian Church of Wales, the Welsh Wesleyan Methodists, the United Reformed Church's Welsh Province and a small group of Baptist congregations) foundered on this history and was rejected by both Anglicans and Presbyterians. The spirit that in the wider ecumenical world produced the Lima document on 'Baptism, Eucharist and Ministry' in 1982, from the Faith and Order Commission of the World Council of Churches, was not greatly in evidence in Wales – at least at the level of institutional contacts; we shall see later that this was, happily, not the whole story. The truth is that, at key points, both Anglicans and Nonconformists seemed to lose sight of what might be entailed in jointly belonging to the Body of Christ, in such a way that the failure or weakening of any constituent part is everyone's problem and everyone's diminution. It is not wholly surprising that what I have described as winning battles and losing wars – short-term triumphalism, in other words – eroded the energy that was needed to confront not the Wales of the sixth or nineteenth or even mid-twentieth century, but the actuality of the drastically impoverished, fragmented and alienated society that was becoming increasingly visible in the Wales of the last decades of the twentieth century and the beginning of the twenty-first – the decades that saw the end of heavy industry, the emergence of third-generation unemployment, the disappearance of much traditional farming and the body blow of the foot-and-mouth epidemic of 2001. By that time, imaginative cooperation between the churches was, thankfully, not an eccentricity; but somewhere along the line crucial ground had been lost to secular influences, despite the lastingly creative work of the mid-century Anglican generation – and indeed the lastingly creative ministry of so many in the Nonconformist world. Energy had not been shared as it might have been between creative Christian communities. As some pointed out, Wales had many of the conditions that might have fostered the emergence of another Iona or even Taizé; yet such a vision for Christian community failed to find traction.[16]

---

[16] See the comment of Dewi Lloyd Lewis in I. T. Rees, *Saintly Enigma*, 109. The sparsity of religious communities in the Church in Wales was a disappointment to many in the

Rival Claims to the Cultural Legacy

Behind the competitive claims to be the natural historic Christian identity of the Welsh nation lies the deeper question of how Welsh identity itself is to be understood – a vastly complex issue, which this chapter cannot begin to address adequately. The disestablishment controversy was significantly fuelled by the bitterness of the debates that developed around Welsh identity in the mid-nineteenth century, debates which, as scholars such as Prys Morgan have amply shown, turned on dramatic changes in how the Welsh language was viewed and how the national story was to be reconstructed (or, more candidly, constructed).[17] The first generations of Nonconformist Revivalism were deeply hostile to local Welsh custom and tradition, largely regarding it as superstitious and immoral; they had no particular interest in the language as such except as a tool for evangelism (and in this they stood in the succession of many previous Welsh Protestant activists). Welsh had survived as a literary language partly because of the Bible of Bishop William Morgan and the Welsh translation of the Book of Common Prayer, and these texts were focal for the great eighteenth-century campaigns for popular literacy which preceded the Methodist Revival and in some ways made it possible.

At the same time, later eighteenth-century antiquarianism prompted some Welsh Anglican clergy to a remarkable burst of activity in conserving and transmitting the remains of older Welsh culture. The notorious Iolo Morganwg, despite his Unitarianism, found enthusiastic allies among the clergy of the established Church in his 'revival' of ancient bardic tradition: Anglican clerics accepted his exuberant fantasies and

province. Small communities of women worked briefly in the south Wales valleys and – for rather longer – in St David's (running the retreat house at St Non's); the Mirfield Fathers occupied St Teilo's Hostel in Cardiff (initially a student hostel, then a retreat house) from 1945 to 1968; and the Society of St Francis, which had run hostels for homeless men in Wales before the Second World War, returned in 1972 to open a house in north Wales. This closed in 1983, though the Swansea-born Brother Ramon, a much-loved and revered spiritual director and writer, lived on for some years as a hermit in the grounds of the Society of the Sacred Cross, a small contemplative women's community in Monmouthshire (see A. Howells, *A Franciscan Way of Life: Brother Ramon's Quest for Holiness* (London: Bible Reading Fellowship, 2018), for a fine portrait of this remarkable figure). Discussions among some south Welsh clergy in the 1970s about the possibility of an Anglican Benedictine foundation in Wales never came to fruition.

[17] See P. Morgan, *Wales: The Shaping of a Nation* (Exeter: David and Charles, 1984); and, for a lively summary account, his long essay, 'From a Death to a View: The Hunt for the Welsh Past in the Romantic Period', in E. Hobsbawm and T. Ranger, eds., *The Invention of Tradition* (Cambridge: Cambridge University Press, 1983), 43–100.

collaborated in the early *eisteddfodau* of Iolo's devising. Clerical poets such as Gwallter Mechain (Walter Davies, 1761–1849) were active in promoting and raising the standards of local *eisteddfodau*, and Bishop Thomas Burgess of St David's, founder of St David's College at Lampeter, though an Englishman with no knowledge of the Welsh language, was the patron of the Carmarthen Eisteddfod of 1819.

The term *hen bersoniaid llengar*, 'the old literary parsons', was familiarly used to designate the group of Anglican clergy in the early nineteenth century who were involved in this cultural revival. The last thing many prominent Welsh Anglicans of this period could be accused of was an indifference to the language and the national heritage as they understood it. But it was indeed a matter of *heritage*, and of a very particular understanding of it. The Anglican cultural revivalists and their lay supporters, many of them aristocrats of English birth or education such as Lady Charlotte Guest and Augusta Waddington (Lady Llanover), were wedded to a romantic picture of rural Welsh life and a fascination with ancient legend; and their politics were unequivocally conservative. Both Charlotte Guest and Lady Llanover devoted a good deal of resource and energy to the education and welfare of the local industrial population (Guest was actively involved in managing the ironworks at Dowlais), but there was something of a gulf between this reality and the imagined Wales of their cultural interests. The critical moment came in 1847 with the report of the Commission of Enquiry into the State of Education in Wales – the 'Treachery of the Blue Books', *Brâd y Llyfrau Gleision*. This document was seen as having been shaped by the interests of landowners and the established Church: it painted a dire picture of ignorance and backwardness, most of it ascribed to a mixture of Nonconformist anti-intellectualism and the stubborn persistence of the Welsh language. Unsurprisingly, it caused outrage in Welsh-speaking communities – but most of all in Nonconformist Welsh-speaking communities, who rallied vigorously in defence of their intellectual *bona fides* and of the language. But this had nothing to do with the sort of cultural identity that had been the focus of Anglican *literati* of the preceding generation; its goal, as Prys Morgan stresses, was to show that Welsh could be as effective a vehicle as English for the conduct of a moral and productive working life acceptable by the standards of Victorian probity. The centre of gravity shifted rapidly, as the defence of Welsh became the project of Welsh Dissent, especially the formidable Calvinistic Methodist community, and a widening gulf opened between Anglicans and 'patriots'.[18]

This meant the creation of a powerful new national mythology: Wales became the model contemporary Christian society, sober and chaste, sabbatarian, economically responsible, socially stable, an example of classical Protestant virtue. A very much chastened interest in poetry and music was encouraged, to avoid the reproach of mindless puritanism (so that, ironically, Nonconformists became the transmitters of the products of an earlier Anglican cultural project, using and developing the sanitised and romanticised models of historical Welshness that had emerged earlier in the century), and the National Eisteddfod was embraced by – and at times almost swallowed by – the Nonconformist establishment. As the nineteenth century wore on, it was this picture that was deployed to argue for the 'alien' character of the Anglican Church in the Principality, overriding the complex history of Anglican involvement in the preservation of national culture. A. G. Edwards of St Asaph, eventually the first archbishop of Wales, wrote indignantly in 1912 of the crucial role played by the Anglican Church in preserving the language: 'It cannot, then, reasonably be denied that the Welsh of today owe the purity and the very survival of their vernacular tongue to the Church which some ignorant people stigmatise as alien.'[19] But the 'alien' reproach was not so easily set aside, chiefly because of the deep-rooted perception that – never mind any number of *personiaid llengar* – the Church's leadership was detached from the mainstream of Welsh life. It was a perception with which it would be hard to argue, given the history of absenteeism and pluralism that had characterised the Welsh episcopate for centuries. A mid-Victorian English commentator, writing of Welsh bishops in general, did not mince his words: 'they have been utterly unlearned in the signs of the times, and have carried the climate of the cloister or the academy into the mountains and valleys of Wales.'[20] This observer, who shows an unusual knowledge of and sympathy with the history of the eighteenth-century Revival, believed that 'Half a century ago [i.e. around 1820–30] Wales might have been preserved

---

[18] P. Morgan, 'From a Death to a View', 94–5.

[19] A. G. Edwards, *Landmarks in the History of the Welsh Church* (London: John Murray, 1912), 237 – an invaluable book for understanding the arguments and mindset current among anti-disestablishment activists at the turn of the century. Edwards had clearly learned the polemical use of statistics and deployed attendance and membership figures with aplomb.

[20] F. Arnold, *Our Bishops and Deans* (London: Hurst and Blackett, 1875), II, 169.

to the Church', and that the advance of education could have made the Anglican liturgy more appealing to 'an increasingly cultivated mind';[21] but he was pessimistic about the chances of any effective Anglican revival in Wales, certainly while the episcopate remained as it was, and his grasp of how and why the language question might matter in any Anglican educational or apologetic strategy was uncertain.

What he did not foresee was that the growing pressure on the Welsh Church from Nonconformity would reinforce the case for more native episcopal appointments and for the general strengthening of discipline and morale in Welsh Anglicanism in the last quarter of the century. Just as the 'Treason of the Blue Books' had consolidated Nonconformist cohesion and confidence, so the growing agitation for disestablishment now consolidated an Anglican political identity. It may seem question-begging to use a phrase such as '*political* identity', but this is not simply about party allegiances in the ecclesiastical struggle. The fact was that by the mid-nineteenth century the Presbyterian Church of Wales was virtually the only distinctively and exclusively Welsh *national* body. There was as yet no Welsh university, and there had not been since the late Middle Ages a distinctive legal system. Whatever might be said by Edwards and others about Wales' debt to the established Church, it was not and never had been a national institution for *Wales*. And the effect of the campaign against disestablishment was to create something of a 'shadow' institutional reality for Welsh Anglicanism, which guaranteed that in due course the independent Welsh province would at least begin with a sense of some corporate identity, the identity of a genuine 'polity'.

The Churches and the Changing Face of Welsh Culture

The point of this digression into the nineteenth century is to help us understand why some of the twentieth-century battles of church life in Wales were configured as they were. As the preceding paragraphs indicate, there was a longstanding tension about what was to be seen as the 'default' position for Welsh Christianity. The difference could be characterised in several ways: a broadly Catholic legacy (with the trace of a Welsh version of Merrie Englandism) versus 'Puritanism', a nostalgia for pre-modernity as opposed to a modern and functionally oriented social imaginary, a theology of sanctifying the whole 'natural' community over against the ideal of a 'gathered' church under godly

[21] Ibid.

discipline. These are all polarities with their roots in the Reformation era, especially in the somewhat diverse spectrum of British reformations in the sixteenth and seventeenth centuries. But what is somewhat different in Wales is the way in which what it *meant* for Anglicans and Nonconformists (particularly Presbyterians) to present themselves as a 'national' Christian body was so heavily conditioned by mutual antagonism and by the changing attitudes to the language. Twentieth-century arguments echo the scripts of the nineteenth century, con sciously and unconsciously. Thus Moelwyn Merchant's appeal, in the quotation at the beginning of this chapter, to a literary and liturgical tradition from the Middle Ages as an element in the creation of a contemporary Welsh Catholic Anglicanism resonates with aspects of the literary antiquarianism of the *hen bersoniaid*; and Edwin Morris' provocative use of 'intruders' for non-Anglican Christians recalls Archbishop Edwards' insistence that Welsh cultural identity owes its survival to the Established Church, as well as his critique of the 'gathered' model of Nonconformist church life and its injurious effect on pastoral ministry.[22] In 1950, Glyn Simon (then dean of Llandaff) made a tactlessly satirical reference to the ceremonial of the Gorsedd, prompting a pained response from the then Archdruid, Cynan, accusing Simon of an ignorance of Welsh culture typical of English Anglican clerics. Simon, who took no prisoners in controversies like this, riposted with a still more pointed critique of the 'pompous nonsense' that surrounded the Eisteddfod, and made much of the fondness of Nonconformist clergy for ersatz vestments and liturgy. Behind the satire and the defensiveness is the odd history of the modern Eisteddfod as partly the creation of Anglican as well as Dissenting antiquarians and its takeover by mainstream Nonconformity.[23] Glyn Simon would have been well aware of the ironies of this history.

But the most potent source of suspicion, the supposed dominance of an English or English-oriented clerical leadership, revived with some force at the time of the election of Edwin Morris as archbishop in 1957 and

---

[22] A. G. Edwards, *Landmarks*, 242–7.
[23] This being said, it is worth noting that Daniel Davies (Bishop of Bangor from 1925 to 1928) had been chair of the Eisteddfod's executive committee in 1912; and his successor at Bangor, C. A. H. Green, welcomed the Eisteddfod to Bangor in 1931 with (characteristically) a High Mass in the Cathedral, and took a full part in the Gorsedd ceremonies (A. J. Edwards, *Archbishop Green*, 77). The Crown and Chair at the National Eisteddfod have gone to Anglican clergy – Euros Bowen, Gwynn ap Gwilym, Aled Jones-Williams – several times in the past seventy-five years.

J. J. A. Thomas as bishop of Swansea and Brecon in 1958: Morris, although he had spent his entire ministry in Wales, was an Englishman, and Thomas a non-Welsh-speaker, and there were widespread reports that comments had been made at the Electoral College that were hostile to or dismissive of the claims of Welsh-speaking candidates for both positions. Glyn Simon incautiously amplified the volume of controversy by publicly stating his unease, and the columns of the *Western Mail* duly filled with correspondence, some of it bearing out the worst anxieties of those unhappy with the decision. Aneirin Talfan Davies of the Welsh BBC, a poet and critic of some renown as well as an exceptionally theologically literate Anglican layman,[24] published a pamphlet on the subject, strongly supportive of Simon, and the controversy produced much bitterness within the Church in Wales as well as reinforcing Nonconformist hostility. One particularly unhappy result was that David Gwenallt Jones abandoned Anglicanism and returned to the Presbyterianism of his youth, accusing the Church in Wales of once again siding with Anglophone privilege.[25] Combined with Morris' inflexibility about the Church in Wales' claims and what seemed to many to be the increasing rigorism about Anglican exclusivity, the controversy about episcopal appointments did a great deal to freeze ecumenical sentiment for many years. And – as had happened in the nineteenth century and in the early days of the autonomous province – the fierceness of pro-Welsh sentiment produced a further disagreeable backlash. When Simon and his successor as archbishop, Gwilym Williams, came out so strongly in support of Welsh-language activists in the 1970s, they will have been sharply conscious of having to make up lost ground in order to avoid a simple reiteration of pre-disestablishment stereotyping. This is explored further in Chapter 15.

[24] His brief book, *Dylan: Druid of the Broken Body – An Assessment of Dylan Thomas as a Religious Poet* (London: J. M. Dent, 1964), cites Etienne Gilson, Thomas Gilby, Gregory Dix, William Temple and others in a strikingly sophisticated and original reading of Dylan Thomas. Once again, this is the cosmopolitan but nationally grounded world of Moelwyn Merchant's generation. Aneirin Talfan (another convert from Calvinistic Methodism) knew Pennar Davies, who was a contributor to *Heddiw*, the cultural monthly founded by Aneirin Talfan in 1937 (it ceased publication in 1942).

[25] D. D. Morgan, *The Span of the Cross*, 2nd ed., 191–3; cf. O. Jones, *Glyn Simon*, 68–71. Aneirin Talfan forwarded his pamphlet to his friend David Jones, who commented on 'irresponsible and ignorant anti-Welsh sentiments' in the press, and added, 'I'd fondly imagined that with Disestablishment the old charges of anglicization and anti-Welshness had largely been disposed of' (A. T. Davies, *David Jones: Letters to a Friend* (Swansea: Triskele Books, 1980), 96). On Gwenallt's return to Nonconformity, see the detailed account in A. Llwyd, *Gwenallt: Cofiant D. Gwenallt Jones, 1899–1968* (Talybont: Y Lolfa, 2016), 289–94.

But what emerges from this episode, and indeed from the whole story we have been examining, is that such stereotypes have been notably hard to change largely because they have generated in reaction such powerful and consoling counter-narratives – the Reformed Christian utopia of the Nonconformist high tide, the uniquely valid Catholic Church of the nation on the Anglican side. The mid-twentieth century saw important qualifications to both. Some Welsh Nonconformist self-understanding acquired a more unconventional political edge in the period, taking to itself the emancipationist and pacifist enthusiasms of the 1960s, and retaining passionate commitment to a simple communitarian vision of small organic and co-operative social and national units – a vision given eloquent expression in the pamphlet written by Pennar Davies in association with other Independent voices, including Gwynfor Evans, leader of the nationalist party, Plaid Cymru – *The Christian Value of the Welsh Language / Gwerth Cristionogol yr Iaith Gymraeg*.[26] And as we have seen, some of the Anglican Catholic advocates of the 1950s and 1960s were, like Glyn Simon, intelligently concerned with both Welsh and wider British cultural life and keen to distance themselves from any residue of the High Toryism of their predecessors. Indeed, in many respects, ironically, the anti-nuclear and anti-racist convictions of Glyn Simon were closer to the politics of a Pennar Davies than to those of many or most of his own flock. But, granted these new refinements in Anglican and Nonconformist self-presentation, the mutually reactive elements in their history died hard; and this had consequences for the wellbeing of the Christian community overall in Wales at a time when secularisation was beginning to prevail.

Hindsight is seductive; and it is no part of my purpose to suggest that decline in Welsh institutional Christianity could have been arrested by more ecumenical imagination. The causes of decline in traditional church attendance and membership throughout Western Europe have common roots in the changing patterns of affiliation and communal identity characteristic of late modern societies; there is no single factor that can be blamed and thus unfortunately no single solution that will reverse the situation overnight.[27] But it is hard not to regret the way in which the enormous theological, cultural and devotional riches of both Christian traditions – not to mention the contribution of the Roman Catholic Church – were not allowed to flower in less reactive modes. One recurrent theme in these pages has been

---

[26] Swansea: Gwasg John Penry, 1967.

[27] For a useful if somewhat dry survey of the social profile of Welsh Anglicanism at the end of the twentieth century, see C. Harris and R. Startup, *The Church in Wales: The Sociology of a Traditional Institution* (Cardiff: University of Wales Press, 1999).

winning battles and losing wars – short-term gains at the expense of 'rival' versions of Christian Welshness; and the other main leitmotif is the way in which this mutual tension and even aggression fostered the creation of historically doubtful narratives designed to legitimise one version of Christian Welshness as primitive, natural and obvious. To note the temptations and the failures of these strategies is by no means to belittle the moral earnestness of the participants in the controversies of both nineteenth and twentieth centuries, to suggest that their theologies were simply deficient or outmoded, or to say that we have nothing to learn from them.[28] The critical point is that the tangled political history of Wales – the heartless and contemptuous neglect of the Welsh Church by the authorities of the English establishment for so much of the post-Reformation period, the crass insensitivity of English government both to the Welsh language and to the social and educational needs of the Welsh people – more or less doomed the different confessional bodies in Wales to a series of sterile collisions, pushing the diverse parties into rivalrous and too often embittered isolation. The legacy of this history has taken a very long time to disappear; and the tragedy is that, if it is now much weaker than half a century ago, that is largely because the entire cultural memory of Welsh Christianity is so much weaker.

And rivalry has never been the whole story. At so many key moments, Christians of differing confessional loyalties have come together in common witness at the local level, and the ecumenical climate – while suffering from the far more widespread lukewarmness about institutional ecumenism overall – is a great deal less frigid. Shared ecumenical pastorates are not a rarity. I have not tried here to outline what might be thought of as a parallel story, the history of twentieth-century Welsh evangelicalism, whose relation to denominational identity since the 1904–5 Revival offers another perspective on what may help to loosen the ties of confessional identity politics for the sake of a more effective missionary engagement.[29] This is largely because, for the greater part of the twentieth century, there was a very limited presence in the Church in Wales of any self-consciously evangelical elements.

[28] To be personal for a moment: I should unashamedly say that I owe my Christian faith to both the confident and expansive Presbyterian chapel of my earliest years and the equally challenging, serious and intelligent Anglican parish of my teens, under the guidance of Anglican clergy very much in the mould of the post-war Church in Wales luminaries we have been discussing.

[29] D. D. Morgan, *The Span of the Cross*, 2nd ed., 213–17 and 248–51, deals with the questions posed by the non-denominational or post-denominational trends in evangelicalism within Nonconformist circles in the mid-twentieth century.

Developments in the late twentieth and early twenty-first centuries have seen some change in this – and in the visibility of charismatic worship and experience in Anglican life, a distinctive if still – in the eyes of some – controversial stimulus to renewal and fresh forms of co-operation. But it may be appropriate to end this sketch with a story about one quite distinctive ecumenical and missionary venture, one that has something inescapably parabolic about it. Between 1989 and 2004, John and Norah Morgans created a Christian community on the Penrhys council estate in the Rhondda. Coming from a Congregationalist background, John Morgans, after a period as Moderator of the United Reformed Church's Welsh province, decided to attempt a new kind of Christian engagement with a community suffering extremes of material and cultural poverty: Llanfair Penrhys (close to the site of one of medieval Wales' most popular Marian shrines) was a worship centre, a focus for social action and support, and increasingly a focus for international interest and involvement, as John sought to make visible the realities of a wider world within the confines of a very challenged local environment. He and Norah built up an extraordinary network of ecumenical connections – with the Cistercian monks of Caldey Abbey, with the Eastern Orthodox Church in the United Kingdom and in Eastern Europe, with the Reformed Church in Hungary and with an assortment of artistic and creative partners. The liturgy that took place in the very simple and beautiful chapel was drawn from a range of historical sources, adapted so as to connect it more directly with what could be digested in the local context but still unashamedly grounded in historic credal faith and practice. A bell from Caldey was hung outside, and the austere interior acquired a couple of icons and a set of seasonal banners to decorate the plain white walls. Young people from the estate were regularly taken on retreat to Caldey and on other visits. The mission of the church was consistently seen as an inseparable union of prayer and service, and the identity of this Christian community was shaped not by intra-Christian competition but by a profoundly theological attention to what it might mean to be the worshipping Body of Christ in the midst of this specific human reality. Llanfair Penrhys emphatically did not turn its back on denominational histories and historic resources, but it did refuse to be pinned down on a map of mutually exclusive territories. The project continues – though the social environment has changed somewhat – as a joint ministry of the Covenanting Churches in Wales.[30]

---

[30] John Morgans has written and published on his own initiative two books about the Penrhys experience – *Penrhys: The Story of Llanfair* (privately published, 1994), and (with

Conclusion

If we ask what a properly Catholic (sacramental, historically continuous and historically literate), Reformed (self-critical and institutionally flexible), mission-oriented Christian community might look like, Penrhys provides a compelling answer to the question. Perhaps as the life of the Church in Wales moves forward, it will be possible to think through more seriously and intensively what a Christian identity will now look like in drastically de-Christianised settings like the council estates of the Rhondda or the gutted town centres of so much of Wales, and in the residually Christian but often equally marginal and deprived rural communities – and to think this through without being imprisoned by a memory of confessional competition or by a myth of any kind of 'given' Welsh Christian identity. Those who treasure the legacy of Timothy Rees, J. C. Jones, Glyn Simon and others – who in their day began to ask how historic Christianity could speak compellingly to a Wales that had in large part long outgrown the traditional, semi-legendary identities of both Anglican and Nonconformist institutions – will pray that the richness of the ethos which at their best these figures fostered and developed still has the capacity to generate a renewed vision of the beauty of holiness and the justice of the Kingdom for the Wales of today and tomorrow.

Norah Morgans) *Journey of a Lifetime: From the Diaries of John Morgans* (Llanidloes: privately published, 2008). In the latter book, pp. 435–60 provide a summary of the vision that animated John and Norah and the development of the project as a whole.

14

The Church and Education

ROSALIND WILLIAMS

The educational landscape of Wales has been characterised by the vision and dedication of many with an honourable and common intent that the gift of education should be the right of every person. Whether we consider Cor Tewdws, founded c. 395, or St Illtyd's School, founded in c. 508, where St David himself is said to have studied, as the early adopters of Welsh education, we can look at our history and confidently see strong links between the Church and education. As we saw in Chapter 1, one of the earliest pioneers of education in Wales was Griffith Jones, who wished to make education accessible to many, allowing them to read the Bible and learn their Catechism, achieved by establishing 'circulating schools'. By the time of his death in 1761, these had taught almost 200,000 people to read. Whilst this chapter focusses on the history of Church in Wales Schools since disestablishment, the contribution of all Christian churches should be acknowledged as they developed early forms of free education, laying the foundation for the next iteration provided by the vision of Joshua Watson (1771–1855) and the so-called Hackney Phalanx (an influential group of Anglican high churchmen).

Church Schools in Wales before 1920

On 16 October 1811, Watson and the Hackney Phalanx established the National Society for Promoting the Education of the Poor in the Principles of the Established Church, throughout England and Wales. Their aim was to establish a church school in every parish. By 1861 there were 12,000 schools 'in union' with the National Society across England and Wales.[1] The practice in Wales was for benefactors or diocesan committees to establish schools which were affiliated to the National Society, and by

---

[1] L. Louden, *Distinctive and Inclusive: The National Society and Church of England Schools 1811–2011* (London: National Society, 2012).

257

1867 there were 808 such schools in Wales. According to one study, the first of these were in Penley and Talwrn Green in Flintshire.[2]

The Schools Sites Act 1841 increased the number of schools established in Wales, but the 1847 commission on education – the 'Blue Books Report' – fuelled debate on the state of education in Wales. The responses to the General Inquiry undertaken by the National Society, a separate parallel inquiry of 1846–7, offered a picture of the achievements of the society, particularly in Wales. As a result, the standing committee of the National Society established a Welsh Education Committee in 1846. It placed the responsibility for Wales with those who lived or owned property in Wales and sought to address the need to train teachers and to establish new schools. To supplement diocesan endowments, a Welsh Education Fund was also established. The Welsh Education Committee identified the need to facilitate the improvement of teacher training and development of Welsh people as teachers. By 1871, the standing committee considered that 'it appears that the Welsh Education Committee has accomplished to a great degree the ends for which it was established ... the change of circumstances has rendered its further continuance unnecessary'.[3] The fund closed in 1872.

The work of the committee had enabled the continued building of new schools and the establishment of Anglican training colleges. The South Wales and Monmouthshire Training College was opened in 1848 to train teachers for church schools in England and Wales. It later became Trinity College, Carmarthen. In 1849, the North Wales Training College in Caernarfon was established, which in 1893 became St Mary's College, Bangor – a Church of England Teacher Training College for women. In 1858, the Model School opened to give students at Trinity College, Carmarthen, real teaching practice.

The (Forster) Education Act 1870 began collaboration between central government and local authorities in the provision of publicly funded education, a mainstay in the years to come. It also made grants of 50 per cent towards the running costs of a voluntary school, which accelerated the building of church schools. The number of schools in Wales in 1879 had risen to 844. Their aim was clear – for example, it was said at the opening of Priory Street Church School in Carmarthen in 1869: 'we are here for the purpose of doing good, and God willing, we will

---

[2] G. E. Jones and G. W. Roderick, *A History of Education in Wales* (Cardiff: University of Wales Press, 1st ed., 2003).

[3] Welsh Education Committee, 'Minutes', vol. 3, 16 June 1871, Archive of the Church in Wales, National Library of Wales, Aberystwyth.

never lose sight of that fact ... the church school is planted here that education shall be associated with religious truth and that education shall be of the highest character'.[4]

However, there was opposition to the bill which became the Education Act 1870 from Nonconformists, especially to the 'Cowper–Temple clause' which became section 14 of the Act. This proposed that religious teaching in state schools be non-denominational, and this still appears in statute today. It was the precursor of the Agreed Syllabus. Section 7 of the Act gave parents the right to withdraw their children from any religious instruction. According to one study: 'when not required by law, [religious education] was virtually universal in board schools ... exposure to the Bible and moral teaching was generally favoured and opt-outs on the part of individuals or institutions were rare'.[5] In turn, the Voluntary Schools Act 1897 provided for a grant of 5 shillings per scholar payable to a voluntary school. These successive steps, whilst in some quarters controversial, provided the seeds of growth for the partnership that continues between church schools and successive governments to the present day. Moreover, the (Balfour) Education Act 1902 provided funds for denominational religious instruction in voluntary elementary schools, and established 'the Dual System' of co-operation between Church and State. It proved very controversial, not least in Wales, where many Nonconformists threatened to refuse to pay rates for denominational schools. It took fifty-nine days of parliamentary debate to agree the final wording – the 1870 Act had required a mere twenty-eight days.

Indeed, such was the outcry that it led to local authorities withholding funding from non-provided schools. The government responded with the Education (Local Authority Default) Act 1904. But this was repealed when the Conservatives lost the election in 1906 and a Liberal government came to power. Nevertheless, there was a continuing discussion about the position of the Church as a partner with the State in education; Kenneth Morgan notes: 'After 1903, Bishop [Alfred George] Edwards became unexpectedly friendly with his old adversary and dialectical sparring partner [David] Lloyd George, in trying to work out

---

[4] See Church in Wales, Bench of Bishops, *Education Review* (Cardiff: Church in Wales, 2009), https://s3.amazonaws.com/cinw/wp-content/uploads/2013/07/edrev-en.pdf.

[5] B. Gates, 'Faith Schools and Colleges of Education since 1800', in R. Gardner, J. Cairns and D. Lawton, eds., *Faith Schools: Consensus or Conflict* (Abingdon: Routledge Falmer, 2005), 19.

a "concordat" over denominational education."[6] Lloyd George, whilst initially sympathising with the local authorities' position, recognised that moving power from the school boards to county councils would cause tension when their priorities differed. The answer was to create a Welsh Department of the Board of Education in 1907. This was a milestone in the devolution of power to Wales.

However, social attitudes and patterns of religious belonging were changing, and the passing of the Welsh Church Act in 1914 was perceived as demonstrating Christian vitality in Wales. Yet, by the date of disestablishment, the ravages of the First World War, a country in recovery, and the social complexion of Wales meant that the newly created Church in Wales inherited an education system that recognised the need for social reform in raising the school leaving age to fourteen, standardising salaries and providing free education. But these aspirational improvements could not compete against post-war austerity. By 1922 the 'Geddes Axe' cut education expenditure by £6.5 million, and once again the Church was required to find the funds to support its schools.[7] The school numbers for 1920 were as follows: county elementary, 1,270; county secondary, 12; Welsh intermediate, 101; Church in Wales elementary, 560; Roman Catholic elementary, 52; and other elementary, 18; the total number for voluntary elementary schools was therefore 630.

The Development of Church Schools and the Challenges They Faced

Church schools embody the commitment to provide education as a form of witness to the Christian faith. After 1920, each diocese held their schools in trust. Some of the buildings were vested in the Representative Body, but day-to-day administration, including teaching religious education, was the duty of the school managers, who were in turn responsible to the bishop and a form of education committee. The local clergy were instrumental in supporting and nurturing schools beyond pastoral care; they sought to assist in finding funding, helping with teaching, and providing the Christian care distinctive of the ethos of church schools.

---

[6] K. O. Morgan, *Rebirth of a Nation: Wales, 1880–1980* (Oxford: Oxford University Press, 1981), 46.

[7] See https://statswales.gov.wales/Catalogue/Education-and-Skills/Schools-and-Teachers/Pre-1974/Schools.

Whilst the Church in Wales developed its unique identity in many areas, and forged new ways of working, the partnership with government and the National Society remained largely unchanged by disestablishment. Welsh education was still the responsibility of the Board of Education in London but the National Society recognised its continuing responsibilities for schools and training colleges in Wales. However, the Representative Body began to assert its own responsibility: the minutes of a meeting of 6 July 1923 record that after disestablishment school sites in Wales were deemed to be vested in the Welsh church commissioners and then the diocesan authority. At this time, a Provincial Church Schools Committee was created by the Governing Body. This gave structure to the provincial and diocesan roles of managing schools. Bishops determined the educational priorities for their own diocese, and a devolved pattern of governance emerged. The condition of schools was still a cause for concern, and a review in 1924–5 classified schools on the basis of their state of repair. This meant that in some areas, significant investment was required. In the Diocese of St David's, for instance, repairs and readjustments needed to church schools were estimated to cost £8,000. In 1927, Bishop David Lewis Prosser established a fund to raise the money. By March 1928, £4,448 had been collected across the diocese, with the rest expected within the year. This was a significant achievement.

The 1920s provide further evidence of the benefits of partnership between government, local authorities and the Church. The Hadow Report of 1926 was the first time a recommendation had been made to establish a system of separate primary and secondary streams of education; it argued that 'the truths of religion and their bearing on human life and thought should be brought home to pupils'.[8] Moreover, teaching 'religious knowledge' developed an important sensitivity among pupils. In addition to a secular government inspection, each diocese inspected religious education and reported to the bishop. In 1928, the register for Rossett Aided School, near Wrexham in the Diocese of St Asaph, for example, stated: 'Diocesan Inspectors on the 19th of November handed out 53 certificates and 3 prizes for Knowledge of the Old and New Testament, Catechism and prayer book. Knowledge described as excellent throughout the school.'[9]

---

[8] Board of Education, *Report of the Consultative Committee on the Education of the Adolescent* (London: HMSO, 1927) (Hadow Report), 189.

[9] R. Lowe, *Reflections of a Bygone Age: A Brief History of Allington and Burton in the Parish of Rossett* (Wrexham: RLP, 1998), 71.

The Welsh Department of the Board of Education was also making changes. By 1927, the Departmental Committee Report on 'Welsh Education and Life' proposed a policy of bilingualism. The subsequent Hadow Reports in 1931 and 1933 proposed changes to primary, infant and nursery schools, and the Spens Report (in 1938) developed the model of secondary education, recommending that there should be different types of secondary school and that the school leaving age should be raised to sixteen.[10] The recommendations of both reports were adopted by later Education Acts. It was clear that the elementary school system was going to change – and, in turn, this would have an impact on the voluntary school system in Wales.

The tensions between church and state education seemed to be diminishing, and a more tolerant policy and practice emerged. There were still challenges to the balance of state grants available to non-provided schools and to the potential loss of their autonomy. Sir Charles Trevelyan, President of the Board of Education, was tasked with developing reform bills that recognised the economic limitations of the time but provided ways to finance improvements to, and the reorganisation of, schools. As a result, the Education Act of 1936, whilst raising the age of compulsory education to fifteen, gave local authorities the power to contribute between 50 per cent and 70 per cent to managers of voluntary schools for building and improvement for senior children. The outbreak of the Second World War resulted in the suspension of the Act – but it had set the precedent for changes that would be proposed by R. A. Butler in 1944. By 1938, the Church in Wales had 501 schools, 59 fewer than in 1920. Given the challenges associated with it, the development of educational provision, and meeting the costs of preserving and improving the school estate, could not be achieved by the Church alone. State and Church would need to work together. Church schools in Wales geographically offered provision in a way that the State could not replicate – but without government grants the Church could not maintain the level of provision.

The National Society also responded to the changing priorities. Its annual report of 1934 states: 'The Church in England and Wales shall be properly represented officially upon the standing committee and in a manner in harmony with modern conditions.' Its president was the archbishop of Canterbury and its vice presidents were the archbishops of

[10] Board of Education, *Secondary Education with Special Reference to Grammar Schools and Technical High Schools* (London: HMSO, 1938) (Spens Report).

York and Wales. The report further states: 'the Society shall as hitherto be a self-governing Society and ... shall operate in England and Wales and not in England alone'.[11] In 1936, the bishops of the Church in Wales attended a conference to 'Consider methods of safeguarding Church Schools', led by John Sankey (by now Viscount), the chair of the National Society. On the recommendation of the conference, Governing Body appointed a provincial Education Committee as a 'consultative and advisory and a central bureau in all matters relating to education throughout the province'.[12]

However, the Second World War brought educational developments to a standstill, and the 1936 Act was suspended. But, during the war, education was seen as key to a national campaign to eliminate the inequalities and anomalies of a fragmented education system. Education needed equality of opportunity, which required partnership and compromise. Voluntary schools were in a poor condition: only 16 per cent of senior schools were voluntary. Conversely, local education authorities did not have the capacity to build small schools to replace those in the voluntary sector. Piecemeal reform had failed, and the dual system needed significant improvement.

As a result, in 1941 the Green Book, 'Education after the War', was issued by the Board of Education and initiated discussion on what changes were needed. At the same time, Richard Austen Butler became president of the Board of Education. He was convinced of the need to overhaul the system but recognised that any change had to be preceded by agreement with the Church. On 13 February 1941, a statement from Lambeth Palace was published in *The Times*. Known as 'the archbishops' five points', it was devised by the archbishops of Canterbury, York and Wales. Archbishop C. A. H. Green was part of these negotiations, and the Church in Wales supported the proposals. The five points were: all children in all schools should receive a Christian education; religious instruction should be an optional subject in training colleges; the existing statutory restriction that religious instruction should be the first or last lesson of the day should be ended; religious teaching should be inspected by Her Majesty's inspectors; and all schools should start the day with a corporate act of worship.

---

[11] National Society for Promoting Religious Education in Accordance with the Principles of the Church of England, *123rd Annual Report* (1934), Lois Louden Archive, Sheppard-Worlock Library, Liverpool Hope University, p. 8.

[12] Church in Wales: Governing Body, 'Minutes', 1936, Archive of the Church in Wales, National Library of Wales, Aberystwyth, Records of the Governing Body of the Church in Wales.

Between 1941 and 1943, careful preliminary discussions were held, including a five-day parliamentary debate in 1942. This ensured accord with the proposals and the white paper *Educational Reconstruction* was published in 1943.[13] The 'Religious Settlement' was a delicately balanced structure which had been created with care over the preceding two years.

Gareth Elwyn Jones and Gordon Wynne Roderick note that 'with the Butler Act the distinctive Welsh system of secondary education coalesced with that of England'. County secondary education in Wales was more advanced than in England but it was an area where the Church in Wales lacked provision. The proposals offered opportunities for growth. In 1938, there had been no Church in Wales secondary schools, but by 1950 there were four. Jones and Roderick further note: 'there were ways in which Wales could try to influence the passing of the Act but Welsh input into policy was limited'.[14] The passage of the bill required compromise and co-operation. What Butler produced was not ideal but it was politically and socially practicable and something with which all partners could co-operate. On 15 December 1943, the Education Bill was introduced. It received royal assent on 3 August 1944.

Church School Autonomy: Relations with Church and State

The Education Act 1944 is seminal. It provided the framework for the Church in Wales to be part of a system where the different school providers could, instead of working in isolation and distrust, engage in partnership and co-operation to improve education for every child. The main provisions of the Act were that: elementary schools were replaced by a tripartite system of primary, secondary and further education; the school leaving age was retained at fifteen; and schools could become voluntary aided or voluntary controlled. If the managers could raise 50 per cent of the costs to bring the buildings up to standard, they would receive a government grant of 50 per cent. In return, a voluntary aided school would retain greater control over its management, including appointing teachers and denominational instruction. In 1959, the sum granted by the government for alterations and improvements was raised to 75 per cent, in 1967 to 80 per cent and in 1975 to 85 per cent. If a school chose to become voluntary controlled, it received 100 per cent of the

---

[13] Board of Education: Welsh Department, *Educational Reconstruction* (London: HMSO, 1943).

[14] Jones and Roderick, *A History of Education in Wales*, 147.

required building costs and financial obligations would be undertaken by the local authority, which would also appoint and dismiss teachers, subject to the right of managers to appoint reserved teachers to deliver denominational instruction should parents request it. The Act also required a daily act of collective worship in every school (and rights of withdrawal), and it created the Agreed Syllabus for Religious Education (and rights of withdrawal), arrangements for inspection and a Central Advisory Council for Wales. There was no transfer of ownership of property of voluntary aided or controlled schools, but the local education authority was represented on the school's governing body – one-third of the membership in an aided school and two-thirds in a controlled school.

The work that went into finding a consensus for the Act is reflected in the official guidance: 'The prominence of voluntary agencies in the sphere of education is partly due to the fact that in the past, when the State was slow to play its part, the burden of providing educational facilities was shouldered by religious bodies, voluntary societies and generous patrons. The educational work of these early pioneers has created not only vested interests but a tradition of voluntary effort which fortunately persists to the present day. This tradition of voluntary effort is characteristic and must be fully appreciated.' Moreover: 'When the time came for the State to undertake fuller responsibility for the educational service it has naturally been reluctant to prejudice merely for the sake of administrative tidiness, the traditional rights of such bodies or destroy the variety which their schools provide in the system as a whole. This reluctance is all the greater where religious belief and freedom and conscience are involved.' And so: 'The result of these provisions of the Act is to ensure that they retain the liberty for the teaching of the tenets of the Church with which they are associated by teachers of their own faith.'[15] This clear assertion by government was that this was a partnership and the educational landscape was enriched by its diversity and strengthened in the delivery of education.

In response to the changes, in 1946 the archbishop of Wales established a Commission on Religious Education, which reported to the Governing Body in September 1947. The report recognised 'an urgent need for the educational work of the Church in Wales to be directed on provincial lines so as to secure unity of purpose while at the same time permitting diversity of method and experiment'. It suggested that a provincial Council for Education should replace the provincial Education Committee (set up in

---

[15] Ministry of Education, *A Guide to the Educational System of England and Wales* (London: HMSO, 1945), 5, 6 and 24.

1936). This new council should: determine the policy of the Church regarding all aspects of religious education; establish a bureau of information to advise on a range of issues, including syllabus, publications and Cymry'r Groes; and have five departmental councils including a Schools' Council and a Council for University and Training Colleges. It also called for the establishment of a Diocesan Council for Education, led by a diocesan director of education, as the diocesan 'authority', answerable to the Diocesan Conference, whom trustees or managers of schools should consult with respect to matters pertinent to running the school.[16] The Governing Body accepted these proposals, and the Council for Education was duly established.

As part of the reconstruction scheme, from 1 January 1948, the Representative Body allocated £400 per year to each diocese to be applied at the discretion of the bishop for the appointment of a director of education, diocesan missioner or director of youth work. This all gave education a clear framework and structure. The inaugural meeting of the Council for Education was held on 17 September 1948; its terms of reference were to 'Promote the educational work of the Church in Wales in primary and secondary schools'. In turn, each diocese had a Diocesan Council for Education and a director of education. The new structures encouraged cohesion and co-operation. The joint syllabus devised by the Dioceses of St Asaph and Bangor was commended for use across the province until a provincial syllabus could be devised and was formally adopted as the provincial syllabus in August 1953. Meanwhile, for controlled schools many local education authorities had adopted the Syllabus of Religious Instruction in the Schools of Wales, which had been prepared by the Welsh Society of the Institute of Christian Education. This was broadly accepted for general use, but in controlled schools it was supplemented by the dean of Bangor's publication, 'A Teacher's Handbook on the Church Catechism'.[17]

In the Diocese of Llandaff, the Association of Day School Teachers, which was established in 1947, became the provincial Guild of Church Teachers in Wales. In 1948, the secular Cyd-Bwyllgor Addysg Cymru (Welsh Joint

---

[16] Church in Wales: Archbishop's Commission on Religious Education and Regulations, 'Report made to the Governing Body of the Church in Wales to provide for the Establishment of a Church in Wales Council for Education and for purposes connected therewith', October 1947, Archive of the Church in Wales, National Library of Wales, Aberystwyth.

[17] Church in Wales: Council for Education, 'Minutes', 5 May 1952, Archive of the Church in Wales, National Library of Wales, Aberystwyth.

Education Committee) was formed, and in 1951 a minister for Welsh Affairs was appointed. It was also at this time, on the recommendation of the minister, that church schools in Wales were formally recognised as 'Church in Wales Schools'. The Education Act gave some opportunity to formulate education policy that recognised the uniqueness of the Welsh language, heritage and culture, and in 1953 the 'Place of Welsh and English in the Schools of Wales' report outlined guidelines for bilingual teaching and teacher training through the medium of Welsh. As a result, Trinity College, Carmarthen, was recommended as a provider of Welsh-medium courses; they began in 1956.[18]

It could be argued that this paradigm shift of policy and practice was a positive development for the Church in Wales. Conversely, whilst the 1944 Act had offered the Church fair opportunities, the rising building costs required to bring schools up to standard, and delays in implementation, imposed a heavy financial burden on the Church. This reduced its capacity to retain or expand its aided schools. As reported to Governing Body in 1960, the numbers of schools in the dioceses were: Bangor, 37 controlled and 3 aided; Llandaff, 9 controlled and 24 aided; Monmouth, 43 controlled and 4 aided (3 temporary); St Asaph, 70 controlled and 37 aided; St David's, 68 controlled and 10 aided; and Swansea and Brecon, 31 controlled and 17 aided. In total, the Church in Wales had 258 controlled schools and 95 aided schools, and, in turn, therefore, the Church supported 353 schools and 26,449 pupils every day.[19]

As the dioceses were now more involved with school managers, syllabus design, inspection and resources, so there was greater accountability and co-operation, and the provincial structure was able to promote the interests of church schools nationally. Yet, for other schools it would not be until 1964 that Wales had its first Secretary of State, and expenditure on certain public services would be delegated from Whitehall to the Welsh Office. So, the 1950s induced 'a mood of optimism, reflected in the growing belief that an improved education system could change society and solve many of its problems'. The fecundity of educational reports and initiatives had a huge impact on the progress of the new education system, mirroring the earlier beliefs of Joshua Watton and the Hackney Phalanx.[20]

---

[18] R. Grigg, *History of Trinity College Carmarthen 1848–1998* (Cardiff: University of Wales Press, 1998), 190.

[19] Church in Wales: Schools Council, 'Minute Books', January 1963, Archive of the Church in Wales, National Library of Wales, Aberystwyth, Board of Mission minutes, Table 15.

[20] Jones and Roderick, *A History of Education in Wales*, 156.

By 1964, the National Society noted in its annual report: 'The separation between Wales and England both ecclesiastically and educationally is growing more clearly recognisable'; and: 'An awakening of the Welsh national consciousness accompanied by a wider desire for national recognition is today an important factor in Welsh life and a sympathetic understanding of this spirit is essential.'[21] In the same year, Governing Body set up a working party to review the Education Council's work. The review commented that, whilst much of the 1947 report was still relevant, there had been a shift in perspective: 'Christian education is not, therefore just "Scripture Knowledge", nor merely teaching about Christian doctrine, Christian behaviour or Christian history, although all these find their proper place within it. It involves much more than that. Christian insight and understanding can relate every branch of knowledge creatively to the whole body of acquired learning.'[22] This was a significant change – from seeing church schools as a catalyst for teaching religious instruction to seeing Christian knowledge as the foundation of learning. Church schools could offer a holistic education based on Christian values and beliefs permeating all aspects of education. The Church in Wales was beginning to develop a broader sense of its witness in education, in partnership with the State, based on a Christian understanding of the nature and purpose of education.

In 1970, the Secretary of State for Wales had assumed responsibility for the education system. Between 1944 and 1990 there was no legal requirement to teach Welsh in primary schools. The Gittins Committee ran a parallel investigation to that of the Plowden Committee into primary education. It delivered similar findings and, in 1967, recommended a completely bilingual system of education in Wales. The Durham Report 1970, advocating the 'Fourth R', suggests that Christian education should be Christ-centred, where the essential and the existential meet. These changes would impact directly on church schools in Wales.[23]

---

[21] National Society for Promoting Religious Education in Accordance with the Principles of the Church of England, *153rd Annual Report* (1964), Lois Louden Archive, Sheppard-Worlock Library, Liverpool Hope University, p. 22.

[22] Church in Wales, Council for Education, 'Report to the Governing Body' (September 1964).

[23] For the Gittins Report, see Church in Wales, *A Manual of Training for Church Schools – Religious Education Syllabus Guide* (Cardiff: Representative Body of the Church in Wales, 1971), https://discovery.nationalarchives.gov.uk/details/record?catid=69791&catln=5. For the Plowden Report, see Central Advisory Council for Education (England), *Children and Their Primary Schools* (London: HMSO, 1967) and www .educationengland.org.uk/documents/plowden/. For the Durham Report, see

The provincial and diocesan structures also worked effectively to enable schools to meet the challenges of an evolving educational system. In the 1970s a provincial director of education was appointed, and the Education Committee worked on revising the syllabus, training diocesan inspectors and Bishop's Visitors, and a continuing building programme. Diocesan Boards of Education were restructured in 1984. The provincial Board of Mission, created in June 1985,[24] had six divisions, one of which was education. It reported to the Governing Body and supported the work of education across the province. The Bench of Bishops and individual Diocesan Boards of Education would embrace these changes and help church schools contribute to the educational landscape in their own contexts. By 1985, 15 per cent of maintained (that is, supported by government grant) primary and secondary schools in Wales were voluntary, and the Welsh Office noted: 'Denominational voluntary schools have played a role in education in England and Wales over a long period and the churches' investment in school building and equipment adds up to a considerable sum.'[25]

The Education Reform Act of 1988 introduced the National Curriculum and maintained the 1944 Act's provision on the place of religious education in the basic curriculum and the daily act of collective worship. In a voluntary aided school, religious education would be in accordance with the trust deed or, in a voluntary controlled or county school, the Agreed Syllabus. The Act recognised that understanding a range of beliefs and perspectives could make a positive impact on the teaching of religious education; and the Agreed Syllabus 'shall reflect the fact that the religious traditions in Great Britain are in the main Christian whilst taking account of the teaching and practices of the other principal religions represented in Great Britain'.[26] It also required each local education authority to have a Standing Advisory Council for Religious Education (SACRE); under the 1944 Act it simply had a power to establish such a body. These councils of all twenty-two local authorities in Wales are members of the Wales

---

Commission on Religious Education in Schools, I. T. Ramsey, ed., *The Fourth R: The Durham Report on Religious Education* (London: SPCK, 1970).

[24] Church in Wales: Board of Mission Division for Education, 'Diocesan Directors of Education, Minute Book 1980–8', BM/1997A/5, Archive of the Church in Wales, National Library of Wales, Aberystwyth.

[25] Department of Education and Science: Welsh Office Guidance, *The Educational System of England and Wales* (London: HMSO, September 1985), 18.

[26] See www.legislation.gov.uk/ukpga/1988/40/part/I/chapter/I/crossheading/religious-education/enacted?timeline=true.

Association of such bodies (WASACRE). The Church in Wales is represented with other denominations on every such council.

The formal inspection of religious education in a voluntary school was required by the Education Schools Act 1992.[27] The inspection evaluates the distinctiveness and effectiveness of a church school. Whilst diocesan inspectors had been undertaking inspections on religious instruction since before disestablishment, the statutory requirement was a positive affirmation that denominational inspection has the same standing as an ESTYN inspection.[28]

The change in government in 1997 led to enactment of the School Standards and Framework Act 1998, the last piece of seminal legislation before Welsh devolution. White papers preceding it had initially seemed to propose a policy detrimental to church schools, which led to pressure from the Bench of Bishops (and from the General Synod of the Church of England). The subsequent wording of the Act offered reassurance, signalled commitment to church schools and ensured the opportunity to develop Wales-specific policy. The Act obliged the governors of schools of a religious character to have an ethos statement. Defining ethos is not straightforward, and living out its elements depends on local context. The agreed ethos statement, found in every Instrument of Government for every Church in Wales school, provides: 'Recognising its historic foundation, the school will preserve and develop its religious character in accordance with the principles of the Church in Wales and in partnership with Churches at parish and diocesan level. The school aims to serve its community by providing an education of the highest quality within the context of Christian belief and practice. It encourages an understanding of the meaning and significance of faith and promotes Christian values through the experience it offers to all its pupils.'[29]

Church Schools since Devolution

The Government of Wales Act 1998 devolved education to the National Assembly for Wales, and, after further legislation in 2006, to the Welsh

---

[27] Section 13 inspections under the 1992 Act gave way to Section 50 inspections under the Education Act 2005.

[28] ESTYN, a crown body established under the Education Act 1992, is independent of the National Assembly for Wales but receives its funding from the Welsh government under section 104 of the Government of Wales Act 1998. The name derives from the Welsh verb *estyn* meaning 'to reach, stretch or extend'.

[29] A similar statement is used by the Church of England.

government which now determines its own policy and practice on the matter. Under this regime, today, the Church in Wales is responsible for 146 schools, serving 27,200 pupils, including 4 secondary schools, and 1 shared Roman Catholic and Anglican secondary school. The six diocesan directors, supported by a provincial director of education policy, liaise directly with the Welsh government and with local authorities in Wales in matters of policy and practice. There is also co-operation with the three Roman Catholic directors of education in Wales and regular joint engagement with both the Catholic Education Service and the National Society.

In 2006, the Bench of Bishops commissioned an Education Review.[30] The resultant report set out a framework as to how the Church in Wales could respond to the changing priorities in its diocesan and provincial contexts. As a result, the Church in Wales Advisory Council for Education was created. This is chaired by the bishop who holds the education portfolio within the Bench of Bishops, and the lead officer is the provincial director of education. The council's members come from each of the six dioceses and include each diocesan director of education and a representative of each Diocesan Board of Education. The council is a vehicle for the Church in Wales to determine its own education policy and be able to influence national policy-making within the terms of the devolution settlement.

In 2006 also, GWELLA (Welsh for 'improvement') was established by the Representative Body to support the statutory denominational inspection processes for the Church in Wales and the training of inspectors. Section 50 inspections under the Education Act 2005 run alongside the ESTYN inspections commissioned by the Welsh government. The GWELLA inspection focusses on the *impact* of a school's distinctive Christian character and collective worship on learners, the *effectiveness* of religious education, and the *effectiveness* of its leadership and management as a *church* school. The process ensures accountability and rigour for church schools to be confident about their mission and service in their own local context.

The seminal document *Faith in Education*,[31] with a foreword by the education minister, was published by the Welsh government in 2011 in partnership with the Church in Wales and Roman Catholic Church. It

---

[30] Church in Wales, Bench of Bishops, *Education Review*.
[31] See https://hwb.gov.wales/curriculum-for-wales-2008/key-stages-2-to-4/faith-in-education.

provides an overview of the role of schools of a religious character and the significant part faith has played in the development of the education system in Wales. It was an important statement of the partnership between Church and State in Welsh education.

The Church in Wales has its own denominational syllabus for religious education (*addysg grefyddol*). Its use is mandatory in voluntary aided schools and optional in voluntary controlled schools.[32] It enables a consistency of approach, ensures a pedagogical rigour in the teaching of religious education, and predicates the commitment of the Bench of Bishops and Governing Body to the Christian distinctiveness of Church in Wales schools. Importantly, the syllabus states: 'In recent years the teaching of religious education has undergone considerable change. It has moved from a concentration on Bible teaching and has developed a broader educational base from which it considers all aspects of religion, celebration, the lifestyles of adherents and beliefs ... The Bible is still studied. It is the source book of the Church's faith and knowledge of its contents is essential to allow the great stories of the faith to be heard, studied and understood ... Pupils should be brought to appreciate the importance of the Christian heritage in Britain and of the differing forms of Christianity in this country and across the world.'[33] Children should also be able to appreciate, respect and understand the beliefs and practices of all faiths, and people of no faith, and to explain their own beliefs with confidence and clarity.

Moreover, since devolution, there has been a complete curriculum review nationally, including the National Exemplar Framework for Religious Education[34] and the review by Professor Graham Donaldson of the Welsh curriculum in March 2014 and the subsequent report 'Successful Futures'.[35] Educational policy and practice in Wales have developed in their own unique context. There are no academies or 'free schools' as in England: these schools are set up by defined groups and funded directly by central government; they operate outside local authority control and have more autonomy than state schools. What is evolving in Wales is a mindset that is not attenuated by trying to remain fixed to what works elsewhere, but an educational landscape that embraces the unique heritage of Wales and seeks to develop learning and knowledge in

---

[32] There had been equivalents issued in 1953, 1963, 1972 and 2003.

[33] See www.churchschoolscymru.org/res/files/Diocese/Syllabus/syllabus.pdf, 7.

[34] See https://hwb.gov.wales/curriculum-for-wales-2008/key-stages-2-to-4/national-exemplar-framework-for-religious-education-for-3-to-19-year-olds.

[35] See https://gov.wales/successful-futures-review-curriculum-and-assessment-arrangements.

an aspirational and self-improving system. The Church in Wales has worked with the Welsh government in the production of the new curriculum and specifically where the teaching of religious education sits among the six 'Areas of Learning Experience'. Its involvement in the creation of the curriculum and engagement with the Welsh government demonstrates, once again, the close working relationship enjoyed between State and Church. It could be suggested that devolution has brought a commonality of approach which would not have previously been possible, for the Church in Wales and the government of Wales to work harmoniously for the common good as stewards of the education system.

The Church and the Universities

The Church in Wales also has a rich history of supporting higher education, post-doctoral research, expertise in theology, and vocations to train for the priesthood or as a teacher, and it has enabled Anglican institutions of higher education to be endowed by it, such as Trinity College (Carmarthen),[36] St Mary's College (Bangor), St Michael's College (Llandaff) and St David's College (Lampeter).[37] The mission and witness of the Church in Wales have also ensured that pastoral care and support have been provided in many ways, at Anglican halls of residence, including Church Hostel in Bangor, which served the University College of North Wales, and Llandaff House, Penarth, for students at the University College of South Wales and Monmouthshire. Providing support to all universities is nowhere better evidenced than in the contribution of university chaplains and local clergy who have established and nurtured official and informal chaplaincy provision across Wales so that students, wherever they choose to study, can cultivate their spiritual learning as well as their academic activities.[38]

Conclusion

We have journeyed briefly through the history of Church in Wales schools with emphasis on the developments since disestablishment.

---

[36] Grigg, *History of Trinity College Carmarthen 1848–1998*.

[37] D. T. W. Price, *A History of St David's University College, Lampeter* (Cardiff: University of Wales Press, 1990).

[38] For examples of chaplaincies, see www.cardiff.ac.uk/study/student-life/student-support/practising-your-religion/chaplaincy; https://bangoranglicanchaplaincy.wordpress.com/; www.uwtsd.ac.uk/faith/lampeter-chaplaincy/; and https://stdavids.churchinwales.org.uk/information/chaplains/.

What is clear is that, even from its early iterations, there has been a wish for education to be freely available, because it is so valuable. The commitment on the part of the Church has persisted across the changing social and economic conditions of Wales. The century has also seen the development of a meaningful partnership between Church and State in the field of education, whose strength is defined by its breadth of experience and practice. The Christian distinctiveness in a church school is still predicated on a firm foundation of Christian values – and the framework developed in education policy and practice has ensured that this has a secure place in the education system. The Church in Wales has invested, at provincial and diocesan levels, in education in the training and practice of those wishing to become teachers, in physical buildings and in the infrastructure of the syllabus and standards. This has demonstrated its commitment both to be an active stakeholder in education and to be a strong partner with civil government, including collaboration making seminal legislation, policy and practice. As the Church in Wales celebrates its first hundred years, we see how its schools have developed as part of a broad education offered in a vibrant Wales, where they are able to serve and witness to our wider communities. Church schools are not just for worshipping Anglicans, nor do they seek to proselytise or convert. Rather, they offer an education to all, of the highest standards based on Christian values at the heart of our communities. They serve the people of Wales and provide an education for all in the context of a clear commitment to Christian values and vision.

15

The Church and the Welsh Language

ENID R. MORGAN

Without the efforts of Reformation lawyers, politicians and the scholar-bishops William Morgan and Richard Davies, the Welsh language would not be alive today. The English prayer books of 1549, 1552 and 1559 had, in Welsh churches, merely replaced one foreign language with another. But these sixteenth-century Welsh leaders knew that the aims of the Reformation could not be achieved in Wales without the Scriptures and prayer book in the language of the people.[1] William Salesbury and others published the New Testament and prayer book in Welsh in 1567. The complete Welsh Bible was produced by Bishop William Morgan in 1588 and his prayer book in 1599, and a Welsh version of the Book of Common Prayer 1662 appeared in 1664. A second edition of the Bible, the 'Parry Bible' published in 1620, was the work not of the bishop of St Asaph, who chaired the enterprise, but of Dr John Davies, rector of Mallwyd, the greatest Welsh scholar of his time.[2] The centenary of the Church in Wales coincides with the 400th anniversary of this enormous volume and will be a subject of national celebration. The modern Beibl Cymraeg Newydd ('New Welsh Bible') was published in 1988.

The Acts of Union (1536, 1542–3) had made one realm of Wales and England, governed by English law, administered by speakers of English, clearly with the intention that Wales should become English-speaking. But the need for Welsh to remain the language of Protestant religion for the foreseeable future caused the Parliament of 1563 to legislate for Welsh translations of Scripture and the prayer book, and so the language of faith, resonant and beautiful, was secured. Because Morgan and Davies were not only learned in classics and theology, but also rooted in Welsh literary tradition, they ensured the dignified use of the language in public, and in the centuries that followed it became a tool of literacy and well of spirituality.

---

[1] E. P. Roberts, 'The Welsh Church, Canon Law and the Welsh Language', in N. Doe, ed., *Essays in Canon Law: A Study of the Law of the Church in Wales* (Cardiff: University of Wales Press, 1992), 151–73.

[2] Gwynn ap Gwilym, *Sgythia* (Caernarfon: Gwasg y Bwthyn, 2017).

From the beginning it was a struggle. There was a dire need to educate Welsh-speaking clergy, to insist on Welsh-speaking bishops and to fight those for whom church livings were things to be grabbed, with many of the gentry successfully getting their hands on church income. By the eighteenth century the Church had became a subservient tool of government, and absentee bishops spent much time in the House of Lords. In Wales the situation was exacerbated both by non-Welsh-speaking bishops and by lay owners of livings, often happy to appoint English relatives to parishes which needed Welsh-speaking clergy. Being literate in Welsh was no way to preferment. Cultured, scholarly, godly men struggled against a hierarchy that was largely indifferent, and against some who regarded the death of the language as something devoutly to be wished.

Thus was the Church alienated from the Welsh-speaking communities which were caught up in the evangelical Revivals of the eighteenth century. The growth of Nonconformity ripened into political protest in the nineteenth century, reaching its highest point in the battle for the disestablishment of the four Welsh dioceses which would become, reluctantly, the Church in Wales. The Church had indeed changed from being *yr hen fam* ('the old mother') to being *yr hen estrones* ('the old foreigner').

A painful turning point came with the publication in 1847 of the report into the state of education in Wales, swiftly dubbed *Brâd y Llyfrau Gleision* (the Treachery of the Blue Books) by its critics, because it blamed the dreadful state of education in Wales on the Welsh language and on Nonconformity. But an English view of Welsh as 'the gibberish of Taffydom' was all too easily internalised by many, and so the report inspired a generation of reformers to seek improvement through English alone, much as was happening to other peoples in Britain's colonies, of which Wales can seem the first.[3]

Contempt for Welsh and Welsh culture was not confined to the established Church. Emrys ap Iwan (Robert Ambrose Jones), scalpel-wielding satirist and Presbyterian minister, was probably the first to refer to the language as a *political* matter. He wrote in 1895:

> *Yr ydym yn methu â gweled bod Eglwys Loegr yn gwneud cymaint i Seisnigo Cymru ag eglwysi Seisnig yr Ymneilltuwyr. Os o wladgarwch y maent yn chwenychu dadsefydlu Eglwys Loegr, dadsefydlent eu heglwysi Lloegraidd eu hunain i ddechrau. Yn boeth y bo'r Eglwyswyr a'r Ymneilltuwyr;*

---

[3] R. R. Davies, *Conquest, Co-existence and Change: Wales 1063–1415* (Oxford: Oxford University Press, 1987).

rhyngddynt â'i gilydd hwy a ddinistrant Gymru os cânt eu ffordd. Nid yw'r helynt sydd rhyngddynt ond ymgecraeth rhwng pechaduriaid a rhagrithwyr. Cenfigen sectol sydd wrth wraidd eu holl regfeydd.[4] (I fail to see that the Church of England does as much to Anglicise Wales as the English chapels of the Non-conformists. If it is for patriotism that they wish to disestablish the Church of England, let them first disestablish their own Englandish churches to start with. To h*** with Churchpeople and Nonconformists; between them they will destroy Wales if they get their way. The quarrel between them is nothing but squabbling between sinners and hypocrites. Sectarian jealousy is at the root of all their cursing.)

In January 1920, the editor of the Anglican Welsh-language monthly magazine *Yr Haul* was still indignant at the way the bill for disestablishment had been hurried through in 1914. Following a conference held in Rhyl in 1919, he complained bitterly about how little had been known about the future Church: *Gwnaed cam gwrthun a di-alw-amdano â'r Hen Fam Eglwys, y rhan dlotaf o Eglwys Loegr.* (A disgraceful and uncalled-for injury was done to the Old Mother Church, the poorest part of the Church of England.) It needs to be remembered that until the 1980s the magazine *Yr Haul* and the newspaper *Y Llan* were the medium for Welsh-speaking Anglicans to argue their cause.

Disestablishment and the Welsh Language

The story of the place of Welsh in the Church in Wales can only be understood in both its social and its political relationships. Thus, the first archbishop of Wales, A. G. Edwards, heard a prominent Welsh Nonconformist, Kilsby Jones, refer to Welsh as a 'barley-bread language'; Edwards himself called it 'a badge of the uneducated'. Even in the 1940s W. H. Harries, Professor of Welsh at St David's College, Lampeter, advised the young G. O. Williams, later archbishop, not to speak in Welsh to his students 'lest he lose their respect'.[5] Even a Welsh accent was derided. When Welsh-speakers came to be considered as potential bishops, H. A. Bruce, Lord Aberdare, protested to Gladstone that the least that could be expected of a bishop was that he be able to address the House of Lords in 'intelligible English'.[6] How astonishing, then, that by

---

[4] Emrys ap Iwan, 'Paham y Gorfu yr Undebwyr', in M. Lloyd, ed., *Erthyglau Emrys ap Iwan* (Wales: Y Clwb Llyfrau Cymraeg, 1936), 23–41.

[5] D. T. W. Price, *Archbishop Gwilym Owen Williams 'G.O.:' His Life and Opinions* (Penarth: Church in Wales Publications, 2017), 12.

[6] R. L. Brown, 'In Search of a Welsh Episcopate', in R. Pope, ed., *Religion and Identity in Wales and Scotland c. 1700–2000* (Cardiff: University of Wales Press, 2001), 84–102.

some residual sense of principle, the newly formed Church in Wales in 1920 declared its intention to have its burdensome Constitution in Welsh as well as in English.

A century later things have changed; there is a Welsh Assembly government, with a declared aim of a million Welsh-speakers. Education in Welsh is available from nursery to post-graduate level. The language is visible, though not reliably, in churches. There is a new generation of confident and committed young translators and lawyers, journalists, academics and entrepreneurs who run their businesses in confident bilingualism. Public bodies are obliged to provide services in Welsh and English.

Lord Justice Sankey, assisted by Bishop John Owen and Charles Green, drafted the Constitution, and presented it in April 1922 to the Governing Body; he waxed lyrical:

> The Church in Wales is a Catholic and National Church; as a National Church we are the old Christian Church in these islands. The saints of the Church of God are sons [sic] of the race. They sleep in Welsh soil, hard by the shrines they loved and served so well. The self-same prayers which moved their lips move ours. Today we are the heirs of their beliefs and their traditions.[7]

Three years later Bishop John Owen wrote to him less romantically: 'I agree with you entirely that the future of the Church in Wales largely turns on its sympathy frankly with all that is sound in Welsh national sentiment; and the love of the Welsh language represents loyalty to its past, the chequered and precious past, of the Welsh nation.'[8] However, as Professor Glanmor Williams wrote, 'the system was more easily established than its ends were attained', adding 'one cannot help feeling that more attention was paid to maintaining the status quo than to envisaging the Church's role in relationship to the life of the Welsh nation'.[9]

Archbishop A. G. Edwards in 1920 took his oath of office on a copy of Salesbury's Welsh New Testament of 1567, but he made the oath in English.[10] Such a gap between symbol and reality quickly became evident with the establishment of two new dioceses. The favoured candidate for

---

[7] Quoted in J. W. Evans and J. M. Wooding, eds., *St David of Wales* (Woodbridge: Boydell Press, 2007), 291.

[8] E. E. Owen, *The Later Life of Bishop Owen* (Llandysul: Gomer Press, 1961), 41.

[9] G. Williams, *The Welsh Church from Conquest to Reformation* (Cardiff: University of Wales Press, 1962), 2–32.

[10] D. Walker, ed., *A History of the Church in Wales* (Penarth: Church in Wales Publications, 1976), 170.

the new Diocese of Swansea and Brecon was the much-loved archdeacon of Gower, Latham Bevan, who was eminently suitable but not a Welsh-speaker. No principle of having Welsh-speaking bishops had been established. Bishop John Owen of St David's, a fluent Welsh-speaker himself, was torn. Lord Justice Bankes thought it wrong to make knowledge of the language compulsory, while Lord Justice Sankey resigned from the Electoral College because he did not want to be involved in the argument. Archdeacon Bevan became the first bishop of Swansea and Brecon. That dilemma has recurred regularly ever since. The inability to give priority to the language also applies less visibly to administration, both at provincial and diocesan level. Although most recent bishops have had some competence in Welsh, not one of the general secretaries has been a Welsh-speaker.

While the Church was struggling to activate its new Constitution and to establish its finances, the economic depression in Wales was deepening. But in the wake of the war there was a considerable resurgence in national awareness.[11] Undeb Cenedlaethol y Cymdeithasau Cymraeg (the National Union of Welsh Societies) had been founded in 1913 and would inspire many new initiatives. It led the Welsh Department of the Board of Education to set up a committee of inquiry 'into the position occupied by Welsh in the schools and education system of Wales, and to advise how its study might best be promoted'.[12] Archbishop Edwards, however, would warn the Association of Elementary Teachers that it was possible to sacrifice the higher interests of people on the altar of 'sentimental devotion to the language'.[13] The inquiry was chaired by Bishop John Owen; its secretary was W. J. Gruffydd, editor of the distinguished cultural periodical *Y Llenor*; his intemperate opinion was that Archbishop Edwards was the most catastrophic man Wales ever saw.

Representatives of the Guild of Graduates of the University of Wales told the inquiry that 'The only truly satisfactory way of raising the status of Welsh was to give it its due status, namely making it the official language of Wales.' The published report:

> viewed with some apprehension the tendency displayed in recent years to appointing monoglot English dignitaries and parish priests to positions in

[11] M. Löffler, *Iaith nas Arferir Iaith Farw yw: Ymgyrchu dros yr Iaith Gymraeg rhwng y Ddau Ryfel Byd*, trans. Geraint H. Jenkins (Cardiff: University of Wales Centre for Advanced Welsh and Celtic Studies, 1995).

[12] Board of Education: Welsh Department, *Welsh in Education and Life* (London: HMSO, 1927).

[13] Brown, 'In Search of a Welsh Episcopate'.

which a knowledge of Welsh would be regarded as indispensable. A policy of this description cannot fail to alienate from the Church in Wales the sympathies of the Welsh-speaking community, and must inevitably hasten the anglicisation of the Church herself, as well as that of the nation as a whole, a result which, in view of her history and traditions, the Church should be the first to deplore.[14]

Another important initiative was the founding in 1922 of Urdd Gobaith Cymru (the Welsh League of Youth) by Ifan ab Owen Edwards to encourage children to take a pride in their language and nationality. A third development was the formation in 1926 of Plaid Cymru, the Party of Wales.

The election, in 1931, of Timothy Rees, a monk from the Community of the Resurrection in Mirfield and a Welsh-speaker from Cardiganshire, to be bishop of Llandâf promised a change. His eirenic attitude to Nonconformity, his warm catholic spirituality and his teaching in the dire circumstances of the Depression all presented a new model for bishops in Wales. His first address to the Governing Body was a vision of what the Church in Wales might be.[15] His early death in 1939 was a tragic loss.

A vignette of the Governing Body in 1935 is provided by Canon D. Parry Jones in his memoirs: *A Welsh Country Parson*.[16] The second archbishop, Charles Green, had told the 300 lay members of the Governing Body in Llandrindod Wells that they were not there because of 'any secular honour'.[17] Amongst the members were 'at least six barons, ten baronets, five knights, eleven titled ladies, three sons of peers, two generals, one vice-admiral, one brigadier-general and sixteen colonels, not to mention majors and captains'.[18]

Meanwhile, a change of mindset was augured when the government went ahead in 1936, despite protests, to found a Royal Air Force bombing school in the heart of the Welsh-speaking community at Pen-y-berth on the Llŷn peninsula.[19] The president of Plaid Cymru, Saunders Lewis, a lecturer in Welsh at the University College of Wales, Swansea, and two other prominent members of the party, the Baptist minister Lewis

[14] Board of Education: Welsh Department, *Welsh Education and Life*, 146–8.

[15] T. Rees, *Sermons and Hymns* (London and Oxford: Mowbray, 1946).

[16] D. Parry Jones, *A Welsh Country Parson* (London: B. T. Batsford, 1975), 109.

[17] A. J. Edwards, *Archbishop Green: His Life and Opinions* (Llandysul: Gomer Press, 1986), 87.

[18] Parry Jones, *A Welsh Country Parson*.

[19] D. Jenkins, *Tân yn Llŷn* (Aberystwyth: Gwasg Aberystwyth, 1937).

Valentine and schoolteacher D. J. Williams, presented themselves at the police station in Pwllheli to announce that they had set fire to some RAF outbuildings at Pen-y-berth. The arson case was heard in Caernarfon and provided a strong platform showing that the issue at stake was the defence of a Welsh-speaking heartland. The jury failed to agree. Dissatisfied with that result, the authorities, despite protests, moved the case to the Old Bailey. The trial, held in English and with an English jury, found the three guilty, and they were sent to Wormwood Scrubs for a year. The government soon found the Llŷn peninsula unsuitable and abandoned the project.

In the wake of Pen-y-berth, a petition was launched to gain official status for the language, and a young lawyer, Dafydd Jenkins, was appointed as secretary. The campaign led to the timid Welsh Courts Act 1942, which allowed the administration of oaths and affirmations in Welsh, for those who could not do so in English, and made the courts responsible for providing and financing a translation service.

By this time, Welsh-speaking Anglican lay people were playing significant roles in Welsh literary and media circles. Aneirin Talfan Davies, son of a Welsh Calvinistic Methodist minister, was one of many converts to Anglicanism at this time. With his brother Alun, he established Llyfrau'r Dryw, an important publishing centre in Llandybie and edited a new literary periodical, *Heddiw*. Eventually he became head of programmes at the BBC in Cardiff. A BBC 'regional' service was established in 1937. Another Anglican, T. I. Ellis, founded Undeb Cymru Fydd (the New Wales Union) in 1941, serving as its secretary for twenty-five years. A Welsh *éminence grise*, Ellis was a member of the ruling bodies of the university in Aberystwyth and the National Library, and a member of the Governing Body and of the Electoral College. His wife, Mari Headley, made a major contribution in her own right, especially in asserting the literary value of the Welsh Anglican tradition.

Rejuvenation and Scandal 1947–1967

In 1947, the Nation and Prayer Book Commission was formed, chaired by the Revd J. C. Jones (future bishop of Bangor), and its report was published in 1949.[20] T. I. Ellis and Mari Headley were members. The tone of the report seems now deferential and circumlocutory. It did declare

---

[20] Church in Wales: Nation and Prayer Book Commission, *Report* (Cardiff: Western Mail & Echo Ltd, 1949), 10, 45.

that the increasing sense of Welsh nationhood of the previous twenty-five years had been largely ignored by the Church, criticised 'the aloofness of the Church from Welsh intellectual life', and called it 'a Church pared down to the bare bones'; moreover: 'We believe that the Welsh way of life, whatever corruptions it admits or whatever virtues it retains, must be the concern of the Church as the agent of God for salvation.' When the commission's report was presented to the Governing Body in April 1950, Edward W. Williamson, Bishop of Swansea and Brecon, used a familiar defence, suggesting that the commission wanted the Church to be 'merely' a means of preserving Welsh.

However, Dr D. Densil Morgan writes of a sense of rejuvenation in Welsh Anglicanism in the period 1950–79: 'Whereas chapel religion was seen to be oppressive and Puritanical, Anglicanism and its Prayer Book Liturgy, sacramentalism and rounded doctrines of creation and incarnation provided a very appealing version of the Christian faith. It presented a viable spiritual alternative for those who were offended by Nonconformity and chose not to succumb to secularism and irreligion.'[21] The Nation and Prayer Book Report recommended the setting up of a triennial Church Congress. But only one was held, in 1953, and its report is a collection of significant lectures (all in English). Sir Idris Bell, much respected former president of the British Academy and acclaimed translator of Welsh poetry, had returned to live in Wales. Reviewing the pre-1920 past, which he saw as the root of current difficulties, he was blunt: 'Not only was the resentment caused by establishment a severe handicap to the work of the Church, but the subjection of the Welsh dioceses to Canterbury and the direction of ecclesiastical policy from England and under English influences tended to raise a barrier between the Church and the great mass of the Welsh people.'[22] He describes the Church's attitude to Welsh as 'Stepmotherly'.

Even less deferential, Dr G. O. Williams, warden of Llandovery College at the time, spoke on 'The Church in Wales and Current Social and Political Trends'.[23] Remembering the hunger marches of the 1930s, he declared, 'Wales must be given more immediate control over her destiny', adding: 'There are two distinct peoples, Welsh and non-Welsh, severed

---

[21] D. D. Morgan, 'The Essence of Welshness: Some Aspects of the Christian Faith and National Identity in Wales c. 1900–2000', in R. Pope ed., *Religion and National Identity: Wales and Scotland, c. 1700–2000* (Cardiff: University of Wales Press, 2001).

[22] Church in Wales, *Cyngres yr Eglwys yng Nghymru: Welsh Church Congress Lectures Delivered at the Congress* (Cowbridge: n.p., n.d.), 83.

[23] Ibid., 96.

not only by suspicion but by a sense of injury and wrong.' Williams was always a reconciler, stressing the need for people with differing attitudes to listen to each other. He had been brought up, like Bishops John Owen and J. C. Jones, in Welsh-speaking Nonconformist Wales, and like others discovered the richness of Anglican liturgy as a student at Oxford. But he was always aware that those who had grown up in other traditions might well hesitate for fear of the Church as an alien institution. Discussing the difficulties inherent in the situation in the Diocese of Bangor, he wrote: 'We are concerned with more than mere intelligibility, for unless in its worship and life the Church offers to God the peculiar gifts and vocation of the Welsh people, she will fail her Lord in two respects. She will not be carrying out her mission to gather the nation together in Christ; and she will deprive the people of the consecration without which nationality becomes an evil instead of a blessing.'[24] His theological point was, 'Our little world in Wales: the greater world outside; one disease, one cure'.[25]

Six years after the Nation and Prayer Book Commission's report, T. I. Ellis published a collection of essays titled *Ym Mêr fy Esgyrn* ('In the Marrow of my Bones'). In two incisive essays he set out a critical account of the first thirty years of the disestablished Church.[26] He saw hope in a new generation who had returned to the Church of their forefathers. The installation of J. C. Jones as bishop in Bangor Cathedral in 1949, when the service was (apart from the legal formalities) conducted entirely in Welsh, had indicated a Catholicity which had room for Welsh, a concept well expressed in a poem by Gwenallt.[27] The early death of J. C. Jones in 1958 from overwork was another grave loss. The *North Wales Chronicle* in January 1959 produced a memorial issue, in which a Methodist elder said 'he belonged to all of us'.

In November 1957, the Electoral College chose Edwin Morris, Bishop of Monmouth, to be archbishop, and three weeks later elected J. J. (Jack) Thomas to be bishop of Swansea and Brecon. Both godly and learned men, neither could speak Welsh. A retrospective account of the election of Edwin Morris by J. S. Peart-Binns cites the bishop of Llandâf, who in his diocesan letter in January 1958 criticised not the individuals concerned, but the Electoral College: 'In a bilingual province it should not be possible to make two elections of this importance in quick succession,

---

[24] G. O. Williams, *The Church's Work* (Caernarfon: n.p., 1959), 73.

[25] Church in Wales, *Cyngres yr Eglwys yng Nghymru*, 103.

[26] T. I. Ellis, *Ym Mêr fy Esgyrn* (Lerpwl: Gwasg y Brython, 1955), 38–59.

[27] D. Gwenallt Jones, 'Catholigrwydd', in D. Gwenallt Jones, *Cerddi Gwenallt: Y Casgliad Cyflawn*, ed. C. James (Llandysul: Gomer Press, 2001), 302.

without apparently allowing for the presence and practice of two languages.'[28] Peart-Binns himself attacked the very concept of confidentiality in the Electoral College: 'The cloak of confidentiality has always been used to cover more than is just and less than is seemly. Secrecy is a breeding ground for mistrust and innuendo.'[29]

A series of hostile letters in the *Western Mail* followed, some from Welsh-speaking clergy keener to defend the Electoral College than the Welsh language. In 1958 a pamphlet titled 'Bilingual Bishops and All That' by 'Theomemphus' was published. Theomemphus was Aneirin Talfan Davies, who continued the critique of T. I. Ellis. The pamphlet is a passionate, Catholic–Anglican piece of writing from a theologically literate layman, who quotes Augustine in defence of the Punic language, T. S. Eliot's *Notes Towards the Definition of Culture* and Simone Weil on the importance of *Roots*. Parts of it could still be an excellent handbook in the training of Welsh ordinands. For Aneirin Talfan the crux of the matter was that: 'in depriving the Welsh-speaking Welshman of a service in his own language, you are impoverishing his act of worship'. In response to the broadcast first sermon of Archbishop Morris, he wrote: 'What we miss in the sermon is a warmth and solicitude for the ancient language which is struggling for survival. There is no attempt to assess the loss suffered by Wales in its Church from the ruthless policies of anglicization carried out by Church and State.'[30] Aneirin Talfan was an ambasssador for the Anglican tradition in contemporary Welsh culture, and argued for more than 'a begrudging and patronising acknowledgment of its existence'. Edwin Morris, not a natural reconciler, thought the pamphlet 'deplorable in tone and content'.[31]

The Years of Turbulence

In 1939–40, despite protests, the War Office had taken over a large area of countryside in Eppynt in Breconshire for artillery training, and had cleared a Welsh-speaking community from their homes for ever. In 1957 Parliament authorised the city of Liverpool to build a reservoir in Tryweryn near Bala, thus drowning the community of Capel Celyn.

---

[28] J. S. Peart-Binns, 'Arglwydd Archesgob Cymru: Alfred Edwin Morris – Election and Aftermath', *Journal of Welsh Ecclesiastical History*, 2 (1985), 67.

[29] Ibid., 57.

[30] Theomemphus [A. T. Davies], *Bilingual Bishops and All That* (Llandybie: Christopher Davies Publishers, 1958), 13 and passim.

[31] *Western Mail*, 23 April 1958, cited in Peart-Binns, 'Arglwydd Archesgob Cymru'.

Despite all Welsh local authorities opposing it, work was completed and a new generation awoke to the vulnerability of its inheritance.

Following Tryweryn, activism intensified. In February 1962, the BBC's annual radio lecture was given by Saunders Lewis. *Tynged yr Iaith* ('The Fate of the Language') proved to be a turning point. The former leader of Plaid Cymru argued that the survival of the language was the single most important political matter in Wales. He laid out a revolutionary campaign of protest to gain equal and official status for the language. A group of students went to discuss action with him and in the summer of 1962 Cymdeithas yr Iaith (the Welsh Language Society) was formed, driven by the conviction that the final crisis of the Welsh language was at hand.

Well before student disturbances in England, the United States and France, young Welsh people knew what change they wanted, and proceeded to challenge the disdain of centuries. A campaign began in late 1962, targeting the Post Office and the tax system, and parents refused to register their babies until it could be done in Welsh. Campaigning moved on to obliterating, with distinctive green paint, English place names and corrupted Welsh ones. Morale was boosted with popular songs. Bewildered magistrates, faced with intelligent and educated young people refusing to pay fines, sent them to prison by the score. There was much jostling and unnecessary rough handling by the police.

The government set up a committee of inquiry chaired by Sir David Hughes Parry. Published in 1965, the report noted that, apart from education, the existence of Welsh had been 'in effect ignored by the British State'. It recommended that there should be a clear, positive, legislative declaration of general application to the effect that any act, writing or thing done in Welsh should have the same force as if it had been done in English.

In 1968, Glyn Simon was chosen archbishop of Wales in succession to Edwin Morris. In 1970 he went to visit the most prominent of Welsh Language Society prisoners in Cardiff gaol, Dafydd Iwan. Simon well understood the value of symbolic and prophetic action: the visit showed concern not only for Dafydd Iwan, but for the language and its campaigners, and proclaimed that here was an issue that was of real concern to the Church. The visit was seen well beyond the church community as a gesture of national leadership. His mantle fell on later archbishops at times when they seemed to speak for the whole of Wales.

These issues were vigorously discussed in *Y Llan* during the 1960s and 1970s. A group of priests, led by Tom Bowen of Llanegwad in the Diocese of St David's, identified sufficiently with the secular campaign to form

Cymdeithas Iaith yr Eglwys yng Nghymru (the Church in Wales' Welsh Language Society) in 1967. One typical occasion of offence had been the celebration in 1967 of the 400th anniversary of the Salesbury translation of the New Testament and Book of Common Prayer. The service in St David's Cathedral had been almost entirely in English. The Revd Terry Thomas, a lecturer in St David's College, Lampeter, wrote a letter of protest. One defensive letter familiarly argued that the Church should not be *merely* a society for the defence of the language. In reply Thomas quoted Paul Tillich's *The Theology of Culture*: 'Every religious act, not only in organized religion, but also in the most intimate movement of the soul, is culturally formed. The fact that every act of man's spiritual life is carried by language, spoken or silent, is proof enough for this assertion. For language is the basic cultural creation.'[32] In 1968, at the National Eisteddfod in Barry, both T. I. Ellis and Bedwyr Lewis Jones delivered passionate lectures on the rich cultural legacy of the Church in Wales.[33] Little had changed when the young lay editor of *Y Llan*, Enid Morgan, wrote six years later: *'Gall ymweld â Thyddewi fod yn fendith i'r Cristion; ond mae'n wayw i'r Cymro'* (Visiting St David's may be a blessing to a Christian, but it is painful for a Welsh-speaker).[34] Such disheartenment was lightened by the impressive example set by the many parish priests who not only learnt liturgical competence in Welsh but also 'crossed the bridge' into the Welsh community and 'went native'.

It was during this period that Welsh-medium primary and secondary schools were multiplying. One of their advocates, Jac L. Williams, Professor of Education at Aberystwyth and a member of the Governing Body, was an inspirational figure in the argument for bilingualism. In matters secular, things were changing, with the establishing of the BBC Council for Wales, the Welsh Committee of the Arts Council, the Welsh Books Council and the Welsh Office.

Equality and Translation

After the scandals of the 1950s and the turbulence of the early 1960s, in 1967 the Church belatedly activated the 1920 promise to translate its Constitution into Welsh, with a surprising consequence. Dafydd Jenkins,

---

[32] M. Wynn Thomas, 'Yr Hen Fam: R. S. Thomas and the Church in Wales', in M. Wynn Thomas, *All That Is Wales: The Collected Essays of M. Wynn Thomas* (Cardiff: University of Wales Press, 2017), 167–8 and notes on 182.

[33] *Y Llan*, 16 August 1968.

[34] *Y Llan*, 14 June 1974.

by then professor of Welsh law at Aberystwyth, was asked to carry out the enormous task and was assisted by Dr Enid Pierce Roberts, lecturer in Welsh in the University College of Wales, Bangor. She, like Dafydd Jenkins, showed a long-lasting commitment both to the Church and to the quality of its Welsh, in a way that was passionate and occasionally acerbic. The work continued from 1965 to 1976. She insisted that 'inelegant prose does little to help clarity of meaning'.[35] Volume I of the Constitution was published in 1972 and volume II in 1980. This Welsh Constitution, of equal validity with the original, was the first considerable legal document in Welsh since the medieval codices known collectively as the Laws of Hywel Dda. Law requires a sophisticated language, both flexible and precise, and thus the language of the Church in Wales' Constitution became the model for the bilingual legislation of the Welsh Assembly from 1999. Two church lawyers, Diocesan (and later Provincial) Registrar David Lambert and the Revd Professor Thomas Watkin, were both involved in this historic process.

In 1975, instant translation facilities were made available in the Governing Body, following the example of the Bangor Diocesan Conference. Bishops such as George Noakes, Alwyn Rice Jones and Saunders Davies and other clergy and laity who belonged to the Welsh-speaking community were glad to make use of it. But there was still a longstanding deference to established usage, with translators often on standby. Amongst campaigners the mocking joke was, 'This is important, so I'll say it in English.'

During the 1970s the campaign for a Welsh television channel began. The 'No' vote in the first devolution referendum in 1979 was a bitter disappointment to many; thereafter campaigning centred even more on the language. In the general election campaign of 1979 the Conservatives promised a Welsh TV channel, a commitment included in the Queen's Speech. Turmoil followed when the new government backed off. Gwynfor Evans, President of Plaid Cymru, pledged to go on hunger strike if the commitment were not honoured. Home Secretary William Whitelaw agreed to meet three mediators whom he later described as 'great leaders in Wales': Cledwyn Hughes (former Secretary of State for Wales), Sir Goronwy Daniel (principal of the University College of Wales, Aberystwyth) and Archbishop G. O. Williams. A week later at a meeting of the Governing Body in Lampeter the news came that the

---

[35] E. P. Roberts, 'The Welsh Church, Canon Law and the Welsh Language'.

government had agreed to a Welsh channel. S4C began broadcasting on 1 November 1982.

Pressure for further parliamentary legislation resulted in the Welsh Language Act 1993, establishing the principle that in Wales both Welsh and English should be treated equally in public business. It was widely regarded as inadequate because of such let-out phrases as 'appropriate in all circumstances' and 'reasonably practicable'. In the Welsh Assembly's Welsh Language (Wales) Measure of 2011, the Welsh Language Board was replaced by a Welsh Language Commissioner; the National Assembly continues with the political process of refining legislation.

Responding to the Language Act 1993, the Church in 2000 produced a set of 'Guidelines for the Provincial Use of the Language'.[36] Like many of the documents produced under the guidance of the Welsh Language Board at that time, it overflows with good will and better intentions. But the Drafting Committee of the Representative Body made it perfectly clear that the Church was not obliged to do anything, since it was not in terms of the law a 'public body'. Then, in 2002, the Revd Gwynn ap Gwilym was appointed a part-time provincial Welsh-language officer, serving not only as a translator, but also as secretary-convener to the Welsh Committee of the Standing Liturgical Advisory Committee. A church website launched in 2006 was largely bilingual. A check of diocesan websites in 2019 showed that the Bangor and St David's websites are bilingual and St Asaph promises to become so, but the other three dioceses have no Welsh other than, oddly, as titles of diocesan magazines. However, the Diocese of Llandaff has published an admirable and practical pamphlet, 'Making Welsh Visible' (2019).[37] One hopes for at least token action in the Diocese of Monmouth and the Diocese of Swansea and Brecon.

Meanwhile, the number of Welsh-speaking ordinands continued to shrink. Archbishop Barry Morgan, forthright and consistent in his support for Welsh, established a Workgroup on Ministry in Welsh with Gwynn ap Gwilym as secretary. The chairman was Cynog Dafis, a founder of Cymdeithas yr Iaith and former Plaid Cymru (and sometime Green Party) MP for Cardiganshire. The report, 'Each in His Own Language' (citing Acts 2:8), was presented to the Governing Body in 2012. The chairman's brief but pungent Foreword noted that the Church

---

[36] See www.churchinwales.org.uk/resources/clergy/welsh-language-guidelines.

[37] For more on this pamphlet, see https://llandaff.churchinwales.org.uk/news/2019/01/making-welsh-visible-in-your-church/.

justifiably has to spend a great deal of money on its architectural heritage, adding 'The Welsh language is a priceless treasure which deserves to be protected and cherished in the same way.' A detailed plan was recommended: a Standing Committee for the Welsh Language chaired by one of the bishops, a full-time provincial language officer, a network of diocesan language organisers, and a full-time provincial translator.[38]

Fortunately, some of the recommendations resonated with the rethinking of clergy training. St Michael's College in Llandâf, with its seminary tradition, has been replaced by St Padarn's Institute, combining residential academic work with practical experience in a parish placement two days a week. Welsh-speaking tutors have been appointed, worship is mainly bilingual, ordinands are obliged to learn Welsh, and Welsh-speaking students are said to be valued. This is beginning to produce research on practical issues for the Church. An as yet unpublished dissertation for St Padarn's Institute, 'Bilingual Worship in the Church in Wales' by Miriam Beecroft, helpfully sets the problem in a wider context. She cites *The Directory for Worship of the Presbyterian Church (USA)*: 'The church is committed to using language in such a way that all members of the community of faith may recognize themselves to be included, addressed, and equally cherished before God.' Beecroft asks: 'If a person lives, thinks, prays and speaks predominantly using the Welsh language, then how is their worship life affected by services conducted predominantly in English?'[39] This is the issue raised by Aneirin Talfan in 1958.

Two events made swift action on the report difficult, the publication of the Harries Review in 2012 and the death of Gwynn ap Gwilym in 2016. The Harries Report was an external review of the Church set up by Archbishop Barry Morgan. He had insisted, as he told this author, that 'the Church cannot go on doing the same thing'. The changes proposed were radical, and affirmed the recommendations of the Welsh Report of 2012. But the language issue could be easily forgotten as each diocese acts in its own way in the flood of other urgencies. The appointment of language officers is beginning to be felt. There are some small heartening signs for Welsh-speaking Anglicans, who sometimes feel they are a suspect minority both in the Church in Wales and in the wider community.

---

[38] *'Pob un yn ei Iaith ei hun' (Actau 2:8)* (Acts 2:8).
[39] Miriam Beecroft, 'Bilingual Worshop in the Church in Wales' (unpublished), Theology for Life dissertation, Module CWTH6002 (St Padarn's Institute, Cardiff, 2017).

The Church and the Arts

It is impossible to do more than give the merest sketch of the arts in connection with the Church in Wales. Churches in Wales are simply not wealthy enough to be regular patrons of major painting, sculpture, architecture and drama. There are exceptions: surely the greatest is the Epstein sculpture dominating Llandâf Cathedral (1957). Its post-Blitz rebuild also gave the opportunity for George Pace to create the St David's chapel, a rare modern architectural and ecclesiastical gem (1953–6). The alterations to St David's Cathedral's cloisters and the former St Mary's College in the 1990s are also done well.

Works of art can surprise visitors to churches, nowhere more so than in the brilliant colours of the reredos at St Woollo's Cathedral, Newport, designed by John Piper and Patrick Reynolds, or Ceri Richards' stark 'Deposition' in St Mary's Swansea (1958). John Piper's stained-glass designs can also be found in St Mary's (1955–6), part of a series of modern glass by various other designers. The most commissioned of modern artists in south Wales has been the stained-glass designer, John Petts, whose work can be seen in many churches. Stained glass is the commonest modern contribution to Welsh churches. While many are stereotypes, striking examples of modernist design can be found.

Good music is naturally associated with cathedrals where festivals have flourished, although only Llandâf has a choir school. Bangor is particularly associated with the composer William Mathias (1934–92). There have also been several musical settings of the new eucharistic services, one by the composer Meirion Williams (1901–76). But Bangor Cathedral's present fine choir has also made a real effort to combine Welsh songs and hymns into the liturgy; and in 2014 the 'Chancellor's Medal for Constancy' among junior choristers was established by the diocesan chancellor, Norman Doe – it is awarded annually. Across mid-Wales and beyond the Christmas Plygain service has been successfully revitalised.

A number of poets have been Welsh clergy or lay people writing in either language. Best known in Wales and beyond is R. S. Thomas (1913–2000). While his poems speak powerfully to both contemporary faith and doubt, his relationship with church institutions was complicated by his devotion to the traditional language of the Book of Common Prayer and his hostility to the liturgical reforms that have swept through the Anglican Communion.[40] A handsome memorial volume to him in Welsh, *Cofio RS: Cleniach yn Gymraeg?* ('Remembering RS: Gentler in Welsh?') shows him smiling and relaxed.[41]

Three other poets who turned to the Anglican Church are significant. The poems of Euros Bowen (1904–88) resonate with an intense religious response to nature. An anthology of his poems and his own translations was published by Church in Wales Publications.[42] The closeness of metaphor and sacrament in his work is cherished also in the work of Gwenallt (David Gwenallt Jones (1899–1968)). His poem on the Lord's Prayer in Welsh in the Church of the Pater Noster in Jerusalem claims resonantly that Welsh is *Un o dafodieithoedd y Drindod* (one of the dialects of the Trinity). But the Edwin Morris rumpus was too much for him, and he departed stormily back to the Presbyterian Church. An obituary in *Y Llan* of January 1969 said: '*Bu'n anffyddiwr, yn Ymneiltuwr, yn Eglwyswr ac yna'n Ymneilltuwr drachefn am fod seisnigrwydd yr Eglwys yn ei gadw draw*' (He had been an atheist, a Nonconformist, an Anglican and then a Nonconformist once more because the Englishness of the Church alienated him).

The third, Gwynn ap Gwilym (1950–2016), whose importance has previously been noted, was a chaired poet who composed and edited several anthologies of poetry. *Gogoneddus Arglwydd, Henffych Well* is a selection of Christian prose and verse published by Cytûn.[43] Its title is the opening line of a Welsh *Benedicite* in the Black Book of Carmarthen, earliest of Welsh manuscripts (c. 1250). His major novel *Scythia*, published posthumously in 2017, tells the story of Dr John Davies, renaissance scholar and rector of Mallwyd.

Welsh poetry has become better known beyond Wales through the work of Anglican interpreters. A. M. (Donald) Allchin (1930–2010), Canon of Canterbury Cathedral, fell in love with the work of Welsh hymn writer Ann Griffiths (1776–1805), and in his *The Dynamism of Tradition* deals with the Welsh poetic Christian tradition in a chapter

---

[40] M. Wynn Thomas, 'Yr Hen Fam: R. S. Thomas and the Church in Wales'; and M. Wyn Thomas, 'R. S. Thomas: A Retired Christian', in M. Wynn Thomas, *All That is Wales*, 185–212.

[41] G. Neigwl, ed., *Cofio RS: Cleniach yn Gymraeg?* (Liverpool: Gwasg y Bwthyn, 2013).

[42] E. Saunders and C. Davies, *Euros Bowen: Priest-Poet / Bardd-Offeiriad* (Penarth: Church in Wales Publications, 1993).

[43] Gwynn ap Gwilym, ed., *Gogoneddus Arglwydd Henffych Well!* (Cardiff: Cytûn: Churches Together in Wales, 1999).

titled 'The Liberating Power of Praise'.[44] Archbishop Rowan Williams' translations have drawn attention to other fine poets, including the mystic Quaker poet Waldo Williams (1904–71), in whose work a resonant phrase like *ehedeg ein hiraeth* ('the flight of our longing') speaks to longing searchers for faith as well as those who are at ease in the language of orthodoxy.[45]

The story of this 'dialect of the Trinity' is not yet finished and hope, unlike *hiraeth*, is a theological virtue.

Conclusion

At a World Council of Churches conference in Brazil in 1996, on the theme of 'One Gospel, Many Cultures', the question was asked of the then still recent Rwandan genocide, 'Who will free us from the lament of history?' *Marwnad Hanes* is a powerful phrase in Welsh and our unofficial, less bloodthirsty national anthem is *Ryn ni yma o hyd* – We're still here. This story, like much church, and indeed human, history is a mix of lament and hope for a new way of human living together. It is a story of a power politics, of enmity and indifference on the one hand, and of resentment, complicity and angry longing on the other. And there needs to be mutual listening and forgiving to flourish into the future. Emblematic of the faith in general, it needs repentance, forgiveness, reconciliation and willingness to act.

---

[44] A. M. Allchin, *The Dynamic of Tradition* (London: Darton Longman and Todd, 1981), 78–93.
[45] See especially R. Williams, *After Silent Centuries* (Oxford: Perpetua Press, 1994), 48–52.

16

The Church, State and Society

JOANNA PENBERTHY

The eight-minute silent film clip recording the highlights of the Enthronement of the Most Revd Alfred George Edwards on 1 June 1920 as the first archbishop of Wales gives some idea of the place in society that the four historic dioceses of the Church of England in Wales had held before disestablishment.[1] The prime minister, David Lloyd George, and George V's nephew, Prince Arthur of Connaught (who after his father, the duke of Connaught and Strathaern, and the king, was the most senior male member of the royal family) were present representing the wider British State. Alongside them were more local notables: the countess of Dundonald of Gwrych Castle, Abergele, and the Lord Lieutenant of Flintshire, Henry Neville Gladstone, son of William Ewart Gladstone. Six thousand people attended, inside and outside the Cathedral of St Asaph. Given that Wales remained firmly part of the British State, with an established church in England, the vestiges of establishment would have been hard to shake off, even were there to have been a will to do so.[2] However, disestablishment had not been sought by the Welsh dioceses themselves, and neither Archbishop Edwards nor his successor, Archbishop C. A. H. Green, were in favour of it.

This sense of establishment continued and continues to this day in a number of ways, most obviously in that ordination in the Church in Wales continues to confer upon the minister the civil status of a registrar, meaning that Church in Wales marriage ceremonies have a secular legal and not simply an ecclesial status. Nonconformist and Roman Catholic ministers may become registrars but this is not automatic. This caused

---

[1] Church in Wales, 'The Historic Ceremony of the Enthronement of the First Archbishop of Wales, 1920, at St Asaph Cathedral, 1 June 1920' (1920), MMS ID 99254367302419, National Library of Wales, and www.youtube.com/watch?v=M0FyVK2q3Qw.

[2] K. Robbins, 'Establishing Disestablishment: Some Reflections on Wales and Scotland', in S. J. Brown and G. Newlands, eds., *Scottish Christianity in the Modern World: In Honour of A. C. Cheyne* (London: Bloomsbury, 2001), 245 and 247.

confusion when in 2013 Prime Minister David Cameron, overstepping his powers, excluded both the Church in Wales and the Church of England from being able to conduct marriages between people of the same sex. Archbishop Barry Morgan immediately took the matter up with the Lord Chancellor and received assurances that, should the Church in Wales decide it wished to conduct same-sex marriages, secondary legislation would be prepared to enable it to do so. The Marriage (Same Sex Couples) Act 2013 then enshrined this guarantee in its provisions. The other so-called vestiges of establishment alongside marriage – such as rights to burial – are also well known (see Chapter 11).

Before disestablishment, as with other Church of England dioceses, the four Welsh dioceses related to wider society in matters generally considered moral, in a number of ways: through their corporate activities, the role of the individual bishops in Parliament and public life, and support for Church of England societies, such as the White Cross League,[3] the Church of England Incorporated Society for the Housing of Waifs and Strays[4] and the Church Army. Each Welsh diocese also ran its own institutions, whether orphanages for the care of babies and children or establishments for unmarried mothers, much like the Magdalen laundries in Ireland, called 'Houses of Mercy', although, in Wales, women and girls were perfectly free to leave. After disestablishment, the Church in Wales' bishops no longer sat in the House of Lords, and it took some time for the Church in Wales' Governing Body to comment on issues of public concern. The involvement of Church of England societies in Wales, however, continued. In 1920, there were five children's homes in Wales,[5] run by the Waifs and Strays Society, three of which were still running until the 1970s or 1980s.

The Church in Wales' dioceses also continued to run their own institutions, established before disestablishment, although some of these now found themselves within a new diocese. For example, the St David's Diocesan House of Mercy at Eastmoor Park, West Cross, opened by the bishop of St David's on 17 October 1891 as a 'House of Penitents',

---

[3] The White Cross League was a society formed to educate young men in matters of moral purity. Its objects were to promote '(1) Purity amongst men; (2) A Chivalrous Respect for Womanhood; (3) The Preservation of the Young from Contamination; (4) Rescue Work; (5) A Higher Tone of Public Opinion': Diocese of St David's, J. Herbert, ed., *St David's Diocesan Directory* (Carmarthen: Spurrell and Son, 1906), Part II, 95.

[4] It later changed its name to the Church of England Children's Society.

[5] It is not clear whether the St David's Church Army Labour and Lodging Home at 12 Rutland Street, Swansea, opened by the Lord Bishop of St David's in 1904, was still open at disestablishment.

whose residents were called 'inmates' in the St David's Diocesan Directory of 1912,[6] was run on the diocese's behalf by the Community of the Name of Jesus. There was also the St David's Orphanage for Girls and Little Boys at Thistleboon, Mumbles, for example. After its foundation in 1923, both these institutions now found themselves within the new Diocese of Swansea and Brecon. However, it is clear from later references to them in the St David's Diocesan Directories and in the minutes of the St David's Moral Welfare Committee that the Diocese of St David's continued to refer women and children to them – and the people of the diocese continued to accept a degree of financial responsibility for them, since fundraising for the institutions carried on within the parishes of the diocese.

The development of the Church in Wales' understanding of its place in relationship to Welsh society over its first hundred years can be traced in a number of ways: the debates held at the Church in Wales' Governing Body; in the topics for which the Church in Wales commissioned reports; in the board and committee structures both of the province and the dioceses reflected in the Diocesan Handbooks; and in those employed to work under provincial and diocesan committees. It is also reflected in the practical work undertaken at diocesan level where pre-disestablishment institutions continued to be supported whilst new ways of working emerged.

The Governing Body and Public Life

The National Assembly of the Church of England (established by Act of Parliament in 1919) was reconstituted in 1970 as the General Synod. Its measures have the same force and effect as an Act of Parliament and may amend or repeal any Act of Parliament concerning the Church of England; but all draft measures require approval by both Houses of Parliament and Royal Assent.[7] In contrast, the Church in Wales acquired an independence after disestablishment which its four historic dioceses had not known before. While the Church in Wales' bishops were no longer part of the House of Lords, the Governing Body potentially provided a forum for bishops and the wider Church to comment on public issues as they saw fit. Yet, the Governing Body minutes before

[6] Diocese of St David's, J. Herbert (Revd), ed., *St David's Diocesan Directory* (London: SPCK, 1912), 263.

[7] N. Doe, *The Legal Framework of the Church of England* (Oxford: Clarendon Press, 1996), ch. 1.

1936 show no evidence of this opportunity having been taken up.[8] Understandably, the early meetings were preoccupied with internal matters. The first recorded debate on a matter of public interest occurred in the September 1936 meeting held at the Pavilion in Llandrindod Wells. The report of the Church in Wales Temperance Society noted with concern that the amount spent out of the public purse in Wales was £83,000,000 less than the Welsh public spent on alcohol. The Mothers' Union, the Girls Friendly Society, the St David's Board of Education, and the Diocesan Bands of Hope, particularly that of the Diocese of Monmouth, are all commended in the report for the work they had undertaken to combat drunkenness.

In so far as it proved difficult to find its corporate voice in public affairs, the Church in Wales continued to relate to wider society primarily through practical action initiated at a diocesan level. However, in April 1939, the Governing Body passed a resolution to set up the Provincial Council for Moral Welfare Work, a term common amongst public and private bodies at the time; its work would be considered today as within the purview of such diverse figures as social workers and probation or housing officers. It was not until 1944 that the first report of the Provincial Council for Moral Welfare Work was presented to the Governing Body, more than ten years after the Moral Welfare Committee in St David's Diocese, for example, had been set up. This 1944 report details the work undertaken by the Moral Welfare Committees in each diocese. Clearly the centre of the Church in Wales' life remained diocesan rather than provincial. In the report which each diocese made to the Provincial Committee, it is clear that the main issue addressed by all is that of illegitimacy. The Diocese of Bangor's committee notes a doubling of the case work in 1943 with respect to 1942; that of Monmouth notes that more girls had been helped than in any previous year. Three of the dioceses note an increase in their staffing levels: St David's appointed a third moral welfare worker to work specifically with local authorities; the Monmouth Shelter took on an extra part-time worker, and Swansea and Brecon, a full-time assistant organiser, noting that Radnorshire County Council also had agreed to work in partnership with the Swansea and Brecon Diocesan Moral Welfare Committee.

Alcohol abuse continued to be of major societal concern at the Governing Body. Before noting the 'moral degradation' to which the

---

[8] Held at the office of the Representative Body of the Church in Wales, 2 Callaghan Square, Cardiff. I am grateful to John Richfield for his work in collating this information.

consumption of alcohol led, the report of the Church in Wales Temperance Society to Governing Body in 1946 drew attention to what they considered the prodigious waste of money, agricultural resources, transport and fuel on producing alcoholic drinks at a time of rationing and scarcity.[9] The concern about the use of alcohol was evident again in a motion put to Governing Body by the bishops of St David's and Bangor in September 1950 deploring the attempt to allow the Sunday opening of public houses in Wales and Monmouthshire and calling for the banning of the sale of intoxicants in private clubs and for an adequate inspection regime.[10] It was not until the Governing Body meeting of September 1972, when the archbishop commended the government's action in supporting the resettlement of Asians fleeing Uganda, that wider societal issues figured in a Governing Body debate. It cannot necessarily be concluded that societal concerns figuring so rarely in these debates in the first fifty years of the Church in Wales' life is an indication of church people's lack of interest in issues of public concern. It might indicate that Church in Wales' clergy and laity were so well integrated within wider society that their social concern was expressed through common political and community channels, although there is nothing on record encouraging clergy or parishioners to take such steps as part of their Christian duty.

By 1975, the renaming of the Provincial Council for Moral Welfare as the Provincial Council for Social Work denoted a change of emphasis. Governing Body's business was still centred mainly on internal church or ecumenical matters, but debates about issues in wider society and the world were beginning to occur. In both Governing Body meetings of 1975, the 'Community Orientation of the Church in Wales' was discussed in the 'Church, Property and People' debate,[11] and business also included reports from the Church and Society Advisory Commissions on the World Food Crisis and on Racism, and from the Working Party on Marriage and Divorce. Twenty or so years later, the frequency of debates on ethical and political issues had increased significantly – topics

---

[9] Church in Wales, 'Minutes of the Church in Wales Representative and Governing Body 1945-8', held at the Provincial Offices of the Church in Wales, 2 Callaghan Square, Cardiff, CF10 5BT, 72–3.

[10] Church in Wales, 'Minutes of the Church in Wales Representative and Governing Body 1949–52', held at the Provincial Offices of the Church in Wales, 2 Callaghan Square, Cardiff, CF10 5BT, 6.

[11] J. Richfield, 'Review of Governing Body Business 2007, 2012, 2016' (2016), 10, held at the Provincial Office, Church in Wales, 2 Callaghan Square, Cardiff, CF10 5BT.

discussed included the National Lottery, climate change, the Jubilee 2000 Drop the Debt Campaign,[12] Church in the Welsh Countryside, the funding of higher education, and the anniversary of the United Nations Declaration of Human Rights.[13] In 1998, the Governing Body heard a presentation on the imminent arrival of the National Assembly for Wales and in 2000 on credit unions.

This increasing interest shown by Governing Body in matters beyond the Church in Wales continued. In 2003, it received reports on climate change, rural communities in Wales, and the Trade Justice Movement. Between 2001 and 2007, nine Private Members' Motions were tabled – three on the relationship between Israel and Palestine, and one each on the Earth Summit, renewable electricity, human sexuality, Make Poverty History, Trident and Zimbabwe. In 2007, Governing Body received its first report on the mobile dental clinic in Gaza,[14] funded by the Church in Wales' Jubilee Fund, set up at the millennium. Concern about climate change continued to be reflected in Governing Body debates, featuring in 2006, 2008, 2010, 2015 and 2016. Aside from the funding of the Gaza dental clinic, the direct practical impact of debates at Governing Body was small, but the tenor of its discussions reflects the increasing sense amongst its members that the Church in Wales should make its voice heard in matters of national and international concern.

Provincial Structures and Public Life

By the early 1980s, the Provincial Council for Social Work had been wound up and the archbishop, the Most Revd Derek Childs, with the support of the Bench of Bishops, set up the Provincial Board of Social Responsibility. It was the interface between the dioceses on matters of public concern and provided a focus of support and discussion. By 1984, the Provincial Board of Social Responsibility had become a division of the newly founded Provincial Board of Mission. Each diocese was represented on the Board of Mission's Division of Social Responsibility by its social responsibility officer, and the Revd Alun Evans became the Church in Wales' first provincial officer for social responsibility. The division became a focus not only for sharing information about and encouraging the specific social responsibility projects being undertaken in each

---

[12] All in September 1996: see ibid., 7.
[13] In April 1998: ibid., 8.
[14] The mobile dental clinic has subsequently been destroyed by hostile action.

diocese but also for joint policy work. The division was allocated a provincial budget which enabled it to commission reports, which were then printed by Church in Wales Publications in Penarth and available to members of the public – thus providing a channel, additional to the Standing Committee of Governing Body or the Bench of Bishops, through which matters of concern might be aired provincially. The division was not afraid to tackle contentious issues. In 1991, it produced a report on 'AIDS/HIV Infection: A Challenge to Care',[15] both educating the Church and encouraging practical action by individual churches and church members to support those with HIV and their families. The following year, a report on genetic screening and therapy was published.[16] These reports were mainly intended to be part of a wider public debate and inform members of the Church in Wales. They were not debated at the Governing Body since only the Standing Committee or members of the Governing Body could table matters for debate.

While this aspect of provincial work continued, the focus began to change. The first provincial social responsibility officers were employed at the Board of Mission to work on policy and to support the project work in the dioceses by providing a forum for dissemination of good practice.[17] However, in 1994 the community development ethos of many of the diocesan projects was having an impact on how the Church in Wales wanted to work at provincial level. As a result, Valerie Martin was employed as the provincial social responsibility officer not only to work as before in policy areas and to staff the meetings of diocesan social responsibility officers but also to roll out a community development programme titled 'Training for Transformation' across communities in Wales. This was to operate alongside the 'Parish Development and Renewal' process which the Board of Mission was using with local church-based groups. Developing resources, such as 'Deal with Debt', to help parishes respond to the needs of local communities and working directly on projects locally also formed part of the provincial social responsibility officer's brief. While these resources were offered, there was no capacity to monitor their use or effectiveness.

[15] Church in Wales: Board of Mission Division for Social Responsibility, *Aids/HIV Infection: A Challenge to Care* (Penarth: Church in Wales Publications, 1991).
[16] Church in Wales: Board of Mission Division for Social Responsibility, *Human Genetic Screening and Therapy: Some Moral and Pastoral Issues* (Penarth: Church in Wales Publications, 1992).
[17] For examples of project work and good practice, see the case study on St David's Diocese below.

Martin also worked with groups establishing credit unions, and with Christian Aid, and she set up links between the Church and the Sabeel Liberation Theology Centre in Jerusalem.[18]

However, by 2000, the Social Responsibility sector of the province was almost entirely wound down when the Church in Wales' Board of Mission (and with it the Division for Social Responsibility) was dissolved by the Bench of Bishops and replaced by the Board of Ministry and Mission, which included not a division but a Bishops' Advisor for Social Responsibility appointed by the Bench. Subsequently, the Board of Ministry and Mission was also in turn wound up, although the role of the Bishops' Advisor continues today. Social Responsibility, then Church and Society, became a portfolio responsibility of one of the six Church in Wales' bishops, with policy work undertaken by the Bishops' Advisor who is responsible to the provincial secretary of the Representative Body and reports to the Church and Society Bishop and to the Bench. In practice, this has meant a significant diminution in the Church in Wales' provincial work in this area, not least because there is no longer a committee, made up of diocesan representatives, accountable for a budget, for whom the officer works and by which work can be both engendered and disseminated.

The growth of social media impacted on the way the Church in Wales corporately responded to societal issues, and personalities became increasingly significant. While the role of archbishop of Wales has always enjoyed respect, that role has become the public face of the Church in Wales through the use of social media. Both Rowan Williams and Barry Morgan were alive to ecumenical sensitivities and strove not to appear to be speaking for Wales as a whole. While this stress on the person of the archbishop gives an envied *entrée* into Welsh life, it has inevitably meant that the Church in Wales' contributions to Welsh public life have been driven by the particular interests and commitments of the individual archbishop. In its relationship with the National Assembly for Wales, the Church in Wales has eschewed any claim to a pseudo-establishment role into which the media often wishes to push it because of the profile of the archbishop of Wales – and the Church allies itself with the work done on wider societal concerns and issues with its ecumenical partners through Cytun – Churches Together in Wales.

---

[18] Sabeel Liberation Theology Centre is a group of local Palestinian Christians based in Jerusalem, who, 'inspired by the life and teaching of Jesus Christ stand for the oppressed, work for justice, engage in peace-building'; see https://sabeel.org.

The Church in Wales had first addressed the importance of managing its public profile by appointing the Revd David Hammond as the first provincial communications officer as early as 1984 – but this role has become all the more critical with the ever quickening development of instantaneous communications. However, in the same way as the title of the provincial officer for social responsibility's post changed to a Bishops' Advisor, so the provincial communications officer's title also changed to Bishops' Advisor. As the public profile of the archbishop grew, so managing this became an increasingly important part of the Bishops' Advisor's role. When the post was advertised in 2006, the job's title was 'Archbishop's Media Officer and Bishops' Advisor for Communication' – but the role was also in effect the press officer for the Church in Wales.[19] Today, the post is called director of communications, and the director answers to the provincial secretary.

While the Church in Wales' voice in Welsh public life has become more confident, it is nevertheless influenced by the *Zeitgeist*. The increasing conservatism that has gradually stifled public debate in the United Kingdom can been seen in the Church in Wales' gradual diminution of support, along with that of the British churches more widely, for the social and political justice agenda that reached its zenith around the millennium, represented, for example, by campaigns such as 'Drop the Debt' and in support for the rights of the Palestinian people. The Church in Wales, like the other churches, is beginning to buy into the move in British political discourse back to a nineteenth-century distinction of deserving and undeserving poor and the move to charity away from justice as an appropriate lens through which to view social problems.[20] While supporting the movement to found credit unions, which saw power firmly placed in the hands of those able to save and take a degree of control over their own lives, was a main focus of the Church in Wales' work in Welsh society in the 1990s, by contrast, an

---

[19] Personal email from Anna Morrell, Director of Communications, Church in Wales, 2 April 2019.

[20] See K. Garthwaite, *Hunger Pains: Life inside Food Bank Britain* (Bristol: Policy Press, University of Bristol, 2016). For the Statement on Visit to the United Kingdom by Professor Philip Alston, United Nations Special Rapporteur on extreme poverty and human rights, see www.ohchr.org/documents/issues/poverty/eom_gb_16nov2018.pdf. For reflections on current social policy from the perspective of the charitable sector, see https://assets.publishing.service.gov.uk/government/uploads/system/uploads/attach ment_data/file/356191/Lecture_-_Dr_Frank_Prochaska.pdf. For an academic reflection on food banks and social policy, see H. Lambie-Mumford, 'The Growth of Foodbanks in Britain and What They Mean for Social Policy', *Critical Social Policy*, 39(11) (2019), 3–22.

encouragement of and support for food banks and night shelters are current today and exemplify rather than challenge the societal move away from a justice-based to a charity-based discourse. This is somewhat offset by the Church in Wales' new partnership with the Children's Society to support an officer who works on the Welsh aspect of specific targeted political campaigns,[21] most recently pressuring the Welsh government and Welsh councils to stop requiring young people who have recently left care to pay council tax.[22]

Practical Action: The Dioceses at Work

Over its first hundred years, the Church in Wales has increasingly learned to relate to Welsh society through public pronouncements by its archbishops, bishops, provincial structures and Governing Body, but its main focus remains practical action at diocesan level, which each diocese has continued to undertake in the public sphere since 1920. The Diocese of St David's serves as a good example of what was happening across the province in this area during the period 1928–70. Despite disestablishment, the role the Church of England societies played within St David's was still clear. In *The Book of the Diocese of St Davids 1928–1929* there were advertisements for the White Cross League,[23] of which the bishop of St David's, David Lewis Prosser, was a vice president, for the Waifs and Strays Society and for the Church Army, which had established the St David's Church Army Labour and Lodging Home at 12 Rutland Street, Swansea, which had been opened by the Lord Bishop of St David's in 1904. As we have seen, the Eastmoor House of Mercy and the Diocesan Orphanage, both established in the Diocese of St David's before disestablishment but located in what became the new Diocese of Swansea and Brecon, continued to be supported financially by parochial collections in St David's. The committees with responsibility for running these – together with the committee set up to support the House of the Good Shepherd, also at Eastmoor, an orphanage established in 1925 – all

---

[21] The officer's salary and pension contributions are paid for by the Children's Society while the Church in Wales provides office space and support.

[22] See www.childrenssociety.org.uk/what-you-can-do/campaign-for-change/a-fairer-start-for-care-leavers. According to a private email from Tom Davies (3 April 2019), as of April 2018, seven councils across Wales had introduced a council tax exemption for care leavers as a result of the Children's Society campaign.

[23] Diocese of St David's, S. B. Williams (Revd), ed., *The Year Book of the Diocese of St David's 1928–1929* (Carmarthen: W. Spurrell and Son, 1928).

continued to be listed in the St David's Directory, but post-disestablishment included representatives from the Diocese of Swansea and Brecon.

The House of Mercy at Eastmoor closed in 1939, but committees for the Diocesan Orphanage at Thistledown and for the House of the Good Shepherd, the management of which had transferred to the Waifs and Strays Society in 1943, continued until the 1950s in the St David's Year Book. The House of the Good Shepherd was subsequently registered as a charity in 1964, under the care of the Children's Society. The closure of the House of Mercy in 1940 meant a lack of provision in the Dioceses of St David's and of Swansea and Brecon for maternity cases and for the care of children under two. At a meeting of the Carmarthen Archdeaconry Case Committee on 28 July 1942,[24] it was noted that maternity cases were being sent to the Salvation Army Home in Cardiff or to a home in Bristol instead.[25] Collectors for the House of Mercy were still listed in the St David's diocesan Year Book of 1942–3 and the funds collected provided for this need as well as for what, as we have seen, was then called moral welfare work in the diocese.[26] At a meeting of the Case Committee for the Archdeaconry of Carmarthen on 2 February 1943, the need for a Babies' Home was noted and Mrs Poole-Hughes (mother of John Poole-Hughes, later bishop of Llandaff 1976–85) proposed that a recommendation be sent to the Home of the Good Shepherd at Eastmoor to provide accommodation for babies as well as children between the ages of two and five.[27]

While the diocesan orphanage at Thistledoon, Mumbles, remained open until at least the late 1930s, in the mid-1930s the focus of the work of the Diocese of St David's changed fundamentally, from running institutions to a more active approach. Listed in the St David's diocesan Year Book 1936–7 for the first time, under the entries for the Bishop's

---

[24] Despite its name, there are no details of individual cases in the case committee minute book. Any correspondence and personal details of adoptees, birth families or adopters are kept secure and are not open to public scrutiny. Only those whose adoption was arranged by the St David's Moral Welfare Committee are entitled to consult the secure sections of these archives.

[25] Diocese of St David's, 'Minute Book of the Case Committee for the Archdeaconry of Carmarthen, 1941–1946', St David's Diocesan Office, Abergwili, Carmarthenshire, SA31 2JG.

[26] Diocese of St David's, 'Minute Book of the St David's Moral Welfare Committee, November 1938–April 1944', St David's Diocesan Office, Abergwili, Carmarthenshire, SA31 2JG, 22.

[27] Diocese of St David's, 'Minute Book of the Case Committee for the Archdeaconry of Carmarthen, 1941–1946'.

Secretary and the Bishop's Messenger, is the diocesan moral welfare worker, Miss V. Maliphant of 2 New Road, Llanelli.[28] Maliphant had begun work on 10 September 1935 partially supported by a grant, from the diocesan Maintenance Committee, of £15.7s.0d,[29] and partially from funds raised in the parishes or at deanery and archdeaconry meetings. Maliphant was the Organising Secretary for the newly created St David's Moral Welfare Committee. Organising Secretaries, for 'preventive and rescue work', had been appointed by dioceses in the Church of England since the end of the nineteenth century.[30] Mrs Davidson, wife of the archbishop of Canterbury, held regular meetings for them at Lambeth Palace from 1912.

In 1917, the archbishop of Canterbury's Advisory Board for Preventive and Rescue Work had been set up,[31] with Mrs Davidson as chair and Miss Jessie Higson as Central Organising Secretary, becoming in 1932 the Church of England Board for Moral Welfare Work. In line with the Church of England's change, a motion was put before the Governing Body of the Church in Wales to ratify the draft constitution for a Provincial Council of Moral Welfare in October 1938 – but this was postponed 'owing to the national crisis'.[32]

A Case Study: St David's Moral Welfare Committee

The St David's Moral Welfare Committee had made its first appearance in the diocesan Year Book in 1936–7,[33] with the bishop, dean, archdeacons and chancellor being *ex officio* members alongside eleven diocesan clerics, Deaconess Williams, Lady Merthyr, thirteen women and

---

[28] Diocese of St Davids, S. B. Williams (Revd), ed., *The Year Book of the Diocese of St David's 1936–1937* (Carmarthen: W. Spurrell and Son, 1936), 11.

[29] Ibid., 184.

[30] A. Sackville, 'The Moral Welfare Workers Association', Professional Associations in Social Work 1900–1990 Working Paper 10 (1987), www.kcl.ac.uk/scwru/swhn/2013/sackville-professional-associations-in-social-work-1900-1990-paper.pdf.

[31] Links between the Church of England Board and Welsh dioceses continued after disestablishment. At a meeting of the St David's Moral Welfare Committee on 24 July 1940, a letter from the Church of England Moral Welfare Committee in support of the archbishop of Canterbury's action with regard to licensed brothels was read aloud ('Minute Book of the St David's Moral Welfare Committee, November 1938–April 1944', 50). At its meeting on 2 February 1942, the committee agreed to send £2 to the Church of England's Moral Welfare Board as a contribution to Miss Higson's retirement present (ibid., 112).

[32] Ibid., from the frontispiece to page 1.

[33] Diocese of St David's, *The Year Book of the Diocese of St David's 1936–1937*, 124.

seventeen deanery collectors. The committee is still in existence and running projects today but under the name adopted in 1975, the St David's Diocesan Council for Social Responsibility. Moral welfare workers, like Maliphant, were employed by religious and non-religious bodies from the 1920s to 1970s across the UK and were one of those categories of practitioner whose work contributed to the development of social work as a profession.[34] The Church in Wales' dioceses, like those of the Church of England, were at the forefront of this development.

In 1940, Miss Maliphant, the Organising Secretary of the St David's Moral Welfare Committee, was joined by an Outdoor Worker, Miss Caroline Jenkins, whom the diocese had put through training at Josephine Butler House, a college which had begun life in 1917 as a training scheme set up by Miss Jesse Higson at St Monica's Refuge in Liverpool. For long periods, the Moral Welfare Committee was able to employ a second Outdoor Worker to work with Maliphant alongside Jenkins, who, after her marriage in 1945, continued to work for the committee until her retirement in 1970. The work was funded by grants from the St David's Diocesan Board of Finance, from funds raised at meetings at which the importance of moral welfare work was spoken about, and from voluntary collections taken up by the network of collectors spread across the diocese, many of whom were clergy wives.

As indicated in the Church of England's original name for what became their Board for Moral Welfare, 'preventive and rescue work', the initial impetus for moral welfare came from the drive against prostitution and the care of both the women caught up in it and the children that resulted from it. While prostitution is not talked about in the minute books of the St David's Moral Welfare Committee, work with unmarried pregnant girls and women, and arranging adoptions, remained a core part of the committee's work from its inception to the 1970s. At a meeting of the Case Committee of the Archdeaconry of Carmarthen on 29 October 1941, Jenkins, the Outdoor Worker, reported that she had been asked by the Public Assistance Board to intervene with regard to the paternity of the child in three cases with which she was dealing – but the committee was clear this was a step too far: 'such work is not within our scope'.[35] While details of specific cases were not included in committee minutes, the categories of cases were noted; and while the care of

---

[34] D. Burnham, *The Social Worker Speaks: A History of Social Workers through the Twentieth Century* (London: Routledge, 2016), 3, 76, 129.

[35] Diocese of St David's, 'Minute Book of the Case Committee for the Archdeaconry of Carmarthen, 1941–1946'.

unmarried mothers and their babies remained the staple work, it was by no means the only type of work undertaken. Indeed, as David Burnham notes with regard to those in the Church of England,[36] the moral welfare workers of the Diocese of St David's were at the forefront of developing the role of probation officers. Both Maliphant and Jenkins were employed as probation officers, the former by Pembrokeshire County Council and the latter by Cardiganshire County Council,[37] dealing with cases involving women and children to the age of seventeen. Higson, Lecturer to the Church of England Moral Welfare Council, in an address to St David's Moral Welfare Committee after its meeting in November 1942, stressed that it was time for moral welfare workers to be released from probation work, which she considered should be carried out instead by fully trained woman probation officers. The committee then wrote to the county clerks asking to discuss the matter. Nothing further was mentioned on the issue, and Maliphant and Jenkins continued to be part-time probation officers for Pembrokeshire and Cardiganshire County Councils.

Nevertheless, a large proportion of the work of the moral welfare workers concerned illegitimacy, and this increased dramatically during the Second World War. In July 1943, it was reported that the committee needed to register as an Adoption Agency under the Adoption of Children (Regulation) Act 1939. This did not meet with unqualified approval. On 23 June 1945, a concern was raised at the committee that the moral welfare workers increased immorality by making it easy for the unmarried mother to get rid of the child, to which Maliphant replied that it was their policy to discourage adoptions and to keep contact between the mother and the child.[38] This reflects the policy, recommended by the Carmarthenshire county medical officer in his quarterly report to the Maternity and Child Welfare and Public Health Committees, based on Circular 2866 issued by the Welsh Board of Health, to encourage birth families to bring up the illegitimate child. In his report, the county medical officer, following the circular's advice to work as closely as possible with voluntary agencies with the relevant expertise in such matters, recommends that the council and the St David's Moral Welfare Committee work together so 'the facilities

---

[36] Burnham, *The Social Worker Speaks*, 57–8.
[37] Diocese of St David's, 'Minute Book of the St David's Moral Welfare Committee, November 1938–April 1944', 68.
[38] Ibid., 10.

available [are] used to the best advantage with the minimum of overlapping'.[39]

While illegitimacy was the usual reason to give a child up for adoption, society was changing. In the early 1950s, the St David's Moral Welfare Committee discussed whether they would arrange adoptions for couples who had offered a child for adoption because they did not consider they could afford to keep the child. A column in the *Daily Telegraph* referring to such cases was glued into the minute book.[40] This trend continued. In 1967, the committee decided that with an increasing shortage of adopters, priority must be given to the unmarried woman, even though the number of married women seeking to give up babies for adoption was growing.[41]

The scope of the moral welfare workers' case-load was broad, and they were an integral part of local social provision. As well as adoptions and maternity cases more generally, the St David's Moral Welfare Committee dealt with 'matrimonial' cases, which presumably referred to domestic violence. In July 1938, the committee decided to write to the magistrates complaining that the sentences handed down for assaults were too lenient. In a meeting of the committee in 1955, Maliphant reported that, of the thirty-two new cases that had been referred to her in the previous quarter, while three came of their own accord, the others were referred to her by medical officers of health, doctors, clergy, children's officers, the National Council for Unmarried Mothers and probation officers. At the same meeting, Mrs Hodges and Mrs Evans, the Outdoor Workers, had, for the same quarter, written 396 letters and made 653 visits between them. The committee minute books detail a year-on-year increase in the case-loads of the moral welfare workers they employed. In 1965, together with the Diocese of Swansea and Brecon, a new shelter was opened for 'moral welfare work'. So heavy was the workload that, in 1968, the secretary of the Adoption Committee, Mrs Webb, wrote to the Moral Welfare Committee asking that the Outdoor Workers be given assistance in both in clerical and case work.[42] By 1969, there were four

---

[39] Quarterly Report of the County Medical Officer of Health, 11 January 1944, ibid., 135.

[40] Diocese of St David's, 'Minute Book of the St Davids Moral Welfare Committee 1951–1955', St David's Diocesan Office, Abergwili, Carmarthenshire, SA31 2JG, 64.

[41] Diocese of St David's, 'Minute Book of the St Davids Moral Welfare Committee 1965–1970', St David's Diocesan Office, Abergwili, Carmarthenshire, SA31 2JG, 56.

[42] Ibid., 100.

workers employed by the Moral Welfare Committee in the Diocese of St David's and two students sent there for training.

Recent Diocesan Social Responsibility Work

All was to change over the next five years and, by 1974, the Diocese of St David's had made the move from 'moral welfare' to 'social responsibility'. Later in the 1970s, new ways of working developed across the province, beginning in the Diocese of Llandaff.[43] The Revd Bill Morgan, a curate in Merthyr Tydfil, asked Bishop John Poole-Hughes for permission to take advantage of the government's Youth Opportunities Projects to help tackle unemployment amongst young people in his area. Bishop John turned to Roger Hughes to help develop the schemes, and together Hughes and Morgan developed training partnerships funded jointly by the government and the Representative Body of the Church in Wales. By 1980, these schemes had proved their worth and Roger Hughes was employed full-time by the Church in Wales to continue their development. Just as the moral welfare workers of earlier times had played a crucial role in the development of probation work in Wales, so the potential of these schemes for reducing reoffending was seen by the Probation Service. In turn, Sylvia Scarf, a senior probation officer and member of the Church in Wales, worked with Roger Hughes to set up Unit II, a work experience and training scheme, as an alternative to a custodial sentence for young men. This worked so well that Nicholas Edwards, Secretary of State for Wales, approached Roger Hughes to develop the schemes further under the newly formed Community Programme for Adults to provide training to prepare unemployed adults to enter or re-enter the workplace. Bishop Poole-Hughes saw the importance of the Church's contribution in this area and set up his own Bishop's Committee on Unemployment. The deputy chair of the Representative Body, Raymond Cory, supported the venture – and what began in the Diocese of Llandaff impacted the work of all four southern dioceses with provincial financial support from the Representative Body.

As prostitution was the major problem in the late nineteenth century, and illegitimacy in the early twentieth, so unemployment was seen as the main problem facing Welsh society in the 1980s. The Diocese of

---

[43] My thanks to the Ven. Roger Hughes for giving generously of his time on 11 February 2019 to explain how these new ways of working developed.

Llandaff addressed this in partnership with the government by providing training. This model of addressing societal needs was the way the Church framed its response to Welsh life from disestablishment onwards. In 1991, the employment schemes had come to an end, but a very successful partnership encouraging community development projects began, funded jointly by the Children's Society and the Church in Wales' Representative Body. Projects were developed in all six dioceses and, by the time the Children's Society withdrew from the partnership in 2001 because of its financial problems,[44] there were 13 projects running and 120 workers employed across Wales.

With the withdrawal of the Children's Society, new charities were quickly established by those two dioceses in which projects were running to ensure their continuance: Faith in Families in Swansea and Brecon[45] and, in St David's, under the auspices of the St David's Diocesan Council for Social Responsibility, Plant Dewi.[46] Faith in Families now runs three family centres in Swansea and one in Brecon offering a range of services across age groups, from childcare to lunch clubs. Plant Dewi runs fifteen family centres and various projects across Carmarthenshire, Ceredigion and Pembrokeshire, with groups for fathers, young parents and families in rural areas. In 2018, Plant Dewi worked directly with 5,000 individuals. As well as Plant Dewi, the St David's Diocesan Council for Social Responsibility supports a farming crisis charity, Tir Dewi, with twenty-four trained volunteers who support farming families facing difficulties.[47]

While community development projects continued in Swansea and Brecon and in St David's, the Diocese of St Asaph employs an engagement officer to encourage Mission Areas to engage effectively with their communities, particularly with those who are marginalised, and to offer training so that Mission Areas have volunteers who are skilled and able to build and sustain projects locally. The engagement officer has developed: a church and community cold weather shelter, working with Housing Justice Cymru; a scheme to make the diocese dementia-friendly, working with the Alzheimer's Society; and a network of providers of packed lunches for children at play schemes in the school holidays. The Diocese of Llandaff social responsibility officer also works at parish level to enable parishes to recognise and respond to the needs of their local communities and to encourage them to see the potential of their

---

[44] See http://news.bbc.co.uk/1/hi/wales/1643851.stm.
[45] See https://swanseaandbrecon.churchinwales.org.uk/faith-in-families/.
[46] See https://stdavids.churchinwales.org.uk/plant-dewi/.
[47] See www.tirdewi.co.uk/en/homepage-1/.

buildings for community use. As in St Asaph, the Llandaff social responsibility officer also works directly with local projects, for example, a project for women and children seeking asylum and an initiative drawing attention to modern-day slavery. Although there is no group or officer in the Diocese of Bangor responsible for social responsibility, one of its three priorities is 'loving the world', and each Ministry Area is invited to map out its current work in this field and outline plans for action in the next three to five years, thus, like St Asaph and Llandaff, rooting its social responsibility work within Ministry Areas. Social responsibility work in the Diocese of Monmouth is also based within Ministry Areas, and the diocese has recently appointed a new archdeacon to develop diocesan work in its post-industrial valley communities.

Conclusion

The Church in Wales marks its centenary in 2020, but the heritage of the dioceses which it comprises stretches back considerably further. The Church's contribution to State and society in Wales grew out of this heritage, and many pre-disestablishment institutions providing social care survived. While the Church in Wales adapted quietly to its new status, the tenor of its relationship with State and society continued as before, mediated by the continuance of the social provision of the dioceses and Church of England societies. We have seen how, in parallel with those in the Church of England, dioceses such as St David's, through their Organising Secretaries and Outdoor Workers, made a considerable contribution to the development of social work and probation services from the 1930s to the late 1960s. As the perception of societal need changed over the years, so did the nature of the provision at diocesan level. Undergirded by the financial support of the province, in the 1980s and 1990s, dioceses developed partnerships with local authorities, government schemes and the Children's Society. In two dioceses, the community development work that began with the Children's Society partnerships continues today, run now by charities set up in the dioceses. Other dioceses have used the community development model to encourage local Ministry Areas to work directly to address locally perceived needs.

While engagement with social needs has been robust at diocesan level, the Church in Wales took some time before finding a provincial voice. Governing Body debates became more outward-looking in the run-up to the millennium and, while that impetus seems to be on the wane, issues concerned with global warming are still regularly addressed. From the mid-1980s, provincial bodies, such as the Board of Social Responsibility, followed by the then Division for Social Responsibility, set up by the Bench of Bishops and financed by the Representative Body, developed a provincial forum not only to discuss societal issues but also as a means by which dioceses could work together and provincial officers work across the six dioceses at local level. This way of working reached its peak in the late 1990s, but has been declining since. Only social policy work now remains with a Bishops' Advisor at provincial level.

Alongside these institutional responses, a core part of the Church in Wales' involvement in Welsh society has been through its people, ordained and lay. Both make contributions to their local area and to the wider world, as they have always done. Parishes today help run food banks, and clergy and parishioners serve as school governors, run community coffee mornings and holiday play schemes, work with voluntary agencies or, like the late Canon Bob Morgan, serve on local councils. While the Church does not have quite the place in society it had at disestablishment, through its work at the diocesan and parish levels, it continues to exercise the responsibility to serve the people and communities of Wales to which it feels called.

PART V

Conclusions

17

The Image of the Church

MARY STALLARD

Drawing on a selection of key themes developed in this book, this chapter focusses on three areas: the concept of image in Christian theology; the image of the Church in Wales inherited at disestablishment and as developed since; and the modern approach of the Church to communicating its image to the wider world. Disestablishment was a unique, and relatively recent, moment of re-formation in the long history of the Church in Wales. In 1920, the Anglican Church in Wales received a new identity and a changed relationship to Wales, the Church of England and the global Anglican Communion. This had a lasting impact upon how the Church in Wales has developed images of itself and how it has been seen by others. What follows, therefore, explores the unfolding awareness of the Church in Wales of its own image and the communication of its ministry, message and values to the wider world.

Image, God and the Church

Image is of great importance to every organisation concerned about how it is perceived and understood. Its image is the general impression presented to the world, the public face by which it is judged. Often regarded as key to effective communication, image is an asset to be maintained and curated. It may be about what is intentionally communicated but it may also be shaped unconsciously or accidentally, and of course it is dependent upon the viewpoint and perception of the audience. A common critique of the work of those concerned with image asks deeper questions about how this connects with substance and values. For Christians, there is also the wider context of image as a theological idea rooted in Scripture.

The biblical accounts of creation tell of a God who creates humanity in the divine image: 'Let us make humankind in our image, according to our likeness.'[1] This is foundational to Christian understandings of the

---

[1] Genesis 1:27.

relationship between humanity and God and gives a further dimension to the concept of image for a church community. Christians
believe humans have a responsibility to reflect the divine image.
Perhaps helpfully, for a body as diverse in tradition as the Church in
Wales, at the heart of this is a concept which affirms divine variety,
which connects with the Christian idea of God-in-community as
Trinity. In the Gospels it appears that Jesus is interested in how he
was understood by those he encountered and the way in which his
friends saw him. At a key moment in his ministry, which led to the
disciple Peter's famous confession of faith on the road to Caesarea
Philippi, Jesus asked his disciples two questions: 'Who do people say
that I am?' and 'Who do you say that I am?'[2]

All this affirms the importance of image for the Christian church as
the Body of Christ, taking Christ, its Head, as the source of its life,
which grows and builds itself up in love as each part plays its proper
role.[3] However, biblical images do not have only positive associations:
they are also closely linked with human stumbling and sin. The Bible
says much about the dangers of false images and warns against vanity
and the veneration of idols or images that misrepresent God.
Christian theology develops this further in the self-emptying love
demonstrated by Jesus, who, for believers, abandoned his own will
and self-interest completely, both in the incarnation – God becoming
human, laying aside divinity – and at the crucifixion, when Jesus
suffered and surrendered his human life. This understanding of the
Christian ideal is sometimes described as *kenosis*, meaning 'self-
emptying',[4] and offers a radical counterbalance to any who might
become overly concerned with their image, or how they are perceived
by others. Nevertheless, the Church in Wales teaches, officially: 'The
Church is the family of God and the Body of Christ through which he
continues his reconciling work'; its mission is 'to be the instrument of
God in restoring all people to unity with God and each other in
Christ'; and the Church in Wales itself 'proclaims and holds fast the
doctrine and ministry of the One, Holy, Catholic and Apostolic
Church'.[5]

---

[2] Mark 8:27b and 29.
[3] Ephesians 4:13, 15–16.
[4] After Philippians 2:7; see also 2:5.
[5] Church in Wales, *The Catechism: An Outline of the Faith, Church in Wales*, BCP (1984),
     vol. II, 690–2, https://s3.amazonaws.com/cinw/wp-content/uploads/2013/07/Catechism-
     English-Text-A4.pdf.

The Changing Images of the Church in Wales

The image of the Church in Wales has changed considerably over the century. Two Church in Wales films display this vividly. The professionally shot motion picture, from June 1920, of the enthronement of Archbishop Alfred George Edwards was probably made at the request of the Church (although its precise origins are unknown).[6] It records pomp and ceremony, an occasion of national significance. It shows important, establishment figures representing both Church and State: the prime minister, the Lord Lieutenant of Flintshire, royal and aristocratic figures, and, alongside the Welsh bishops, the archbishops of Canterbury and York and the bishop of London. The participants are smartly dressed, with all sorts of clerical, legal and military garb on display. But it is striking today to note the familiar elements one hundred years later: the clerical choir dress, the style of procession, and the great sense of ceremony are all still maintained at major Church in Wales events today. What is noticeably different is the complete absence of women in the processions and the predominance of men. And the film has no sound but its subtitles are all in English, not in Welsh. The film communicates that what began at disestablishment was the emergence of a church with a place still closely connected to the heart of power and the establishment.

In contrast '2020 Vision Summer 2014' is a film commissioned by the Church in Wales in 2014 to help its six dioceses to prepare to celebrate the centenary of disestablishment.[7] It communicates a very different vision of 'church' than that in 1920, including its more marginal position in society. With an image of a small girl re-enacting the parable of the sower, this film communicates that the Church in Wales needs to grow and change to speak its gospel message effectively. Relatively few shots of traditional churches are included, and local people, rather than celebrities, predominate. A range of male and female clergy are included who by their dress and language appear to represent a breadth of traditions. The film centres on local church outreach work, with people speaking Welsh as well as English. It offers a vision of 'church' as outward-looking, engaging with local communities. Indeed, the strapline of '2020 Vision' is 'serving community, inspiring

---

[6] Church in Wales, 'The Historic Ceremony of the Enthronement of the first Archbishop of Wales at St Asaph Cathedral June 1st, 1920', MMS ID 99254367302419, National Library of Wales, and www.youtube.com/watch?v=M0FyVK2q3Qw.

[7] Church in Wales, '2020 Vision Summer 2014 (Golwg 2020)', 2V Studios, Pontypool 2014, www.churchinwales.org.uk/news/2014/09/film-shows-2020-vision-progress/.

people, transforming church'.[8] This image is also reflected in modern diocesan 'straplines': Llandaff's is 'where faith matters'; Bangor has 'worshipping God, growing the church, loving the world'; Swansea and Brecon uses an emblem of a tree with the words 'gathering, growing, going'; St David's has 'growing hope' written under a Celtic cross, encased in a flame; St Asaph combines the crossed keys, from its crest, with the words 'unlocking our potential'; and Monmouth has 'becoming the people God calls us to be'.[9] They are in Welsh and English.

Between the years these two films were produced, as we have seen in this book, the image of the Church in Wales changed in a variety of more particular ways. After 1920, the Church in Wales continued to be seen as part of the establishment, 'Tory and toff',[10] even: the members of Governing Body included a significant number from the ranks of the aristocracy; the Constitution was drafted by senior members of the civil judiciary; and legal vestiges of establishment continued (and do so today) in relation to marriage and burial. By the end of the century, though, the image had changed: while civic services are still held in Welsh cathedrals,[11] the range of participants at them is more diverse; social class is no longer perceived as a prerequisite to membership of the institutions of the Church at all its levels, provincial, diocesan and local. Whilst there are notable examples of its public appraisal and criticism of the social and economic conditions in Wales across the century, in the past few decades it has become commonplace for the Church to debate and pronounce critically, and for its view to be sought, on political issues. As Archbishop Barry Morgan said to Governing Body in 2008: 'The fact of the matter is that the Church in Wales is concerned about every aspect of life in Wales and has a worshipping congregation and building in virtually every single community in Wales. As a result of this, the Bishops are talking to Cabinet Ministers about a whole range of issues to do with the life of Wales.'[12]

---

[8] See www.churchinwales.org.uk/review/.

[9] See www.churchinwales.org.uk/#ciw-diocese-map.

[10] See for this image J. Davies, *A History of Wales* (London: Allen Lane, 1993), 539; and S. J. Taylor, 'Disestablished Establishment: High and Earthed Establishment in the Church in Wales', *Journal of Contemporary Religion*, 18(2) (2003), 235–6.

[11] For example, the image of a Church at ease with royalty appears in film footage from 1955, showing the Queen and Prince Philip leaving St David's Cathedral accompanied by the Dean: Pathé Newsreels, 'Royal Tour of Wales (Long Version)', British Pathé (11 August 1955) 3.11, www.Britishpathe.com.

[12] Archbishop Barry Morgan, 'Presidential Address to Governing Body', April 2008, summary in Church in Wales: Governing Body, *Highlights* (Penarth: Church in Wales

At the beginning of the century the Church in Wales was perceived in large measure to be Anglophile: there was at best ambivalence and at worst hostility to the Welsh language; the outlook of church leaders was often considered to be 'too English'; and the Constitution was not translated into Welsh until some fifty years after disestablishment. Today, however, the principle of equilingualism is embedded, enhancing the Welsh image of the Church – in governance, liturgy and education – and it still claims to be the ancient church of the land.

Across the century there have been subtle changes in the image of the Church in terms of its allegiance to or preference for 'parties' within it, of those who stand in an evangelical, liberal or catholic tradition. In the early years, a dominant image of the Church was that it was in the high-church or catholic tradition: it embraced the Oxford Movement; it was reluctant to meddle with the inherited liturgical texts; and it was conservative in its approach to reform of the Constitution. In the past fifty years or so, however, we have seen the development of an image which is more pluralistic and diverse theologically, with: the growth of the evangelical or low-church movement; the rise of liberalism and perhaps a decrease in clerical and lay numbers in the catholic tradition (played out in debate about the composition of the Doctrinal Commission); and the emergence of a more professionalised approach to theological enquiry, a move to which academic theologians have contributed greatly.

In the decades after disestablishment, the Church was imagined as predominantly clerical, hierarchical and male-led: there was a culture of lay deference to the clergy, especially the bishops. For Archbishop C. A. H. Green in his book on the Constitution, the episcopate was the essence and fount of all ministry in the Church; and so any constitutional, doctrinal or liturgical developments were a matter for the initiative of the Bench of Bishops. But in the second half of the century, particularly the last three decades, a new, more equal, modern and inclusive image has developed, with: the ordination of women as bishops, priests and deacons; greater informal consultation over matters of debate across the province; a greater awareness among the bishops that their authority is perceived as not unlimited; and an increase in lay ministries and a move towards greater collaboration between clergy and laity. The former perception of the Church as episcopally governed and synodically guided has been replaced by a culture of the Church as episcopally led and synodically governed.

Publications), April 2008; full text, Church in Wales, 2 Callaghan Square, Cardiff, CF10 5BT, p. 2.

Another strong image represented in the chapters of this book concerns the Church in its relations with wider society. In 1920, many saw the Church as a victim of aggression by the State – the State had disestablished and disendowed it – and in the first fifty or so years the Church was viewed as hostile to other denominations in Wales and then a reluctant collaborator, struggling for natural rights to the faith of the nation; the Church was perceived very much as a minority (and its naming as the 'Church in Wales' rather than the 'Church of Wales' was intimately linked to debate about its image in this context);[13] and the Church generally engaged in its social responsibility work unilaterally without explicit collaboration with wider society. In the past fifty years or so, however, the image of the Church has changed to that of an institution keen to engage, co-operate and collaborate with society, in, for example, the provision of education in church schools, in the provision of social responsibility work and, after devolution, in working with the National Assembly for Wales and Welsh government.

Images of the Church in Wales and its relationship with the Church of England have also changed. Initially, the Church was seen as waiting upon the English Church as the stimulus for developments in Wales, such as in the field of liturgical innovation. However, as the decades unfolded, the Church in Wales became more confident about its own capacity to innovate, and did so in a number of fields before the Church of England, such as: its own ecumenical law with the covenanting churches in the 1970s; the ordination of female deacons in the 1980s; and the introduction of a disciplinary tribunal at the millennium. At the same time, however, even though there has been a dramatic decline in the number of its members and its clergy (though there was an increase in numbers in the 1960s), the Church in Wales still, like the established Church of England, considers itself to have a ministry to the whole nation, whose people have direct access to its ministrations and pastoral activity.

Then there is the image of the Church in Wales as a member of the worldwide Anglican Communion, that is, part of a large family of churches in the Western Christian tradition, which trace their development from the practice, liturgy and tradition of the Church of England following the sixteenth-century Reformation. Anglican identity is always and in every place complex and hard to define. However, the image of the Communion itself is that of 'a fellowship of churches within the One, Holy,

[13] *Cambria Daily Leader*, 5 October 1917, 3.

Catholic and Apostolic Church, characterised by their historic relationship of communion with the See of Canterbury'; individually, the churches 'uphold and propagate the historic faith and order' in communion with each other but also autonomously.[14] In turn, the 'five marks of mission' developed by the Anglican Consultative Council since 1984 go to the heart of Anglican identity, namely: to proclaim the Good News of the Kingdom; to teach, baptise and nurture new believers; to respond to human need by loving service; to seek to transform unjust structures of society, to challenge violence of every kind and to pursue peace and reconciliation; to strive to safeguard the integrity of creation and sustain and renew the life of the earth.[15] Another key feature is diversity; and: 'In diverse global situations Anglican life and ministry witnesses to the incarnate, crucified and risen Lord, and is empowered by the Holy Spirit. Together with all Christians, Anglicans hope, pray and work for the coming of the reign of God.'[16] The Church in Wales has been an active participant in the Anglican Communion throughout the past century. The election of a Welsh archbishop, Rowan Williams, to Canterbury, and thus as the spiritual leader of the Communion from 2002 to 2012, highlighted one of the contributions of the Church in Wales to, and affirmed its status as an active member of, the Communion.

The Church and the Media

Throughout the century, the Church in Wales has had a strong profile and a privileged place in emerging forms of national and local media – and in recent years it has sought to develop a more professionalised approach to communicating itself to and in the media. Before 1920, the weekly church newspaper *Y Llan*, published in Rhyl and widely circulated throughout Wales from 1881, contained a cornucopia of local,

---

[14] Anglican Communion Legal Advisers Network, *The Principles of Canon Law Common to the Churches of the Anglican Communion* (London: Anglican Communion Office, 2008), Principle 10 and Definitions.

[15] Anglican Consultative Council, 'The Five Marks of Mission' (adopted by the Lambeth Conference 1988), www.anglicancommunion.org/mission/marks-of-mission.aspx.

[16] Anglican Communion, Theological Education for the Anglican Communion (TEAC), 'The Anglican Way: Signposts on a Common Journey', *TEAC Anglican Way Consultation Singapore* (May 2007), www.anglicancommunion.org/media/109378/The-Anglican-Way -Signposts-on-a-Common-Journey_en.pdf. For diversity, and how this may be rooted in the classical Anglican triad of Scripture, reason and tradition, see the Lambeth Commission on Communion, *The Windsor Report* (London: Anglican Communion Office, 2004), 46–54.

district, national and international news, with Welsh-only and English-only contributions side by side; and it presented the Church as highly engaged with these various levels of life. Issues of *Y Llan* from 1919 portray a Church keen to work through the financial complexities of disestablishment and with a high level of administrative organisation, but also focussed upon its work of evangelism and mission, including among young people.[17] Similar images appeared in *Y Dywysogaeth* ('The Principality') and then later *Y Llan a'r Dywysogaeth* ('The Church and the Principality'), which together ran from 1870 until 1955. *Y Llan* was later revived as a Welsh-language publication of the Church in Wales with a more focussed Christian and Welsh-language agenda, but this publication ceased in 2006, by which time its circulation had dwindled to only 400 copies.

At significant moments, the Church in Wales has also made interventions in the press that have had a strong, positive impact, such as, for example, the letter from Glyn Simon, Bishop of Llandaff, to the *Western Mail* following the Aberfan disaster in 1966.[18] And Archbishop G. O. Williams is remembered for his vocal support of the Welsh language; he opposed moves by Prime Minister Margaret Thatcher to downplay its official status, and argued for the Welsh-language television channel, Sianel Pedwar Cymru, S4C (Channel Four Wales). Less helpful to its image have been the ways in which some internal debates, short-comings and controversies of the Church have been portrayed in the media. Anna Morrell, Director of Communications for the Church in Wales, comments: 'we are . . . easy prey for negative stories. We have been pilloried in the media for discrimination against women and same-sex couples', such as in debates about the ordination and representation of women in the Church and its attitude to human sexuality;[19] one example is the publicity that surrounded the consideration of Jeffrey John, Dean of St Albans, for the office of bishop of Llandaff.[20]

---

[17] Revd Canon Edwards, 'The Disendowment of the Church in Wales', *Y Llan*, 31 October 1919, 2; Revd R. E. Roberts, 'The Mission of the Welsh Church', *Y Llan*, 12 December 1919, 2.

[18] A. O'Callaghan, 'Aberfan 50 Years on: How the Press Covered the Disaster and the Aftermath', Wales Online, 17 October 2016, updated 20 October 2016.

[19] A. Morrell, e-mail interview, 31 January 2019.

[20] See for example, M. Shipton, 'The Furious Letter of a Gay Cleric to Bishops Who Rejected Him', 20 March 2017, www.walesonline.co.uk/news/wales-news/furious-letter-gay-cleric-sent-12769110; H. Sherwood, 'Anglican Clergyman Accuses Church in Wales of Homophobia', *Guardian*, 19 March 2017.

It is hard to measure the impact of negative media attention on the Church. But the increasing attention given by the Church in Wales to media relations in recent years perhaps indicates a growing awareness of the importance of co-ordinated and clear communication for the Church's image and reputation. According to Morrell: 'The Archbishop ... is assumed to be not just the spokesperson for the Church or even for Welsh Christians but for faith generally in Wales ... As an organisation, we get more than our fair share of publicity in Wales – both positive and negative ... Bishops are the go-to spokespeople on many issues of the day – they offer an alternative voice to politicians.'[21] This view is evident in Archbishop Morgan's words to Governing Body in 2008: 'bishops ... tackle issues of nationhood, health, prosperity, education, community, housing, the poor, culture, the environment and governance – all the issues in fact that are crucial to a nation's wellbeing'.[22]

Surprisingly, it was not until 1992 that the Church appointed a provincial media officer. Until this time media engagement seems to have been handled without a clear strategy, with bishops and clergy making their own responses when approached by journalists, or speaking out publicly as issues arose. The beginning of this proactive approach can be traced to proposals from a Working Group on the Future Role of the Archbishop, developed as Archbishop George Noakes was succeeded by Archbishop Alwyn Rice Jones, and presented at the Governing Body in 1992.[23] As part of a package of measures to support the role, it was agreed that the archbishop's staff should include a media officer. The thinking appears to have been to protect the archbishop's time more than to develop a communications strategy. Indeed, in its communications posts, there has been a gradual move away from deploying ordained staff and an increasing reliance on personnel with journalism and media training. This appears to show a commitment to cultivate a more professional image in the media.

The Revd David Williams was the first media officer for the Archbishop in 1992. He pioneered the role after serving as director of the Provincial Board of Mission. He was succeeded by Siôn Brynach (2000–6) who brought experience of media work from previous careers in communications and public relations. During his time the role was

[21] A. Morrell, e-mail interview, 31 January 2019.

[22] Archbishop Barry Morgan, Presidential Address, Governing Body, April 2008.

[23] Church in Wales: Working Group on the Future Role of the Archbishop, 'Report, Minutes of Governing Body, 22–3 April 1992', Cardiff, Item 11, 8–10.

extended to include greater collaboration with those having a diocesan communications brief. Brynach was involved in managing the Church's commentary on and engagement with political issues, most notably devolution and the Cymru Yfory (Tomorrow's Wales) campaign in which the Church was an active participant through the work of Archbishop Morgan.[24]

As the election of Rowan Williams as archbishop of Canterbury in 2002 attracted positive media attention to the Church,[25] Archbishop Barry Morgan continued to develop these media relations. Morrell comments that Morgan had 'a media profile on a par with a party political leader – he was almost the "commissioner for faith". During his tenure, we had BBC TV and radio coverage of every Governing Body meeting – mainly his presidential addresses.'[26]

The media has also presented an image of the Church as a body seeking to engage with issues that sometimes divide Christians. Recently, this was apparent following discussion at Governing Body 2018 of possible, formal provision for same-sex partnerships. It led to the headline 'Church in Wales to Consider Allowing Gay Marriage' from Premier News,[27] and a progressive view of the Church. Wales Online reported the same debate, stressing the view that the bishops were united in concern about the lack of provision for same-sex couples. Within this article there is some acknowledgment of alternative voices within the Church in Wales but the overall image reported is of a Church that is seeking to be inclusive.[28]

The increasing ease of access and contribution to broader media networks over the past thirty years have enabled the Church in Wales to communicate its message and to reach out to a wider audience. It has also exposed it to greater public scrutiny. An article published in the *Daily Express* about declining church attendance in Wales titled 'Death of the Church: Attendance Plummets to Size of Pontefract Threatening Sunday Worship' demonstrates the vulnerability of having a public platform. The article gives a disparaging

---

[24] Cited in Archbishop Barry Morgan, Presidential Address to Governing Body, April 2008.
[25] See for example BBC News: www.bbc.co.uk/news/uk-17399403.
[26] A. Morrell, e-mail interview 31 January 2019.
[27] A. Williams, 13 September 2018, www.premier.org.uk/News/UK/Church-in-Wales-to-consider-allowing-gay-marriage.
[28] D. Williamson, 12 September 2018, 'Gay Marriage in Welsh Churches? Welsh Bishops Say It Is "Unjust" Not to Provide for Same-Sex Couples', www.walesonline.co.uk/news/wales-news/gay-marriage-church-wales-15139880.

report of part of a meeting of the Governing Body in September 2016, at which members were seeking to address declining attendance figures by considering plans for renewal and growth; and yet this headline, sparked by that debate, arguably added to the Church's marginal image.[29]

Over the years the Church in Wales has made many contributions, in both Welsh and English, to radio and television broadcasts.[30] On television, ordinands in training for ministry in the Church in Wales featured in *Vicar Academy*, broadcast in 2012 on BBC Wales. This four-part series followed a small group of students through their studies. It presented a rather bleak picture of the Church as a struggling organisation, but the cohort of trainees gave a generally upbeat account of their experiences of ministerial training. On S4C, *Parch* (Reverend), a Welsh-language drama by Fflur Dafydd, presented a fictional story about Myfanwy, a priest serving in a rural Welsh parish. In its first series, this too presented an image of a typical parish church with a tiny congregation, but it presented a sympathetic picture of the priest, portraying ministry in a generally positive light. *Parch* was warmly received and returned in a further two series in which Myfanwy took on a new role in community chaplaincy, a newer form of engagement pioneered by Church in Wales clergy.[31]

Online, the Church receives both praise and criticism. At the time of writing, the BBC News website lists a wide range of news items under the heading 'Church in Wales'. The first fifty stories listed range from criticism of the Church regarding the deployment of retired clergy, to praise for its social enterprise projects. Of the stories listed on 11 April 2019, fourteen give a broadly positive account of the Church's work, shining a spotlight on projects such as local church initiatives assisting people living with dementia, while seven offer negative or critical perspectives drawing attention to church failures in practice or policy. There are five stories about the attitude of the Church in Wales to sex or sexuality, eleven about gender, four about graveyards and trees, and six about the Church's

---

[29] K. Mansfield, 'Death of the Church: Attendance Plummets to Size of Pontefract Threatening Sunday Worship', *Daily Express*, 1 October 2016.

[30] For example, 'The Last Words of St David', *Sunday Worship*, BBC Radio 4, 24 February 2019, 08.10 am., led by the Very Revd Dr Sarah Rowland Jones with Joanna Penberthy, Bishop of St David's.

[31] *Parch* was broadcast from 2015 to 2018, and used Canon Dr Manon Ceridwen James as Religious Advisor.

positive social projects such as helping the homeless or environmental campaigns.[32]

The Church's increasing engagement with digital communication has developed since 2007. Anna Morrell continued to be the Archbishop's Media Officer and Bishops' Advisor for Communication and is now the Church in Wales' director of communications. This role is now located more remotely from the archbishop, with the Information and Communication Technology department at the Representative Body offices in Cardiff. Morrell reports that there is an intentional shift in this new alignment to enable broader communication with the whole church in line with the provincial strategy,[33] and to have a less hierarchical focus following the recommendations of the Harries Review 2012.[34] Dioceses and local Ministry and Mission Areas are also making effective use of the most modern forms of communication, reflected in the detailed advice provided on the Church in Wales website.[35]

In recent years the Church in Wales has developed its website, first created by Revd David Neale in 1998, then adapted and updated in 2002 by Revd Dr John Baldwin. It had a major relaunch at Governing Body in 2007 after further work by Matt Knight, Creative Resources Officer. The present design was launched in 2013 and is currently undergoing further work to keep pace with changing technology and developing Church plans. The website is presented in English and Welsh. This form of communication is replicated in the dioceses and cathedrals, and in many cases by parishes and ministry or mission areas across the province.

The Church in Wales has also grown increasingly adept at developing its professional networks of communication. This has led to it becoming a trusted resource for media contacts such as the Religious Progammes Department at the BBC in Cardiff, which has strong links with the Provincial and Diocesan Offices. The Church in Wales presents itself with confidence as a leading faith voice in Wales. There remains a stereotype that the Church is old-fashioned and less than comfortable with the fast-moving news world of technology, but there are also many individuals and

---

[32] 'Church in Wales U-turn over "Too Old" Ceredigion Vicar': www.bbc.co.uk/news/uk-wales-45978920; see also 'Dementia Projects for Church in Wales Parishes': www.bbc.co.uk/news/uk-wales-39816093.

[33] A. Morrell, e-mail interview 31 January 2019.

[34] Church in Wales, *Review* (July 2012), www.churchinwales.org.uk/review/, 4.

[35] Parochial Administration, Chapter 6, 'Communication', and Clergy Handbook, Section 3, Procedures, 'Social Media Policy': www.churchinwales.org.uk.

communities engaging with newer forms of communication and making positive steps to spread good news throughout Wales.[36]

Conclusion

As I began to write this chapter, I had a chance encounter with someone who had attended the Church in Wales' conference 'The Time is Now', in Llandudno in November 2014, which was part of responses to the Church in Wales' *Review* of 2012. The conference involved people from all over Wales who were invited to explore how the Church might respond to the call of God today and flourish and grow in prayer and service. The man I met is a businessman, with marketing and management skills. He explained his professional journey as one in which he has had to translate, transfer and transform his career to adapt to changing local and global markets. As a Christian he is also committed to exploring his faith, perhaps making a similar journey of change. He has been nurtured at times by the Church in Wales although, like many today, he has not felt confined to a single tradition but has also found a home in other Christian churches and currently worships with a Methodist congregation in north Wales. He was interested in what had become of all those discussions he had heard about in Llandudno with regard to forming Ministry Areas – and he wanted to know if the Church has stayed true to the ideas and visions explored then. He asked searching questions about how the Church, with its six diverse dioceses and many local churches, is managing to offer a coherent brand. He was interested and enthusiastic about the good he has experienced in the Church in Wales and expressed his hopes for continued ecumenical co-operation. His questions and desire to know more about what is happening say something about the ongoing challenge for the Church of enabling effective communication about its image, identity and engagement. After his enthronement in 2017, Archbishop John Davies spoke about the importance of refreshing the image of the Church in Wales.[37] And it seems this is happening already: an emerging, modern, confident image is perhaps reflected in the recent move of the Provincial Offices from a Victorian house in Cathedral Road, Cardiff, where it was located for almost a hundred years, to newly built, rented premises at Callaghan

---

[36] See: @ChurchinWales on Twitter; The Church in Wales on Facebook.
[37] 'New Archbishop Wants to "Refresh" Church in Wales', 2 December 2017, www .bbc.co.uk/news/uk-wales-42167184.

Square in the heart of the city.[38] This was a bold move highlighting graphically the potential the Church in Wales has always had, to be courageous in moving forward, using its resources well to help others know the God of hope and to serve the world effectively and with a generous heart.

[38] Church in Wales, 'Provincial Office Move', Provincial Press Release, 21 September 2017, updated 25 September 2017, www.churchinwales.org.uk/news/2017/09/provincial-office -move/.

18

The Church of the Future

JOHN DAVIES

My responsibility, in concluding this very welcome volume, is, I believe, to be encouraged both to comment and to pose questions which might possibly be challenging, even painful. I hope they will emerge from what follows. I pose them not to be provocative, but to recognise a plain truth: one hundred years on from its birth, the Church in Wales is right to remember, celebrate and mark the events, engagements and activities of those years, but it must not merely look back. Remembrance, different from simply remembering, requires more than acts of memory – it demands commitment to what lies ahead, for 'no one who puts a hand to the plough and looks back is fit for the kingdom of God'.[1]

The final verses of the Gospel according to St Matthew contain the best-known version of what is frequently referred to as 'The Great Commission':

> Now the eleven disciples went to Galilee, to the mountain to which Jesus had directed them. And when they saw him, they worshipped him, but some doubted. And Jesus came and said to them, 'All authority in heaven and on earth has been given to me. Go therefore and make disciples of all nations, baptizing them in the name of the Father and of the Son and of the Holy Spirit, teaching them to observe all that I have commanded you. And behold, I am with you always, to the end of the age.'[2]

Whether the incident, as recorded several decades after the first Christian Pentecost, was a historic event does not, for our purposes, matter. What does matter is the evident conviction, one that underpinned the life of the early church, that its duty, its joy and its sole purpose were to act upon the Great Commission by making disciples, disciples who would be faithful in word and deed to all that Jesus had commanded and taught.

[1] Luke 9:62.
[2] Matthew 28:16–20.

What the infant church was not told explicitly to do was to become an institution. Institutional religion had, at different times in the history of the People of God, become hugely discredited, and the target of excoriating condemnation by the prophets and by Jesus himself. Nevertheless, the church would, relatively soon, become an institution, with structures for governance and administration, orders of ministers, processes for discipline and for the defining and refining of doctrine among its notable characteristics. It would possess, enshrined in its documents, its rites and its ceremonies, the fruit of the labours of great minds and of pious, holy souls.

Such an outcome was, frankly, inevitable. Any society, whether sacred or secular, needs its structures and disciplines, its rules, its rulers and its rule-making processes, lest its life should rapidly become chaotic and, possibly, even unfaithful to the vision of its founders and unfaithful to its founding purpose. Societies need organisation. There is, however, a dangerous side to the coin of organisation, namely, that the existence and functioning of everything designed, created and put in place – whether deliberately or out of necessity – to support the fulfilment of the vision and purpose may end up actually obscuring them, thus diminishing the vigour of that which it was intended to sustain. The structures may become ends in themselves rather the means of achieving or supporting the one true end. The plot, as they say, is lost, with the institution becoming internalised: self-interested, self-perpetuating, inward-looking and losing sight of its external purpose which, in the case of the Church, is the fulfilment of the Great Commission.

Densil Morgan appositely reminds us in Chapter 3 of this book of the view expressed by J. I. Morgans and P. C. Noble that, entering upon the twenty-first century, 'While the churches debated details of belief, church discipline and ministry, the world journeyed rapidly towards secularism.' Whilst apportioning blame or attributing responsibility for this evidently accurate state of affairs is all too easy, I will lean, and lean most definitely, in the direction of saying that I do not, for a moment, believe this to be the entire responsibility or the complete fault of a world deliberately setting its face against the Gospel or becoming increasingly hostile to the teachings of Christ. Far from it. I turn, again, to Scripture, to the Acts of the Apostles, to reflect upon the opinion of Gamaliel, 'a Pharisee in the council, a teacher of the law, held in honour by all the people'.[3] When intervening in the debate about how the apostles should be punished for

---

[3] Acts 5:34.

their defiant teaching, he warned his fellow members of the council that 'if this plan or undertaking is of men, it will fail; but if it is of God, you will not be able to overthrow them'.[4] If the Church is, in places, failing today, then Gamaliel challenges it, in those places, to ask whether it has lost its vision of God and God's kingdom, and whether it is living out its days as a mere institution. Would it be too discourteous to suggest, constructively one hopes, that in such places the Church may have become deaf to the Great Commission or at least a little hard of hearing? How does such a suggestion sit with the Church in Wales as we mark its foundation one hundred years on?

There can be no doubt, and we have already read, that the Church in Wales was created and came into being, if not wholly formed then certainly partly formed, as an institution. It subsists as such. Emerging from another institution, the Church of England, with layers of already existing diocesan and other complementary structures, constituent parts, governance systems and accompanying complications, it had to be created thus; the model was already there, and radical departure from it would have been unthinkable and quite un-Anglican. Yet, when it was born, when it emerged, it did so, some would argue and argue strongly, with the innate possibility and opportunity of being set free from shackles. These shackles, they would also argue, had led to it becoming a mere adjunct of its much larger if, oddly, younger 'parent', the Church of England. They had caused it, during its time as four dioceses in the Province of Canterbury, to become forgetful, if not entirely then certainly significantly, of its rootedness in the Age of the Saints of Wales and its acquiescing in the imported practices and spiritual disciplines of those such as the Cistercians and Benedictines.

Religious diversity on a scale barely, if at all, understood by the English Church, the radically differing approaches of Anglicanism and Nonconformity, and cultural and linguistic diversity – fuelled, at the end of the nineteenth century and in the early twentieth, by political expediency and no small touch of guile – combined, however, to create a set of circumstances which, I believe, had buried within them, invisible to many eyes, seeds of hope and promise. Were the four dioceses *actually* a 'problem child', better left to its own devices, perhaps to wither and perish? There may have been those who believed this. But once battles were fought, once the die was cast with the passing of the Welsh Church Act 1914, there were at least some who would not see it that way, who had

---

[4] Acts 5:38b–39a.

a very different view. They recognised those seeds of hope and promise for something new. Whether they were seeds of hope and promise simply for a shiny, new institution to be born, or whether they were seeds of hope and promise for the renewal of commitment to the Great Commission, remained to be seen.

Clearly, as we have read, there was, at the time of disestablishment, huge anxiety that the province of the Church in Wales should not only survive after the prolonged labour pains that preceded its birth, but that it should also be able and equipped to thrive. The disestablishment settlement did not guarantee this, and disendowment threatened it. Much hard work had to be done and was done to set in place as secure a set of foundations as might realistically be required. That work was well rewarded and the institution was able, thanks not least to determined characters such as Sankey, Atkin, Bankes and Morgan, to stand on its own feet. This very fact, and the success of the appeals launched to provide financial viability and security, were all the more remarkable when viewed against the background of international conflicts and the political tensions of the time, as well as the biting poverty, depression and deprivation visited upon so many individuals and families in Wales.

How, then, has the institution fared? Has its first hundred years enabled the Great Commission to be heeded and to continue to be heeded? Is it embedded in our life and have we evidence that its plans for the future are built around a real desire to take it further? There are clear and positive indications. The Prefatory Note to the Constitution of the Church in Wales, found in both of its volumes, and to which Norman Doe draws attention in Chapter 5, explicitly states that the Constitution exists to serve the sacramental integrity and good order of the Church and to assist its mission and its witness to the Lord Jesus Christ. It goes on to affirm that the chief features of the law of the Church in Wales – a number of its structures and practices – identify it as part of the worldwide Anglican Communion. The purpose of the Governing Body is to provide for 'the general management and good government of the Church'.[5] The Representative Body is required to manage the resources of the Church 'to effect the purposes of the Archbishop, Bishops, Clergy and Laity of the Church in Wales'.[6] The Constitution also requires the Parochial Church Council to promote 'the whole mission of the church,

---

[5] Constitution II.12.
[6] Constitution III.16.

pastoral, evangelistic, social and ecumenical',[7] and among the duties of churchwardens it states that 'they shall use their best endeavours to ... encourage the parishioners in the practice of true religion'.[8] The Church in Wales' *Review*, the report published and received in 2012, reminded the province that its fundamental purpose is to proclaim the Gospel and draw people into the life of Christ – the Great Commission, articulated locally. And the rites of ordination, the bidding at services of licensing or induction, and assorted other doctrinal statements and documents, both liturgical and administrative, are peppered with similar exhortations and affirmations. So, the Church in Wales certainly articulates itself on paper as faithful and as a vehicle for faith, a 'Jesus movement', committed, as some of the rites put it, to proclaiming the faith afresh in each generation.

Reflecting upon the chapters in this book, I guess that it is the yardstick 'proclaim the faith' against which I would want to measure and evaluate the activities of which those chapters speak in order to answer the question posed above – whether the Church in Wales, in the hundred years of its life, has been faithful to its core task. To paraphrase the question, is the Church in Wales a family of faithful Christians or a grouping of habitual churchgoers, or a mixed bag?

If we take Gamaliel at his word, we could argue, and with some justification, that a faltering and declining institution is a sign of a failure to be faithful, and that history is calling the Church in Wales to return to its core business, to rediscover its brand identity. I would hope that, in affirming evangelism, living and teaching the Gospel, as its primary task, the Governing Body of the Church in Wales, in April 2017, put down a careful and clear marker calling the Church to evaluate, and to continue to evaluate, its performance as a community of faithful evangelists. In doing so, one might wonder whether the Church was implicitly recognising that, perhaps, a deal of its activity had been focussed elsewhere and in directions other than the core business of fulfilling the Great Commission.

On becoming archbishop, I said, on a number of occasions, that *rehabilitation*, making the Church fit for purpose and deliberately refocussing on a more evident return to its original purpose, was needed. This would mean recognising that, whilst set in Wales, whilst committed to the culture, society, identity and people of Wales, and whilst steadfastly affirming a bilingual policy, the Church is about the Gospel, and about

---

[7] Constitution IVC.8(3)(a).
[8] Constitution IVC.13(4).

preaching not itself, but Jesus Christ, as Lord, with the Church as servant of others. 'The Son of Man came not to *be* served but *to* serve',[9] and the Church must have the same intention. In what it has done over one hundred years, and as set out and discussed in the chapters of this book, has the Church in Wales so organised and managed itself, so worshipped, so engaged with the world through works and words of goodness, love and truth, as to demonstrate a clear commitment to be a family of faith?

As we have seen, in what it has done in fields such as education, social responsibility, charitable outreach, culture, language, and community engagement and development, the Church in Wales has served the localities in which it is set. It has sometimes done so in partnership with other agencies, other churches and, at other times, on its own. It would assert and argue vigorously that it has done all of this as a response to the Gospel imperative to serve after the example of Christ and as a witness to God's love for the world and its people. But do not numerical decline, some unacceptable ignorance of both Scripture and the most basic tenets of the faith and, in some places, a lamentable absence of teaching and study at any level, suggest that the Church has wandered into an area where some might not be able to distinguish it as a 'Jesus movement', but might simply see it as a voluntary offshoot of secular civic social services, within which people, admittedly of a good heart and mind, give of their time because they have that time to give, rather than as a direct consequence of their desire to follow Christ in serving others?

Some of the judgments or suggestions which I have made in this chapter may be viewed and rightly critiqued as somewhat too broad-brush and far too general. They may be seen to be dismissive of much hard work and social engagement, even discourteous to some things undertaken in good faith. But the questions which I have sought to ask are, I believe, being answered; and the answers being given are evidence of the Church in Wales being ready and awake to engage in real self-evaluation, and both to reassess and return more consciously and deliberately to its calling to make disciples. Among the evidence are to be found: the affirmation of the ministry of all the faithful, lay and ordained, which recognises that each and every gift of ministry is not the possession of any one group; the variety of callings and ministries being discerned, trained for and provided; the commitment to providing both contemporary and traditional worship, well done; welcoming

---

[9] Matthew 20:28a.

buildings; a real appetite, at a number of levels, for achievable and realistic ecumenical working and worshipping with Christians of other denominations; careful auditing and targeting of resources locally and provincially; the encouragement to team-working across larger areas, rather than isolation behind impenetrable parochial boundaries.

Particularly welcome for me is the growth of interest and participation in theological study through initiatives such as 'Theology for Life'. Introduced earlier this decade, this course of study is now managed and overseen by St Padarn's Institute (itself set up in 2016) and is delivered in a variety of venues across the province. It aims to deepen theological thinking, and to facilitate and foster the growth of disciples, equipping some, but not all of them, to become participants in Ministry Teams emerging in a number of areas across the province. There are currently well over 200 people across the province studying part-time on the course and, in addition, others who are in training on the course for licensed ministry full-time in the Church.[10]

Also most welcome is the province's 2020 Vision through which, following the 2012 review, the Church in Wales is committed to taking a fresh look at its structures and ministry. It will, I hope, help it to see more clearly how it can best serve Wales in the twenty-first century, making best use of the Church's rich resources – material, financial and human. The Vision has been summarised as enabling the Church to be the prayerful heart of the community, sharing the Christian message in a way that engages, inspires and transforms. Some of the changes envisaged are recognised to be radical, pushing the boundaries of long-established traditions, while others were developments of ministry that were already taking place. All, however, are changes which the Church in Wales itself has identified as some of the means by which it hopes to re-energise and reinvigorate its life and ministry across the nation.

These and other developments are all evidence of something which gives me hope for the future, namely a renewal of a commitment to Christ's Great Commission. I end with a final reference to Scripture: 'Every scribe who has been trained for the kingdom of heaven is like the master of a household who brings out of his treasure, what is new and what is old.'[11] So, in reviewing this past hundred years, in the

---

[10] As we see elsewhere in this book, St Padarn's is the 'training arm' of the Church in Wales which delivers theological training across the wide spectrum of ministry, lay and ordained.

[11] Matthew 13:52.

studies contained in this book, we can properly remember, celebrate and mark much that has been brave, visionary and worthwhile. But, as we do so, we must confidently look forward further with bravery and vision to more years of faithful service rooted in courageous and loving commitment to that same Great Commission.

BIBLIOGRAPHY

Primary Sources

Anglican Communion Sources

Anglican Church of Australia, 'Canons and Rules', www.anglican.org.au/canons-and-rules.

Anglican Communion: Theological Education for the Anglican Communion, 'The Anglican Way: Signposts on a Common Journey', *TEAC Anglican Way Consultation Singapore* (May 2007), www.anglicancommunion.org/media/109378/The-Anglican-Way-Signposts-on-a-Common-Journey_en.pdf.

Anglican Communion Legal Advisers Network, *The Principles of Canon Law Common to the Churches of the Anglican Communion* (London: Anglican Communion Office, 2008).

Anglican Consultative Council, 'The Five Marks of Mission' (adopted by the Lambeth Conference 1988), www.anglicancommunion.org/mission/marks-of-mission.aspx.

Anglican–Roman Catholic International Commission, 'Walking Together on the Way: Learning to Be the Church – Local, Regional and Universal. An Agreed Statement of the Third Anglican–Roman Catholic Commission' (ARCIC-III) (2018).

Church of England, 'Admission of Baptised Children to Holy Communion Regulations' (2006).

Episcopal Church (USA), 'Constitution and Canons', www.episcopalchurch.org/posts/publicaffairs/episcopal-church-constitution-and-canons-2018.

Lambeth Commission on Communion, *The Windsor Report* (London: Anglican Communion Office, 2004).

Lambeth Conference, Resolution 9.III (1920), www.anglicancommunion.org/media/127731/1920.pdf.

Scottish Episcopal Church, 'Code of Canons', www.scotland.anglican.org/who-we-are/publications/code-of-canons/.

Church in Wales: Provincial Sources

Cathedrals of the Church in Wales: Report of the Review Group, The (June 2016).

Church in Wales, '2020 Vision Summer 2014 (Golwg 2020)', 2V Studios, Pontypool 2014, www.churchinwales.org.uk/news/2014/09/film-shows-2020-vision-progress/.

The Book of Common Prayer for Use in the Church in Wales (Penarth: Church in Wales Publications, 1984).

The Catechism: An Outline of the Faith, Church in Wales: https://s3.amazonaws.com/cinw/wp-content/uploads/2013/07/Catechism-English-Text-A4.pdf.

The Church in Wales Today (Penarth: Church in Wales Publications, 1990).

'Clergy Handbook', www.churchinwales.org.uk/resources/constitution-handbooks/clergy-handbook/.

'Constitution', www.churchinwales.org.uk/structure/representative-body/publications/downloads/the-constitution/.

Cyngres yr Eglwys yng Nghymru: Welsh Church Congress Lectures Delivered at the Congress (Cowbridge: n.p., n.d.).

Daily Prayer (Norwich: Canterbury Press, 2010).

'Ethical Investment Policy of the Representative Body of the Church in Wales' (approved by Governing Body, April 2016), https://llandaff.churchinwales.org.uk/parish-resources/.

'Guidance: Parish Green Guide' (undated); 'Care of Area Deanery and Parish Records' (2013, updated 2017); 'Parochial Fees Guidance' (2015); 'Parsonage Security' (undated); 'Mediation Service' (2014); 'Code of Practice on Episcopal Ministry' (2014), www.churchinwales.org.uk/structure/representative-body/publications/downloads/.

The Holy Eucharist in Modern Language (Penarth: Church in Wales Publications, 1984).

'The Historic Ceremony of the Enthronement of the First Archbishop of Wales, 1920, at St Asaph Cathedral, 1 June 1920', MMS ID 99254367302419, National Library of Wales, and www.youtube.com/watch?v=M0FyVK2q3Qw.

A Manual of Training for Church Schools – Religious Education Syllabus Guide (Cardiff: Representative Body of the Church in Wales, 1971) (Gittins Report), https://discovery.nationalarchives.gov.uk/details/record?catid=69791&catln=5.

'Minutes of the Church in Wales Representative and Governing Body, 1945–8 and 1949–52', held at the Provincial Offices of the Church in Wales, 2 Callaghan Square, Cardiff, CF10 5BT.

The Official Handbook of the Church in Wales (Cardiff, 1930).

An Order for the Holy Eucharist (Norwich: Canterbury Press, 2004).

The Ordination of Women to the Priesthood: The Record of the Debate during the April 1975 Governing Body Debate of the Church in Wales (Penarth: Church in Wales Publications, 1975).

'Parochial Administration', www.churchinwales.org.uk/resources/constitution-handbooks/parochial-administration-handbook/.

'Representative Body', www.churchinwales.org.uk/structure/repbody, and www.churchinwales.org.uk/structure/representative-body/publications/downloads/review/.

'Retirement of Archbishop Barry Morgan', www.churchinwales.org.uk/news/192017/01/archbishop-of-wales-retires/.

Review (July 2012), Report of the Review Group, Commissioned by the Church in Wales, Lord Harries of Pentregarth, Professor Charles Handy, and Professor Patricia Peattie, www.churchinwales.org.uk/review/.

'Same-Sex Marriage', www.churchinwales.org.uk/faith/believe/bench_samesex marriage/; www.churchinwales.org.uk/news/ 192018/09/church-to-explore-formal-provision-for-same-sex-couples/; and www.churchinwales.org.uk /news/2016/04/same-sex-marriage-statement/.

Services for Christian Initiation (Norwich: Canterbury Press, 2006).

The Welsh Church Year Book, 1929 (Cardiff: Representative Body of the Church in Wales, 1929).

Women and the Ministry (Penarth: Church in Wales Publications, 1972).

Church in Wales: Archbishop's Commission on Religious Education and Regulations, 'Report, made to the Governing Body of the Church in Wales to provide for the Establishment of a Church in Wales Provincial Council for Education and for purposes connected therewith', October 1947, Archive of the Church in Wales, National Library of Wales, Aberystwyth.

Church in Wales: Archbishop's Commission on the Boundaries and Structures of the Church in Wales, *Report* (1980).

Church in Wales: Bench of Bishops, 'Children and Holy Communion: Guidelines and Resources for Parishes' (2001).

Education Review (Cardiff: Church in Wales, 2009), https://s3.amazonaws.com /cinw/wp-content/uploads/2013/07/edrev-en.pdf.

'Marriage and Divorce: Guidelines' (1998).

'Minutes', 14 January 1969 (Cardiff: Church in Wales Representative Body, 1969), contained in file 'Standing Doctrinal Commission' (1969–2013).

'A Pastoral Letter from the Bishops of the Church in Wales to All the Faithful Concerning Admission to Holy Communion' (September 2016), www.churchinwales.org.uk/news/2016/09/confirmation-no-longer-required-for -holy-communion-bishops-letter/.

Church in Wales: Board of Mission Division for Education, 'Diocesan Directors of Education, Minute Book 1980–8', BN/1997A/5, Archive of the Church in Wales, National Library of Wales, Aberystwyth.

Church in Wales: Board of Mission Division for Social Responsibility, *Aids/HIV Infection: A Challenge to Care* (Penarth: Church in Wales Publications, 1991).

Human Genetic Screening and Therapy: Some Moral and Pastoral Issues (Penarth: Church in Wales Publications, 1992).

Church in Wales: Church Schools Wales, www.churchschoolscymru.org/res/files/Diocese/Syllabus/syllabus.pdf.

Church in Wales: Council for Education, 'Minutes', 5 May 1952, Archive of the Church in Wales, National Library of Wales, Aberystwyth.

Report to the Governing Body of the Church in Wales (September 1964).

Church in Wales: Governing Body, *Highlights* (Penarth: Church in Wales Publications), April 1967, October 1969, May 1970 and August 1980; *Highlights* (Cardiff: Church in Wales Publications), May 1987, September 2002, www.churchinwales.org.uk/structure/representative-body/publications/downloads/highlights/.

'Minutes', 1936, Archive of the Church in Wales, National Library of Wales, Aberystwyth.

Church in Wales: Nation and Prayer Book Commission, *Report* (Cardiff: Western Mail & Echo Ltd, 1949).

Church in Wales: Schools Council, 'Minute Books', January 1963, Archive of the Church in Wales, National Library of Wales, Aberystwyth.

Church in Wales: Working Group on the Future Role of the Archbishop, 'Report, Minutes of Governing Body, 22–23 April 1992', Cardiff, Item 11, 8–10.

Church in Wales: Youth Council, *Cymry'r Groes 1951* (Cardiff: Church in Wales, Provincial Youth Council, 1951).

Gittins Report, *see* Church in Wales, *A Manual of Training for Church Schools – Religious Education Syllabus Guide*.

Harries Report, *see* Church in Wales, *Review*.

Morgan, Archbishop Barry, 'Presidential Address to Governing Body, September 2003', www.churchinwales.org.uk/structure/representative-body/publications/downloads/theology-wales-back-issues/theology-wales-the-church-and-homosexuality/presidential-address-archbishop-barry-morgan/.

'Presidential Address to Governing Body, April 2008', summary in Church in Wales: Governing Body, *Highlights* (Penarth: Church in Wales Publications), April 2008; full text, Church in Wales, 2 Callaghan Square, Cardiff, CF10 5BT.

'Presidential Address to Governing Body, April 2014', www.churchinwales.org.uk/structure/bishops/sermons-and-addresses-archbishop-barry-morgan/presidential-address-governing-body-april-2014.

Official Report of the Proceedings of the Convention of the Church in Wales Held at Cardiff (Cardiff, 1917).

St Deiniol's Group, *Crossing Thresholds: The Licensed Ministry of Women in the Church in Wales: 1884-2014* (Cardiff: Church in Wales Publications, 2014).

Church in Wales: Diocesan Sources

Diocese of Bangor, 'Guidelines for Governance in Ministry Areas' (2013).

Diocese of St David's, 'Minute Book of the Case Committee for the Archdeaconry of Carmarthen, 1941–1946', St David's Diocesan Office, Abergwili, Carmarthenshire, SA31 2JG.

'Minute Book of the St David's Moral Welfare Committee, November 1938– April 1944', St David's Diocesan Office, Abergwili, Carmarthenshire, SA31 2JG.

'Minute Book of the St David's Moral Welfare Committee, 1951–1955', St David's Diocesan Office, Abergwili, Carmarthenshire, SA31 2JG.

'Minute Book of the St David's Moral Welfare Committee, 1965–1970', St David's Diocesan Office, Abergwili, Carmarthenshire, SA31 2JG.

J. Herbert (Revd), ed., *St David's Diocesan Directory* (Carmarthen: Spurrell and Son, 1906).

J. Herbert (Revd), ed., *St David's Diocesan Directory* (London: SPCK, 1912).

S. B. Williams (Revd), ed., *The Year Book of the Diocese of St David's 1928–1929* (Carmarthen: W. Spurrell and Son, 1928).

S. B. Williams (Revd), ed., *The Year Book of the Diocese of St David's 1936–1937* (Carmarthen: W. Spurrell and Son, 1936).

Other Materials

Board of Education, *Report of the Consultative Committee on the Education of the Adolescent* (London: HMSO, 1927) (Hadow Report).

Secondary Education with Special Reference to Grammar Schools and Technical High Schools (London: HMSO, 1938) (Spens Report).

Board of Education: Welsh Department, *Educational Reconstruction* (London: HMSO, 1943).

Welsh in Education and Life (London: HMSO, 1927).

Central Advisory Council for Education (England), *Children and Their Primary Schools* (London: HMSO, 1967) (Plowden Report), www.educationengland.org.uk/documents/plowden/.

Central Church Committee for Defence and Instruction, 'Mass Meeting of Churchmen in the Royal Albert Hall on February 20, 1912' (London: Central Church Committee for Defence and Instruction, 1912).

Commission of Enquiry into the State of Education in Wales, *Report* (London: HMSO, 1848).

Commission on Religious Education in Schools, I. T. Ramsey, ed., *The Fourth R: The Durham Report on Religious Education* (London: SPCK, 1970).

Covenanted Churches of Wales: 'The Gathering: Summary of Recommendations' (Cardiff: Covenanted Churches of Wales, 2012), www.cydgynulliad.org.uk/.

Daniel, D. R., Letter to Thomas Rees, 16 October 1914, Bala-Bangor MSS 65, Bangor University Archives.

Department of Education and Science: Welsh Office Guidance, *The Educational System of England and Wales* (London: HMSO, September 1985).

Donaldson, G., 'Report on the Welsh Curriculum', March 2014, https://beta .gov.wales/sites/default/files/publications/2018–03/succesful-futures-a-sum mary-of-professor-graham-donaldsons-report.pdf.

Durham Report, *see* Commission on Religious Education in Schools, I. T. Ramsey, ed., *The Fourth R: The Durham Report on Religious Education*.

Ecumenical Panel, *A Statement of Principles of Christian Law* (Rome, 2016).

Faith Communities Forum, 'Terms of Reference': https://gov.wales/faith-communities-forum/terms-of-reference.

Hadow Report, *see* Board of Education, *Report of the Consultative Committee on the Education of the Adolescent*.

Interfaith Council for Wales, 'Constitution', revised and adopted July 2018.

Jenkins, Alfred, Letter to Owen Prys, sometime in 1917, Owen Prys Papers 22283, Calvinistic Methodist Archives, National Library of Wales, Aberystwyth.

Ministry of Education, *A Guide to the Educational System of England and Wales* (London: HMSO, 1945).

National Assembly for Wales: Constitutional and Legislative Affairs Committee, *Report on the Inquiry into Law-Making and the Church in Wales* (June 2013).

National Society for Promoting Religious Education in Accordance with the Principles of the Church of England, *123rd Annual Report* (1934), Lois Louden Archive, Sheppard-Worlock Library, Liverpool Hope University.

153rd Annual Report (1964), Lois Louden Archive, Sheppard-Worlock Library, Liverpool Hope University.

Pathé Newsreels, 'Royal Tour of Wales (Long Version)', British Pathé (11 August 1955), 3.11, www.Britishpathe.com.

Plowden Report, *see* Central Advisory Council for Education (England), *Children and Their Primary Schools*.

Royal Commission on the Church of England and Other Religious Bodies in Wales and Monmouthshire, *Report* (London: HMSO, 1910).

Sankey, J., *Diaries*, Bodl. MS Eng. Hist. e. 271 (1917); e. 272 (1918); e. 273 (1919); e. 274 (1920) (Bodleian Library, University of Oxford).

Spens Report, *see* Board of Education, *Secondary Education with Special Reference to Grammar Schools and Technical High Schools*.

Welsh Education Committee, 'Minutes', vol. 3, 16 June 1871, Archive of the Church in Wales, National Library of Wales, Aberystwyth.

Secondary Sources

Abraham-Williams, G., ed., *Towards the Making of an Ecumenical Bishop in Wales / Tuag at Benodi Esgob Ecwmenaidd yng Nghymru* (Penarth: Enfys – The Covenanted Churches in Wales, 1997).

Allchin, A. M., *The Dynamic of Tradition* (London: Darton Longman and Todd, 1981).

Arnold, F., *Our Bishops and Deans* (London: Hurst and Blackett, 1875).

Bebbington, D. W., 'Edward Miall', *Oxford Dictionary of National Biography* (Oxford: Oxford University Press, 2004).

Beecroft, Miriam, 'Bilingual Worship in the Church in Wales' (unpublished), Theology for Life dissertation, Module CWTH6002 (St Padarn's Institute, Cardiff, 2017).

Bell, G. K. A., *Randall Davidson* (Oxford: Oxford University Press, 1952).

Bell, P. M. H., *Disestablishment in Ireland and Wales* (London: SPCK, 1969).

Benson, E. W., 'The Church in Wales: Shall We Forsake Her? A Speech to the Church Congress at Rhyl, Tuesday, 9 October 1891' (London: Church Defence Association, 1891).

Binns, J. S., *Alfred Edwin Morris: Archbishop of Wales* (Llandysul: Gomer Press, 1990).

Bishop, E., *Liturgica Historica* (Oxford: Oxford University Press, 1918).

Boneham, J., 'Isaac Williams and the Welsh Tractarian Theology', in S. J. Brown and P. B. Nockles, eds., *The Oxford Movement: Europe and the Wider World 1830-1930* (Cambridge: Cambridge University Press, 2012), 37–65.

Brierley, P., *Major UK Religious Trends 2010 to 2020* (Tonbridge: Brierley Consulting, 2010).

Brown, R. L., *Evangelicals in the Church in Wales* (Welshpool: Tair Eglwys Press, 2007).

In Pursuit of a Welsh Episcopate (Cardiff: University of Wales Press, 2005).

'In Search of a Welsh Episcopate', in R. Pope, ed., *Religion and Identity in Wales and Scotland c. 1700-2000* (Cardiff: University of Wales Press, 2001), 84–102.

ed., *The Letters of Edward Copleston* (Cardiff: South Wales Record Society, 2003).

'Pastoral Problems and Legal Solutions', in Doe, ed., *Essays in Canon Law*, 7–24.

A Social History of the Welsh Clergy (Welshpool: privately published, 2017).

The Welsh Evangelicals (Welshpool: Tair Eglwys Press, 1986).

Bull, P. J., *Catalogue of the Papers of John Sankey (1866-1948)* (Oxford: Bodleian, 1973).

Burnham, D., *The Social Worker Speaks: A History of Social Workers through the Twentieth Century* (London: Routledge, 2016).

Caird, D., *Church and State in Wales: The Case for Disestablishment* (London: Liberation Society, 1912).

Cameron, G. K., 'The Church in Wales, the Canons of 1604 and the Doctrine of Custom' (LLM Dissertation, University of Wales, Cardiff, 1997).

'Locating the Anglican Communion in the History of Anglicanism', in I. S. Markham, J. B. Hawkins, J. Terry and L. N. Steffensen, eds., *The Wiley-Blackwell Companion to the Anglican Communion* (Chichester: Wiley-Blackwell, 2013), 3–14.

Chadwick, O., *A History of the Popes 1830–1914* (Oxford: Oxford University Press, 1998).

The Victorian Church 1860–1901 (London: SCM Press, 1987).

Chandler, L., 'Governing Body of the Church in Wales: April and September 2016', *Ecclesiastical Law Journal*, 19 (2017), 73–7.

Chapman, M. D., S. Clarke and M. Percy, eds., *The Oxford Handbook of Anglican Studies* (Oxford: Oxford University Press, 2016).

Chapman, T. R., *Un Bywyd o Blith Nifer: Cofiant Saunders Lewis* (Llandysul: Gomer Press, 2006).

Cragoe, M., 'George Osborne Morgan, Henry Richard and the Politics of Religion in Wales 1864–1874', *Parliamentary History*, 19 (2000), 118–30.

Cranmer, F., M. Hill, C. Kenny and R. Sandberg, eds., *The Confluence of Law and Religion: Interdisciplinary Reflections on the Work of Norman Doe* (Cambridge: Cambridge University Press, 2016).

Cripps, H. W., *A Practical Treatise on the Law relating to the Church and Clergy* (London: Sweet & Maxwell, 1849).

Crockford's Clerical Directory (London: Oxford University Press, 1953–4).

Daniel, C., 'Wales: Catholic and Nonconformist', *Blackfriars*, 38(444) (1957), 100–11.

Daniel, J. E., 'Diwinyddiaeth Cymru', *Yr Efrydydd*, 5 (1929), 118–22, 173–5, 197–203.

Davie, G., 'Establishment', in M. D. Chapman, S. Clarke and M. Percy, eds., *The Oxford Handbook of Anglican Studies* (Oxford: Oxford University Press, 2016), 287–300.

Religion in Britain since 1945: Believing without Belonging (Oxford: Blackwell, 1994).

Davies, A. T. [under the pseudonym Theomemphus], *Bilingual Bishops and All That* (Llandybie: Christopher Davies Publishers, 1958).

Davies, A. T., *David Jones: Letters to a Friend* (Swansea: Triskele Books, 1980).

Dylan: Druid of the Broken Body – An Assessment of Dylan Thomas as a Religious Poet (London: J. M. Dent, 1964).

Davies, C., *Mothers' Union Alive* (Cowbridge: D. Brown, 1993).

Davies, D. P., 'Welsh Anglicanism: A Renewed Church for a Reviving Nation', in N. Yates, ed., *Anglicanism: Essays in History, Belief and Practice* (Lampeter: Trivium Publications, 2008), 105–23.

Davies, G., *The Chosen People: Wales and the Jews* (Bridgend: Seren, 2002).

The Dragon and the Crescent: Nine Centuries of Welsh Contact with Islam (Bridgend: Seren, 2011).

Davies, J., *A History of Wales* (London: Allen Lane, 1993).

Davies, N. A., *A History of Ecumenism in Wales, 1956–1990* (Cardiff: University of Wales Press, 2008).

Davies, P., *Diary of a Soul*, trans. H. Hughes (Talybont: Y Lolfa, 2011).

Davies, R. R., *Conquest, Co-existence and Change: Wales 1063–1415* (Oxford: Oxford University Press, 1987).

Davies, R. T., 'Some Reflections', in Doe, ed., *Essays in Canon Law*, 191–4.

Doe, N., *Canon Law in the Anglican Communion* (Oxford: Clarendon Press, 1998).

  Christian Law: Contemporary Principles (Cambridge: Cambridge University Press, 2013).

  'The Contribution of Common Principles of Canon Law to Ecclesial Communion in Anglicanism', in Anglican Communion Legal Advisers' Network, *The Principles of Canon Law Common to the Church of the Anglican Communion*, 97–124.

  ed., *Essays in Canon Law: A Study of the Law of the Church in Wales* (Cardiff: University of Wales Press, 1992).

  'The Instruments of Unity and Communion in Global Anglicanism', in I. S. Markham, J. B. Hawkins, J. Terry and L. N. Steffensen, eds., *The Wiley-Blackwell Companion to the Anglican Communion* (Chichester: Wiley-Blackwell, 2013), 47–66.

  Law and Religion in Europe (Oxford: Oxford University Press, 2011).

  The Law of the Church in Wales (Cardiff: University of Wales Press, 2002).

  The Legal Architecture of English Cathedrals (London: Routledge, 2017).

  The Legal Framework of the Church of England (Oxford: Clarendon Press, 1996).

  'Rediscovering Anglican Priest-Jurists I: Robert Owen', *Ecclesiastical Law Journal*, 21 (2018), 54–68.

  'Richard Hooker: Priest and Jurist', in M. Hill and R. H. Helmholz, eds., *Great Christian Jurists in English History* (Cambridge: Cambridge University Press, 2017), 115–37.

Eckerdal, E., 'Apostolic Succession in the Porvoo Common Statement: Unity through a Deeper Sense of Apostolicity' (PhD Thesis, Uppsala University, 2017), http://uu.diva-portal.org/smash/record.jsf?pid=diva2%3A1129750&dswid=-9729.

Edwards, A., 'Introduction', *Inter-Faith Wales: Building Trust and Respect between People of All Faiths throughout Wales* (Cardiff: Interfaith Council for Wales, 2008).

Edwards, A. G., *Landmarks in the History of the Welsh Church* (London: John Murray, 1912).

  Memories (London: John Murray, 1927).

Edwards, A. J., *Archbishop Green: His Life and Opinions* (Llandysul: Gomer Press, 1986).

'Building a Canon Law: The Contribution of Archbishop Green', in Doe, ed., *Essays in Canon Law*, 49–67.

The Seven Bishops (Newport: Diocese of Monmouth, 1996).

Edwards, J. H., *The Life of David Lloyd George* (London: Waverley Book Company, 1913).

Ellis, T. I., *Ym Mêr fy Esgyrn* (Lerpwl: Gwasg y Brython, 1955).

Emrys ap Iwan, 'Paham y Gorfu yr Undebwyr', in M. Lloyd, ed., *Erthyglau Emrys ap Iwan* (Wales: Y Clwb Llyfrau Cymraeg, 1936), 23–41.

Evans, D., *Cymru mewn perygl! Defodaeth yr un a Phabyddiaeth* (Dolgellau, 1869).

Evans, G., *The Christian Value of the Welsh Language / Gwerth Cristionogol yr Iaith Gymraeg* (Swansea: Gwasg John Penry, 1967).

Evans, J. W. and J. M. Wooding, eds., *St David of Wales* (Woodbridge: Boydell Press, 2007).

Freeman, P., '*Baner y Groes*, a Welsh-Language Tractarian Periodical of the 1850s', *Cylchgrawn Llyfrgell Genedlaethol Cymru*, 32 (2001–2), 305–16.

'The Response of Welsh Nonconformity to the Oxford Movement', *Welsh Historical Review*, 20(3) (2001), 435–65.

Gainer, J., 'John Sankey and the Constitution of the Church in Wales' (LLM Dissertation, University of Wales Cardiff, 1994).

Garner, P., 'The Reader: An Exploration of the History and Present Place of Reader Ministry in the Church of England' (PhD Thesis, University of Leeds, 2010), http://etheses.whiterose.ac.uk/1913/1/READER_ministry_THESIS_master .pdf.

Garthwaite, K., *Hunger Pains: Life inside Food Bank Britain* (Bristol: Policy Press, University of Bristol, 2016).

Gates, B., 'Faith Schools and Colleges of Education since 1800', in R. Gardner, J. Cairns and D. Lawton, eds., *Faith Schools: Consensus or Conflict* (Abingdon: Routledge Falmer, 2005), 14–35.

Gibbard, N., *R. B. Jones: Gospel Ministry in Turbulent Times* (Bridgend: Bryntirion Press, 2009).

Girard, R., *Violence and the Sacred*, trans. P. Gregory (Baltimore: Johns Hopkins University Press, 1977).

Green, C. A. H., *The Church's Title to Its Endowments* (London: Central Church Committee for Defence and Instruction, 1909).

The Setting of the Constitution of the Church in Wales (London: Sweet & Maxwell, 1937).

Grigg, R., *History of Trinity College Carmarthen 1848–1998* (Cardiff: University of Wales Press, 1998).

Grubb, N., *Rees Howells: Intercessor* (Cambridge: Lutterworth Press, 2013).

Gwynn ap Gwilym, ed., *Gogoneddus Arglwydd Henffych Well!* (Cardiff: Cytûn: Churches Together in Wales, 1999).

Sgythia (Caernarfon: Gwasg y Bwthyn, 2017).

Harris, C. and R. Startup, *The Church in Wales: The Sociology of a Traditional Institution* (Cardiff: University of Wales Press, 1999).

Hill, M. and N. Doe, 'Principles of Christian Law', *Ecclesiastical Law Journal*, 19 (2017), 138–53.

Hill, M., R. Sandberg and N. Doe, *Religion and Law in the United Kingdom* (Alphen aan den Rijn: Wolters Kluwer, 2nd ed., 2014).

Hill Fletcher, J., *Motherhood as Metaphor: Engendering Interreligious Dialogue* (New York: Fordham University Press, 2013).

Howells, A., *A Franciscan Way of Life: Brother Ramon's Quest for Holiness* (London: Bible Reading Fellowship, 2018).

Hughes, T. O., *Winds of Change: The Roman Catholic Church and Society in Wales, 1916–1962* (Cardiff: University of Wales Press, 1999; 2nd ed., 2017).

Jackson, B., *Leading One Church at a Time* (Cambridge: Grove, 2018).

James, J. W., *A Church History of Wales* (Ilfracombe: Stockwell, 1945).

Jenkins, D., *Tân yn Llŷn* (Aberystwyth: Gwasg Aberystwyth, 1937).

Jones, B. Pierce, *How Lovely Are Thy Dwellings* (Newport: Wellspring Publications, 1999).

The Spiritual History of Keswick in Wales, 1903–1983 (Cwmbran: Christian Literature Press, 1989).

Jones, D. C., 'Evangelical Resurgence in the Church in Wales in the Mid-Twentieth Century', in A. Atherstone and J. Maiden, eds., *Evangelicals and the Church of England in the Twentieth Century: Reform, Resistance and Renewal* (Woodbridge: Boydell Press, 2014), 227–47.

'Evangelicalism and Fundamentalism in Post-War Wales, 1947–1981', in D. Bebbington and D. C. Jones, eds., *Fundamentalism and Evangelicalism in the United Kingdom during the Twentieth Century* (Oxford: Oxford University Press, 2013), 289–308.

'Lloyd-Jones and Wales', in A. Atherstone and D. C. Jones, eds., *Engaging with Martyn Lloyd-Jones: The Life and Legacy of 'the Doctor'* (Nottingham: Apollos, 2011), 59–90.

'Pentecostalism', in R. C. Allen, D. C. Jones and T. O. Hughes, eds., *The Religious History of Wales: Religious Life and Practice from the Seventeenth Century to the Present Day* (Cardiff: Welsh Academic Press, 2014), 131–46.

Jones, D. Gwenallt, *Cerddi Gwenallt: Y Casgliad Cyflawn*, ed. C. James (Llandysul: Gomer Press, 2001).

Jones, E., *Croesi Ffiniau: Gyda'r Eglwys yn y Byd* (Swansea: Gwasg John Penri, 2000).

Jones, G., *The Dragon Has Two Tongues*, ed. T. Brown (Cardiff: University of Wales Press, revised ed., 2001).

Jones, G. E., *Which Nation's Schools? Direction and Devolution in Welsh Education in the Twentieth Century* (Cardiff: Cardiff University Press, 1990).

Jones, G. E. and G. W. Roderick, *A History of Education in Wales* (Cardiff: University of Wales Press, 1st ed., 2003).

Jones, O. W., *Glyn Simon: His Life and Opinions* (Llandysul: Gomer Press, 1981).

Saint Michael's College Llandaff 1892–1992 (Llandysul: Gomer Press, 1992).

Jones, P., *The Governance of the Church in Wales* (Cardiff: Greenfach, 2000).

Jones, R. Tudur, *Faith and the Crisis of a Nation: Wales 1890–1914*, ed. R. Pope (Cardiff: University of Wales Press, 2004).

Ffydd ac Argyfwng y Genedl (Swansea: Ty John Penry, 1982).

'The Origins of the Nonconformist Disestablishment Campaign 1830–1840', *Journal of the Historical Society of the Church in Wales*, 20 (1960), 39–76.

Jones, S. H. and L. J. Francis, 'The Fate of the Welsh Clergy: An Attitude Survey among Male Clerics in the Church in Wales', *Contemporary Wales*, 10 (1997), 182–99.

Lambie-Mumford, H., 'The Growth of Foodbanks in Britain and What They Mean for Social Policy', *Critical Social Policy*, 39(11) (2019), 3–22.

Lane, M., 'The Legal Extent of the Disestablishment of the Church in Wales' (LLM Dissertation, Cardiff University, 2018).

Lewis, A. T., 'The Case for Constitutional Renewal in the Church in Wales', in Doe, ed., *Essays in Canon Law*, 175–89.

Lewis, E., *John Bangor – The People's Bishop: The Life and Work of John Charles Jones, Bishop of Bangor 1949–1956* (London: SPCK, 1962).

Prayer Book Revision in the Church in Wales (Penarth: Church in Wales Publications, 1958).

Lewis, G., *Lord Atkin* (London: Butterworths, 1983).

Llwyd, A., *Gwenallt: Cofiant D. Gwenallt Jones, 1899–1968* (Talybont: Y Lolfa, 2016).

Llywelyn, D., *Sacred Place, Chosen People: Land and National Identity in Welsh Spirituality* (Cardiff: University of Wales Press, 1999).

Llywelyn, J., *Pilgrim of Peace: A Life of George M. Ll. Davies, Pacifist, Conscientious Objector and Peace-Maker* (Talybont: Y Lolfa, 2016).

Löffler, M., *Iaith nas Arferir Iaith Farw yw: Ymgyrchu dros yr Iaith Gymraeg rhwng y Ddau Ryfel Byd*, trans. Geraint H. Jenkins (Cardiff: University of Wales Centre for Advanced Welsh and Celtic Studies, 1995).

Louden, L., *Distinctive and Inclusive: The National Society and Church of England Schools 1811–2011* (London: National Society, 2012).

Lowe, R., *Reflections of a Bygone Age: A Brief History of Allington and Burton in the Parish of Rossett* (Wrexham: RLP, 1998).

Merchant, M., *Fragments of a Life* (Llandysul: Gomer Press, 1990).

Morgan, B., 'The Church in Wales', in I. S. Markham, J. B. Hawkins, J. Terry and L. N. Steffensen, eds., *The Wiley-Blackwell Companion to the Anglican Communion* (Chichester: John Wiley, 2013), 452–63.

Morgan, D. D., *Barth Reception in Britain* (London: T. & T. Clark, 2010).

Cedyrn Canrif: Crefydd a Chymdeithas yng Nghymru'r Ugeinfed Ganrif (Cardiff: University of Wales Press, 2001).

'Christianity and National Identity in Twentieth-Century Wales', *Religion, State & Society*, 27(3/4) (1999), 327–42.

'The Essence of Welshness: Some Aspects of the Christian Faith and National Identity in Wales c. 1900–2000', in R. Pope, ed., *Religion and National Identity: Wales and Scotland, c. 1700–2000* (Cardiff: University of Wales Press, 2001).

'Lampeter, Mirfield and the World: The Life and Work of Bishop Timothy Rees (1874–1939)', *Welsh Journal of Religious History* (2013), 100–17.

Pennar Davies (Cardiff: University of Wales Press, 2003).

The Span of the Cross: Christian Religion and Society in Wales, 1914–2000 (Cardiff: University of Wales Press, 1999; 2nd ed., 2011).

Wales and the Word: Historical Perspectives on Welsh Identity and Religion (Cardiff: University of Wales Press, 2008).

Morgan, F., *A Short Summary of the Constitution of the Church in Wales* (Cardiff: Western Mail Ltd, 1920).

Morgan, K. O., *Freedom or Sacrilege: A History of the Campaign for Welsh Disestablishment* (Penarth: Church in Wales Publications, 1966).

Rebirth of a Nation: Wales, 1880–1980 (Oxford: Oxford University Press, 1981).

Wales in British Politics, 1868–1922 (Cardiff: University of Wales Press, 1963; rev. ed., 1980).

Morgan, P., 'From Death to a View: The Hunt for the Welsh Past in the Romantic Period', in E. Hobsbawm and T. Ranger, eds., *The Invention of Tradition* (Cambridge: Cambridge University Press, 1983), 43–100.

Wales: The Shaping of a Nation (Exeter: David and Charles, 1984).

Morgan-Guy, J., 'The Visit of the Eastern Metropolitans and Patriarchs to St David's Cathedral in 1925, a Lecture Given to the Cathedral Friends, September 2014', in *Friends of St David's Cathedral: Annual Report 2015* (St David's: St David's Cathedral, 2015).

Morgans, J. I., *Penrhys: The Story of Llanfair* (privately published, 1994).

Morgans, J. I. and N. Morgans, *Journey of a Lifetime: From the Diaries of John Morgans* (Llanidloes: privately published, 2008).

Morgans, J. I. and P. C. Noble, *Our Holy Ground: The Welsh Christian Experience* (Talybont: Y Lolfa, 2016).

Morris, A. E., *The Church in Wales and Nonconformity: Being the Second Visitation Charge of Edwin, Lord Bishop of Monmouth* (Newport: A. T. W. James, 1949).

Morris, E., *The Christian Use of Alcoholic Beverages* (Risca: Starling Press, 1961).

Morris, J., 'Anglicanism in Britain and Ireland', in J. Morris, ed., *The Oxford History of Anglicanism, Volume IV: Global Western Anglicanism, c. 1910–Present* (Oxford: Oxford University Press, 2017), 397–436.

Morris, R. M., ed., *Church and State in 21st-Century Britain: The Future of Church Establishment* (London: Palgrave Macmillan, 2009).

Neigwl, G., ed., *Cofio RS: Cleniach yn Gymraeg?* (Liverpool: Gwasg y Bwthyn, 2013).

O'Leary, P., 'Religion, Nationality and Politics: Disestablishment in Ireland and Wales', in J. R. Guy and G. Neely, eds., *Contrasts and Comparisons: Studies in Irish and Welsh Church History* (Llandysul: Gomer Press, 1999), 89–114.

Owen, E. E., *The Later Life of Bishop Owen* (Llandysul: Gomer Press, 1961).

Owen, J., *The Principles of the Welsh Disestablishment Bill* (Cardiff: Western Mail Ltd, 1909).

Owen, R., *Institutes of Canon Law* (London: John Hayes, 1884).

Parri, H., *Cannwyll yn Olau: Stori John Puleston Jones* (Caernarfon: Gwasg y Bwthyn, 2018).

   Gwn Glân a Beibl Budr: John Williams Brynsiencyn a'r Rhyfel Mawr (Caernarfon: Gwasg y Bwthyn, 2014).

Parry, R. Ifor, *Ymneilltuaeth* (Llandysul: Gomer Press, 1962).

Parry Jones, D., *A Welsh Country Parson* (London: B. T. Batsford, 1975).

Paterson, R., 'The Church in Wales', in C. Hefling and C. Shattuck, eds., *The Oxford Guide to the Book of Common Prayer: A Worldwide Survey* (Oxford: Oxford University Press, 2006), 426–30.

Peart-Binns, J. S., 'Arglwydd Archesgob Cymru: Alfred Edwin Morris – Election and Aftermath', *Journal of Welsh Ecclesiastical History*, 2 (1985), 55–86.

   Edwin Morris, Archbishop of Wales (Llandysul: Gomer Press, 1990).

   Gravitas with a Light Touch (Durham: Memoir Club, 2009).

   'Martinet and Shepherd: John Morgan Archbishop of Wales', *Welsh Journal of Religious History*, n.s. 4 (2004), 41–64.

Phillimore, R., *Ecclesiastical Law* (London: Sweet & Maxwell, 1873; 2nd ed., 1895).

Pope, R., *Building Jerusalem: Nonconformity, Labour and the Social Question in Wales, 1906–1939* (Cardiff: University of Wales Press, 2nd ed., 2014).

   'Dolur Dwfn Diffyg Ystyr: J. R. Jones a Chrefydd', in E. Gwynn Matthews, ed., *Argyfwng Hunaniaeth a Chred: Ysgrifau ar Athroniaeth J. R. Jones* (*Astudiaethau Athronyddol*, vol. 6) (Talybont: Y Lolfa, 2017), 31–59.

Price, D. T. W., *Archbishop Gwilym Williams, 'G.O.': His Life and Opinions* (Cardiff: Church in Wales Publications, 2017).

   'The Contribution of St David's College, Lampeter, to the Church in Wales, 1920–1971', *Journal of Welsh Ecclesiastical History*, 1 (1984), 63–83.

   A History of St David's University College, Lampeter (Cardiff: University of Wales Press, 1990).

A History of the Church in Wales in the Twentieth Century (Penarth: Church in Wales Publications, 1990).

'The Modern Diocese of St Davids', in W. Gibson and J. Morgan-Guy, eds., *Religion and Society in the Diocese of St Davids 1485–2011* (Farnham: Ashgate, 2015), 202–32.

Rees, I. T., *Saintly Enigma: A Biography of Pennar Davies* (Talybont: Y Lolfa, 2011).

Rees, J. Lambert, *Timothy Rees of Mirfield and Llandaff: A Biography* (London and Oxford: Mowbray, 1945).

Rees, T., *Sermons and Hymns* (London and Oxford: Mowbray, 1946).

Reichel, O. J., *The Canon Law of Church Institutions* (London: SPCK, 1922).

Richards, T., *The Puritan Movement in Wales* (London: National Eisteddfod Association, 1920).

Religious Developments in Wales (1654–1662) (London: National Eisteddfod Association, 1923).

Richfield, J., 'Review of Governing Body Business 2007, 2012, 2016' (2016), held at the Provincial Office, Church in Wales, 2 Callaghan Square, Cardiff, CF10 5BT.

Robbins, K., 'Establishing Disestablishment: Some Reflections on Wales and Scotland', in S. J. Brown and G. Newlands, eds., *Scottish Christianity in the Modern World: In Honour of A. C. Cheyne* (London: Bloomsbury, 2001), 231–54.

Roberts, E. P., 'The Welsh Church, Canon Law and the Welsh Language', in Doe, ed., *Essays in Canon Law*, 151–73.

Roberts, G. T., *The Language of the Blue Books: The Perfect Instrument of Empire* (Cardiff: University of Wales Press, 1998).

Rowland Jones, S., ed., *An Ecumenical Bishop for Wales?* (Cardiff: Church in Wales Publications, 2002).

Sackville, A., 'The Moral Welfare Workers Association', Professional Associations in Social Work 1900–1990 Working Paper 10 (1987), www.kcl.ac.uk/scwru/swhn/2013/sackville-professional-associations-in-social-work-1900-1990-paper.pdf.

Saunders, E., *A View of the State of Religion in the Diocese of St David's* (Cardiff: University of Wales Press, [re-print] 1949).

Saunders, E. and C. Davies, *Euros Bowen: Priest-Poet / Bardd-Offeiriad* (Penarth: Church in Wales Publications, 1993).

Shortt, R., *Rowan's Rule: The Biography of the Archbishop* (London: Hodder and Stoughton, 2008).

Simon, G., *Then and Now* (Penarth: Church in Wales Publications, 1961).

A Time of Change: The Second Visitation Charge of the Bishop of Llandaff (Penarth: Church in Wales Publications, 1966).

Snell, K. D. M. and P. S. Ell, *Rival Jerusalems: The Geography of Victorian Religion* (Cambridge: Cambridge University Press, 2000).

Taylor, S. J., 'Disestablished Establishment: High and Earthed Establishment in the Church in Wales', *Journal of Contemporary Religion*, 18(2) (2003), 227–40.

Thomas, D., 'Liturgical Revision in the Church of Wales' (1977), www.churchservicesociety.org/journals/volume-07-number-02-nov-1977/liturgical-revision-church-wales.

Silyn (Cofiant Silyn Roberts) (Liverpool: Gwasg y Brython, 1957).

Thomas, D. R., *A History of the Diocese of St Asaph* (Oswestry: Caxton Press, 1913).

Thomas, M. Wynn, 'Yr Hen Fam: R. S. Thomas and the Church in Wales', in M. Wynn Thomas, *All That Is Wales: The Collected Essays of M. Wynn Thomas* (Cardiff: University of Wales Press, 2017), 165–83.

'R. S. Thomas: A Retired Christian', in M. Wynn Thomas, *All That Is Wales: The Collected Essays of M. Wynn Thomas* (Cardiff: University of Wales Press, 2017), 185–212.

Thomas, P. E., 'Doctrine of the Church', in S. W. Sykes and J. Booty, eds., *The Study of Anglicanism* (London: SPCK, 1988), 249–62.

Turton, D. W., *Clergy Burnout and Emotional Exhaustion: A Socio-psychological Study of Job Stress and Job Satisfaction* (Lampeter: Edwin Mellen Press, 2010).

Van Espen, Z. B., *Jus Ecclesiasticum Universum*, 5 vols. (Louvain, 1753).

Viator Cambrensis [pseudonym], *The Rise and Decline of Welsh Nonconformity* (London: Sir Isaac Pitman and Sons Ltd, 1912).

Wakefield, G., *An Outline of Christian Worship* (Edinburgh: T. & T. Clark, 1998).

Walker, D., ed., *A History of the Church in Wales* (Penarth: Church in Wales Publications, 1976).

Ware, T., *The Orthodox Church* (London: Penguin Books, 1997).

Watkin, T. G., 'The Constitution of the Church in Wales', https://law.gov.wales/constitution-government/intro-to-constitution/ecclesiastical-church-in-wales/the-constitution-of-church-in-wales.

'Disestablishment, Self-Determination and the Constitutional Development of the Church in Wales', in Doe, ed., *Essays in Canon Law*, 25–48.

The Legal History of Wales (Cardiff: University of Wales Press, 2007).

'Vestiges of Establishment', *Ecclesiastical Law Journal*, 2 (1990), 110–15.

Welby, J., Speech, Muslim Council of Wales' Interfaith Dinner, 2 October 2015, www.archbishopofcanterbury.org/speaking-and-writing/speeches/archbishop-justin-addresses-muslim-council-wales.

White, S., *The Churchyards of the Church in Wales* (Bangor: Welsh Legal History Society, 2018).

Williams, D. D., ed., *Thomas Charles Edwards* (Liverpool: National Eisteddfod Transactions, 1921).

Williams, G., *Wales and the Reformation* (Cardiff: University of Wales Press, 1997).

The Welsh Church from Conquest to Reformation (Cardiff: University of Wales Press, 1962).

Williams, G. A., *When Was Wales?* (London: Penguin Books, 1985).

Williams, G. O., *The Church's Work* (Caernarfon: n.p., 1959).

Williams, H., 'St David's and Disestablishment: Reassessing the Role of Bishop John Owen', in J. Morgan-Guy and W. Gibson, eds., *Religion and Society in the Diocese of St David's 1485–2011* (London: Ashgate, 2015), 179–202.

Williams, J., *Digest of Welsh Historical Statistics* (Cardiff: Welsh Office, 1985).

Williams, R., *Addresses and Sermons delivered by the Most Revd and Rt Hon. Dr Rowan Williams while Archbishop of Wales* (Cardiff: Church in Wales, 2003).

After Silent Centuries (Oxford: Perpetua Press, 1994).

'Foreword', in Doe, *The Law of the Church in Wales.*

'Simon, (William) Glyn Hughes', *Oxford Dictionary of National Biography* (Oxford: Oxford University Press, 2004).

Wright, C., 'The English Canon Law Relating to Suicide Victims', *Ecclesiastical Law Journal*, 19 (2017), 193–211.

Wyn, Hefin, *Ar Drywydd Niclas y Glais: Comiwnydd Rhonc a Christion Gloyw* (Talybont: Y Lolfa, 2017).

INDEX

equilingualism, 112, 319
Erastianism, 241
ESTYN, 270
Ethical Investment Group, 118
Eucharist, the, 188, *see* Holy
  Communion
Evangelical Alliance Wales, 61
Evangelical Fellowship, 57, 167
Evangelical Movement of Wales, 56, 57
Evangelicals, 163, 186
evangelism, 57, 99, 112, 117, 118, 138,
  146, 180, 196, 247, 322, 333
evangelistic workers, 156
Evans, Alun, 298
Evans, Gwynfor, 59, 253, 287
Evans, Bishop John, 16
Evans, Mrs, 307
Evening Prayer, 66, 73, 183, 187, 190,
  192, 204
excommunication, 213

faculty jurisdiction, 97
Faith Communities Forum, 231, 342
Faith in Families, 309
farming, 246, 309
fees, 124
Feilding, Lord, 35
Fellowship of Reconciliation, 49
First World War, 28, 45, 47, 126, 196,
  241, 260
Fleetwood, Bishop William, 16
Forster Education Act 1870, 36
Froude, Hurrell, 35

Gamaliel, 330, 333
Garmon (Germanus), Bishop, 10
Gaza dental clinic, 298
Geddes Axe, 260
Gee, Thomas, 37, 40
Geiriadur Beiblaidd (Biblical
  Dictionary), 54
General Committee on Mutual
  Understanding and Co-
  operation, 225
George V, King, 293
Giraldus Cambrensis, 9
Girls Friendly Society, 296
Gladstone, Henry Neville, 151, 293

Gladstone, Sir William, 74
Gladstone, William Ewart, 22, 27, 30,
  40, 293
Global Anglican Future
  Conference, 220
Glyndŵr University, Wrexham, 127
God, xvii, xviii, 29, 34, 46, 49, 52, 55, 58,
  72, 73, 88, 95, 96, 104, 139, 144,
  154, 155, 156, 167, 169, 180, 193,
  194, 196, 197, 198, 199, 200, 202,
  204, 205, 208, 224, 226, 228, 232,
  234, 235, 236, 258, 278, 282, 283,
  289, 315, 316, 318, 321, 327, 329,
  330, 331, 334
Gorsedd of Bards, 113
Gospel, the, 14, 34, 39, 53, 115, 147, 165,
  195, 200, 235, 333
Governing Body, 64, 88, 89, 92, 97, 122,
  152, 202
Government of Wales Act 1998, 270
Graham's Factory Bill 1843, 36
grammar schools, 18, 20
Great Commission, the, 329, 330, 331,
  332, 333, 336
Green, Bishop (and Archbishop)
  C. A. H., 41, 67, 94, 102, 103, 106,
  108, 125, 147, 165, 181, 183, 241,
  263, 278, 280, 293, 319
Griffith, John, 21
Griffiths, Ainsley, 174
Griffiths, Ann, 291
Griffiths, David, 19
Griffiths, James, 52
Gruffydd, W. J., 54, 279
Guest, Charlotte, 248
GWELLA, 271
Gwenallt, 54, 291, *see* Jones, David
  Gwenallt
Gwynn ap Gwilym, 190, 288, 289,
  291

Hackney Phalanx, 257, 267
Hadow Report 1926, 261
Hammond, David, 301
Handy, Charles, 76, 115, 340
Hardie, Keir, 52
Harries, Lord, Pentregarth of, 76
Harries, W. H., 277